The Farthest Place

MW01169922

The Farthest Place

The Music of **John Luther Adams**

Edited by Bernd Herzogenrath

Northeastern University Press
Boston

NORTHEASTERN UNIVERSITY PRESS

An imprint of University Press of New England

www.upne.com

© 2012 Northeastern University

All rights reserved

Manufactured in the United States of America

Designed by Eric M. Brooks

Typeset in Arnhem and Aeonis

by Passumpsic Publishing

University Press of New England is a member of the
Green Press Initiative. The paper used in this book meets
their minimum requirement for recycled paper.

For permission to reproduce any of the material in this
book, contact Permissions, University Press of New England,
One Court Street, Suite 250, Lebanon NH 03766; or visit
www.upne.com

Library of Congress Cataloging-in-Publication Data
The farthest place: the music of John Luther Adams /
edited by Bernd Herzogenrath.
      p. cm.
Includes bibliographical references and index.
ISBN 978-1-55553-762-3 (cloth: alk. paper)—
ISBN 978-1-55553-763-0 (pbk.: alk. paper)—
ISBN 978-1-55553-764-7
1. Adams, John Luther, 1953– —Analysis, appreciation.
I. Herzogenrath, Bernd, 1964–.
ML410.A2333F37   2011
780.92—dc23   2011040642

5 4 3 2 1

* For
Frank
and
Janna

Contents

Acknowledgments

I would like to thank UPNE (in particular Richard Pult) for giving me and us the opportunity to work on this labor of love for John Luther Adams, and all those wonderful people who contributed to this volume—it has been a pleasure!

Most of all I would like to thank John himself for support, encouragement, and practical help—highly appreciated!

While working on this book project, two important and life-changing things happened to me: in the summer, our little daughter Janna was born . . . she's our cute little *clinamen*, the tiny little thing that makes life swerve into unforeseen directions. And in the early morning hours of Christmas Eve, my beloved little brother Frank died, after more than four years of living under the shadow of an incurable, malignant brain tumor. I can only now, in retrospect, see how brave he had been all those years. Frank now has gone farther than the farthest place, and my only hope is that this turns out to be the closest place as well. It is to Janna and Frank that I dedicate this book.

Some of the essays in this book already had a previous life:

Alex Ross's "Song of the Earth" was published in *The New Yorker*, May 12, 2008. http://www.newyorker.com/reporting/2008/05/12/080512fa_fact_ross, reprinted with kind permission of the author.

Peter Garland's "For Lou Harrison" is reprinted from the liner notes for *John Luther Adams—For Lou Harrison* (New World Records 80669-2). © 2007 Anthology of Recorded Music, Inc. Used by permission.

Part of Bernd Herzogenrath's "Introduction" and "The 'Weather of Music': From Ives to Adams" was already published as "The 'Weather of Music': Sounding Nature in the 20th and 21st Centuries." *Deleuze|Guattari & Ecology*. ed. Bernd Herzogenrath. Houndmills: Palgrave Macmillan, 2009, 216–32. Reprinted with kind permission.

All illustrations are reprinted with kind permission of John Luther Adams, and Taiga Press, with the exception of figure 5.2, which is copyright 2008 Lisa Tolentino Esler and is reprinted with kind permission.

* Introduction

John Luther Adams is a singular voice in contemporary music. This book is the first critical anthology about the work of a composer the critic Alex Ross has called "one of the most original musical thinkers of the new century."

Like Henry David Thoreau, Charles Ives, and John Cage, Adams inhabits both the periphery and the center of his times. Adams lives and works in Alaska, and his music echoes the open spaces of the far North. He is anything but a regionalist, however. He aspires to integrate his art into the larger fabric of life, believing that "music can provide a sounding model for the renewal of human consciousness and culture" (*The Place* 1).

Adams does not *represent* nature through music. He creates tonal territories that resonate *with* nature — immersive listening experiences that evoke limitless distance, suspended time, deep longing and even transcendence. As the composer writes about the northern landscape, "the feeling of endless space is exhilarating. *This* is what I want to find in music!" (*Winter Music* 69).

Adams's explorations began some thirty-five years ago, with a cycle called *songbirdsongs*, setting his "translations" of bird songs within open-ended musical landscapes. In his opera *Earth and the Great Weather*, Adams weaves recordings of wind across the tundra, ice melting, thunder and glaciers booming, with ritual drumming, ethereal music for strings, and the chanting of Alaska Native people into "a journey through the physical, cultural and spiritual landscapes of the Arctic" (Young 40).

During recent years, Adams has added a scientific perspective to his fascination with nature, which also reflects his stance toward the relationship between the "two cultures":

Science examines the way things are. Art imagines how things *might* be. Both begin with perception and aspire to achieve understanding. Both science and art search for truth. Whether we regard truth as objective and demonstrable or subjective and provisional, both science and art can lead us toward a broader and deeper understanding of reality. Even as they augment our understanding, science and art heighten our sense of wonder at the strange beauty, astonishing complexity, and miraculous unity of creation. (*The Place* 10)

Thus *Strange and Sacred Noise*, for example, an extended ritual for percussion, is inspired by elemental noise in nature and by chaos theory, blending the composer's ideal of "sonic geography" with "sonic geometry"—mathematical forms (fractal geometry, the Cantor set) made palpable in sound.

Adams—much like the philosopher Gilles Deleuze—is interested in "the relations between the arts, science, and philosophy. There is no order of priority among those disciplines" (*Negotiations* 123) for either Deleuze or Adams. The relationship is not a simple one-sided affair—as Adams has recently stated in a video clip, "Art and science have lots to say to one another. What is music but audible physics?" ("A Sonic Geography"). Whereas science involves the creation of functions, of a propositional mapping of the world, and art involves the creation of blocs of sensation (or affects and percepts), philosophy involves the invention of concepts. According to Deleuze / Guattari, philosophy, art, and science are defined by their relation to chaos. Whereas science "relinquishes the infinite in order to gain reference" (*What Is Philosophy?* 197), by creating definitions, functions, and propositions, art "wants to create the finite that restores the infinite" (197)—and it was exactly this creation of *finite* objects that bothered Cage (e.g. in "4:33"), a problem that Adams ingeniously "fixed" in his installation *The Place Where You Go to Listen*. In contrast, "philosophy wants to save the infinite by giving it consistency" (197).

Yet, since "sciences, arts, and philosophies are equally creative" (5), it might be fruitful, as Deleuze proposes, "to pose the question of echoes and resonances between them" (*Negotiations* 123)—to pose the question of their ecology, which is what much of Adams's work does.

As Deleuze specified in one of his seminars, "between a philosophical concept, a painted line and a musical sonorous bloc, resonances emerge, very, very strange correspondences that one shouldn't even theorize, I think, and which I would prefer to call 'affective' . . . these are privileged moments" ("Image Mouvement Image Temps").[1] These moments privilege an affect where thought and sensation merge into a very specific way of "doing thinking" *beyond* representation and categorization, a moment that might be called "contemplation," which also fittingly describes the "audience's" approach to Adams's *The Place Where You Go To Listen*, which transforms the rhythms of night and day, the phases of the moon, the weather, earthquake data, and disturbances in the earth's magnetic field into an ever-changing ecosystem of sound and light. As Deleuze / Guattari argue in *What Is Philosophy?*, "Philosophy needs a nonphilosophy that comprehends it; it needs a nonphilosophical comprehension just as art needs nonart and science needs nonscience" (218).

Friedrich Nietzsche, in his unpublished early notebooks dating from the period of his *Unfashionable Observations* [1872–73], relates the true philosopher to the scientist and the artist as listener (it is as if Cage is present in these lines): "The concept of the philosopher . . .: he tries to let all the sounds of the world reverberate in him and to place this comprehensive sound outside himself into concepts" (19[71], 115) . . . whereas the artist lets the tones of the world resonate within him and projects them by means of percepts and affects. So, the sound-art practice of Adams becomes research and philosophy, and vice versa—John Luther Adams, artist-philosopher-scientist.

Rainer Maria Rilke, in his 1919 essay "Primal Sound" (*Urgeräusch*) described an experience he had as a young boy when introduced to a phonograph for the first time, seeing how the needle produced sounds out of grooves in a wax cylinder, grooves that the recording of actual sounds had put there in the first place. Years later, while attending anatomical lectures in Paris, Rilke connected the lines of coronal suture of the human skull to his childhood observations—"I knew at once what it reminded me of: one of those unforgotten grooves, which had been scratched in a little wax cylinder by the point of a bristle!" (22). From this incident, Rilke derives the following "experimental set-up": "The coronal suture of the skull (this would first have to be investigated) has—let us assume—a certain similarity to the closely wavy line which the needle of a phonograph engraves on the receiving, rotating cylinder of the apparatus. What if one changed the needle and directed it on its return journey along a tracing which was not derived from the graphic translation of a sound, but existed of itself naturally—well: to put it plainly, along the coronal suture, for example. What would happen?" (23). Rilke's obvious answer is, of course: noise, music— sound! Probing further, Rilke asks himself, "what variety of lines then, occurring anywhere, could one not put under the needle and try out? Is there any contour that one could not, in a sense, complete in this way and then experience it, as it makes itself felt, thus transformed, in another field of sense?" (23).

In a letter, Rilke specifies this idea. Writing to Dieter Bassermann, Rilke speculates on "set[ting] to sound the countless signatures of Creation which in the skeleton, in minerals . . . in a thousand places persist in their remarkable versions and variations. The grain in wood, the gait of an insect: our eye is practiced in following and ascertaining them. What a gift to our hearing were we to succeed in transmuting this zigzag . . . into auditory events!" (*Letters* 391–92).

And with Nietzsche, we could add: "Images in human eyes! This dominates all human nature: from the *eye*! The *ear* hears sounds! A completely different, wonderful conception of the same world" (19 [66], 113).

It is such an unheard-of world that John Luther Adams's music makes come to life—and in 2010, he was awarded the Nemmers Prize in Music Composition "for melding the physical and musical worlds into a unique artistic vision that transcends stylistic boundaries."

The Farthest Place: The Music of John Luther Adams includes essays from scholars, critics, composers and performers, merging theoretical and historical observations, musical and environmental issues, with analytical discourse and very personal commentaries on Adams's music and thought.

In the early spring of 2008, Alex Ross traveled to Fairbanks to meet Adams and talk to him about his work. He visited the site of Adams's remarkable real-time installation, *The Place Where You Go to Listen*, held long conversations with him at his studio, and went for a drive with him south to Lake Louise, on the far side of the Alaska Range from Fairbanks. In the resulting essay—"Song of the Earth"—Ross attempts to sum up the life and work of this remarkable American composer, showing how he relates to the great experimental tradition in American music while evoking his Alaskan home in an extraordinarily distinctive musical language. Adams explains his own music best: "All along, I've had this obsessive, delusional idea that I could somehow be outside culture, which is, of course, patently absurd. But I could at least hold the illusion of being outside culture, where culture is put in proper perspective."

Captivated by the Arctic North, its indigenous cultures and wintry landscapes with their special light, colors, and sounds, Adams has established himself as a composer most strongly associated with a place: Alaska. A passionate environmentalist who moved to Alaska in the 1970s, Adams has paid tribute to his chosen environment in compositions that are exceptional in their diversity and consistency in relation to his concept of "sonic geography." In her essay "Music as Place, Place as Music," Sabine Feisst examines how Alaskan landscapes shaped Adams's creative voice. Two early nature-inspired pieces and four major works are investigated to demonstrate different imprints of the North and different compositional approaches: *Earth and the Great Weather*, a unique nonnarrative music theater piece indebted to Alaskan indigenous cultures and soundscapes; *In the White Silence*, a seventy-five-minute-long musical tableau glorifying the color white and silence, dominant features of Arctic landscapes; *Strange and Sacred Noise*, a concert-length cycle of six movements for percussion quartet drawing on the sonic violence of nature and fractal geometry; and *The Place Where You Go to Listen*, a sound installation at the Museum of the North which makes Interior Alaska's geophysical forces audible.

The music of Adams is simply and logically constructed, but operates on such a vast scale that we don't experience it as simple or logical. At a given moment an Adams piece presents us with an image of eternity: an unchanging sonority, or a complex of repeating, out-of-tempo ostinatos. Changes of texture and sonority come, but we cannot hear them coming nor predict their arrival. The pattern of changes makes logical sense to one who analyzes the score, and thus views the music, as it were, from a bird's-eye view; but the listener, close to the music's surface — like a hiker working her way across Adams's beloved Alaskan landscape — must submit to the vastness, the unknowability, the richness of the textures and patterns, the accidental coincidences of large-scale process. Still, there are clues embedded in the music that mark the trajectory of that process, and the well-informed listener is like a hiker with a road map in his head, and who occasionally glimpses a landmark.

Kyle Gann's essay "Time at the End of the World" takes its cue from Adams's credo in *Winter Music*: "I aspire to music that is both rigorous in thought and sensuous in sound" (140). Focusing on that separation (and ultimate reunion) of the intellectual (or spiritual) and the sensual, Gann creatively reads this into an almost neurological perspective, claiming that Adams writes music for the two hemispheres of the brain, the "the logical, time-assessing left brain and the contour-intuiting, lost-in-the-moment right brain." Instead of aiming at an easy harmony between the two strategies and temporalities that Gann observes (which bear a close resemblance to the Bergsonian distinction between *temps* and *durée*: time as compartmentalized and spatialized "logical units" such as seconds, minutes, hours, and time as duration, which is an indivisible continuum and as such has to be experienced), Adams holds up and builds on this tension, creating a sublime encounter in which the intellect alone fails at understanding and gives way to a more intense and affective experience.

Gann's essay follows these ideas through an analysis of some of Adams's core works: *Dream in White on White* (1992), *Clouds of Forgetting, Clouds of Unknowing* (1991–95), *In the White Silence* (1998), and *for Lou Harrison* (2003–4).

Peter Garland's essay on Adams's *for Lou Harrison* examines the structural elements of the work, but its more important focus is on the sociocultural and spiritual influence of Harrison's life on Adams. In the early 1950s Harrison composed his *Four Strict Songs* for male voice and orchestra based on his own texts. These texts outlined an ecological consciousness with a strong Native American influence that was far ahead of its time, and Harrison's music and life represented an alternative to the academic and alienating *zeitgeist* that dominated those years. The influence of Lou Harrison is one key to Adams's achievement, both in this piece and in his work as a whole.

Steven Schick's "Strange Noise, Sacred Places" is an on-the-ground look at the relationship between two of Adams's major works for percussion ensemble and the natural world. The two pieces, *Strange and Sacred Noise* and *Inuksuit* probe Adams's relationship to silence, noise, and the ecology of percussion music. *Strange and Sacred Noise*, Adams's 1997 sixty-five-minute percussion quartet, was used as a test case to examine the receptivity of natural environments to composed percussion music. With a team led by Robert Esler, percussionists took *Strange and Sacred Noise* on a tour of extreme outdoor performance sites: from the Anza Borrego desert, to the New Hampshire woods, Ohio farmland, and finally, to the tundra near Denali in Alaska. In each instance the organic rapport between percussive noises of the music and the sonic elements of the natural world served to reinforce Adams's notions of a grand continuity—between "composed" and "naturally existing" music; between noise and silence; and between the interventions of humans and the world upon which their interventions are visited.

The wisdom gleaned from the performances of *Strange and Sacred Noise* in outdoor environments informed the composition of a new work for percussion, *Inuksuit*, which was purposely designed for outdoor performance. *Inuksuit*, literally "in the capacity of the human," is scored for between nine and ninety-nine percussionists and posits a dynamic, mutually informative rapport between action and site. It is, in the composer's words, "site determined."

"Strange Noise, Sacred Places" is a practical philosophy—a performer's view of the music of Adams as told from the perspective of Steven Schick. Schick is a percussionist with nearly forty years of experience performing, recording, and commissioning contemporary percussion music, and was the primary performer advocate and presenter of the first performances of *Inuksuit* at the Banff Centre for the Arts in June 2009.

The percussion music of Adams starts with noise, and in the attempt to manage and leverage that noise for the purposes of art it crosses paths with a wide variety of musical, social, scientific, and cultural ideas. It is the music closest to the poetic vision of Harry Partch, who said, "Once upon a time / There was a little boy / And he went outside." If outside has been the longstanding goal of percussion music, Adams might just, finally, get us there.

The idea that the sounds of the environment, the "echology," or the soundscape, is a form of music has been with us since Thoreau, since John Cage, since R. Murray Schafer, and it has long been a fragile message that few of us truly hear. Adams has heard it much more strongly than most composers because listening to his place has truly led him to change his own music. As David Rothenberg muses in his essay "Go There to Listen: How Music Based on Nature Might Not Need Natural Sounds," any composer who decides to construct her music out of direct inspiration from nature has to make a choice: shall I compose right from natural sound as raw musical material, or shall I emulate, evoke, be inspired by nature, as Cage spoke "in its manner of operation," an idea that goes back to Aristotle? Adams chooses to base *The Place Where You Go to Listen* on the purest kind of electronic sounds: pink noise. The genius of the composer is to work out a system that combines simple enough sounds into a greater whole, sounds simple enough to need to be combined with other simple sounds. The history of music could thus be said to be a simplification of the pure wild noise of the world into refined pure tones, ready to be assembled into melodies and scales, based on order, system, consistency, something in human sound that nature cares little for. With this view in mind, one could say Adams's music has gotten more normal, more traditional, over time, while at the same time coming to sound totally unlike anyone else's.

One of the things that a music fanatic can hope to come across is something fresh and mysterious—music that instills a sense of hope, wonder, and possibility. As Glenn Kotche, percussionist, composer, and drummer, famously, of Wilco, enthusiastically admits, the music of Adams does just that for him. In writing about the drum quartets that play such an integral part in Adams's seminal work *Earth and the Great Weather: A Sonic Geography of the Arctic*, Kotche discusses his feeling that rhythm is at the core of the one-time rock drummer Adams's achievement of what every musician and composer aspires to, but only the greatest are able to accomplish: finding one's own sound. Adams's quartets can stand independent of the whole in which they are embedded as fresh and exhilarating sonic places. These places also provide a foundation on which his subsequent work has been built and by which it continues to be influenced. The unique rhythmic qualities of this music are, in Kotche's opinion, a creative trailhead that opened up new realms of discovery for the composer—replete with a new set of unanswered questions to pursue. As a result, Adams has created a more sensual and physical world through his percussion music; a place of discovery, substantive innovation, and purity of spirit. This music addresses the essence of drumming—sound and time—and audible processes are replaced by the exploration of psychoacoustic properties, with the performance environment playing an integral role in the overall experience of the works. Adams does this with dedication and a degree of bravery not experienced in our generation. He followed these questions up, and the results landed him in a truly unique place he can call his own.

In music we do not often encounter auras. In *The Mathematics of Resonant Bodies*, however, Adams surrounds the percussion with prerecorded sonorous auras. For a performer these extra-musical sounds both confuse and excite the interpretive intellect. It is clear that *Mathematics* is not a tape piece or a piece for percussion and electronics (or insert whatever technological rhetoric you like). It is a piece for percussion and auras. In any field other than contemporary music this notion would seem ridiculous. But for performers like Robert Esler, it is an open invitation to *play*. How do you *play* with an aura?

In his essay "How Do You *Play* with an Aura? The *Mathematics of Resonant Bodies*," Esler introduces the idea that performance is a means toward an experience, which is ultimately derived from the notions of play. The auras of this work extend conceptually beyond their prerecorded isolation and are open to a wider interpretive scope. A performer is not just given a task by the composer; rather, they are designers of an experiential construct.

While interpreting *Mathematics*, Esler immediately realized this role was essential. How does one re-perform the natural abstractions of the North that have gone in—and come out of—Adams's mind? As a percussionist, Esler has no mechanism to re-perform a calving glacier with his tiny drums and tam-tams. He is too weak. So he had to *play* with the concept. The auras of *Mathematics* are easy to perform with but difficult to accept beyond their prerecorded absoluteness. They are concrete. How was one supposed to put life into them? Esler's essay discusses the way he chose to *play* with the conceptual and musical aspects of this epic work and how he eventually was led to perform the work outdoors, in the desert, under the glaring sun.

Qilyaun (1998) is scored for either four percussionists playing bass drums or a single performer with digital delay and surround system. Commissioned by the Fairbanks Symphony for percussionist Scott Deal, *Qilyaun* received its premiere on April 18, 1998. As Deal himself in his essay observes, the work, along with *Strange and Sacred Noise*, is informative as a departure from Adams's earlier percussion works (the quartets from *Earth and the Great Weather* and *Coyote Builds North America*), where percussion instruments are employed as melodic chamber instruments, toward his later works (*Mathematics of Resonant Bodies*, *Red Arc Blue Veil*), in which they become generative devices of ecstatic noise.

Deal participated in lengthy discussions during the compositional phase of the piece, and these discussions informed his essay on the creation of the work. Deal's essay also provides an analysis of its form and rhythmic devices, as well as technical specifications and performance notes for the piece as a solo work and as a quartet.

Since 1999, the majority of Adams's output has been what Todd Tarantino in his essay calls "color field compositions." These pieces feature limited harmonic activity and no traditional sense of phrase or tonal trajectory. In their overall sound, they are inscrutable, presenting a series of slowly shifting singularities enlivened by surface disturbances. Owing to the absence of a theoretical framework for understanding these pieces, criticism and analysis tends to be limited to bland generalities about their "timeless" nature or "Arctic" colors; similarly, conductors and performers can only "play the notes" and Adams himself assumes the mantle of a mystic channeling an environment rather than a composer manipulating sounds for a desired end. In his essay, Tarantino dissects the color field compositions in order to develop a typology of Adams's techniques and approaches. He then takes this taxonomy and demonstrates how Adams composes: by using his personal compositional language to create narrative and large-scale form.

It would be easy to get lost in the romance of the backstory that has grown up around Adams, a composer inextricably tied up in postcard-ready images of the natural beauty that surrounds him in his home state of Alaska. Remarkably, this awe-inspiring landscape does not overwhelm his musical voice. It delivers him back to what he knows is his primary work—the solitary, introspective task of putting notes on paper. Adams, willing to sit and listen and wait for the music in his surroundings, has long taken the idea of *place* as his starting point. The songs of birds, the weight of ice, and the richness and power of the aurora borealis across the night sky feed his imagination. Yet his work is not landscape painting but an aural expression of a very personal experience of his environment. Hints of this remain in his poetically suggestive titling style: *In the White Silence* and *Earth and the Great Weather*, for example, reflect that touchstone.

Yet for all this dedication to quiet introspection and meditative observation, Adams is a compelling storyteller, particularly when it comes to a discussion of his musical interests. Seated on a grass-covered hill in New York City's Central Park in April 2010, he spoke with Molly Sheridan about his orchestral work *The Light Within* (also available in a chamber version) and the strong links it shares with previous compositions in the his catalog such as *The Light That Fills the World*, *Dark Waves*, and *Red Arc/Blue Veil*. In the edited transcript of the conversation included here, Adams also reflects on how these works fit into his larger catalog and addressed some of the deeper motivations behind his output.

Over the course of the past decade, Adams has become increasingly focused upon the creation of music that utilizes unified "fields" of harmony and timbre. To create these fields, Adams avoids the use of overt melodies or instrumental elements that easily delineate themselves from one another. Through primary score analysis, preexisting literature, and personal interviews with the composer, Dave Herr's essay "Timbral Listening in *Dark Waves*" examines the relationship between timbre and light in Adams's recent compositions, focusing on *Dark Waves*, a 2007 composition scored for orchestra and electronics, and two pianos and electronics. Herr's essay is the first large-scale piece of writing about *Dark Waves*. Herr analyzes the techniques through which Adams unifies harmonic and timbral material and live instrumental and electronic elements in both scorings of the piece, and how a constantly expanding "field of light" serves as a metaphor for human optimism in the face of environmental and political threat. This field of light is examined using a bottom-up approach that views the expanding timbres as developments from "points of germination," and a top-down approach that views all sounds within the piece as the result of a process of filtration akin to the filtration of colored noise. Herr also discusses the piece's chiastic form, which evokes the natural phenomenon of a "solitary wave" and places *Dark Waves* within a series of pieces built on an identical structure.

Robert Carl's essay "Place and Space: The Vision of John Luther Adams in the Ultramodernist Tradition" places Adams's roots within the American experimentalist tradition. He traces the composer's connection to the "maverick" composers of the early twentieth century, who promoted a distinctly American form of modernism (as well as to their successors). The transcendentalist visions of Charles Ives and Carl Ruggles; the comprehensive practice of Henry Cowell (unifying the parameters of pitch, duration, and color); Conlon Nancarrow's creative use of strict algorithms; James Tenney's combination of stasis and development in ergodic form: all of these find their very personal synthesis in Adams's work. Carl also suggests how "experimentalism" is not adequate as a sole description, as the visionary quality of music stemming from the ultramodernist tradition is also key to its impact and success. It is this combination of elements plainspoken, transcendental, and inventive that makes for a distinctly American music, of which Adams is a major heir.

Carl concludes by showing how these elements interweave, via an analysis of the composer's grand and spacious electroacoustic installation *Veils*.

In his installation *The Place Where You Go to Listen* (2006), Adams wires meteorological stations and seismic and electromagnetic stations throughout Alaska into a permanent "sound machine" through which climatic and geological data are transposed into tonal sculptures. Real-time data are collected, coordinated, and made audible through pink noise filters. In 1852, Henry David Thoreau describes an "accidental music" that is created by the wind "playing" on telegraph wires. In both cases, as Bernd Herzogenrath, in his essay "The Weather of Music: Sounding Nature in the Twentieth and Twenty-first Centuries," shows, nature itself creates a kind of "ambient music," sounds based on a nature / culture continuum—an ecology of music. Based on Thoreau's sonic aesthetics, a genuine American tradition of avant-garde composers from Charles Ives through John Cage to Adams makes "nature" the focus of compositorial reflection / contemplation, not so much in the way of program music, but as a physical and acoustic phenomenon—the "musicalization of nature" is complemented by the "naturalization of music."

Thirty years separate Adams's *songbirdsongs* (1974–79, rev. 2009) and *Inuksuit* (2009), yet the two pieces seem like siblings in their musical materials, compositional approach, and ecological philosophy. In both works, as David Shimoni argues in his essay "*songbirdsongs* and *Inuksuit*: Creating an Ecocentric Music," Adams goes beyond "authentic" representations of natural sounds.

Using indeterminate structures, he enables his performers to incorporate the natural world more as a partner than as a resource. *songbirdsongs* consists of nine pieces for piccolos and percussion, each featuring the song of at least one bird species. By providing the performers with only an event map, individual musical phrases, and performance instructions that reflect the singing behavior of each featured bird species, Adams preserves the essential freedom of birdsong. *Inuksuit*—for nine to ninety-nine percussionists—is Adams's first piece specifically intended for outdoor performance. With its combination of manmade sounds derived from the natural world, formal structures derived from inuksuit (human-made stone configurations in Arctic landscapes), and the natural sounds and acoustics of the performance site, *Inuksuit* enables listeners and performers to experience a place more fully, while subtly presenting a narrative of life on Earth. In these two pieces Adams creates ecocentric music that encourages us to contemplate our position in the biosphere.

For over thirty years the works of John Luther Adams have revealed a unique musical vision. Adams's diverse body of work spans not just compositions and sound recordings, but also theatrical performances, sound and light installations, and print and web publications. Noah Pollaczek's bibliography represents the most complete inventory of Adams's output to date. In the first three parts—works, discography, and writings—the many strands of the composer's *oeuvre* are explored, followed by a concluding section which documents the numerous creators who have produced writings and audiovisual materials concerning Adams's work. Through hundreds of entries encompassing a multiplicity of media, this bibliography aims to be a resource that will serve researchers and appreciators of John Luther Adams's work well into the future.

Note

1. My translation of: "Alors je dirais que le concept philosophique n'est pas seulement source d'opinion quelconque, il est source de transmission très particulière, où entre un concept philosophique, une ligne picturale, un bloc sonore musical, s'établissent des correspondances, des correspondances très très curieuses, que à mon avis il ne faut même pas théoriser, que je préférerais appeler l'affectif en général. . . . Là c'est des moments privilégiés." Gilles Deleuze, "Image Mouvement Image Temps." Cours Vincennes—St Denis: le plan—02/11/1983. www.webdeleuze.com/php/texte.php?cle=69&groupe=Image%20Mouvement%20Image%20Temps&langue=1 (last accessed Feb 10, 2011).

Works Cited

Adams, John Luther. *Winter Music: Composing the North*. Middletown, Conn.: Wesleyan University Press, 2004.

———. *The Place Where You Go to Listen: In Search of an Ecology of Music*. Middletown, Conn.: Wesleyan University Press.

———. "A Sonic Geography of Alaska" online video, directed by Steve Elkins, http://vimeo.com/3019076 (last accessed Feb 10, 2011).

Deleuze, Gilles. *Negotiations 1972–1990*. Translated by M. Joughin. New York: Columbia University Press, 1995.

———. "Image Mouvement Image Temps." Cours Vincennes—St Denis : le plan—02/11/1983. www.webdeleuze.com/php/texte.php?cle=69&groupe=Image%20Mouvement%20Image%20Temps&langue=1 (last accessed Feb 10, 2010)

Deleuze, Gilles, and Félix Guattari. *What is Philosophy?* Trans. Hugh Tomlinson and Graham Burchell. New York: Columbia University Press, 1994.

Nemmer Prize Committee Announcement. http://www.northwestern.edu/newscenter/stories/2010/04/nemmersprize.html (last accessed Feb 10, 2011)

Nietzsche, Friedrich. *Writings from the Early Notebooks*. Ed. Raymond Geuss and Alexander Nehamas. Trans. Ladislaus Löb. Cambridge: Cambridge University Press, 2009.

Rilke, Rainer Maria. "Primal Sound." *The Book of Music and Nature: An Anthology of Sounds, Words, Thoughts*. Ed. David Rothenberg and Martha Ulvaeus. Middletown, Conn.: Wesleyan University Press, 2001, 21–24.

———. *Letters of Rainer Maria Rilke. Vol. II: 1912–26*. Trans. Greene Jane Bannard. Leiserson Press, 2007.

Young, Gayle. "Sonic Geography of the Arctic: An Interview with John Luther Adams." *Musicworks* 70 (1998): 38–43.

1 * Song of the Earth

When I took a trip into the Alaskan interior several years ago, I didn't get to see the aurora borealis, but I did, in a way, hear it. At the Museum of the North, on the grounds of the University of Alaska in Fairbanks, the composer John Luther Adams has created a sound-and-light installation called *The Place Where You Go to Listen*—a kind of infinite musical work that is controlled by natural events occurring in real time. The title refers to Naalagiagvik, a place on the coast of the Arctic Ocean where, according to legend, a spiritually attuned Iñupiaq woman went to hear the voices of birds, whales, and unseen things around her. In keeping with that magical idea, the mechanism of *The Place* translates raw data into music: information from seismological, meteorological, and geomagnetic stations in various parts of Alaska is fed into a computer and transformed into an intricate, vibrantly colored field of electronic sound.

The Place occupies a small white-walled room on the museum's second floor. You sit on a bench before five glass panels, which change color according to the time of day and the season. What you notice first is a dense, organlike sonority, which Adams has named the Day Choir. Its notes follow the contour of the natural harmonic series—the rainbow of overtones that emanate from a vibrating string—and have the brightness of music in a major key. In overcast weather, the harmonies are relatively narrow in range; when the sun comes out, they stretch across four octaves. After the sun goes down, a darker, moodier set of chords, the Night Choir, moves to the forefront. The moon is audible as a narrow sliver of noise. Pulsating patterns in the bass, which Adams calls Earth Drums, are activated by small earthquakes and other seismic events around Alaska. And shimmering sounds in the extreme registers—the Aurora Bells—are tied to the fluctuations in the magnetic field that cause the northern lights.

The first day I was there, *The Place* was subdued, though it cast a hypnotic spell. Checking the Alaskan data stations on my laptop, I saw that geomagnetic activity was negligible. Some minor seismic activity in the region had set off the bass frequencies, but it was a rather opaque ripple of beats, suggestive of a dance party in an underground crypt. Clouds covered the sky, so the Day Choir was muted. After a few minutes, there was a noticeable change: the solar harmonies acquired extra radiance, with upper intervals oscillating in an almost melodic fashion. Certain that the sun had come out, I left *The Place*, and looked out the windows of the lobby. The Alaska Range was glistening on the far side of the Tanana Valley.

When I arrived the next day, just before noon, *The Place* was jumping. A mild earthquake in the Alaska Range, measuring 2.99 on the Richter scale, was causing the Earth Drums to pound more loudly and go deeper in register. (If a major earthquake were to hit Fairbanks, *The Place*, if it survived, would throb to the frequency 24.27Hz, an abyssal tone that Adams associates with the rotation of the earth.) Even more spectacular were the high sounds showering down from speakers on the ceiling. On the web site of the University of Alaska's Geophysical Institute, aurora activity was rated 5 on a scale from 0 to 9, or "active." This was sufficient to make the Aurora Bells come alive. The Day and Night Choirs follow the equal-tempered tuning used by most Western instruments, but the Bells are filtered through a different harmonic prism, one determined by various series of prime numbers. I had the impression of a carillon ringing miles above the earth.

On the two days I visited *The Place*, various tourists came and went. Some, armed with cameras and guidebooks, stood against the back wall, looking alarmed, and left quickly. Others were entranced. One young woman assumed a yoga position and meditated; she took "The Place" to be a specimen of ambient music, the kind of thing you can bliss out to, and she wasn't entirely mistaken. At the same time, it is a forbiddingly complex creation that contains a probably unresolvable philosophical contradiction. On the one hand, it lacks a will of its own; it is at the mercy of its data streams, the humors of the earth. On the other hand, it is a deeply personal work, whose material reflects Adams's long-standing preoccupation with multiple systems of tuning, his fascination with slow-motion formal processes, his love of foggy masses of sound in which many events are unfolding at independent tempos.

The Place, which opened on the spring equinox in 2006, confirms Adams's status as one of the most original musical thinkers of the new century. At the age of fifty-five, he has become a chief standard-bearer of American experimental music, of the tradition of solitary sonic tinkering that began on the West Coast almost a century ago and gained new strength after the Second World War, when John Cage and Morton Feldman created supreme abstractions in musical form. Talking about his work, Adams admits that it can sound strange, that it lacks familiar reference points, that it's not exactly popular—by a twist of fate, he is sometimes confused with John Coolidge Adams, the creator of the opera *Nixon in China* and the most widely performed of living American composers—and yet he'll also say that it's got something, or, at least, "It's not nothing."

Above all, Adams strives to create musical counterparts to the geography, ecology, and native culture of his home state, where he has lived since 1978. He does this not merely by giving his compositions evocative titles—his catalogue includes *Earth and the Great Weather, In the White Silence, Strange and Sacred Noise, Dark Waves*—but by literally anchoring the work in the landscapes that have inspired it.

"My music is going inexorably from being about place to becoming place," Adams said of his installation.

I have a vivid memory of flying out of Alaska early one morning on my way to Oberlin, where I taught for a couple of fall semesters. It was a glorious early-fall day. Winter was coming in. I love winter, and I didn't want to go. As we crested the central peaks of the Alaska Range, I looked down at Mt. Hayes, and all at once I was overcome by the intense love that I have for this place—an almost erotic feeling about those mountains. Over the next fifteen minutes, I found myself furiously sketching, and when I came up for air I realized, There it is. I knew that I wanted to hear the unheard, that I wanted to somehow transpose the music that is just beyond the reach of our ears into audible vibrations. I knew that it had to be its own space. And I knew that it had to be real—that I couldn't fake this, that nothing could be recorded. It had to have the ring of truth.

Actually, my original conception for *The Place* was truly grandiose. I thought that it might be a piece that could be realized at any location on the earth, and that each location would have its unique sonic signature. That idea—tuning the whole world—stayed with me for a long time. But at some point I realized that I was tuning it so that this place, this room, on this hill, looking out over the Alaska Range, was the sweetest-sounding spot on earth.

Adams blends in well with the proudly scruffy characters who populate the diners and bars of Fairbanks. Tall and rail-thin, his handsomely weathered face framed by a short beard, he bears a certain resemblance to Clint Eastwood, and speaks in a similarly soft, husky voice. He's not unworldly—he travels frequently to New York, Los Angeles, Amsterdam, and other cultural capitals—but he is happiest when he goes on extended camping trips into the wilderness, especially to the Arctic National Wildlife Refuge. He exudes a regular-guy coolness that is somewhat unusual in contemporary composers.

He lives on a hill outside Fairbanks, in a sparsely furnished, light-filled split-level house, much of which he designed and built himself. He shares it with his second wife, Cynthia Adams, who has been the mainstay of his occasionally precarious existence since the late nineteen-seventies. Cindy, as spirited as her husband is soft-spoken, runs GrantStation, an internet business that advises nonprofit organizations across the country. To many locals, the Adamses are best known for serving on the board of the Alaska Goldpanners, Fairbanks's amateur baseball team. When they go shopping at Fred Meyer, the all-purpose store in town, they are peppered with questions about the state of the team.

Like many Alaskans, Adams migrated to the state from a very different world. He was born in Meridian, Mississippi; his father worked for AT&T, first as an accountant and later in upper management, and the family moved often when he was a child. Much of his adolescence was spent in Millburn, New Jersey, where he developed a passion for rock and roll. He was the drummer in several bands, one of which, Pocket Fuzz, had the honor of opening for the Beach Boys in a local New Jersey show.

Frank Zappa caused a violent change of perspective. In the liner notes to Zappa's 1966 album *Freak Out!* Adams noticed a quotation: " 'The present-day composer refuses to die!' — Edgard Varèse." Adams went hunting for information about this mystery figure, whose name he pronounced "Var-EE-zee." A friend, the composer Richard Einhorn, discovered a Varèse disk in a Greenwich Village record shop, and the two braved the sonic hailstorms of *Poème électronique*. Adams was soon devouring the music of the postwar European and American avant-garde: Karlheinz Stockhausen, Iannis Xenakis, György Ligeti, and, most important, John Cage.

"Once I discovered that stuff, I rapidly lost interest in the backbeat and the three chords," Adams said. "I was still in bands, but they kept getting weirder and weirder. In the last band, a trio called Sloth, we were trying to work with open-form scores and graphic notation."

In 1969, the family moved again, to Macon, Georgia. Adams enrolled in Westminster Academy, an elite boarding school, from which he failed to graduate. "I was your classic problem kid," he said. "My grades were O.K.; it was my behavior that was the problem." At the age of sixteen, he fell in love with a young woman named Margrit von Braun — the younger daughter of Wernher von Braun, the godfather of the American space program. Not surprisingly, the German émigré and the American teenager didn't get along. In 1969, Adams says, he was impressed more by the Miracle Mets than by the first moon landing. Nonetheless, he and Margrit married, and for several years he coexisted uneasily with her powerful father.

In 1971, Adams moved to Los Angeles to study music at CalArts. One teacher there, the composer James Tenney, became a significant mentor; Tenney's wild imagination was balanced by the mathematical rigor of his methods. Likewise, beneath the dreamlike surfaces of Adams's work are mathematical schemes controlling the interrelationship of rhythms and the unfolding of melodic patterns. At CalArts, the novice composer also familiarized himself with the oddball heroes of the American avant-garde: Harry Partch, who adopted a hobo lifestyle during the Great Depression; Conlon Nancarrow, who spent the better part of his career writing pieces for player piano in Mexico City; and Lou Harrison, who sought musical truth in the Indonesian gamelan tradition. Adams calls them "composers who burned down the house and started over."

Perhaps Adams's most crucial encounter was with Morton Feldman, the loquacious New Yorker whose music has an otherworldly quietude and breadth. On a Columbia LP he heard Feldman's *Piece for Four Pianos*, in which four pianists play through the same music at different rates, floating around each other like the arms of a Calder mobile. That work galvanized Adams, teaching him that music could break free of European tradition while retaining a sensuous allure. One of his first characteristic pieces, for three percussion players, bears the Feldmanesque title *Always Very Soft*, although the seamlessness of the construction—accelerating and decelerating patterns overlap to create a single, ever-evolving sonority—hints at a distinct sensibility.

Southern California also brought Adams in contact with the environmental movement. He became obsessed with the plight of the California condor, which was facing extinction. Several expeditions into the Los Padres National Forest, where the last wild condors lived, led him to make his first attempt at "nature music"—a cycle of pieces entitled *songbirdsongs*. Olivier Messiaen had been taking inspiration from birdsong for decades. With "the self-consciousness of the self-styled young iconoclast," Adams says, he went out of his way to avoid Messiaen's influence, and his own personality emerged in the unhurried pacing of events and the wide-open sense of space.

By the mid-seventies, Adams was working with the Wilderness Society and other conservation groups. At the time, one of their major projects was lobbying for the Alaska Lands Act, whose purpose was to protect large tracts of the state from oil drilling and industrial development. Adams first went to Alaska in 1975, and returned in 1977 to spend a summer in the Arctic. His marriage to Margrit von Braun unraveled that year. Around that time, he met Cindy, who was also an environmental activist. They fell in love during the long battle for passage of the Alaska Lands Act, which President Carter signed into law in 1980.

What Adams needed most, after a turbulent decade, was solitude. During the first decade of his relationship with Cindy, he lived in a rudimentary cabin in the woods outside Fairbanks, a mile from the nearest road. "It was my Thoreau fantasy—cutting wood and carrying water," he told me. The fantasy subsided when Cindy suggested in a non-roundabout way that he should either join her full time—by now the couple had a son, Sage—or go his own way. In 1989, he moved out of the woods, and has never returned to his old cabin.

Adams embraced his new life in Fairbanks, but he still struggled to find his way as a composer. The eighties were, he now says, "lost years": he made various attempts to write orchestral pieces that would reach a wider audience, and, though he was pleased with the work, he didn't feel that it was entirely his. At times, he wondered whether he would make more headway in New York or Los Angeles. In this same period, not incidentally, John Adams, of Berkeley, California, found fame with *Nixon in China*. The two composers had known each other since 1976; they moved in the same circles, and one week they stayed together at Lou Harrison's house. Nevertheless, the phenomenal success of the Californian Adams pushed the Alaskan Adams to differentiate himself, not only by using his middle name but by finding territory he could call his own.

"In a way, that experience challenged me to reëvaluate my whole relationship to the idea of success," he says. "Maybe it confirmed my outsider resolve — 'No, I'm not moving from Alaska; this is who I am, this is where I belong, this is what I'm supposed to be doing' — but most of all it helped my sense of humor. For me, finally, it's kind of worked out. John is always very gracious. We occasionally exchange e-mails about the latest incidents of mistaken identity. Recently, someone thought he was me. Very sweet."

By the 1990s, Adams had begun to carve out a singular body of work, which can be sampled on recordings on the New World, New Albion, Cold Blue, Mode, and Cantaloupe labels. First came a conceptual Alaskan opera entitled *Earth and the Great Weather*, much of which is given over to the chanting of place-names and descriptive phrases from the native Iñupiaq and Gwich'in languages, both in the original and in translation. One mesmerizing section describes various stages of the seasons: "The time of new sunshine," "The time when polar bears bring out their young," "The time of the small wind," "The time of eagles." The music runs from pure, ethereal sonorities for strings — tuned in a scheme similar to that of the Aurora Bells in *The Place* — to viscerally pummeling movements for quartets of drums.

In the next decade, Adams further explored the sonic extremes that he had mapped out in his opera. *In the White Silence*, a seventy-five-minute piece for harp, celesta, vibraphones, and strings, is derived from the seven notes of the C-major scale; in a striking feat of metaphor, the composer equates the consuming whiteness of midwinter Alaska with the white keys of the piano. *Strange and Sacred Noise*, another seventy-five-minute cycle, evokes the violence of changing seasons: four percussionists deploy drums, gongs, bells, sirens, and mallet percussion to summon up an alternately bewitching and frightening tableaus of musical noises, most of which were inspired by a trip that Adams took up the Yukon River in spring, when the ice was collapsing. Whether unabashedly sweet or unremittingly harsh—*Clouds of Forgetting, Clouds of Unknowing*, a memorial to the composer's father, manages to be both at once—Adams's major works have the appearance of being beyond style; they transcend the squabbles of contemporary classical music, the unending arguments over the relative value of Romantic and modernist languages.

The sense of vastness, separateness, and solitude is even more pronounced in Adams's recent electronic compositions. A 2005 installation entitled *Veils*, which has appeared in several venues in America and Europe, uses a "virtual choir" of ninety polyphonic voices, and unfolds over a span of six hours. *The Place*, meanwhile, could continue playing at the Museum of the North for decades to come. Both Cage and Feldman talked about making music that you can live with, much as you can live with visual art; *Veils* and *The Place* execute that idea with uncommon vigor. Adams is an avid art-viewer, and is particularly keen on the second generation of American abstract painters: Frank Stella, Ellsworth Kelly, Jasper Johns, and Joan Mitchell. There are more art books than music books on the shelves of his studio, a neat one-room cabin that faces south, toward the Alaska Range.

Adams says, "I remember thinking, To hell with classical music. I'm going into the art world; I'm going to do installations. But I was really just interested in working with new media. And it doesn't matter what I think I'm doing. The work has a life of its own, and I'm just along for the ride. Richard Serra talks about the point at which all your influences are assimilated and then your work can come out of the work."

Although Adams is content to write for electronics, small ensembles, and percussion groups, he still longs to write for larger forces, and, above all, for orchestra. For most of the eighties, he was the timpanist for the Fairbanks Symphony, which, at the time, was led by the conductor, composer, and environmental activist Gordon Wright. During Adams's cabin-in-the-forest period, Wright was living nearby, and the two became close friends, often trekking into the wilderness together. Once, they drove into the Alaska Range while listening to Bruckner's Eighth Symphony, music that has the weight of mountains. "This may be where our musical worlds meet," Adams said to him.

Wright died in 2007, near Anchorage, at the age of seventy-two; he was found one night on the deck of his cabin. A few days later, the Anchorage Symphony played the première of Adams's *Dark Waves*, an extraordinary piece for orchestra and electronics, which the composer dedicated to Wright. One of the most arresting American orchestral works of recent years, it suggests a huge entity, of indeterminate shape, that approaches slowly, exerts apocalyptic force, and then recedes. Every instrument is, in one way or another, playing with the simple interval of the perfect fifth—the basic building block of harmony—but at the climax the lines coalesce into roaring dissonances, with all twelve notes of the chromatic scale sounding together.

Adams is now contemplating a large-scale work in the vein of *Dark Waves*. It might bring him into a Brucknerian or even Wagnerian realm. Wagner's *Parsifal* is one of three opera scores in Adams's library; the others are Mussorgsky's *Boris Godunov* and Debussy's *Pelléas et Mélisande*. He speaks with awe — and a little envy — of the resources Wagner had at his command. A few years ago, Adams went to see *Die Walküre* at the Metropolitan Opera, and departed with his mind full of fresh longings.

"I thought, This couldn't be repeated," Adams told me. "Wagner kind of caught the perfect wave. But I did wonder what kind of opportunities exist for us, right now." He sat still for a moment, his blue-gray eyes drifting. I sensed some wordless, high-tech, back-to-the-earth *Parsifal* waiting to be born.

Knowing of Adams's love for Alaska's remotest places, I asked him to take me to one of them. His favorite place on earth is the Brooks Range, the northernmost extension of the Rocky Mountains, but that area was inaccessible when I visited. Instead, we went south, to Lake Louise. Snowy weather blocked most of the mountains as we drove, although looming white shapes occasionally pierced the flurries. "Aw, that's nothing," Adams would say, slipping into the role of the hardened Alaskan lifer. "Foothills. The big guys aren't coming out."

Lake Louise is framed by several of North America's grandest mountain ranges: the Alaska, the Chugach, the Wrangell-St. Elias, and the Talkeetna. The native word for this kind of place is *chiiviteenlii*, or "pointed mountains scattered all around." The lake was covered with ice four feet thick, and, after spending the night at a local lodge, we went for a walk. The sun was burning faintly through the mist above. Periodically, a curtain of snow descended and the shores and islands of the lake disappeared from view. I noticed that Adams was listening closely to this seemingly featureless expanse, and kept pulling information from it: the fluttering of a flock of snow buntings, the low whistle of wind through a stand of gaunt spruce, the sinister whine of a pair of snowmobiles. He also noted the curiously musical noises that our feet were making. Tapping the crust of snow atop the ice, under which the wind had carved little tunnels, he compared the sounds to those of xylophones or marimbas. Meanwhile, a dog had wandered out on the ice and was howling to itself. "He has some fantasy he's a wolf," Adams said. He yelled at the dog to go home.

Adams recalled the Yukon River trip that led him to write *Strange and Sacred Noise* and other tone poems of natural chaos. "When the ice breakup comes, it makes incredible sounds," he said. "It's symphonic. There's candle ice, which is crystals hanging down like chandeliers. They chime together in the wind. Or whirlpools open up along the shore or out in the middle of the river, and water goes swirling through them. Or sizzle ice, which makes a sound like the effervescent popping you hear when you pour water over ice cubes. I have literally hundreds of hours of field recordings that I made back in the *Earth and the Great Weather* period, in the early nineties. I keep thinking that maybe one day I could work with some of that material — maybe try to transcribe it, completely remove it from the original reality, extract the music in it."

We were standing on a tiny island, where cormorants had built a network of nests. Adams had discovered these nests on a trip to the lake a few weeks earlier. One of the nests had slid off the ridge onto the lake, and we carried it back to land.

"All along, I've had this obsessive, delusional idea that I could somehow be outside culture, which is, of course, patently absurd," he said. "But I could at least hold the illusion of being outside culture, where culture is put in proper perspective. That's why I am so concerned with the landscape. Barry Lopez" — the author of the epic travelogue *Arctic Dreams* — "says that landscape is the culture that contains all human cultures, all forms and artifacts and culture and language. Maybe it's just a hippy-dippy sixties-seventies thing, but, to tell the truth, I was never such a good hippie."

Adams is well aware of the naïveté, sentimentality, and outright foolishness that can attach to fantasies of dropping out of society in search of "the real." But that same naïveté can lead to work of intimidating power, especially when it is wedded to artistic craft. In this regard, Adams cites another of his heroes, the poet John Haines, who, after the Second World War, took up residence in a one-room cabin he built off the Richardson Highway, south of Fairbanks, and stayed there for some twenty years, living off the land in time-honored fashion. Not long before Adams moved to Alaska, he read Haines's first book, *Winter News*, falling under the spell of poems such as "Listening in October":

There are silences so deep
you can hear
the journeys of the soul,
enormous footsteps
downward in a freezing earth.

In a collection of writings entitled *Winter Music*, Adams cites, among other reasons for moving to the state, the richness of its silences. He writes, "Much of Alaska is still filled with silence, and one of the most persuasive arguments for the preservation of the original landscape here may be its spiritual value as a great reservoir of silence."

Haines was then eighty-three years old and had recently endured a near-fatal bout of pneumonia, but he still welcomed visitors, especially those who bring a good bottle of whiskey. On our visit, Adams asked Haines to recite one or two of his poems. Haines proceeded to chant several of them in a courtly, melancholy voice, somewhat in the manner of William Butler Yeats delivering "The Lake Isle of Innisfree." He ended with "Return to Richardson, Spring 1981," which looks back fondly and sadly on the homestead period, when "our life [was] like a boat set loose," and evenings were spent reading books since forgotten:

In this restless air I know
On this ground I can never forget
Where will I set my foot
With so much passion again.

After a pause, Adams said, "That hurts." We talked for a few more minutes, Adams gave Haines the whiskey, and we said goodbye.

On the way to Lake Louise, we passed Haines's old homestead. The highway now cuts close to the house, ruining its magnificent isolation. Alaska's "great reservoir of silence" is disappearing; even in the farthest reaches of the Brooks Range, Adams commented, you will sooner or later hear the drone of a snow machine or the hum of a small plane. Adams spoke also of the scary pace of climate change, of how the thaw now comes as much as a month earlier than it did when he moved to the state. He talked about various future projects—including an outdoor percussion piece for the Banff Centre, in Alberta, Canada, which was to become *Inuksuit*—and explained why his work was becoming more global in focus.

"I tried to run away," Adams said. "I hid for quite a while. I had a rich life; I had incredible experiences, a very slow development of a certain musical world. I wouldn't trade it for anything. But I can't live there anymore. Because, in a sense, it doesn't exist anymore. A piece like *In the White Silence* is almost—I didn't realize this at the time—almost an elegy for a place that has disappeared."

Sabine Feisst

2 * Music as Place, Place as Music
The Sonic Geography of John Luther Adams

My work has long been grounded in the physical, cultural, and spiritual landscapes of the North, and an ideal of "sonic geography," a music of place. Living in Alaska for most of my creative life, I've come to measure everything I do—in fact, all human invention and activity—against the overwhelming presence of this place. This has profoundly influenced the atmosphere and the scale of my work.

* JOHN LUTHER ADAMS, quoted in Young, 39

John Luther Adams is an American composer whose life and music are both uncompromising and unique.[1] Born in Meridian, Mississippi, he grew up in homogeneous suburban surroundings in the South and on the Northeastern seaboard. After living in overdeveloped Southern California, however, he turned toward environmentalism, eventually finding his spiritual home in Alaska in the 1970s. In a musical career that began with rock drumming and song-writing in his teens, and continued with compositional studies with James Tenney and Leonard Stein at the California Institute of the Arts, Adams has established himself as the composer most strongly associated with Alaska.

The Arctic North, its landscapes and cultures, became the major inspirational source for most of Adams's compositions. Unlike many other nature-inspired composers—Claude Debussy, Ives, Sibelius, and Alan Hovhaness among them—Adams has consistently explored the idea of "sonic geography" and frequently paid tribute to his chosen environment in his compositions. Building on the American experimental tradition established by Ives, Cowell, Partch, Cage, La Monte Young and others, Adams evokes Northern landscapes through experimental musical means. He uses recorded sounds of the Arctic and draws on the music, language and poetry of indigenous Eskimo and Indian peoples. He invokes the color white, the special light and the spaciousness of Arctic landscapes through just intonation, sustained tones, tone clusters, modal harmony, static textures, delicate instrumentation and extended lengths approaching Feldmanesque dimensions. The following paragraphs shed light on two early pieces and focus on four major works, *Earth and the Great Weather*,

In the White Silence, *Strange and Sacred Noise*, and *The Place Where You Go to Listen* with special consideration of Adams's notion of "sonic geography."

Early Works

songbirdsongs (1974–1980) for piccolos, percussion, and ocarinas and *Night Peace* (1976–1977) for solo soprano, two choirs, harp, and percussion, belong to his early and pre-Alaskan œuvre—both written after his studies at CalArts during a time when Adams was becoming active with environmental groups in the South and in the Rocky Mountain West. Both works were inspired by nature, the former by the songs of North American birds and the latter by the nocturnal landscape of the Okefenokee Swamp in South Georgia. *songbirdsongs* is a still-growing collection of miniature pieces of variable form, duration, and instrumental combinations, which feature free translations rather than literal transcriptions of birdsongs.[2] Each song is devoted to specific birds such as the field sparrow, Carolina wren, or tufted titmouse, and is provided with its own "performance kit."[3] A brief poetic description evocative of the birds' environment precedes a limited body of precisely notated, rhythmically and melodically fixed motives and brief phrases in which intonation, tempo, repetition, order, and combination are indeterminate. The interplay between the instruments should be spontaneous, reflecting an antiphonal character. Preconceived structures should be avoided.[4]

While *songbirdsongs* involves indeterminacy, spontaneity, and varied and vivid rhythms, *Night Peace*, a quiet one-movement piece, dispenses with indeterminate aspects with regard to performance. *Night Peace* is based on very limited pitch material (the tones of an extended F-sharp minor chord), sustained notes, and silences of a single wordless melody, sung by the solo soprano only once in its entirety—at the end of the piece. Throughout the piece fragments of this melodic line appear within a sparse and static texture and occasionally conglomerate in a dissonant chord or cluster. The static texture is interspersed by more animated pentatonic harp motives, repetitive patterns in the harp and vibraphone, and colorful appearances of timpani, cymbals, tamtam and wind chimes. The timbral contrasts, the occasional loosening up of the static texture as well as the antiphonal use of the wordless parts, create a certain spatial effect. Both of these works document two chief characteristics of Adams's later music: an attempt to capture natural phenomena and landscapes musically, and a determination to deal economically with musical materials.

Earth and the Great Weather

Written between 1989 and 1993, *Earth and the Great Weather: A Sonic Geography of the Arctic* is an impressive and ambitious music theater work inspired by the landscapes of the Arctic National Wildlife Refuge, and constitutes a mature realization of Adams's idea of "sonic geography." This composition began as a thirty-minute piece for the public broadcasting series *New American Radio* and grew into a seventy-five-minute music theater work, commissioned by the Alaska Festival of Native Arts and premiered in 1993 in Fairbanks by Adams and his ensemble. Written for four narrators, a vocal, string and percussion quartet, recorded environmental sounds and digital delay, *Earth* received after further performances in Alaska, Canada, Scandinavia and Western Europe its British premiere in 2000 at the Almeida Festival in London in a new production by stage designer Peter Mumford.[5]

The work's title is derived from a poem by the Inuit shaman Uvavnuk. Reflecting an individual's intense identification with nature, this poem in its Iñupiaq form opens *Earth* and is recited at the end of the work in its English translation:

The great sea has set me adrift.
It moves me like a weed
in a great river.
Earth and the great weather move me,
have carried me away
and move my inward parts with joy.[6]

The libretto dispenses with plot, narrative, and characters. Instead it consists of six so-called "Arctic Litanies," incantations of indigenous names for places, birds, mammals, plants, seasons, and weather in the Arctic, all emphasizing a sense of place. While the poem and most lists of names for natural phenomena refer to no *specific* places in the Arctic, the title and opening phrase of the first litany "The Place Where You Go to Listen" is a literal translation of the Iñupiaq Native place name Naalagiagvik, and can be considered a motto for the whole work.[7] The Arctic Litanies are in English and Latin, but above all in Iñupiaq, the language spoken by the Iñupiat people living in extreme Northern Alaska, and in Gwich'in, the language spoken by the northern Athabascan Indian people living in Northeast Alaska and Yukon. The litanies are often simultaneously read in two or three languages, but are not necessarily literal translations of each other. In fact not all of the names are translated or are even translatable. The two indigenous languages are primarily used to evoke a "poetry of place," whereas the English language and the Latin scientific binomials for plants and birds (only used in the fifth and sixth litanies) add contrasting color and rhythm and provide Western listeners with two additional semantic layers (Adams, "Composer's Notes" 7). The juxtaposition of four languages, however, results in a hybrid, multilingual text pointing to the coexistence and interpenetration of different cultures in Alaska.

The "Arctic Litanies" are freely recited, whispered, or chanted over a string and vocal background. Derived from the sounds of Aeolian wind harps recorded by the composer in the Brooks Range of northernmost Alaska, the atmospheric, seemingly improvised but rigorously formal and precisely notated string accompaniments are called "Aeolian Dreams." They are frequently heard as background to the voices, environmental sounds and drum pieces, and represent the foundation of the whole work.[8] Adams employs just intonation. Based on the first eight uneven harmonics of a low D (D, A, F#, C, E, etc.) on a double bass (IV string), the pitch material is produced from retuned open strings and natural overtones up to the 105th harmonic (the seventh harmonic of the fifteenth harmonic).[9]

In the first "Aeolian Dream" ("The Place Where You Go to Listen") these pitches are woven into drone-like, sustained open sounds and scintillating textures of natural harmonics. Herein string players make use of "harmonic bowing": bowing near the bridge with slight modifications in bow pressure, direction, and speed. This section, which dispenses with traditional motivic-thematic patterns, consists of an arch-like form with an overall textural and dynamic crescendo at its beginning and a decrescendo at its end. It also incorporates a continuous stream of interior crescendo-decrescendo gestures decreasing in size from eight-bar to one-bar sections. In the second "Dream" ("Pointed Mountains Scattered All Around"), the pitch material is worked into oscillating rising and falling glissandos on natural harmonics. The notation provides an approximate fingering for the contrapuntally layered unbroken rising and falling glissandos on natural harmonics, with the highest note as the sounding harmonic closest to the bridge and the lowest note as the harmonic closest to the nut. The score also reveals tone painting and *Augenmusik* pictorial graphic traits (see Figure 2.1).

The vocal quartet (two sopranos, alto, bass) accompanies the strings in all but one of the seven "Aeolian Dreams," singing the libretto portions in Iñupiaq and Gwich'in. Using the same pitch material as the strings, the singers lend depth to the strings' ethereal sonic texture and echo the spoken text. The indigenous words are set syllabically. Repetitive, sustained open sounds, often divided into unusual durations, dominate most settings. In some of the vocal quartets Adams requires special vocal expression, ranging from "sotto voce" in the fifth "Aeolian Dream" ("River With No Willows") to the imitation of the strings' "seagull" glissandos in the sixth "Aeolian Dream" ("One That Stays All Winter"). Further both the vocal and string quartets are expanded to a virtual choir and orchestra (sixteen parts and sixteen voices) through three tiers of

FIGURE 2.1. *John Luther Adams,* Earth and the Great Weather, *"Pointed Mountains Scattered All Around," strings and voices (mm. 9–16).*

TABLE 2.1. Structural Layout of "Drums of Winter" from *Earth and the Great Weather*.

	Introduction	A	B	C	D
MM-Tempo Modulation	1/4 note = 90	1/4 triplet = 136	1/4 note = 90	1/4 note = 113	1/4 note = 90
Pulse Modulation	1/4 Notes	1/4 Note Triplets	1/4 Notes	8th Note Quintuplets → 8th Notes	8th Notes → 8th Note Quintuplets
Pulse Ratios	3 (+2)	3	5:3	5:3	5:3
+ Common Pulse ÷ Divided Pulse	+	÷	÷	+	÷

E	F	G	H	I	J
1/4 note = 158	1/4 note = 90	8th note = 203	1/4 note = 90	8th note = 203	8th note = 203
8th Note Septuplets → 8th Notes	8th Notes → 8th Note Septuplets	8th Note Nonuplets → 8th Notes	8th notes → 8th Note Nonuplets	8th Note Nonuplets → 8th Notes	Same
3:5:7	5:7	3:5:7:9	7:9	3:5:7:9	3:5:7:9
+	÷	+	÷	+	+

digital delay, producing dense and complex canonic structures and a surround sound effect.

Earth falls into ten major sections played without interruption. The "Aeolian Dreams" and "Arctic Litanies" are linked by overlapping recorded natural sound (wind, thunder, melting ice, booming glaciers, birdcalls) and interspersed with three large, vigorous pieces for percussion. Entitled "Drums of Winter," "Deep and Distant Thunder," and "Drums of Fire, Drums of Stone," these pieces require the largest possible selection of tom-toms and bass drums.

Emerging from recorded sounds of thunder, each of the percussion pieces embraces rhythmic elements derived from traditional Iñupiat or Gwich'in dance music. "Drums of Winter" and "Drums of Fire, Drums of Stone" make use of asymmetrical cells from Iñupiat music. In "Drums of Winter," for instance, the asymmetries are created through additive rhythms and divided rhythms (ever-changing rhythmic combinations of two and three in groups of three, five, seven, and nine) and through constant tempo modulation. Throughout the piece, common pulse sections alternate with segments featuring divided pulse, and both textures gradually gain in complexity (see Table 2.1). The common pulse sections reveal more and more frequent change of meter and dense textures due to the increasing division of longer rhythmic values and the

FIGURE 2.2. *John Luther Adams*, Earth and the Great Weather, *"Drums of Winter,"*
(mm. 130–137/letter I).

superimposition of rhythmic layers (see Figure 2.2 and Table 2.1: Ratio pulse of letters C, E, G, I, J).[10] At the same time the common pulse textures get faster from section to section (see Table 2.1: letters C, E, G, I, J). Gradual acceleration is another typical feature of Iñupiat drumming.

In contrast, the segments with divided pulse (A, B, D, F, H) retain the same tempo and never deviate from their 4/4 meter. In these passages Percussion I and II feature rhythmic counterpoint with ratios of 5:3, 5:7, and 7:9 while Percussion III and IV provide a tremolo background.

In comparison "Deep and Distant Thunder" uses relentless steady drumbeats typically found in Gwich'in music, and Adams utilizes once again intricate cross-rhythms such as three-against-four-against-five-against-six. As rigorously structured as the "Aeolian Dreams," "Deep and Distant Thunder" is marked by frequent changes of meter, complex multilayered rhythms, and shifting pulse. All three percussion pieces are, according to Adams, "informed by the elemental power of natural forces in the Arctic and by the ecstatic power of Inuit drumming and dancing" (Adams, Preface to "Three Drum Quartets" 1).

In *Earth* Adams's idea of music as place or "sonic geography" is suggested in multiple ways. First, Arctic landscapes are vividly evoked through the verbal articulation of places and natural phenomena. Second, features of Arctic soundscapes, taped natural sounds, indigenous languages, and elements of Alaska Native music predominate. Third, the pitch material of the entire work is derived from Aeolian harp sounds recorded in the Brooks Range. Fourth, static textures, non-narrative concepts, non-developmental harmony, reiterative techniques, and extended length suggest vast spaces and time at a standstill. Adams likes to compare the "Aeolian Dreams" to plains and the percussion interludes to rising mountains (Adams, "Composer's Notes" 7). Fifth, space is simulated through a digital delay system and speakers surrounding the audience.

Critical of the passive perception of landscape from a distance, whether from paintings, photography, and films, or through the window of a speeding car, Adams sought "to move away from music *about* landscape, toward music which in a certain sense, *is* landscape." (Adams, "Resonance" 10). Adams attempted to overcome or expand the dimension of program music not only by avoiding musical narrative, but also by extending the work's length—thus challenging the traditional way of listening.[11] Both the "Arctic Litanies" with their invoking of multilingual names underlain by ethereal sonic strata, and the percussion interludes with their pulsing rhythms, convey a ritualistic ambiance. Enveloping the listener in spatially distributed sounds, *Earth* requires a deep attentiveness or contemplative attitude from the listener. Adams emphasized: "I want to immerse the listener in a place of suspended time and endless space. I want music to be wilderness. And I want to get hopelessly lost in it" (Adams, *Winter Music* 75).

When one considers *Earth*'s ritualistic quality and Adams's borrowings from non-Western traditions, one might infer that the composer exoticizes Alaska. Adams, however, goes beyond a mere evocation of an exotic locale. *Earth* rather appears to be what Ralph P. Locke calls a "consciously multicultural" work from a "composer with feet in two different cultures" (Locke 460). By the time Adams conceived *Earth* he had lived in Alaska for more than ten years and had studied various Arctic cultures and communicated and worked extensively with indigenous Alaskans.[12] "The longer I walk the ground of my home, Alaska, the more I admire and respect the musics of its indigenous Eskimo and Indian peoples; musics which sound so fully the sympathetic resonances of thousands of years of living and listening in this place" (Adams, "Resonance" 13). Adams involved four Arctic natives as collaborators and narrators in *Earth*: James Nageak, Doreen Simmonds, Adeline Peter Raboff, and Lincoln Tritt. And interestingly, Alaska Natives were present at performances of the work in Fairbanks (1993) and Anchorage (1995). One Iñupiaq who attended the latter performance remarked that he "kept going back and forth into the spirit world" (Dunham 62). But as Jonathan Bellman pointed out, the idea of "musical exoticism" depends on "who is doing the composing and who is doing the listening" (Bellman x). In general, however, borrowings from Alaska Native music in *Earth* appear in abstracted, fragmented form and remain a rarity within Adams's œuvre.

Earth owes its origin at least in part to Adams's commitment to environmentalism. In the mid-1970s he worked as a wilderness guide and for the Alaska Coalition, which at that time was struggling for the passage of the "Alaska Lands Act," eventually enacted to preserve large wilderness areas, including the area now known as the Arctic National Wildlife Refuge. Recently threatened again by renewed pressure for oil exploitation, the Arctic Refuge was *Earth*'s inspiration. The work is dedicated to Adams's wife Cynthia, a professional environmentalist who worked with him at the Northern Alaska Environmental Center. *Earth* also points to Adams's interest in acoustic ecology, pioneered by R. Murray Schafer, and his concern for the ecologically fragile state of Northern soundscapes. *Earth*'s recorded sounds originated from Adams's Alaska Soundscape Project, which was inspired by Schafer's World Soundscape Project and equally dedicated to the periodical recording of environmental sounds.[13] Since *Earth* reflects upon the preciousness and equality of human and non-human life and the priceless values of the Arctic's eco-regions and thus resonates with the philosophies of deep ecology and bioregionalism, this work was considered an environmentalist statement and Adams was soon classified as a "Green" composer (Morris 131). Yet Adams maintains: "*Earth and the Great Weather* is not an intentionally political work. In it, my intention was not so much to make a specific statement about, or even to evoke a specific place. Rather, I hope to take the listener through strange and beautiful landscapes which embrace places both real and imaginary" (Adams, "Resonance" 16).[14]

In the White Silence

Shortly before Adams began composing *Earth*, he wrote the one-movement orchestral work *The Far Country of Sleep* (1988), dedicating it to the memory of Feldman, whose works Adams has long viewed as sublime soundscapes. This work became the first of a series of meditative orchestral works in one movement forming sonic equivalents to the treeless and windswept expanses of the Arctic, and depicting sonic environments with an enveloping presence. Constantly growing in length, subsequent works include *Dream in White on White* (1992), *Clouds of Forgetting, Clouds of Unknowing* (1991–95), *In the White Silence* (1998), and *for Lou Harrison* (2003). As *Clouds* was composed following the death of his father, *Silence* is a memorial to Adams's mother, who died in the fall of 1996. While these two works share the same number of instruments and a similar form, they are very different from one another with regard to sound and orchestration. *Silence* actually evolved from *Dream*, a fifteen-minute piece for string quartet, harp (or piano), and string orchestra.[15] Like *Dream*, *Silence* reveals Adams's fascination with the color white, a dominant feature of Arctic landscapes. Yet as Adams explains: "White is not the absence of color. It is the fullness of light. As the Inuit have known for centuries, and as painters from Malevich to Ryman have shown us more recently, whiteness embraces many hues, textures, and nuances" (Adams, Preface to score of *In the White Silence*).[16] Whiteness is evoked in *Silence* in several ways. Above all, the instrumentation (celesta, harp, orchestra bells, two vibraphones, and strings) produces luminous and iridescent sonorities. Further, the work features durations consisting of whole and half notes ("white notes") and is based, like *Dream*, exclusively on the non-chromatic "white" tones (the "white" keys of the piano). The frequent use of perfect intervals, harmonics, and unstopped string tones, however, connote the color white as well.

The title of the piece reveals another important aspect of the piece: silence. Adams explains: "As Cage reminded us, silence does not literally exist. Still, in a world going deaf with human noise, silence endures as a deep and resonant metaphor . . . Silence is not the absence of sound. It is the presence of stillness" (Adams, Preface to score of *In the White Silence*). Although silence and stillness contradict the basic premises of music, they are evoked through various compositional means.[17] The dynamic range of *Silence* is subtle and unobtrusive, with piano and pianissimo predominating. Stillness is further suggested through static textures of densely layered sound, sustained tones, short repetitive patterns, and long rising and falling modal lines (while conventional leading-tone-driven developmental melodic and harmonic syntax is avoided).

Stillness is also conveyed through the piece's symmetrical and arch-like rondo form with three basic rotating textures. The opening texture (A), consisting of dispersed tone clusters, consistently recurs between two different subsidiary textures and concludes the piece. Of the two subsidiary textures, one reveals a chorale-like texture (B) and the other, long contrapuntally interwoven lines (C). Sequences of ABA textures recur five times and alternate with the C-texture. The cyclical changes of the piece's texture often occur subtly and kaleidoscopically due to the delicate juxtaposition and superimposition of different patterns and are comparable to changes of a vista. *Silence* opens with sustained spacious pianissimo tone clusters in the string orchestra that recede to the background when the string quartet adds a slightly more intense layer of mezzo-piano clusters and the harp injects bright ascending eighth-note motifs. Then two additional colorful strata emerge: the celesta intersperses ascending scale-like motifs and the vibraphones add a soft, dense, and continuous tremolo cluster sound. Later in the piece, the B- and C-textures show intricate polymetric and polyrhythmic relationships between various strata, culminating in what Adams calls "allover counterpoint," a technique pointing to Cowell's innovative ideas and to "allover" structures (dense tangles without a center or hierarchy) in the poured paintings of Jackson Pollock (see Figure 2.3).

As in *Earth*, in *Silence* Adams evokes the idea of music as place through spatially deployed sound to enhance the perception of background and foreground strata. The strings are divided into an orchestra seated in a wide arc upstage providing a gleaming background with soft sustained non-vibrato sonorities and a quartet seated in a small arc downstage playing always with vibrato and more volume. The vibraphones, bells, celesta, and harp are placed mid-stage between the orchestra and quartet and their contrasting sonic layers add to the spatial feel as well. The orchestra's and quartet's mostly inert, dispersed tone clusters, often embracing all seven pitches of the diatonic scale, are frequently topped by a layer of shimmering harmonics. Interestingly, Adams conceives of these as "clouds": "There's so much 'air' between the tones."[18] He used "clouds" in *Dream* for the first time. In *Silence*, however, they become more expansive and more densely layered.

Space or spaciousness is further suggested by the work's extended dimension of time. *Silence* slowly unfolds over the course of about seventy-five minutes. Its expansive length, non-dramatic structure and absence of goal-directed motion reveal Adams's desire to create music as an "immeasurable space" and to transcend the conventional boundaries of musical composition.[19] "I want

FIGURE 2.3. *"Allover Counterpoint,"* *excerpt from the second to last C episode (N1)* *of* In the White Silence.

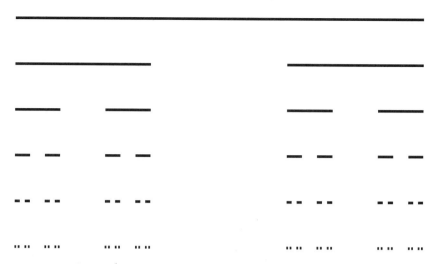

FIGURE 2.4. *Cantor dust.*

to leave the composition, the 'piece' of music, for the wholeness of music," declared Adams. The opening indication of *Silence* reads "Timeless . . ." Hence the listeners should not perceive the piece as a sound object apart or a musical narrative proceeding from A to B. Rather, they should inhabit time and sound like a place devoid of beginning and end (as emphasized by the title *In the White Silence* rather than "The White Silence"). To Adams "the experience of listening is more like sitting in the same place as the wind and weather, the light and shadows slowly change." (Adams, Preface to *The Light*).

Strange and Sacred Noise

In the 1990s Adams became gradually fascinated with more abstract and complex aspects of nature. His growing interest in the sonic violence of nature and the power of primordial noise such as thunder, river ice breaking up, and the crashing of glaciers into the sea led him to study chaos theory, fractal geometry, and the science of complexity and to develop his concept of "sonic geometry." As a consequence he focused on chromaticism, dissonance, and ultimately noise. *Clouds of Forgetting, Clouds of Unknowing*, a spacious and dissonant piece in which he began to explore "more abstract dimensions of places and presence," was the first step in this direction. However, *Strange and Sacred Noise* (1991–97), a concert-length cycle of six movements for percussion quartet, is one of Adams's first attempts to find sonic equivalents of simple, linear fractals. The first and last movements (". . . dust into dust . . ." and ". . . and dust rising . . .") are based on the Cantor set and Cantor dust (the Cantor set's two-dimensional version), fractals modeling the behavior of electrical

...dust into dust...

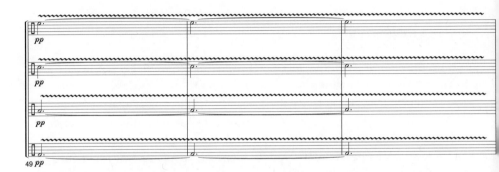

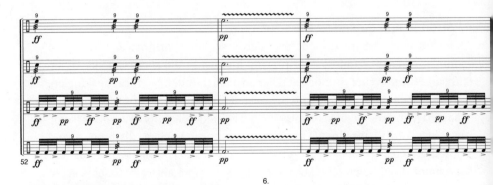

6.

* From E through H; an accented note is
played ff and an unaccented note is played
pp.

FIGURE 2.5A. *John Luther Adams,* Strange and Sacred Noise, *"... dust into dust..."*
(mm. 46–54/letter E).

...dust into dust...

Q

154

157

160

18.

FIGURE 2.5B. *John Luther Adams,* Strange and Sacred Noise, *"... dust into dust..."* *(mm. 154–62/letter Q, the negative image of the E section).*

FIGURE 2.6A. *Menger sponge.*

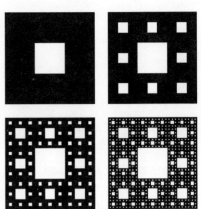

FIGURE 2.6B. *Sierpinski carpet, original solid square with three iterations.*

noise. "... dust into dust ..." for two snare drums and two field drums explores the dynamic form of the Cantor set, whereby in an infinite process, line segments are divided into two segments by the removal of their middle third (see Figure 2.4).[20]

This procedure is simulated in musical time by accented rhythms that, step by step, are replaced by drum rolls. The rolls (which are intermittent in nature as well, containing within them innumerable short rests) are in turn replaced by silence.[21] The initial patterns gradually dissolve into drum rolls and then silence, whereupon the process is reversed. In addition, Adams contrasts this procedure by using "positive" and "negative" forms of the fractal. "Positive" refers to sounding statements and "negative" to silence analogous to the images of the Cantor dust, which can be viewed as negatives, whereby the distribution of filled out and blank space is reversed (see Figures 2.5a and 2.5b).[22]

The fourth movement of *Noise* ("triadic iteration lattices") is scored for four sirens and grounded in the Sierpinski gasket, a self-similar structure of triangles reiterated in smaller and smaller dimensions.[23] Herein continuously rising and falling glissandi reflect the triangles' diagonals. The musical form portrays three dimensions of the Sierpinski gasket through three interlocking "iterations" each embracing 128 measures.[24] The second iteration represents an inversion of the first statement, an up-and-down glissando. And the third iteration is a negative form of the first iteration.

The fifth movement, "clusters on a quadrilateral grid" (for four percussionists playing four marimbas, four vibraphones and four sets of orchestra bells) was inspired by the Menger sponge, a quadrilateral with an infinite surface

TABLE 2.2. Formal layout of "Clusters on a Quadrilateral Grid" from *Strange and Sacred Noise*.

	Iteration Series I—Marimbas							Iteration Series II—Vibraphones							
	Rolled Clusters							Hammered Clusters							
	+ (positive)			– (negative)				+				–			
Iteration: C-0	C-1	C-2	C-3	C-0	C-1	C-2	C-3	C-0	C-1	C-2	C-3	C-0	C-1	C-2	C-3
Rehearsal letter:	A	B	C	D	E	F	G	H	I	J	K	L	M	N	O

	Iteration Series III—Orchestra Bells							Iteration Series IV—Marimbas							
	Faster Hammered Clusters							Rolled Clusters							
	–				+				–				+			
C-3	C-2	C-1	C-0	C-3	C-2	C-1	C-0	C-3	C-2	C-1	C-0	C-3	C-2	C-1	C-0
P	Q	R	S	T	U	V	W	X	Y	Z	AA	BB	CC	DD	EE

area and a volume of zero, and by the Sierpinski carpet (the two-dimensional version of the Menger sponge) (see Figure 2.6a).[25] These fractals and their first three iterations are musically translated into small, dense tone clusters composed from a field of twenty-seven chromatic pitches and organized in measure-units and durational groups of twenty-seven, nine, and three, numbers reflecting the structure and proportions of the Menger sponge and Sierpinski carpet (see Figure 2.6b). The grids of the Sierpinski carpet, C (0), C (1), C (2), and C (3)—once again used in positive and negative forms—are interpreted as coordinate systems in which the x-axis is time (with twenty-seven small squares corresponding to twenty-seven measures) and the y-axis is pitch (comprising twenty-seven chromatic pitches).

Formally this movement falls into four series of iterations. Each series is differently scored and consists of four "positive" and four "negative" iterations (see Table 2.2). The piece opens with the musical reading of the original solid square (C-0) and presents a full static field of soft tremolo clusters embracing all twenty-seven chromatic pitches from A through b' over the course of twenty-seven measures. The four players each use four mallets, so that a maximum of sixteen tones can be articulated at any given moment. Each of the following positive iterations (C-1, C-2, C-3) of the first series shows a gradual textural transformation involving a decrease in the clusters' density and size and subtle changes in the clusters' rhythmic articulation—all in accordance with the filled-out and blank spaces on the grids. The negative iterations manifest

clusters

28

37

46

62.

FIGURE 2.7A. *John Luther Adams,* Strange and Sacred Noise, *"clusters on a quadrilateral grid," the positive version of C(2) (mm. 55–81/letter B).*

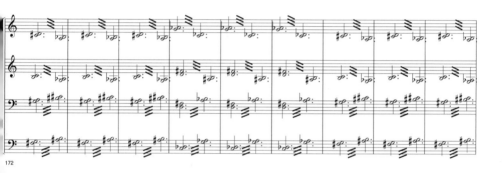

67.

FIGURE 2.7B. *John Luther Adams*, Strange and Sacred Noise, *"clusters on a quadrilateral grid," the negative version of C(2) (mm. 163–89/letter F).*

strong textural contrast. C-1 negative (letter E) is made up of a nine-measure-long dense tone cluster segment preceded and followed by nine measures of silence. In C-2 negative (letter F) a nine-measure-long cluster section is surrounded by segments in which silence and cluster sonorities alternate in three-measure units (see Figure 2.7).

The second series is an octave higher than the first; the third series, a retrograde of the second, is yet another octave higher; and the last series is a retrograde of the first in its initial register. The two middle series display rhythmic acceleration and dynamic intensification pointing toward the fractals' gradually decreasing interior dimensions.

Noise features geometric formalism, with the symmetry of the forms only occasionally disturbed. Inspired by the spring break-up of ice on the Yukon River, this music, however, also conveys a strong elemental and ritualistic impact due to the enormous dynamic range, from near inaudibility to the threshold of pain, the vigor of relentlessly rattling snare drums, rolling tam-tams, howling sirens, or thunderous bass drums, and the spatially deployed percussion instruments (surrounding the audience). Moreover, Adams wants this percussion work to be perceived as "places," as he points out: "Ultimately, I've come to regard the six sections of *Strange and Sacred Noise* not so much as musical compositions or pieces, but as places . . . places for listening, places in which to experience the elemental mystery of noise" (Adams, "Strange and Sacred Noise" 146). Since *Noise*, "sonic geometry" has remained an important concept for Adams in addition to "sonic geography."

The Place Where You Go to Listen

With his continuous sound-light installation, *The Place Where You Go to Listen* (2005), titled after the Iñupiaq name Naalagiagvik—a place on the Arctic coast—Adams offered his most intriguing realization of "sonic geography" to date. This sonic and visual environment, permanently installed at the Museum of the North in Fairbanks since the spring equinox of 2006, reflects the geography of Interior Alaska (from the Alaska Range's crest to that of the Brooks Range, including most of the Yukon River basin). It makes audible in real time this region's cycles of daylight and nighttime; phases of the moon; meteorological, seismic, and geomagnetic activities; and the aurora borealis.

Adams's *Place* draws on real-time digital data streams (numerical maps) of this region's geophysical forces, which are continuously fed into a computer and "orchestrated" with electronic sounds.[26] As in his six-hour sound installation *Veils* of 2005, Adams uses pink noise (a variation of white noise) as his point of departure, from which he obtains through filtering and tuning processes (subtractive sound synthesis) the desired tones and timbres. A "Day Choir" and

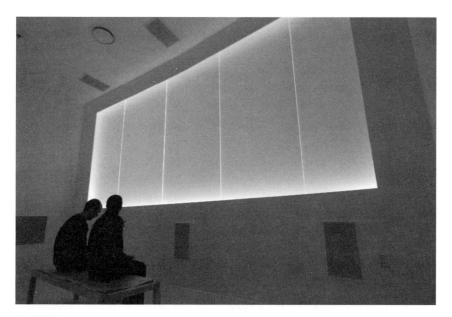

FIGURE 2.8

a "Night Choir" of virtual voices feature sustained chords based on a respective overtone and undertone series on G, which change according to the phases of the sun and darkness. The "Voice of the Moon" traces the positions and phases of the moon through a month-long glissando of a narrow band of pink noise. The so-called "Earth Drums" with their low-frequency roars sonify Interior Alaska's many small earthquakes while the "Aurora Bells," shimmering high-pitched sonorities in just intonation prompted by geomagnetic fluctuations, are a sonic translation of the aurora borealis, the northern polar lights in the sky. During a sunny day a listener is typically confronted with an ongoing sensuous drone, with bright and clearly defined voices embracing a range of up to four octaves, that may be temporarily muted by passing clouds or dramatically punctuated by rattling drums triggered by strong seismic activity and/or shimmering bell tones set off by geomagnetic disturbances. Yet such changes are controlled by nature and unpredictable.

With this work, Adams undoubtedly comes closest to his vision of creating music with a place-like enveloping presence. Unlike most of his other pieces, *The Place* is devoid of beginning, middle, and end, as it resonates the ever-changing natural events, 24/7, all year long, year after year, transcending in expansive length La Monte Young's "Dream House" and "eternal music" projects. The fact that this music is not portable, emanates from fourteen surround-sound speakers, and features specially designed visual components, including five glass panels with constantly changing colors in response to the cycles of the sun, further enhances this work's sense of place (see Figure 2.8).

As Adams's *Place* is directly tied to the natural world, grafted onto Interior Alaska's ecosystem, it helps listeners to establish a special connection with this place or restore their "lost connection [to] a place they inhabit." It also allows audiences to enhance their awareness of this place's geophysical activities and unique ecology. Adams's work has drawn countless visitors to the museum, including numerous Alaskans, and prompted them to spend extended periods listening to Interior Alaska's natural events.

Another musician fascinated by the North, Glenn Gould, remarked in his radio documentary *The Idea of North* (1967), "Something really does happen to most people who go into the north—they become at least aware of the creative opportunity which the physical fact of the country represents, and, quite often I think, come to measure their own work and life against that rather staggering creative possibility—they become, in effect, philosophers." Adams's conceptions about "sonic geography" are exceptional in their consistency and diversity and in their relationship to Arctic landscapes. They have resulted in an ever-growing range of fascinating works for solo instruments, ensembles, and orchestra. His music embraces works of miniature-like conciseness and great extension. Though marked by meditative qualities, and fine-spun, sustained sounds, his music also displays explosive, reiterative, and percussive elements and is distinguished by formal and structural rigor as well as by a sensual sound image rich in nuances and colors. As Adams proceeds in his explorations of "sonic geography" he is guided by a vivid musical imagination and moral strength nourished by the extraordinary landscapes of Alaska.

Notes

1. John Luther Adams is not to be confused with the John Adams of *Shaker Loops* and *Nixon in China*. Due to the international success of *Nixon in China*, when the latter became a household name, the former began to use his middle name Luther to avoid confusion. Incidentally, both Adamses met each other in the 1970s and shared interest in the music of John Cage, Morton Feldman and Steve Reich. Both avail themselves of certain elements of minimal music, though each does so in his own distinctive way (Salzman).

2. Although Adams completed nine pieces published in two volumes of four and five *songs*, there are sketches for more than thirty other *songbirdsongs*.

3. The expression "performance kit" was often used by Lou Harrison.

4. Like Messiaen, Adams spent much time in the field studying the sounds of birds, but tried to escape Messiaen's influence by intentionally ignoring his birdsong works. Neither was Adams, when composing *songbirdsongs*, aware of such works as Cage's *Bird Cage* (1972) or Einojuhani Rautavaara's *Cantus Arcticus* (1972).

5. The version performed at the Almeida Opera Festival included newly composed choral parts.

6. This poem was translated from Iglulik Inuktitut into Danish by the Arctic explorer and ethnologist Knud Rasmussen, then translated into English, and from English into Iñupiaq by James Mumigaaluk Nageak.

7. Inuit place names such as "The Place Where You Go to Listen" are more subjective in tone, denoting a deep knowledge and authentic experience of place. In 2005 Adams titled his sound installation for the Museum of the North in Fairbanks *The Place Where You Go to Listen*. *Earth*'s first two Arctic Litanies contain further names of specific places on the north and south slopes of the Brooks Range.

8. British choreographer Rosemary Lee based a dance on *Earth*'s "Aeolian Dreams."

9. Due to the use of an unusual tuning system and natural harmonics, Adams employs a notation showing the sounding pitches with Roman numerals indicating the string and Arabic subscripts showing the number of the harmonic.

10. This technique brings to mind some of Henry Cowell's rhythmic theories from *New Musical Resources* (1930), whereby whole notes are often continuously divided into different numbers of equal durations.

11. However, many of La Monte Young's works and Philip Glass's *Einstein on the Beach* involve greater length and are performed without interruptions.

12. Adams collaborated with the musician Joe Beetus, a Koyukon elder, when writing the score for the public television series *Make Prayers to the Raven* (1987) about the Koyukon Athabascans of Interior Alaska. He worked with the Yu'pik dancer, singer, and drummer Chuna McIntyre on a growing collection of *Alaskan Dances* based on indigenous songs. Adams also worked with poets and writers such as John Haines and Barry Lopez, all closely associated with Alaska.

13. The "World Soundscape Project" was founded in 1971 at Simon Fraser University, British Columbia, Canada, to draw attention to so-called "soundscapes" and to document the acoustic elements of the environment on tape. Later the term "soundscape" was also applied to musical compositions sonically evoking landscapes.

14. Compared to *Earth*, R. Murray Schafer's composition *North/White* (1973) for orchestra, inspired by Canada's Arctic landscapes, is a much more overtly political work. Herein the noise of a snowmobile and of various metal objects is used to disturb the delicate sonic texture of the piece and to highlight the acoustic pollution of the Canadian North through snowmobiles, pipelines, highways, and runways.

15. *In the White Silence* (1998) was premiered in the year of its completion and recorded for New World Records (New World Records 80600–2) by the Oberlin Contemporary Music Ensemble, conducted by Tim Weiss in the Finney Chapel in Oberlin, Ohio.

16. Many of Adams's works suggest—due to their static character and pictorial quality—associations with painting, namely the non-representational visual art of Kasimir Malevich, Robert Ryman, Jackson Pollock, and Mark Rothko, all of whom used color as subject. According to Adams, "Malevich's *White on White* and the paintings of Robert Ryman were touchstone images for *Dream* and *Silence*."

17. Of course, musically it is easier to depict sonic aspects of nature: bird calls or characteristics of motion-oriented landscape such as murmuring brooks.

18. John Luther Adams to author, May 31, 2003. "Clouds," another visual metaphor

and landscape component, brings to mind La Monte Young's use of the word for dense harmonies embracing a wide range of pitches.

19. In 2002 Adams completed a piece for chamber ensemble entitled *The Immeasurable Space of Tones*. Interestingly, Adams's desire to write works of extended duration converge with Mark Rothko's expressed need to paint large pictures: "I paint very large pictures. I realize that historically the function of painting large pictures is painting something very grandiose and pompous. The reason I paint them, however—I think it applies to other painters I know—is precisely because I want to be very intimate and human. To paint a small picture is to place yourself outside your experience, to look upon an experience as a stereopticon view or with a reducing glass . . . However, you paint the larger picture you are in it. It isn't something you command" (Rothko quoted in Waldman 62). Perhaps for this reason *Silence* and other works by Adams have been perceived as "sounding images" and as large time canvases consisting of multiple quasi-symmetrically organized panels where broad washes of harmony and timbre replace developmental and narrative patterns (Gann).

20. The Cantor set is named after the German mathematician Georg Cantor (1845–1918).

21. See in comparison Tom Johnson's ideas and realizations of Cantor sets in his handbook *Self-Similar Melodies* (Paris: Editions 75, 1996). Since Benoit Mandelbrot's path-breaking publication *The Fractal Geometry of Nature* (1982) many other composers —among them György Ligeti, Jean-Claude Risset, Elliott Sharp, and Charles Wuorinen —have become fascinated with fractals and translated them into music. *Strange and Sacred Noise* was premiered by the Percussion Group Cincinnati in Cincinnati in 1998 and recorded for Mode Records (CD/DVD Mode 153) in 2005.

22. Adams also used "negative" forms of fractals in two other movements of this cycle: ". . . and dust rising . . ." and "clusters on a quadrilateral grid."

23. The Sierpinski gasket is named after the Polish mathematician Waclaw Sierpinski (1882–1969).

24. Adams uses the term "iteration" for every musical statement including the first.

25. The Menger sponge is named after the Austrian mathematician Karl Menger (1902–85) who developed this fractal solid.

26. This intricate enterprise required the collaboration of meteorologist James Brader, seismologist Roger Hansen, scientist Dirk Lummerzheim, physicist John Olson, mathematician Curt Szuberla, and the computer programmers Jim Altieri, Josh Stachnik, Roger Topp, and Debi-Lee Wilkinson.

Works Cited

Adams, John Luther. Preface to *Earth and the Great Weather*. Fairbanks: Taiga Press, 1993.

———. Preface to "Three Drum Quartets" from *Earth and the Great Weather*. Fairbanks: Taiga Press, 1993.

———. "Resonance of Place: Confessions of an Out-of-Town Composer." *The North American Review* 179, no. 1 (Jan.–Feb. 1994): 8–18.

———. "Composer's Notes to *Earth and the Great Weather. A Sonic Geography.*" New York: New World Records, 80459-2, 1994.

———. "Strange and Sacred Noise." In: *Northern Soundscapes.* Yearbook of Soundscape Studies, vol. 1, ed. R. Murray Schafer and Helmi Järviluoma. Tampere, Finland: University of Tampere, 1998, 143-46.

———. Preface to *In the White Silence.* Fairbanks: Taiga Press, 1998.

———. Preface to *The Light That Fills the World.* Fairbanks: Taiga Press, 2000.

———. *Winter Music. Composing the North.* Middletown, Conn.: Wesleyan University Press, 2004.

Alburger, Mark. "A to Z. Interview with John Luther Adams." *21st Century Music* 7, no. 1 (2000): 1-12.

Bellman, Jonathan, ed. *The Exotic in Western Music.* Boston: Northeastern University Press, 1998.

Dunham, Mike. "Anchorage." *Opera News* 60, no. 3 (1995): 62.

Gann, Kyle. "Sounding the Image." *The Village Voice* 37, no. 5 (1992): 86.

Gould, Glenn. *The Idea of North, Solitude Trilogy. Three Sound Documentaries.* Toronto: CBC Records/Les Disques SRC, PSCD 2003-3, 1992.

Harley, Maria Anna. "Ritual und Klanglandschaft. Zur Musik von R. Murray Schafer." *MusikTexte* 67/68 (1997): 25-26.

Locke, Ralph P. "Exoticism." In *The New Grove Dictionary of Music and Musicians,* 2nd edition, ed. Stanley Sadie, vol. 8. London and New York: McMillan, 2001.

Morris, Mitchell. "Ecotopian Sound or The Music of John Luther Adams and Strong Environmentalism." In *Crosscurrents and Counterpoints: Offerings in Honor of Bengt Hembraeus at 70,* ed. Per F. Broman, Nora A. Engebretsen and Bo Alphonce. Göthenborg: University of Sweden, 1998, 29-41.

Salzman, Eric. "Two John Adamses." *Stereo Review* 46, no. 10 (1981): 140.

Schafer, R. Murray. *The Tuning of the World.* New York: Alfred Knopf, 1977.

Waldman, Diane. *Mark Rothko, 1903-1970. A Retrospective.* New York: Harry N. Abrams, 1978.

Young, Gayle. "Sonic Geography of the Arctic: An Interview with John Luther Adams." *Musicworks* 70 (Spring 1998): 38-43.

3 * Time at the End of the World
The Orchestral Tetralogy of
John Luther Adams

*I aspire to music which is both rigorous in thought
and sensuous in sound.*

* JOHN LUTHER ADAMS

John Luther Adams is a reasonably tall man who lives in an enormous state: Alaska. He enjoys crawling over that state's wilderness landscape and encountering bears, nearly horizontal sunrises, fields of ice crystals, avalanches, and other phenomena that many of us would be happy to stay at home and read vivid descriptions of. From the air (from former Governor Sarah Palin's helicopter, for instance), Adams must look like an ant traversing a vast white expanse whose larger contours stand outside his perception. He enjoys that experience of disappearing into something beyond human scale. He's one of the few artists around who still likes to talk about that ultimate nineteenth-century artistic category "the sublime."

And that's the experience Adams often gives us in his music. We start listening and the sonic surface is sensuous and beautiful, but the pacing is too vast to hear "around the corner." At a given moment an Adams piece presents us with an image of eternity: an unchanging sonority, or a complex of repeating ostinatos. Changes of texture and sonority come, but we cannot hear them coming nor predict their arrival. The pattern of changes makes logical sense to one who analyzes the score, and thus views the music, as it were, from a great enough height to encompass the entire form; but the listener, close to the music's surface, can only surrender to the sensuousness of the moment, reconstructing large-scale recurring patterns in memory, if at all.

As the statement quoted above implies, Adams writes music for both halves of the brain: the logical, time-assessing left brain and the contour-intuiting, lost-in-the-moment right brain. Unlike more conventional classical music, however, he does not appeal to both in a unified way. In a piece of music from the eighteenth through early twentieth centuries, a motive or theme might be introduced, then repeated, varied. These repetitions and variations keep the passage of time pinned down in the ear's imagination. A reappearance of the theme in its original form (or key) might signal the approach of a closing section. Certain chord progressions suggest, via a familiar and learned syntax, an increase in tension or a prolonged resolution—also markers of the passage of time. At the same time, these elements are fused to other factors less easy to articulate: gestural contours, mood, atmosphere, heights and depths of register, a feeling of stability or instability. In competently written conventional music, these left-brain and right-brain factors work hand in hand, inseparably, to convey the music's meaning.

In the works of Adams here considered (and not only those), the fine line between these syntactic and sensuous factors is intentionally widened into a gulf. Sensuous aspects are accessible at every moment; the work's large-scale logic, however, is confined to rare changes, inscrutable at first but gradually revealing their trajectory over a half-hour, an hour. The listener, or analyst, who knows how the pieces work, can take pleasure in tracking the progress of the form, but in the process of listening must still submit to the vastness, the unknowability, the richness of the textures and patterns, the accidental coincidences of large-scale process. No matter how familiar one is with the piece, there is no humming along, almost no anticipating the next turn. In places the complexes of layered multitempos and independent processes become sufficiently absorbing that the attention is barely adequate to take in the pleasures of the moment. You lose yourself in the attempt to grasp the complexity of the phenomena. One listens to an Adams piece, as one might move to Alaska, because the pleasure of *comprehending* seems inferior: one wants to feel the full force of the mystery. That the whole ultimately makes sense, that it condenses into a unitary gesture, becomes a matter of rather abstract thought, perhaps even of faith—and perhaps that faith itself allows one to surrender to the unmediated details. It is almost as though a single phrase of Mozart, coherent in itself, were slowed down across an hour and blown up through several octaves of register so we could view it from the inside, as a flea might view a Cezanne that it was wandering across. Past a certain point, as Morton Feldman noted, form becomes scale.

"Rigorous in thought" and "sensuous in sound"—but not on the same scale, nor in the same way. The rigor and sensuousness are separated out, and reuniting them in the imagination becomes the mystery, the challenge, of the music.

Adams has spoken of his three orchestral works *Clouds of Forgetting, Clouds of Unknowing* (1994–95), *In the White Silence* (1998), and *for Lou Harrison* (2003–4) as a trilogy, a phase in his output. The phase really stems from a shorter work that provided a template for the others: *Dream in White on White* of 1992, which is therefore also included here. This article will explore the distribution and development of techniques, ideas, and methods used in these four works. Since the respective lengths of these four pieces are (proceeding chronologically, and based on the first commercial recordings) seventeen, sixty-one, seventy-five, and sixty-three minutes, this is a massive amount of music, more than three-and-a-half hours' worth. Nevertheless, as even the vast state of Alaska can be mapped on a page, the principles of these pieces are simple and systematic enough that we can outline them in some detail in the course of a few pages.

Dream in White on White

Dream in White on White presents three layers of activity. First enters a series of chords in the string orchestra, whose changes every two and two-thirds measures outline a slow pulse of (at quarter = 48) thirteen and one-third seconds, only four and a half chords a minute. These chords continue into m. 73, providing a mystical background for the entering harp and string quartet—much as the string orchestra (or quintet) in Ives's *The Unanswered Question* provides a background for the trumpet and woodwinds. Starting at m. 87, higher and quicker chords in the string orchestra, initially stacked in fourths and metamorphosing into stacked fifths, move at a rate of every one and one-third measure, or every six and two-thirds seconds—double the previous tempo. These chords continue to m. 119. At mm. 128–46 the string orchestra plays a series of repeated ostinati, analogous to earlier activity in the string quartet. At m. 159 the string orchestra chords return at the original tempo and spread of range, continuing to the end at m. 206. A schematic summarizing this information can be seen in Figure 3.1, with the string orchestra part along the bottom.

Most, though not all, of the string orchestra chords contain all seven notes of the natural white-key scale. Adams uses several strategies to maintain pitch saturation, with a variety of spacings and interval colors. Ninths, both major and minor, are particularly emphasized, giving a stretched, oversize quality to the virtual canvas on which the music is written. In the beginning one finds an alternation of fourths and sixths making up those ninths; later (in the middle section) stacked fourths leading to fifths, as mentioned; and toward the end, stacked sevenths. At the beginning the chords rise in parallel stepwise motion, and a phenomenon such as the Shepard's Scale is suggested, an illusionary phenomenon in which high notes seem to disappear from audibility but actually leap to lower octaves, low notes appearing from quasi-inaudibility in the same way. The entire available pitch spectrum is activated.

The string quartet layer enters second, at first consisting merely of two-measure chords, articulating a subtle pulse three-quarters as fast as the string orchestra (changing every ten seconds) and thus a 3-against-4 rhythm.

EXAMPLE 1. Form in *Dream in White on White*

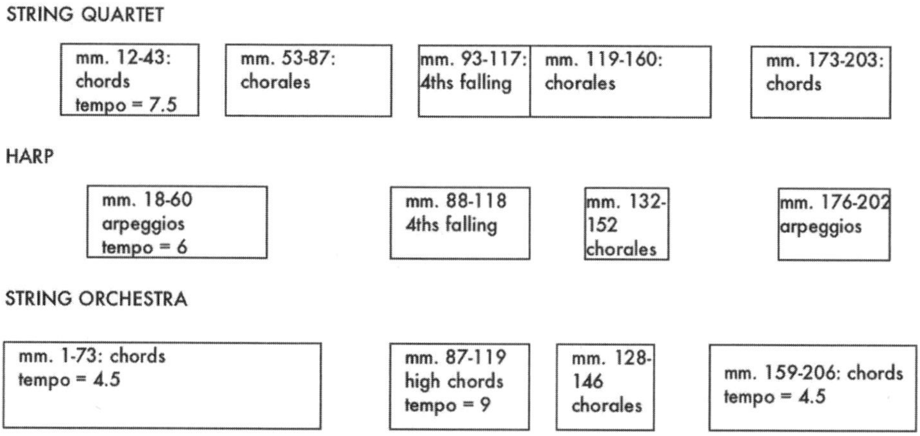

STRING QUARTET

| mm. 12-43: chords tempo = 7.5 | mm. 53-87: chorales | mm. 93-117: 4ths falling | mm. 119-160: chorales | mm. 173-203: chords |

HARP

| mm. 18-60 arpeggios tempo = 6 | mm. 88-118 4ths falling | mm. 132-152 chorales | mm. 176-202 arpeggios |

STRING ORCHESTRA

| mm. 1-73: chords tempo = 4.5 | mm. 87-119 high chords tempo = 9 | mm. 128-146 chorales | mm. 159-206: chords tempo = 4.5 |

FIGURE 3.1

Like the orchestra chords, these exhibit both saturation and consistency: all stacked in fifths at the beginning, then in fourths and sixths, and so on. A few measures after the string quartet begins the harp comes in, with the first true foregrounded figures: a series of four-note phrases in both hands, in quintuplet eighth-notes, in a repeating isorhythm that comes every sixteen quintuplet eighths, or every 1.6 measures. Pitch content in the harp is consistent with that of the string chords, beginning in rising fifths, and often but not always comprising the entire scale in each gesture. In every eight measures there are three string orchestra chords, four string quartet chords, and five harp figures, after which the pattern repeats again.

At measure 53, as the harp and orchestra continue uninterrupted, the solo quartet initiates a new phase by playing lines in regular quarter notes. Adams labels this section the "Lost Chorales." All four instruments play rising four-note figures in a step-leap-step pattern, but the two violins pause on each last note to make a five-beat pattern, while the viola and cello play four-beat phrases. Adams plays around with the phrase lengths, increasing it to six and five, then back to five and four.

After a pause at m. 86 comes a new section (mm. 87–118) titled "Fourths, falling. . . ." Over the faster, higher chords in the string orchestra, the harp indeed plays two lines of mostly falling fourths in quintuplet quarter-notes; this is then imitated, quasi-canonically, by the pizzicato solo first violin and viola. The second violin and cello then enter with mostly rising fifths ("and Fifths rising . . .," the composer adds in the score), in triplet half-notes. Among all the plucked notes Adams creates a tempo complex of 3-against-4-against-5.

This texture comes to a rather abrupt end at m. 119, where a new, higher set of chorales begins in the string quartet, again with the same polyphony of four- against five-beat phrases. At m. 128 the string orchestra enters with its own chorales, mimicking the rhythms of the quartet but at a triplet-half-note tempo, 3/4 as fast. At last the harp joins them with its own chorales in quin- tuplets at m. 132, completing again the 3-against-4-against-5 tempo complex, now involving the entire ensemble. The string orchestra drops out, and then the harp, and at m. 189 comes a brief final section that is basically a recapitula- tion of the first section in texture and rhythm (though with intervallic differ- ences as noted above for the string orchestra, similarly varied in the harp and quartet).

Within the piece's relatively brief span of seventeen minutes, Adams has created a symmetry entirely based on the rhythm 3-against-4-against-5. In the slow outer sections, that polyrhythm (expressed in string chords and the harp's melodic phrases) spans a repeating period of eight measures. In the faster middle sections—the first one throwing the symmetry off a little with its slower chords—the 3-against-4-against-5 takes place within each measure. The sections are differentiated by intervallic content, but not yet in a linear manner (as will be true in the later works). The entire piece expresses a single idea, creating internal variety through changes of speed and interval content in four large canvases, the first and last nearly identical. The map is simple, the symmetry clear, but even within seventeen minutes the ear loses itself in relatively unarticulated textures.

Clouds of Forgetting, Clouds of Unknowing

The basics of *Dream in White on White* would later be expanded into a major orchestral essay in *In the White Silence*, but first Adams created a massive ode to the chromatic scale: *Clouds of Forgetting, Clouds of Unknowing*. Begun in 1991, written mostly in 1994–95, *Clouds of Forgetting* is a sixty-three-minute, almost all-inclusive paean to the basic materials of the twelve pitches of the octave. As the piece starts with a unison and passes through progressively larger intervals up to an octave, familiar chords and scales make their appearances like char- acters in a wordless opera. A mixture of major and minor seconds bring the octatonic scale into play; major and minor thirds blossom into triads; and so on, each element reappearing when the intervals' inversions come around in a kind of harmonic palindrome.

The piece begins with vibraphone, celesta, piano, and violins on a unison middle C, articulated in one of the two small-scale rhythms that will run almost throughout the piece: 4:5:6:7 (the other is 2:3:4:5). Pitches are added a half-step upwards at a time, until by m. 36 a twelve-pitch cluster is reached. From this point onward, each section will concentrate on either one or two primary intervals, moving in stages from half-steps up to major sevenths. Meanwhile, the piece moves among four textural paradigms.

The first is sometimes indicated by the word "rising" in the title: for instance, "Major Seconds, rising." These move among tremolos, sustained chords, and polytempo ostinatos, alternating among the winds, percussion, brass, and strings. At any given time in these sections, ostinatos, tremolos, and sustained chords are all present, but every two to four measures they switch among the various sections of the orchestra. There are eight such sections, found at the following rehearsal letters (which run from an unmarked section before A, then A through Z, and AA through FF, making thirty-three sections in all):

TABLE 3.1

Reh. let.	Title	mm.	length in mm.	Dominant Interval size in 1/2-steps
A	untitled	37–70	34	1
D	Major Seconds, rising	102–130	29	2
J	Forgotten Triads	271–298	28	3,4
L	Lost Chorales	309–328	20	4,5
T	Chorales return	517–537	21	7,8
V	Triads, remembered	550–577	28	8,9
BB	minor sevenths, rising	743–770	28	10
EE	Major Sevenths, rising	822–857	36	11

One quickly notices a rough symmetry among the sections, including, within a couple of measures per section, their lengths. The first and last "Rising" sections employ only one interval each, the middle four employ two intervals. "Forgotten triads" at J is balanced by "Triads, remembered," at V, "Lost Chorales" (a name repeated from *Dream in White on White*) by "Chorales return." All eleven intervals are represented, and the major third (4) and minor sixth (8) appear in two sections each. Details within the eight sections can be elaborated in this way:

A—Chromatic cluster chords.

D—Major Seconds, rising: whole-tone cluster chords; both whole-tone scales appear within each texture, however, separated by register, for full twelve-pitch saturation.

J—Forgotten Triads: each sonority consists of four augmented, major, or minor triads, usually registrally separated. In augmented triad sonorities, all twelve pitches are present; since the twelve pitches of the scale cannot be divided among four major triads, or four minor triads, there is some pitch duplication and incomplete saturation in these sonorities.

L—Lost Chorales: patterns of four notes in alternating major thirds and perfect fourths produce two types of chord: major-minor triads (e.g, E♭-G-C-E) and minor seventh chords in open position (e.g., F-B♭-D-G). Four chords are present in each sonority, sometimes overlapping in pitch, and given the intervallic constraints, sometimes not all twelve pitches are present.

T—Chorales Return: Like Lost Chorales, only with chains and sonorities of minor sixths and perfect fifths. Similar sonorities result, though in wider spacings. Sometimes intervals are inverted (rising minor sixth into a falling minor third, or rising fifth into a falling fourth) to keep the pitches within the ranges of the instruments.

V—Triads, Remembered: Like Forgotten Triads, with augmented, major, and minor triads, though with ostinatos and chords voiced in major and minor sixths rather than thirds.

BB—Minor Sevenths, rising: Like Major Seconds, rising, only with mostly minor sevenths; some sevenths are inverted to falling major seconds due to limitations of instrument range.

EE—Major Sevenths, rising: once again, complete chromatic saturation with as many melodic and harmonic major sevenths as possible.

The second texture type is uniformly referred to as "Clouds": seemingly pulseless tremolos alternating among mallet percussion, strings, and winds. Clouds in each area of the orchestra overlap in twos and threes with clouds in other areas. There are eight of these sections: B, E, H, M, S, W, Z, and CC. All except the middle two alternate two intervals.

TABLE 3.2

Reh. let.	Title	mm.	length in mm.	Int. size in 1/2-steps
B	Clouds of mixed seconds	71–96	26	1,2
E	Clouds of seconds and thirds	131–173	43	2,3
H	Clouds of mixed thirds	220–270	51	3,4
M	Clouds of perfect fourths	329–370	42	5
S	Clouds of perfect fifths	471–516	46	7
W	Clouds of mixed sixths	578–620	33	8,9
Z	Clouds of sixths and sevenths	685–727	43	9,10
CC	Clouds of mixed sevenths (floating)	771–796	26	10,11

EXAMPLE 2. Pitch row rotation from "in time" sections, *Clouds of Forgetting, Clouds of Unknowing*

FIGURE 3.2

Note that the symmetry of these sections is thrown off by the disparity in length between the third and sixth, H and W (51 versus only 33). These clouds (sometimes marked "timeless") account for more than a third of the work's length (310 out of 906 mm.), and are its most characteristic texture.

The third type, the "In time . . ." sections, come as interruptions in the otherwise continuous texture. Most of them begin and end with rests, between which melodic gestures are articulated at several tempos at once. The melodic gestures are all based on melodic rows that follow a pattern of increasingly large rising intervals, starting with half-step, whole-step, minor third, major third, and so on, adding one new interval with each new "In time" passage. Adams's method is to use the available pitches as a pitch row, cycling through them by dropping the first note in the first gesture, the first two notes in the second gesture, and so on, building up a new pattern of this kind at the end (one thinks of the rotation method in some of Stravinsky's twelve-tone usage). The method is clear in Figure 3.2, an excerpt from the first violin line from the penultimate "In time" section (this method of note permutation will be used more pervasively in *for Lou Harrison*).

There are eleven "In time" sections, though the sixth and seventh are not designated as such ("Floating" is their performance direction), and they are the only elements that throw off the piece's formal symmetry. The first contains only two pitches in its row, the second three, the third four, and so on, with the result that overall the sections (but not systematically) increase in length:

TABLE 3.3

Sec.	Mm.	Length	Pitches
C	97–101	5	C, Db
F	174–178	5	Bb, Cb, Db
I	299–308	10	G, Ab, Bb, Db.
K	371–380	10	D#, E, F#, A, C#
N	412–422	11	Bb, Cb, Db, Fb, Ab, Db
P	412–422	11	E, F, G, Bb, D, G, C#
R	454–470	17	Bb, Cb, Db, Fb, Ab, Db, G, D
	With sustained chords in the strings.		
U	538–549	12	D#, E, F#, A, C#, F#, C, G, D#
X	621–643	23	G, Ab, Bb, Db, F, Bb, E B G, E
	With tremolo sonorites in the piano and chords with trills in the woodwinds.		
AA	728–742	15	Bb, Cb, Dd, Fb, Ab, Db, G, D, Bb, G, F
DD	797–821	25	C, Db, Eb, Gb, Bb, Eb, A, E, C, A, G, F#
	With sustained string chords and mallet-percussion tremolos.		

In Adams's world, it makes a kind of sense that the "In time" sections serve as markers of the passage of time by increasing in length and number of pitches, while the "timeless" sections mostly preserve symmetry of length. Note another symmetry among sections in the opening pitches of each row, which spell out a palindrome too vast to be perceived as such: C, Bb, G, D#, Bb, E, Bb, D#, G, Bb, C.

What we'll call the "Bell" sections are characterized by sustained or tremolo chords in the winds and strings and foregrounded patterns in the mallet percussion and piano. There are only four such sections:

TABLE 3.4

Sec.	Title [or performance direction]	Mm.	Length
G	diminished bells	179–219	41
O	Turbulent Changes	381–411	31
Q	["Heavy and Measured, again"]	423–453	31
Y	and bells, again	644–684	41

The outer sections here, at G and Y, have polytempo ostinatos in the mallet percussion and piano; the inner ones, at O and Q, have heavy repeated chords (also spelling out polyrhythms among the percussion), and constitute a pair of stormy climaxes for the entire piece, with only a brief "In time" section between them, like the eye of a hurricane. In "diminished bells" and "and bells again" the ostinatos and chords are made up of diminished seventh chords,

EXAMPLE 3. *Clouds of Forgetting, Clouds of Unknowing*:
Textural and intervallic structure

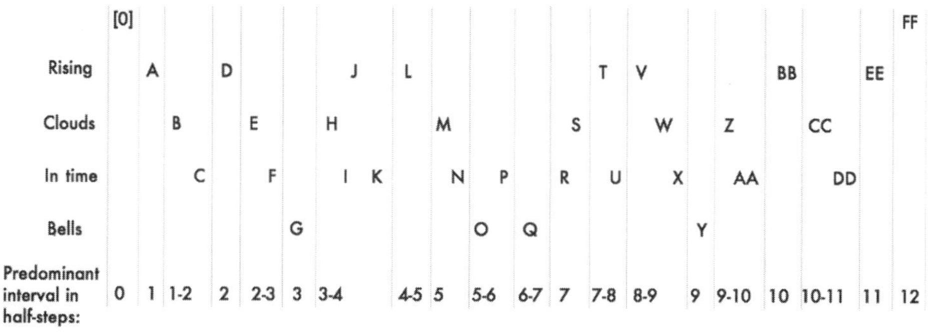

	0	1	1-2	2	2-3	3	3-4	4-5	5	5-6	6-7	7	7-8	8-9	9	9-10	10	10-11	11	12
	[0]																			FF
Rising		A		D			J	L				T	V				BB		EE	
Clouds			B		E		H		M		S			W	Z			CC		
In time				C		F	I	K		N	P	R		U	X		AA	DD		
Bells						G				O	Q					Y				
Predominant interval in half-steps:	0	1	1-2	2	2-3	3	3-4	4-5	5	5-6	6-7	7	7-8	8-9	9	9-10	10	10-11	11	12

FIGURE 3.3

minor seventh chords, half-diminished sevenths, and dominant sevenths, all emphasizing minor thirds. In the first section these various arpeggios rise, in "and bells again" they fall—rising sixths being replaced by falling thirds for (perhaps) playability's sake. The first "Turbulent Changes" section contains chords of perfect fourths and tritones, the second of tritones and perfect fifths, marking the midpoint of the intervallic expansion (I've kidded Adams that when I start hearing tritones I know his pieces are half over—but it actually only applies to a few works).

Figure 3.3 shows the form of the piece as revealed in the distribution of textural types: the introductory and closing addition and subtraction of pitches, the "Rising" sections, the "Clouds," the "In time" passages, and percussion-dominated "Bells" sections. Along the bottom runs a tabulation of predominant interval sizes in half-steps associated with each section. Reading the diagram with the "In time" sections omitted makes it easier to see the underlying symmetrical structure.

Clouds of Forgetting, Clouds of Unknowing is intriguingly both symmetrical and non-symmetrical. With the partial exception of the "In time" passages, the pattern of textures is a palindrome, and seconds at the beginning are balanced by sevenths at the end, thirds by sixths, triads echoed by triads, octatonic scales by octatonic scales, and so on. Yet the expansion of dominant intervals from unison up to octave is unidirectional (if subject to the symmetry of the musical octave itself). Since a crescendo in the size of melodic leaps is easier for the listener to register than a palindrome of textures and section lengths, the work sounds a little more like a representation of an expanding universe than a closed system, though both aspects are present at once.

In the White Silence

In 1998 Adams vastly expanded the materials of *Dream in White on White* into a much larger work, *In the White Silence*. The earlier work's seventeen minutes became seventy-five minutes. *Dream* starts with chords and arpeggios moving out of phase, changes into chorales, and returns to chords and arpeggios. *In the White Silence* replicates and repeats this process five times, adding a new element between the repetitions, a chamber-like polyphony of similar melodies at the simultaneous different tempos implied by various tuplets. Using A to represent the out-of-phase chords, B for the chorales, and C for the new multitempo polyphonic texture, the four can be simply represented (reading horizontally across each line) as:

TABLE 3.5

A	B	A'	C
A	B	A	C
A	B	A	C
A	B	A	C
A'	B	A	

Of course, each section does not return verbatim, but is transformed somewhat at each new repetition.

The A sections are all based on a large-scale structural cross-rhythm, too large to easily hear as such, of 3-against-4-against-5. That is, a hypermeasure of either sixteen or twenty-five measures is divided into three, four, and five equal parts by different parts of the ensemble:

* Sustained chords in the string orchestra change three times in each hypermeasure.
* Chords in the string quarter change four times, their onset accompanied by arpeggios or scales in the harp.
* Tremolo chords in the vibraphones change five times in each hypermeasure, their onset accompanied by gestures in the celesta.

All of the A sections use a 16-mm. hypermeasure except for the second and penultimate (marked as A' above), which use a 25-mm. unit. In the 16-mm. sections, the string orchestra chords last five and one-third measures each. The string quartet chords last four measures, each marked by a harp gesture eight notes long. The vibraphone chords last three and one-fifth measures, each marked by an eight-note-long celesta gesture. In the two sections with 25-mm. hypermeasures, those durations are eight and one-third, six and one-quarter, and 5 mm. respectively, and the harp and celesta gestures are expanded to fifteen notes.

Within each of the five major divisions of the piece, the A sections are formally paired in a series of textural palindromes. The first of each pair (1, 3, 5, 7, and 9) starts with several string orchestra chords (usually four), adds in the string quartet chords and then the percussion, as the string orchestra chords drop out. Following the chorale section, the second A section (2, 4, 6, 8, and 10) starts with the entire orchestra at once, and the percussion and then string quartet drop out, leaving only the string orchestra chords.

Within each A section, the string orchestra chords move in parallel. The sonorities are organized by use of various intervals, as shown in Fig. 3.4. Once stated, each chord is moved in parallel by a systematic interval pattern that hits all scale degrees and (except for the second A section) returns to the original transposition level. (Unlike working in the chromatic scale, where a succession of major seconds, minor thirds, and so on will not hit every note of the scale, a diatonic scale can be saturatedly traversed by a series of repetitions of any interval—making no distinction, of course, between major and minor seconds, or thirds, sixths, or sevenths, as they fall in the scale.) Chords in A sections 1, 3, 5, 6, 8, and 10 use all seven pitches of the diatonic scale; those in sections 2, 4, 7, and 9 have duplications and at least one omission.

The harp and celesta gestures mark the clearest means of following the interval expansion through the work. Their rising gestures in the A sections are generated from the following intervals:

A1   seconds
A2   seconds and thirds alternating
A3   thirds
A4   thirds and fourths alternating
A5   fourths
A6   fifths
A7   fifths and sixths alternating
A8   sixths
A9   sixths and sevenths alternating
A10   sevenths

Adams has to forgo alternating fourths and fifths because they would produce octaves on alternate notes, and fail to generate the entire scale. The first six A-section celesta entrances are given in Fig. 3.5. Notice that octaves and other melodic turns are used to keep melodies within the range of the instrument. Also, the opening harp gesture employs ninths rather than seconds—possibly because simple scales on the harp lack the definition they have on the celesta.

The B sections I refer to as chorales because they closely resemble the "Lost Chorale" sections of *Dream in White on White* (though they are not labeled

EXAMPLE 4. *In the White Silence* string chords and intervallic pattern of movement

FIGURE 3.4

EXAMPLE 5. *In the White Silence*, first A-section celesta entrances

FIGURE 3.5

as such here). Each one starts with the solo string quartet playing lines at a quarter-note pace, five-beat phrases in the violins against four-beat phrases in the viola and cello. As Fig. 3.6 shows, variations among the chorales loosely follow an intervallic logic expanding from an emphasis on seconds to one on thirds, then fourths, fifths, and sevenths. In the fourth B section, the emphasis on fifths progresses to one on sixths. Here we find a similar reliance on interval expansion as a directional force, as in *Clouds of Forgetting*, though not carried out with as much systematic consistency.

The C sections all consist of eight individual solo lines—vibraphones 1 and 2, celesta, harp, and the four players of the string quartet—two each in the 4, 5, 6, and 7 tempos. As in the "In time" sections of *Clouds of Forgetting*, the melodies are all based around a pitch row based on expanding and contracting interval sizes, from a second up to a seventh, as shown in Figure 3.7. Adams uses the row flexibly, inverting a rising sixth into a falling third, and so on. Each section starts on the same pitch level: the seconds and sevenths all involve E and F, the fourths and fifths D and A, the thirds and sixths F and A. The vibraphones, celesta, and harp articulate these patterns in steady quarter-notes (or tuplet quarter-notes). The strings rise and fall through arithmetically expanding and contracting series, adding one note unit to each successive note or subtracting it, as shown in Figure 3.8. Such melodies sometimes begin in the middle of the duration sequence.

The distribution of these lines is visible in Figure 3.9. Note that the relative

EXAMPLE 6. Chorales, *In the White Silence*

FIGURE 3.6

EXAMPLE 7. *In the White Silence*, contracting/expanding melody

FIGURE 3.7

EXAMPLE 8. *In the White Silence*, expanding rhythmic series

FIGURE 3.8

placement is more or less symmetrical (though less so in the first section), and that the later each instrument enters, the sooner it departs. Usually each percussion line (counting harp as percussion) is paired in its entrances and exits with a member of the quartet: the harp is always paired with the cello, the viola with one of the vibraphones, the celesta with Violin 1 in every section except the second. At the beginning of the first section is a momentary Violin 1 solo with the celesta, giving the basic melodic pattern; this is alluded to at the end of the first section, and repeated at the end of the last C section. In addition, the tempos are distributed according to the following pattern, each instrument sharing a tempo with the instrument with which it enters and exits:

TABLE 3.6

C Section #	1	2	3	4
Vib. 1	6	6	7	5
Vib. 2	5	4	4	4
Cel.	7	7	5	6
Harp	4	5	6	7
Vn. 1	7	4	5	6
Vn. 2	6	7	4	5
Viola	5	6	7	4
Cello	4	5	6	7

Perhaps because so simple an alternation of textures sets up a mild expectation (though strong by Adams's standards) of continuation, he ends the piece with a thirteen-measure coda: the only concession to concert-music framing found in any of the pieces under discussion here. One final gesture starts with a flurry of percussion, rising melodies brought back in the harp and celesta, and two string orchestra chords, the last one dying away. As in *Dream in White on White*, the music alternates among a few easily characterized panels of sound. As in *Clouds of Forgetting*, a large-scale intervallic expansion is evident, if one listens for it, among the A sections, in the expansion of intervals from seconds to sevenths in the harp and celesta; and in the B sections in the intervals

EXAMPLE 9. *In the White Silence*: Proportional Graph of Instruments in Section C

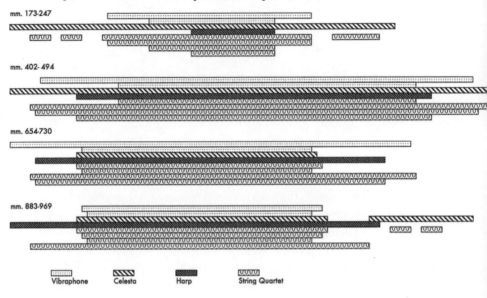

FIGURE 3.9

emphasized in the chorales. Overall the section lengths are sufficiently undif-
ferentiated as to probably be experienced as functionally identical, though the
floating, polytempo C sections are always the longest:

TABLE 3.7 [section]

A:	62		57		62		41		62		41
B:		53				51				56	
C:				75				93			
A:		62		41		59		43	13 (coda)		
B:			49				69				
C:	77				87						

This is *Dream in White on White* greatly expanded, and given more of a time
orientation via the methods developed in *Clouds of Forgetting*.

For Lou Harrison

As *In the White Silence* represents a formal simplification compared to *Clouds
of Forgetting, for Lou Harrison* is, structurally, even simpler. The form is a simple
alternation of textures: ABABABABA. Each A section is 88 mm. long and each B
section 134 mm.: although each B section begins with a four-measure gesture
that serves as a final flourish for the preceding A section. Forming a link be-

tween the A-B pairs, these flourishes continue the texture of the A section, but announce the changed harmonic content of the newly arrived B sections.

Each section is couched entirely in a five-, six-, or seven-note scale, as follows:

TABLE 3.8

Section	Scale	Major-key key signature
A1: mm. 1–88	C D Eb F G Ab Bb	Eb
B1: mm. 89–222	C Db Eb F Ab Bb	Ab/Db
A2: mm. 223–310	C D E F# G A B	G
B2: mm. 311–444	C D E F# G A B	G
A3: mm 445–536	C Db Eb F Ab	Ab/Db
B3: mm. 537–666	C D Eb F G Bb	Bb/Eb
A4: mm. 667–754	C Db Eb F Gb Ab Bb	Db
B4: mm. 755–888	C Eb G Ab Bb	Eb/Ab
A5: mm. 889–983	C D Eb F G Bb	Bb/Eb

The variety is presumably inspired by the five-pitch slendro scale and the seven-pitch pelog scale of Indonesian gamelan music, Harrison having been one of the primary Western composers for the gamelan orchestra. Note that C is the only pitch common to all nine sections, all other pitches appearing in one section or another; it is also the pitch in the bass at the beginning of each section, and from which each section appears to grow.

The A sections are all marked by groups of rising melodic figures that occur independently among the two pianos, the violins of the string quartet, and the viola and cello of the string quartet. Rather than create some large cross-rhythm, as in *In the White Silence*, Adams resorts here to a simpler system of distribution that results in much the same effect: the violin duo, the viola/cello duo, and each of the pianos begins its upward arpeggios in phrases either four, five, six, or seven measures long, staggered so as to be nonsynchronous. Phrases in the first A section are distributed thus:

TABLE 3.9

Vns.	6	7	4	5	7	4	5	6
VaVc	5	6	7	4	6	7	4	5
Po1	7	4	5	6	4	5	6	7
Po2	4	5	6	7	5	6	7	4
Vns	4	5	6	7	5	6	7	4
Va/Vc	7	4	5	6	4	5	6	7
Pno1	5	6	7	4	6	7	4	5
Pno2	6	7	4	5	7	4	5	6

Likewise, and again, all four layers are at perceived different tempos, in tuplets of four, five, six, or seven notes to a half-note. The music washes up over and over in nonsynchronous waves.

The A sections are roughly differentiated by emphasis on various intervals, but there is no consistent intervallic expansion as in the earlier two works; indeed, the varied number of pitches available in each section militates against any such consistent process. Section A1 relies on alternating seconds and thirds, A2 on seconds and fourths, and the later sections use wider intervals but are not so simply characterized. Instead, each section relies upon a pitch row that is rotated through one note at a time, as in both previous works. Thus, in *Clouds of Forgetting*, the interval expansion was a strict and determinative process; one might imagine that even a listener who didn't know what was going on might notice the chromatic scales at the beginning, the whole steps soon after, the leaping major sevenths at the end, and figure out the overall structure. In *for Lou Harrison*, the interval expansion is background, a starting point for the composer but almost unavailable to the ear. The listener gets less guidance about where he is in the piece, and surrenders to a potentially endless process.

The five A-section rows are as in Figure 3.10. All gestures in all instruments consist of sixteen notes, so in the fourteen-note rows the last two get repeated in each phrase (in a different octave); in the fifteen-note rows, the last note gets repeated.

The four B sections are fundamentally isomorphic, differentiated primarily by their harmonic and interval content. The events in each section can be summarized as follows:

1 The pitch spectrum changes with the initial four-measure flourish (except between the second A and second B, which use the same scale).
2 As the string orchestra holds chords that slowly shift in an eight-measure polyrhythm divided 3:4:5, Piano Two begins a pair of quasi ostinatos (the same pitches aren't always repeated, but the contours are) in quarter-notes, nine-beat phrases in the right hand, eight-beat in the left.
3 The orchestral cellos and violas begin similar 8:9-beat phrases, only in quintuplet quarters, after which the violins repeat this process in sextuplets.
4 Piano 1 enters with similar phrases in septuplets.
5 As all these quasi ostinatos continue in a 4:5:6:7 polyrhythm, the string quartet players enter one by one in a tempo canon (though not a completely strict one) based on a recurring isorhythm. The cello measures the rhythm in quarter-notes, the viola in quintuplet quarters, the second violin in sextuplets, and the first violin in septuplets.
6 The string quartet lines are spaced so that they reach a convergence point

EXAMPLE 10. *For Lou Harrison*, A-section pitch rows

FIGURE 3.10

36 measures after the cello's entrance, all moving to the next isorhythm at the same time. This convergence point comes near the center of the B section and forms a subtle climax both in terms of register and density.

7   All instruments drop out in reverse order of entry: first the string quartet one by one, then Piano One, the string orchestra lines melt back into chords, and these and Piano Two's quarter notes continue to the onset of the next A section.

Differences among the sections, aside from the pitch content as noted earlier, have mainly to do with the intervallic emphasis and the isorhythms employed by the string quartet lines:

TABLE 3.10

Section	isorhythm	intervals emphasized
B1:	1 2 4 6 3 5 7 8	thirds and fourths
B2:	1 3 5 7 2 4 6 8	fifths
B3:	1 2 5 6 3 4 7 8	fifths and sixths
B4:	1 3 4 7 2 5 6 8	fifths and sixths

Thus, in its simplicity, *for Lou Harrison* is a more austere work than its companions in the cycle, even though arguably no less sensuous. The timbral palette is more limited (merely strings and pianos), and although the harmonic colors change with each section across a more tonally differentiated spectrum, there is no overall directional process to follow aside from the simple alternation of sound panels, which, for any internal cues given the listener, could go on forever. The endlessly rising gestures create an uplifting feeling, and the overlapping phrases in the A sections resonate on a more human scale than the layerings of *Clouds* or *White Silence*. Nevertheless — and much as in Feldman's far darker final magnum opus *For Samuel Beckett* — the lack of directionality submerges the listener in an experience to which he can only surrender to timelessness, like sitting at the edge of a beach and feeling the waves wash up over and over.

In the early twenty-first century, Adams's search for even more sublime proportions and processes would lead him to electronic sound installations. The most ambitious of these yet — indeed, it is difficult to see how it could be surpassed in scale — is *The Place Where You Go to Listen*, a permanent installation at the University of Alaska's Museum of the North. *The Place* is an open-ended, eternal web of slowly metamorphosing sounds, dependent on and altered by data being streamed in from seismological and geomagnetic monitoring stations. Two sustained chords called "The Day Choir" and "The Night Choir," based respectively on an overtone series and an undertone series, move around the room's fourteen speakers in a way that tracks the current positions of the sun and moon. Since Fairbanks, the Museum's location, is near the Arctic Circle, "The Night Choir" is far more prominent in winter, "The Day Choir" in summer. Booming low tones are triggered in real time by seismic activity. Bell sounds occur when the aurora borealis is active. The overall sound, its center of gravity glissandoing periodically and contrapuntally across four octaves, can also be muted by the passage of clouds overhead.

Variety in *The Place Where You Go to Listen* is infinite; it fluctuates from summer to winter, day to night, fair weather and foul, and will never be exactly the same twice. One feels like an ant crawling, not across a mere Cezanne, but across the state of Alaska itself. Even its composer will not live long enough to experience more than a fraction of the piece's moods and patterns (in real time, that is; privately he has the capacity to computer-simulate any number of potential seasons and states of motion). Adams has also made comparatively diminutive installations, titled *Veils* and *Vespers*, with similar processes, but on six-hour repeating cycles. Even so the ear wanders through these massive sonic landscapes with little feel for what's coming next or how to locate oneself in the overall process.

Some listeners to these sound installations are eager to know how they work; others don't want to know, preferring to simply immerse themselves in inscrutable sonic sensuousness. But here, as in the orchestral pieces, the deepest meaning comes from knowing and hearing on different levels, from the discontinuity between logic and sound, time and eternity, structure and surface. It is because we know or can make inferences about how this music works, but while listening can only surrender to the sonority, that it engages our entire brain while tantalizingly thwarting a final resolution. It tells us that time and eternity are the same: if only we were equipped to perceive it.

4 * for Lou Harrison

I n 1953 (the year John Luther Adams was born), Lou Harrison, then a young composer still in his thirties, came home to California after a decade on the East Coast—first in New York City and then at Black Mountain College in rural North Carolina. Back on the West Coast he eventually settled in Aptos, a small coastal community near Santa Cruz. Lou's "Chinese poet" hermitage was up on the hill, just a short distance from the Pacific Ocean. He and Bill Colvig were still in that tiny house when John and I and others—two generations now after Lou—first met him in the 1970s. By then he was an "elder" (a status we are rapidly approaching!) and an iconic figure in Western American culture. As such, his life and work represented an alternative to the career and reputation machine of New York, and his example was a profound inspiration to several of us younger composers. We were all products of the social and cultural up-heavals of the 1960s—too young to have been original participants, but old enough to be thoroughly influenced and enthused by the incredible cultural-imaginative expansion that era represented. By the time we came of age in the early seventies, much of that original energy had become diffused (and already commercialized and exploited), and the dominant ethos of those years was the idea of "going back to the land." What that represented was a dropping out of the "rat race" of mainstream society and its values and the development of a personal and cultural self-sufficiency. Lou had done precisely that, twenty years before. By the early seventies, with the Vietnam War soon to be wind-ing down, and the American working class as prosperous (and conservative) as it ever had been, environmentalism came to the fore as the cutting edge of radical politics, replacing old-fashioned Marxist paradigms or the conflicts, so prominent in the sixties, of the so-called generation gap. Twenty years earlier, roughly around that same year 1953, Lou Harrison had written one of his major works, albeit one that is rarely performed and little known today, the *Four Strict Songs* (1951–55) for male voices with orchestra. In his own words, these were "Making-things-right-&-good-again Songs, after the examples of Hozhonji-Songs from Navaho"—almost twenty years before "ethnopoetics" and Jerome Rothenberg's *Technicians of the Sacred* anthology that was to have such an in-fluence on our generation.

In 1953 Gary Snyder, future spokesperson for the West Coast poetic and environmental counterculture, was a starting-out poet and hermit summer fire lookout in the Cascades of Northern Washington. (Fire lookout was a job, in fact, that Lou recommended to us as good for composers; his long-time partner Bill Colvig was a Sierra Club guide and legendary mountaineer.) So Lou's *Four Strict Songs* are a landmark piece, not just in music, but also in the environmentalist, ethnopoetic, alternative-culture vision that emerged on the West Coast of the United States in the 1950s. There were antecedents, of course — Robinson Jeffers and Jaime de Angulo and Henry Cowell — but after World War II it was a brand new ball game, as they say; and Lou, along with Harry Partch and certain poets of the so-called San Francisco Renaissance, was one of its early pioneers. Back when it was lonely to be so. So when someone like John Luther Adams arrived on the scene in the mid-1970s, it was not simply a case of a young talented composer — though it was certainly that, too — but more deeply, he was someone that Lou had been waiting for, ever since those difficult years of the 1950s. A cultural (and might I say spiritual — " 'spiritual' is a word that has been much abused these days," Lou once said to me) heir, through whom this legacy and tradition that Lou represented would be passed on and continued. Lou lived to see his vision and life's work — and his struggles and sacrifices — vindicated, and he died in 2003 a deeply respected and beloved figure. We hear that love and respect in John Luther Adams's *for Lou Harrison*. In talking about John and his piece, I am going to use as section headings the titles of each of the *Four Strict Songs*: our generation's environmental, cultural, spiritual manifesto, first elaborated by Lou more than a half century ago.

Here Is Holiness

Lou's *Four Strict Songs* make reference to a Native American spirituality and reverence for all forms of life and manifestations of living energy, and it is clear that such an attitude has influenced John deeply too. Titles of his works alone illustrate that: *songbirdsongs*, *Forest Without Leaves*, *Earth and the Great Weather*, *The Light that Fills the World*, among others. John's contact with the indigenous cultures of Alaska have also influenced his concept of sound as sacred (*Strange and Sacred Noise*) — one hears the booming resonance of Yup'ik and Iñupiaq drumming in John's percussion works (the "Jekyll and Hyde" contrast to his quieter, more contemplative pieces, as he jokes — but they still belong on the same continuum of the power and mystery of sound, albeit sometimes on opposite ends of that spectrum). Another source of strength and inspiration is in the land itself — the "Mountains and Rivers Without End" (to borrow a phrase from Gary Snyder) of Alaska and the American West. Charles Olson proclaimed in his 1947 landmark essay on Melville, *Call Me Ishmael*, "I take SPACE to be the central fact to man born in America" and "America completes her West only on the coast of Asia." The indigenous world of John's Alaska is quite literally close to our Asian origins as Americans (the original Bering Strait!), and Alaska may now be the last place in the United States where Olson's vision of American SPACE still rings true. With the incredible surge in population in the U.S. since the 1960s, it's starting to feel a bit crowded down here in the Lower 48; and our generation (John and I are a year apart) may have been the very last to have experienced that sense of space and its corollary—personal and imaginative freedom. The classic novel of mid-century America, after all, was Kerouac's *On the Road*, a paean to precisely that. And even though in John's hometown, Fairbanks, it's perhaps a case of "one can't see the forest for the trees," his love for the open spaces and sheer magnificence of Alaska is well documented in his writings. His recent installation piece at the University of Alaska Museum, *The Place Where You Go to Listen* (which I have only read about), is a poem to Alaska: its weather, the long days and nights, the magical aurora borealis of the Northern sky, and even the seismic energies in the Alaskan earth itself. Here is Holiness, indeed.

Here Is Nourishment

Obviously this sense of place, and being in the midst of a culturally and ecologically rich environment, alongside all other living beings and spirits (we know about "spirits")—all this is very nourishing, creatively. When I most recently saw John, at the very end of summer 2006, I commented that winter was coming on; and that unlike our friends in academia who often compose during their "free" time in the summer, winter for us was the time when we settled in to compose. He nodded, in total understanding and agreement. The darkness of winter (and nowhere is it darker than Alaska), not to mention the cold, provides a time and space to go inward, and for that special intimacy and solitude that is so conducive to creativity. I heard a news story a few weeks ago about all these urban artists who go to retreats like the MacDowell Colony to create. Composers like John and me come *home* to create. That sense of place, of intimacy, of your own carefully set up creative environment, both in exterior and interior terms—I don't think either of us would trade that for any "artists' colony." The sounds I hear now in spring are the returning ducks and geese, and my next-door neighbors include a pair of nesting bald eagles. I'm sure John has similar companionship. It certainly beats what Lou Harrison once called, in reference to New York City, "the group chattering of the metropolis." And yet John, wisely, has never let himself be content—as he could have been—with being a big frog in a small pond, as far as Alaska goes. He has kept his perspective and ambition intact (which time and his own achievement have validated). We wouldn't be talking (writing) about him today otherwise. So—in a kind of opposite direction from those urbanites who go to the wilderness and the art colonies to seek inspiration and the time and space to create—John makes his regular pilgrimages to New York and the "urb" to recharge his creative batteries, going to museums and concerts, meeting people, making the necessary career connections. To then: go home. To compose. Here is nourishment.

Here Is Tenderness

This is the trickiest one. Hard as it may be to believe—since it is such a natural and taken-for-granted aspect of folk and popular musics—tenderness, and things like melody, simplicity, and clarity, were actually *forbidden* when we were coming up as young students (though, fortunately, not by our teachers). Of course, by the late sixties, early "minimalism" was beginning to subvert all that—and Lou Harrison's music was full of such clarity and tenderness, which was one of the reasons it attracted us so much. Back in the fifties and sixties, music was all about structure and analysis—and complexity.[1] Now, there's nothing wrong with any of that. One look at the score of *for Lou Harrison* reveals that despite its clarity, there is structure and complexity—just as there are in the colors and form of a Mark Rothko painting. There is also a very sensual approach to sound that invites the listeners in, rather than repelling and baffling them with obtuseness, aggressiveness, or a merely intellectual complexity. Many of these latter types of composers have become very defensive and, safe in their academic refuge, blame the listeners rather than themselves, and scornfully talk about "naive and sentimental" music. With these kinds of attitudes, in a mere fifty years composers have become virtually irrelevant figures in contemporary society. *for Lou Harrison* is neither naive nor sentimental—though I don't have a problem with that sometimes either (remember: rules are not chains!). But there is a great deal of emotion, and of tenderness—for Lou, and for the listeners who will be moved by this music. This type of expressivity is not to be confused with any sort of "New Romanticism." The latter is a neoconservative response to this communication crisis, a falling back into old formulas of stylistic and rhetorical gestures. Authentic emotion is always fresh: that is the magic and the constantly renewing originality of art; and without a love for the listeners (who else does one write music for?—not just for the sake of theory or analysis, for god's sake!), music becomes only stale technique. In the academic manner in which music is taught and judged these days, we too often confuse technical competence with real creativity—but in the end, the discerning public knows the difference. So here is tenderness, and beauty.

Here Is Splendor

So here we have John's sixty-three-minute piece, *for Lou Harrison*. It is one continuous work, though it is clearly divided into nine sections. There are two basic ideas that alternate: ABABABABA. In this regard, the structure of the piece is quite audible. What this does is create a sense of stasis, even though within each section there is constant movement. This static quality, combined with the formal simplicity and transparency, gives the work a monumental, almost monolithic character. This piece is therefore not about melodic/thematic or dramatic development in a conventional (musical) narrative sense. Like the use of paint and color in a Rothko painting, the thematic and dramatic elements—which actually abound—are instead embodied in the sound materials themselves. We are invited into that sound world and hence, the listening experience becomes meditative, as much sensual as intellectual/cognitive. The hour-long length of *for Lou Harrison* contributes to that also. This is music to get lost in—while at the same time, due to the formal clarity, you always know where you are. I immediately heard two images, two kinds of energy, in the different sections. The principal idea in both sections is that of ascending and constantly overlapping melodic lines. There is a rhapsodic and ecstatic quality that links this music to the legacy of Carl Ruggles (who once wrote in a letter to Dane Rudhyar: "Music is no better than it sounds"—which expresses another essence of this piece). I would describe these two energies/images as "Tidal" and "River." The A sections have a more rapid momentum—both in terms of ascent and overlap. The musical lines swell and accumulate more quickly and then climax and fall back, to once again repeat that momentum. I hear waves building and breaking. In the B sections, I hear the steady flow and inexorable motion and swell of a river (John referred to it as a "processional"). The musical lines are longer, slower; and even though the accumulation and overlapping build to a greater fullness, this energy does not spend itself like waves; rather it subsides. I know it is perhaps dangerous to indulge in such analogy, but I think this helps clarify matters for the general readership.

This is a fun musical score to study, and there is a wealth of "shop talk" for composers here. The instrumentation calls for a string quartet, along with a string ensemble (violins one and two, violas, cellos, and basses) of optional size, plus two pianos. These constitute three autonomous units within the ensemble as a whole. In a real sense these are three simultaneous quartets, as the pianos play continuous single lines in each hand—that is, four lines. The basses of the string ensemble add depth and find their counterpart in the deep bass notes of Piano Two in the "River" sections. This instrumental configuration thus represents another element of clarity within the constantly shifting textures. Furthermore, in the string quartet during the "Tidal" sections the two violins are always paired, as are the viola and cello. This mirrors the two pianos, who are always kept distinct in their musical roles. Due to their sustain, strings tend to create a denser texture of sound than the more percussive quality of the pianos. This creates another level of contrast and clarity. Between the string quartet and the string ensemble there is a fascinating shift of foreground-background. In the "Tidal" sections the string ensemble provides a solid, though openly voiced and transparent, background, against which the paired melodic lines of the quartet (violin one / violin two, viola / cello) ascend and overlap. In the "River" sections the string ensemble itself takes over this function of overlapping lines, and the string quartet shifts to a background function (one of the most interesting moments in the piece, for me), adding melodic fragments and emphases that appear and disappear in the larger texture. Sometimes it is hard to distinguish the string quartet lines against the massed string ensemble; but like any key ingredient in a recipe, you would immediately notice if they weren't there. The string ensemble creates continuity between sections by gradually reverting to its background function at all the transition points. This way the alternation of sections is seamless, also kept so by the steady presence of the pianos. Yet within this stasis and steady repetition, there is constant change. The pitches—in terms of scales, and intervals—always vary, as does the harmonic foundation. Sometimes the intervals—the space between notes—are close and dense sounding; at other times they are more open, airy, ringing. In the "Tidal" sections, the possible combinations of overlappings are continuously alternated. This creates two interesting effects: first, shifting bands of tonal/textural color, and second, an almost verse/quatrain structure. This quality of a "poetic line" of different lengths (longer in the "River" sections, shorter in the "Tidal") is one of the first things I heard in the piece.

This quatrain effect is achieved by a structural symmetry in the "Tidal" sections. First, all the instruments more or less sound and ascend together. Then there are three "phrases" of ascent/overlap, each with a different tonal/textural combination, followed by all the instruments together again. If you call the unison part a "refrain" and the three following elaborations "verses," you get a structure of: opening refrain, three verses/refrain, three verses/refrain, three verses/refrain, three verses/refrain. That basic, that ingenious: again the combination of complexity and clarity that defines this piece. Like the alternating bands and planes of color in a Rothko painting: If you think that's simple, well, take another look.

There is a further element in this clarity-complexity scheme: tempo—the speeds at which these melodic lines ascend and mingle. Taking as a basis the idea of four beats per measure (4/4 time), other lines play against that with various groupings and speeds of five, six, and seven notes. That thickens the texture, makes it less measured, predictable, and plodding—and creates a sense of different rates of acceleration or deceleration. Yet John keeps these tempo ratios fairly simple and obvious enough so that neither the musicians nor the listeners get lost. He avoids sonic "mud," while adding yet another layer of rhythmic fluidity.

Finally, there is one almost surprising aspect which links John's piece to Lou Harrison's music. John wrote in a letter: "Shortly after Lou died, I dreamed I was rehearsing a new piece for chorus and gamelan . . . I was convinced this was the memoriam I would compose for Lou . . . but I've never composed for gamelan, and in the months following . . . I came to feel it would be presumptuous for me to compose a gamelan work in memory of the master of the American Gamelan . . . One evening . . . I stopped. Suddenly it struck me that the interlocking layers of repeated melodic cells, the longer phrases punctuated by gong-like octaves in the low register of the piano, the stately pacing and solemn tone of the whole thing sounded a lot like Javanese Gamelan."

The "gongs" John refers to are in the "River" sections, and their regularity mirrors their function in Javanese gamelan music, to mark off time. This also helps to anchor the performers, who are playing in these 5, 6, 7 relationships against the 4-beat. To me this is stunning—as the simplest ideas often are. As I was working on this essay, I recalled a mesostic that John Cage had written in honor of Lou ("Many Happy Returns"), and I was struck by the fact that Cage described the same river/ocean imagery in talking about Lou's music that I have been using here. He wrote that its quality, quantity, and variety

> make it Resemble
>   a rIver in delta.
>   LiStening to it
>   we becOme
>   oceaN.

I could say the same about John's *for Lou Harrison.* Here's a music full of energy that is never frenetic; brimming with emotion, but without bombast. Here is Holiness, Nourishment, Tenderness.

Here is Splendor.

Note

1. Even the supposedly freer aleatory music suffered from this too: the idea that a piece is somehow "justified" by its "explanation."

5 * Strange Noise, Sacred Places

Zoom in on composer John Luther Adams. His fingers press a set of earphones tightly against his ears and his eyes squeeze shut as he tries to hear through the recorded marimba sound to the faint buzz of distortion in the audio signal. He calls me over to take a listen. "Is that a rattle in the resonator tube, or do we have a microphone problem?"

I listen for a while as Eric Schultz, our recording engineer, pans back and forth between the overhead microphones and a pair he has placed under the instruments to catch the resonance. I hear something between a buzz and a swish, and shrug. "Actually, I think it might be the wind, John."

"Well, whatever it is we can deal with it in post-production."

I glance quickly at my watch, worried about the time. It's after 3:30 a.m. The brief dusk that counts for night in the Alaskan summer is over and there is a forecast for rain in the morning.

We are five percussionists who have come to Alaska to film a performance of John Luther Adams's *Strange and Sacred Noise*, the stunning hymn of noise and redemption written for the Percussion Group Cincinnati in 1997. Our concert hall and recording studio is the flat top of a west-facing bluff in the Maclaren Valley not far (by Alaskan standards) from Denali National Park. Here we have positioned the nearly fifty percussion instruments called for in John's seven-movement, sixty-five-minute-long piece, carrying them over more than a mile of muddy trails from the roadside parking area. As we record in the constant light of the subarctic solstice the tundra around us teems with life. There are migratory birds: loons, ptarmigan, and plovers—the greatest long-distance flyers of them all. They make their summer homes here in the mosses, shrubs, and grasses that comprise the soft tundra floor. In Alaska's lower elevations the forest is called taiga, mostly dwarf versions of spruce, birch, aspen, and willow. (The permafrost shortens root systems and in a counterbalancing gesture lowers the canopy.) Here at more than four thousand feet the landscape is even scruffier and dotted with small ponds. The largest of these is a small mountain lake that has been chosen as the focal point for an antiphonal movement for four sirens. Even in late June it is still ringed with ice. We haven't seen any big animals except for a stray moose that popped up suddenly in front of Eric's ATV and scared them both. However, the standing water and daytime temperatures warming to the mid-fifties mean a near-constant plague of mosquitoes. In much of the world the mosquito is a small, relatively timid insect requiring at most an occasional swat. In Alaska, however, the biomass of mosquitoes is greater than that of caribou. Mosquitoes swarm in bloodthirsty black clouds around anything that is warm and stationary, say in our case a group of percussionists standing at a marimba.

Temperatures have fallen to well below freezing overnight, but by the time John and I finish our conversation about the buzzing marimba the sun has peeked out from behind Mount Hayes. Across the wide Maclaren Valley a ridge of slate gray hills begins to glow in hues of pink and amber and signals that time is fleeting. John motions towards a set of vibraphones perched at the edge of a rocky outcropping. Percussionists, camera operators, sound engineers, and assorted friends are suddenly in motion. Sleeping bags have kept us warm during the break but now they are shoved aside and cups of tea quickly brought to boil. Eric coils microphone cable as four camera operators collapse their tripods. Percussionists grab new sets of sticks, and we're on the move.

John is leafing through the score to the next movement of his piece. He pauses briefly, looks up at me with a shy smile and asks under his breath, "What the hell are we doing here?"

Freeze the frame. The time stamp is a little before 3:45 a.m. on June 24, 2008.

Dr. Esler's Project

One of the percussionists in this scene is Dr. Robert Esler, the catalyst and primary force behind the performance of *Strange and Sacred Noise* on the tundra. Towards the end of his doctoral studies in percussion with me at the University of California, San Diego, Rob started to feel a little itchy. At the source of the itch was the ill-fitting relationship between music and the place in which it is made. "Place" mattered, it seemed to Rob. We'll get back to Dr. Esler in a moment. But let's start by saying that it hasn't been only to Esler that "place" and its implications for artmaking has had traction. In recent years place has been at the center of a number of hot topics within academic circles. For starters, there have been experiments in the multisite, cyber-emplacements of "telematic" performances. Sophisticated musicians like bassist Mark Dresser and composer/accordionist Pauline Oliveros have led the way by mapping our singular notions of "a place" onto a new space of multiplicity, creating in effect "place-ness." In many respects these artists are closer to the classical Roman linkage of *images* (visualized ideas) and *loci* (multiple places) than anyone since Quintilian. Place has also been of central concern among scholars and students of the African Diaspora and African-American music in general. As

George E. Lewis points out in his wonderful book "A Power Stronger than Itself," the African-American musical experience has been forged in large part from a sense of loss, in particular the loss of land—of place. From the savage displacement of slavery to its twentieth-century counterpart—the tragic story of stolen land and Klan terrorism that we euphemistically call "The Great Migration"—the place-less place has been home to many African-Americans and by extension to some of the most vital music of the twentieth century. And among my graduate students at UC-San Diego "place" is treated as a natural outgrowth of the ne plus ultra of contemporary theoretical concerns: situation. Under the prevailing rules of engagement an argument must be situated in order to be valid. (As a result I often see papers that read like assemblages of framing mechanisms: "in the Lacanian sense," or "as Deleuze pointed out," and so forth.) In such discourse "place" functions far beyond the boundaries of simple location and has become a critical vector in the creation of a new hyper-situation.

Notions of "place" are everywhere in the latest scholarship, but there is still a lot of traditional significance to the word. As a now-grown farm boy I am skeptical of any use of the word "place" that requires the use of quotation marks or italics. For me, "place" is also just plain place. Un-italicized and un-theorized. In fact for much of my life place has had the most basic of meanings: 640 acres of dirt, a rectangle of rich northern Iowa farmland that is our family farm. My father worked this land—corn, soybeans, hogs, and turkeys. And my brother owns it to this day. The farm provided a constant reminder of the tangibility of place since bits of it routinely needed to be scrubbed from under the fingernails or scraped off the bottoms of shoes.

Just plain place has also had central importance in the life of John Luther Adams. Nearly forty years ago he traded a rather suburban existence in New Jersey and Southern California for the distinctly un-suburban boreal forest of central Alaska. And when he arrived as a new recruit in the small army of environmentalists who mobilized northward to protect Alaska's great open spaces he found, as he has told me many times, his true home. Over the years no other composer has been as associated with Alaska as John has been. In fact very few composers have ever been more associated with any place than John has been with Alaska. Vienna had its first and second schools, Paris had Les Six, and New York its Bang on a Can gang. But as rooted in a place as these musicians were, the relationship between John and Alaska is different, deeper. It's not just more powerful, but also more singular. Cities like New York, Paris, or Vienna are by definition catch basins of multiplicity, sites often of unremarkable geography where liveliness derives from a crisscrossing of the diversities within a continually mutable population. New York is a greater city than, say,

Des Moines, not because the sycamores of Central Park are more imposing than the oaks of Iowa but because New York's large population and effusion of varied and vital energies lead to complexity and an abundance of options. In other words, it's not place but plentitude that defines the core identity of great cities. But the unremittingly singular stamp of Alaska, in particular of its wilderness, offers stark and limited choices.

Adams's options in Alaska were few indeed: he might have chosen to become a musical chronicler of the north, the Villa-Lobos of the tundra so to speak, by quoting Inuit music and alluding to windswept vistas. But after 1997 and the composition *Strange and Sacred Noise* it became clear that he chose another path. By avoiding the most literal influences of his place he moved beyond a music inspired by place to a music that was in fact a place unto itself. In his music sonic forces interact more like the vectors of weather patterns or the arcs of migration or reforestation than traditional notes, rhythms, and scales. The irony here is bittersweet: by living fully in Alaska John Luther Adams created a music in which Alaska became irrelevant. This thought occurred quite strongly on the ridge overlooking the Maclaren Valley as we played *Strange and Sacred Noise*. Neither the recursive overlapping of the four snare drums in *. . . dust into dust . . .* nor the wailing of the four sirens in *triadic iteration lattices* seemed to imitate natural sounds. They are not the musical representations of glaciers calving or wind howling. But neither do they sound like concert music. In essence this music asks us to suspend our usual need to categorize experiences as either "natural" or "constructed," and creates instead a linkage between the two. In this pipeline between the natural and constructed world, this "poly-place" as it were, we were left with many questions. What would happen, we wondered, if we took a piece of music that was heavily influenced by wild places and played it not in the anonymous confines of a concert hall where performers and listeners are purposely insulated from the outside world, but played it instead outdoors in the wild? Would music born in the wild seem to belong there—perhaps in a musical version of *Free Willy*, the heroic story of a piece born in the wilderness, held for a while in the captivity of the concert hall and released to cavort again with the moaning winds and drifting snows? Or would the self-conscious constructions of music seem out of place among the swarming mosquitoes and patrolling grizzly? As the agents of this music would we seem out of place?

These questions lay at the foundation of Robert Esler's project. His experiment was to reverse the equation of the concert hall, which is a single space designed to be the home of multiple and widely varied pieces of music. Instead Rob took us on a tour in which a single piece was played in four very different outdoor performance sites. *Strange and Sacred Noise* was particularly well suited to the experiment. As a quartet it was small enough to be readily portable. It was also expandable. With its six movements and five different arrangements of percussion instruments it was the perfect vehicle for platoons of percussionists, which became a valuable aspect since in every one of our outdoor performances more than four percussionists wanted to be involved.

Beyond practical issues of size, *Strange and Sacred Noise* offers ready access to many of today's most interesting questions in percussion. Starting with the intense noises of snare drums in the first movement and moving through the filtered "tonal noises" of tam-tams and tomtoms the piece arrives at its midpoint in a long movement for the pure tones of pitched instruments before returning to snare drums. This classic percussive arc from noise to tone and back again afforded a perfect testing ground for the receptiveness of outdoor environments to various degrees of spectral saturation. Cutting another way, the piece becomes a double-tour of the other classic percussive binary: vertical and horizontal. The opening snare drum music, largely polyphonic, leads to the horizontal swelling of tam-tam rolls, returns to polyrhythm in the tomtom movement, flattens again to horizontal in the melodic rise and fall of four sirens, and finalizes with the polyphony of the snare drum music. Verticality with its implications of attack, polyphony, and stacking, counterpoised with the melodic and textural aspects of horizontality, outlined a complex web of musical vectors. We hoped that these and other embedded cycles would make *Strange and Sacred Noise* a revealing test case for outdoor performances.

On the inside cover of the score, Adams describes movements of *Strange and Sacred Noise* and the structural models employed in each:

> *. . . dust into dust . . .* is a sonic equivalent of the "Cantor Dust"—a fractal of the behavior of electrical noise—articulated by two snare drums and two field drums.
>
> *solitary and time-breaking waves* (after James Tenney) is scored for four tam-tams. Waves of intensity with varied periods gradually drift together, cresting in a massive tsunami of sound.
>
> *velocities crossing in phase space* (after Conlon Nancarrow and Peter Garland)—for six tomtoms and four bass drums—is a canon in continuous waves of acceleration and ritardando, modeled after Nancarrow's *Canon X* and Garland's *Meditation on Thunder*.
>
> *triadic iteration lattices* (to Edgard Varèse and Alvin Lucier)—for four sirens—traverses an expanding field of rising and falling glissandi. The piece is modeled on the Serpienski Gasket: an Eiffel Tower of reiterated, telescoping pyramids.
>
> *clusters on a quadrilateral grid* (to Morton Feldman) is scored for four

marimbas, four vibraphones and four sets of orchestra bells. It is the sounding of the Menger Sponge: an enigmatic quadrilateral with an infinite surface area and a volume of zero.

...*and dust rising*... is scored for two snare drums and two field drums. Out of silence, points of dust emerge to become relentless, reiterated noise.

The first outing of the Esler Project was a performance by the University of California, San Diego percussion group, red fish blue fish, in the badlands of the Anza-Borrego desert near San Diego. Esler and red fish blue fish joined forces again in a performance near Sandwich, New Hampshire, in the halcyon days of autumn in a northern forest. A third performance included percussionists from Akron and took place in the rolling, wooded farmland of Ohio. And, finally, we headed north to the tundra and our performance and filming at the Maclaren Valley.

We started in late February, 2006, when a group of six percussionists and about twenty friends trekked east from La Jolla to the desert in San Diego county, unloaded a fully packed cargo truck, and carried drums, gongs, and marimbas to an exposed perch on an east-facing cliff in the Anza-Borrego desert. As the sun began to set and hawks soared in the final updrafts of the day we had a spectacular view of the subtle colorations of the California desert as it went from brown to umber to dark purple. The sights were glorious. Unfortunately the sonic results were a little less glorious. We were too exposed, too far away from rock faces and canyon walls that might have provided natural reverberation and sonic warmth. The pitched instruments—marimbas, vibraphones, and glockenspiels—suffered the most, and by the time their moment came the late-afternoon desert wind had started to blow in earnest. What little sound reached the small group of listeners through the Aeolian mesh amounted to a vestigial high whistling decorated only occasionally by actual notes. Yet afterward we were pleased, euphoric even. It seemed like something true had happened; not something vague or theoretical but a real thing.

Among the positive aspects, we found that in the desert we listened more closely to the music and to each other than we had in our indoor concerts. We had to. The normal interactions of chamber music that are nearly second nature in a concert hall require intense focus outside. The concentrated focus on music was its own reward, but it also seemed transposable to the outside sounds. I doubt I have ever been as aware of natural sounds—the tightly braided band of wind noise or the sudden clattering sound of a rock rolling down the hillside—as I was on that day. I also had a flash of insight into Carnegie Hall where the occasional external noises of subway trains can only be

82 * SCHICK

called disturbances. In the desert, however, environmental noises did not disturb. After all they were not the outsiders, we were. And while it's hard not to resent the subway at Carnegie, the desert wind seemed perfectly contented that we were there. In spite of our general disappointment with *Strange and Sacred Noise* as a musical experience, some aspects actually worked better outdoors. The polyphony was remarkably apparent in the desert. For example the thundering movement scored for tomtoms and bass drum, *velocities crossing in phase-space*, often sounds like a noise-cloud—not unlike Xenakis's *nuages* from *Persephassa*—when played in a moderately resonant hall. Our performance outdoors dried it up nicely, and revealed an intricate weave of accelerating and decelerating lines. Likewise, every snare drum and glockenspiel attack was rendered, as they say, as clear as a bell.

However, as clear as the polyphony may have been, the desert is no place for Bach. There were serious problems with balance. In addition to problems resulting from the lack of natural reverberation, such that an instrument set near a cliff face or even positioned next to a flattish rock projected much better than one left completely in the open, there was also distortion across register. Registral extremes, the highest glockenspiel notes and the lowest tam-tam and bass drum, which often predominate in concert settings to the point of serious musical imbalance, lost their teeth outdoors, and one heard mostly attacks in the middle registers. (This makes one marvel at the enormous sonic force in a peal of thunder such that it can project booming low frequencies over great distances!) The absence of sheer percussive force also made for problems of identity and scale. Percussionists are used to being the merchants of terrifying sounds. We can produce a range from soft to loud that no other acoustic instrument can match, and when we want to have the last word we can always play loud enough to get it. So we were humbled by the experience of driving a tam-tam or bass drum to its maximum volume only to produce a polite whirring or clattering noise. Of course this is largely a question of scale. A bass drum sounds grand within the framework of the small spaces and the otherwise quiet sounds of a concert hall, but the same sound can seem pretty puny in the midst of more than 600,000 unfenced acres of desert. It's the same principle that made Walt Disney's Sleeping Beauty castle loom over the orange groves of Anaheim, while its much larger parent, King Ludwig's "Neuschwanstein," is dwarfed by the Bavarian Alps. By going outside we had abandoned control over the management of scale and in turn lost our prerogative to be the biggest, most impressive thing around.

The most complex experiences in the Anza-Borrego desert came in the two movements for snare drum quartet, ... *dust into dust* ..., and ... *and dust rising*. Here, thanks to the absence of resonance in the outdoor environment, the impact of individual strokes and their vertical relationships were strikingly clear, especially in less dense passages and when listeners were not far from the drums. But with increased density or greater distance the snare drums blended at times so well with the ambient sounds that they literally melded with the wind. In a recent conversation, Bernhard Wulff, the visionary German percussionist and musical thinker, warned me of difficulties in fore- and background relationships when the sonic qualities of a composition to be played outdoors are too similar to the sounds of the environment. The noise floor will swallow the music, he said. Herr Wulff should know after thirteen years of organizing the outdoor festival "Roaring Hooves" in the Gobi, not to mention a set of concerts he presented in seaside caves in Vietnam and assorted performances closer to home in the Black Forest. Wulff notes that the most successful performances he organized in the Mongolian desert would certainly include the bongo movement from Steve Reich's *Drumming*, some brass music of Janacek, and one he could not resist: *Density 21.5* in honor of Henry Miller's *With Edgar Varèse in the Gobi Desert*. These pieces feature the common sonic elements of precise attack, robust sound mass, and spectral clarity such that they stand in relief against the more diffuse and noisy background of the environment. Confusion of the music with the noise floor is only a problem, however, if one's goal is to differentiate the two. It's true that if you want to hear a piece of music against the backdrop of the desert then indeed a good idea would be to program, say, the Stravinsky *Octet* or Janacek *Sinfonietta*. Thanks to the inherent contrasts between the noise environment of the outdoor site and the unambiguous, spectrally coherent qualities of the instruments, the ear can easily separate musical sounds from nonmusical noises. (In this regard our experience of the four sirens in *triadic iteration lattices* from *Strange and Sacred Noise* in Alaska was an unqualified success since sirens are noisemakers explicitly designed to be heard in contrast to unpredictable interference from outside noise.) If the goal is not to hear "a piece of music played in the desert," however, but rather to hear "the desert played by a piece of music," then the fact that the sounds of massed snare drums and the noises of nature are easily confused with each other is hardly a problem. I'm not sure which is more beautiful: to be unsure of whether you're hearing a snare drum roll or a rock slide, or suddenly to be aware of rhythm in the sound of the wind.

At first I was skeptical of the idea that we might be able to "play the desert" using the snare drum as a mallet. But in spite of doubts there *was* something different about playing outdoors. I swear that we often found ourselves in the midst of magical moments where the natural world seemed to be singing along with us as we played. Or perhaps we bade it sing. The most memorable of these moments came before the beginning of our performance amid a kaleidoscope of fall colors in the New Hampshire woods in late September of 2006. This trek was significantly more arduous than the one near San Diego. The load-in was over nearly a mile of uneven ground, across a collapsing wooden fence, along a shallow ridgeline and down a tricky slope before finding our performance sites tucked in the crooks and narrows of a small stream. The marimbas and vibraphones were set on a small sand bar in the middle of the water, and a line of tam-tams receded on a slant atop the opposing high ground. Snare drums were nestled into a rock alcove near a bend in the creek while the tomtoms were positioned in a small open space. All in all, the site was a lot like a small amphitheater; it was relatively sheltered and the natural enclosures of the small valley and surrounding rocks made it far more satisfying than the desert in terms of sound reinforcement. As you might expect, as a "concert" our afternoon was a success. Sonically it felt much less like an experiment and much more like a reasonable alternative to the stage. Add to that an audience of between fifteen and twenty who drove the five hours from either Boston or New York to share in the event (the Brazilian percussionist Eduardo Leandro flew his small plane from Amherst) and things seemed pretty festive.

We decided to start the day with a performance of . . . *having never written a note for percussion*,[1] a tribute to its composer James Tenney who had died a few weeks earlier. There were enough performers among the percussionists and audience members for fifteen or so musicians to be spread out into the forest—we had made the decision to be far enough apart to hear nearby players but not see them. So we found our spots and started to play, tentatively at first, beginning with the softest tremolo we could make on our instrument and then with increasing force to maximum volume and back again, over the course of about fifteen minutes. Conditions were perfect. The woods were hushed, the air completely still. As we finished there were perhaps thirty seconds of silence and then a single gust of wind blew through the creek bed, rustling the leaves and rippling the water before going quiet for the rest of the day. The intervention felt otherworldly. And suddenly I was trapped: I was a classically trained musician and professor at a research university, participating in Rob Esler's project as his thesis supervisor and out of my devotion to the music of John Luther Adams. I wanted our experiences to be quantifiable—a little quirky perhaps, but still somehow academic. Yet I was sure I had just heard the spirit of James Tenney in that sudden breeze. The world, which so often seems anonymous, had become amniotic. Air was no longer vague ether but was suddenly alive, and it was singing along with us. Of course, I told myself quickly, this wasn't *real* magic. We had simply manipulated the psychoacoustics of the perceptual frame. As our performance decayed into nothingness we had transferred the intense listening that music demands to the near-silence of the woods. We put a loupe to a world of ambient sounds so that a sudden gust of wind was no longer a background phenomenon, but now within the musical frame, something foreground and intended. This seemed to make sense, and for the moment at least I felt back on firm academic footing.

In search of the comforting architecture of theory I started to examine our outdoor experiences of *Strange and Sacred Noise* in light of John Luther Adams's compositional strategies. Music starts with noise, as John has said in many ways. By "noise" he means saturated, chaotic waveforms, just as any acoustician would define it, but he also means noise as simply another name for the audible world, from the singing of birds to the thumping of our hearts and the hiss in our ears. If noise equals "the world," it's tempting to understand Adams's view of noise as the audible poetry of a savage natural state, the noble opposite of the man-made. But this view would be wrong. In John's music noise is not *found* but *made*. In *Strange and Sacred Noise*, and its sister work for solo percussion *The Mathematics of Resonant Bodies* (2002), Adams begins by constructing noise, engineering it to create spectral saturation in instrument-specific ways. With four snare drums, for example, noise means unison strokes at roughly the speed of nine beats per second, with tam-tams a dense tremolo, and with marimbas a complex chord. This noise then is not accidental—not unintended or collateral, not *natural*—but the entirely purposeful, self-consciously created product of compositional process. As such, noise in Adams stands for the exercise of craft and in these pieces is the emblem of tradition and civilization, not nature.

Once a substrate of noise has been built Adams begins a rigorous process of fenestration, of carving windows in the constructed noise. So, in the beginning there is noise. Then it is carved away to produce texture, then line, and then a set of increasingly sparse points that approach silence. Fenestration in the two snare drum movements from *Strange and Sacred Noise* is driven by Adams's translation of the "Cantor Set" and "Cantor Dust" into musical form. In summary, the "Cantor Set" begins with a line segment. From this segment the middle third is removed, then from each of the remaining two segments the middle third is removed, and from the remaining segments the middle third is removed, and so on into infinity. Progressing in a series of self-similar shapes, each successive removal comes closer to nothingness as a final, but ultimately unreachable, goal. Elsewhere, in *clusters on a quadrilateral grid*, a long movement for pitched percussion instruments, the model is the "Menger Sponge," an extension of the "Cantor Set" into three dimensions—in the composer's description, a cube with an infinite surface area and a volume of zero. Here again a saturated spectral space is created, this time as complex harmony in dense clusters of rolled marimba music. Again the middle third of a phrase

clusters

E

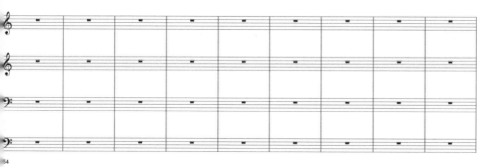

FIGURE 5.1

is manipulated, although in *clusters on a quadrilateral grid* the middle third remains and the outer two thirds are removed, serving to create silence more quickly than in the snare drum movements.

Fenestration reveals the dynamic interplay between noise and silence in Adams's music. Noise is made and manipulated in order to create silence. And then when played outdoors, the vibrant silence is used to frame and enliven the noises of the background. In the case of the snare drum and keyboard movements the silences are long—nearly thirty seconds. And in the New Hampshire woods, just as we heard at the end of . . . *having never written a note for percussion*, they were luminous, full of wondrous small sounds. Was this, I wondered, the musical equivalent of the sculptures of Henry Moore where the work consists as much in the shape of the unfilled space as in the shape of the stone? In an indoor performance of *Strange and Sacred Noise* the unfilled bars would have been simply empty (plus of course the acoustical chaff of air moving and electronics humming). Played outdoors the silences became anything but empty and, in the intense quality of listening they engendered, produced a sense of awakening to the natural acoustical world.

These were the acoustical aspects; then there are the rhetorical aspects of silence. With each successive fenestration Adams creates silence but he also distances himself from a "constructed" noise. Again it is tempting to construct a facile binary: If noise is the product of compositional craft then, inversely, approaching silence means an ever greater distance from construction and, therefore, ever greater proximity to nature. If this were truly the case one could imagine with a composer as attuned to nature as John Luther Adams that soon we would have pieces that consisted largely if not completely of silence. But John Cage's most famous experiment not withstanding, silence has proven to be too unconditional and unmalleable a state to be readily sustained as material within a piece of composed music. In the case of Adams's percussion music it seems that noise functions affectively as stasis—for all of the chaos of its waveforms, structurally it is a point of repose. It is tonic. Silence on the other hand is comprised of a more perishable commodity and functions in his music as the force of dissonance. This means that silence is a state through which one passes and rarely, if ever, is sustained as actual *material*. Indeed even the most famous devotees of silence from Feldman and Cage to Thomas DeLio and others have not been able to sustain silence in durations beyond a minute or two.[2] Silence simply does not lend itself to shaping, to elongation, or to paraphrase. It is too categorical, too uncompromising. Or, as Mark Rothko famously put it: "Silence is so accurate."

However one might describe silence, its growing importance in Adams's percussion music was becoming evident—and problematic. For most listeners noise and silence occupy mutually exclusive zones, and if the truth were told mainstream musical tastes don't want very much of either. But by employing a purposeful compositional strategy in which noise is a given point of departure and silence is an inevitable goal, John Luther Adams embraces a view in which silence and noise, far from being unrelated opposites, are structurally twinned. In his music the weight of silence as *absence* is inversely proportional, and perceived to the same degree, as noise is felt as *presence*. Thus silence and noise, while functionally inverted, are ontologically indistinguishable. Each is the systematic, man-made invention of a composer. For a musician like John Luther Adams, a person as formed by and indebted to the natural world as any I know, this conundrum grated. If neither noise nor silence stood for nature, then where was nature to be found in his percussion music? Perhaps as a response to this question a frequent trope in our conversations became that John's music was no longer "about place," but had "become place." In other words, nature did not have to be sought; it was not a separable identity but an intrinsic and inextricable part of any musical creation. However, Dr. Esler's project of taking *Strange and Sacred Noise* into natural settings seemed to disallow this rhetorical sleight of hand. We all knew that there was an extraordinary resonance between John's music and the natural world. We had experienced it for ourselves in the California desert and the forest of New Hampshire. So as we packed our instruments in the soft fading light of a New England autumn day, we knew that there was only one way to probe this central issue. There was only one direction to go and that was north. North towards the place where noise and silence make their home. North to the tundra.

Noise on the Tundra

Return to the freeze-frame. The time stamp still reads a little before 3:45 a.m. on June 24, 2008. We are deeply cold.

The evening began smoothly enough. In fact the entire trip to Alaska began auspiciously as my plane touched down in Fairbanks exactly at the stroke of the summer solstice. I was met by the other members of our team of percussionists: Rob Esler and his fiancée Lisa Tolentino, who had played in each of the outdoor performances; Morris Palter, another former student and head of the University of Alaska percussion program; and Doug Perkins, a founding member of the wonderful So Percussion group. Filmmaker Len Kammerling and composer Eric Schultz, who would serve as recording engineer, also joined. We all went immediately to the Museum of the North to see John's stunning interactive sound and light installation, *The Place Where You Go to Listen*. The installation is housed in a small room in which a light and sound design changes in response to the real-time input of seismic, electro-magnetic, lunar and solar

FIGURE 5.2

data drawn from all over Alaska. In my first experience with *The Place* a sudden rumbling and darkening drew our attention to a corner of the room and prompted John to announce that we had just experienced an earthquake in the Aleutians. When we entered *The Place Where You Go to Listen* roughly ninety minutes after the summer solstice, the room was humming in consonant bands of filtered noise and glowed with an intense yellowish-orange. We were watching and listening to Alaska at the zenith of its short summer.

By now the *Strange and Sacred Noise* drill was clear. After two days of rehearsal and an afternoon of instrument-packing and loading we were ready for the long drive south into the Alaska Range. Frequent squalls in Fairbanks seemed intent on reminding us that we were sure to find the most demanding outdoor performance conditions yet. But as we departed Fairbanks the weather began to clear, and after stopping briefly en route to visit the single-room homestead where the poet John Haines lived after moving to Alaska in 1947, we arrived at the performance site in plenty of time to offload the instruments, tents, and cooking gear before eating supper.

John's idea was roughly to encircle the four-acre site with seven sets of instruments at a distance of between fifty and one hundred yards from one another. The site was a patchwork of fairly flat but rocky outcroppings separated by lower grassy areas and occasionally by rather steep rills overgrown with scrubby brush. We started by placing the small group of snare drums on a slight rise at the southern end of site. From there a line of equidistant tamtams bowed slightly outward along a west-facing ridgeline and connected the snare drum station to another slight rise on the north where we positioned the set of tomtoms and bass drums. The site then spiraled inward on grassier land toward a small mountain lake at the center, which served as the locus for the antiphonal movement for four sirens at the midpoint of the piece. On higher ground above the lake was our large screened tent with folding tables and chairs where musicians and crew could eat and stay warm. A gradually opening arc of marimbas, vibraphone, and glockenspiels led away from the tent on a bias back toward the snare drums.

In retrospect I realize that this arrangement outlined a roughly shaped labyrinth of percussion instruments with the snare drums at the entry point and the lake at the center. There were gaps along the pathway on account of the practical need for flat performance sites, but there was a clear inward curve. There was also the sense that each movement of the piece was a step along the path of the labyrinth, one leading to another and to another and another. Every labyrinth features a beguiling set of contradictions: sometimes you have to turn your back on what seems to be the shortest path in order to find the most direct one; at other times what appear to be two adjacent and proximate pathways are really very far apart. Our labyrinth of percussion sounds was no less fascinating. The goal was to link seemingly incompatible sounds along a single logical pathway of sonic equivalencies. This was a formidable challenge since in purely spectral terms the outermost point of snare drums and center of the labyrinth with its sirens are as far apart as it's possible to be. What linked these sounds, and therefore allowed them to coexist in the same musical space, was the parity of their sonic *presence*. The instrumental sets were not similar but they were equivalent. Here equivalency was the product of a balance between percussive impact and spatial amplitude. A tight circular arrangement of snare drums takes up very little physical space but occupies a large virtual space on account of the spectral density and sheer noise of its music. Inversely the sirens at the center were completely devoid of attack and noise but compensated by means the architectural amplitude of their positioning around the lake.

We originally planned to distribute the instruments to their respective sites that evening, cover them with tarps and then start recording early the next morning. But as we cleared the dinner dishes and started stepping off the performance space the sky was perfectly clear and the light magical. By 8:30 p.m. with the sun still high in the sky at sixty-four degrees north latitude, and a decidedly mixed forecast for the morning, we quickly opted to begin playing as soon as possible. Len assured us that even in the middle of the night there would be enough light to film. We attacked the piece and recorded the first few movements very quickly. The most difficult moments were not musical but involved holding our positions at the beginning and end of each movement. As soon as Len shouted, "cut," musicians and camera operators waved their arms and legs wildly and clouds of well-fed mosquitoes rose into the sky. Between each movement there was a pause of about an hour as microphones, cabling, the recording desk and two car batteries needed for power were carried from one installation to another across the brushy, uneven terrain and through nearly impenetrable swarms of bugs. Following the sound gear came the four camera operators and Len, who set up the shots as we finalized the positions of instruments and did a quick sound check.

We were fantastically lucky with the light. The line of tam-tams in the second movement glowed bronze in the back-lit twilight, and by the time we reached the tomtom movement the sun had set briefly, leaving Mount Hayes ringed in volcanic red behind us. Each movement was attacked with vigor; and each was recorded in a single take.

Then suddenly, as it seems in every performance of *Strange and Sacred Noise*, the emotional turning point of the piece came in the siren movement. There were problems. It wasn't so much that the music was difficult, but we struggled with our small red plastic sirens, and it was getting very cold. Standing in icy puddles at the edge of the lake our body heat leached quickly through our thin rubber boots. This time we had to wait much longer than usual for the recording equipment to be set. Clearly the best place for the microphones in an antiphonal recording would have been the middle of the lake. But that wasn't possible, so Eric devised an ingenious linkage between his equipment and the built-in microphones of the cameras in order to balance the four widely dispersed sound sources. But it all took time. The movement was further slowed because the large distances between us made playing together extremely tricky. In the end we opted for a conductor, Rob I think, who was stationed just out of camera range. As we waited it got progressively darker and colder. The scene emerges in my memory now as the four of us, isolated and exhausted, etched as pewter silhouettes against the pale reflected light of the snow-covered mountains behind us. It was a moment of alone-ness that reinforced John's view that an interpreter of his music is a solitary vertical presence in a mostly horizontal sonic landscape, the musical analogue of the vertical zip in a Barnett Newman painting. It was not easy, but eventually we were ready to play. And the music that came out of that difficult moment proved, again, that ease is the enemy of art.

Unfreeze the frame.

John and I have finished our conversation about the marimba sound. By now we are well past the sirens and are abandoning the marimbas and moving to the vibraphones. In an hour or so we'll be on to the glockenspiels and then the snare drums again. We'll be finished soon. The sun is now fully out and the temperatures are climbing. This bit of good news is tempered by the reappearance of mosquitoes. We hadn't noticed that they had disappeared—but where?—in the cold night. But with the sun in our faces now, first one and then two and then many appeared on our music, then our ears and hands, then the backs of our necks. The warming day also seemed to welcome the clangorous vibraphone music and the pure, crystalline glockenspiel sounds. Attacks ricochet off nearby rocks as though, like the mosquitoes, reverberation and sonic warmth had somehow disappeared into the midnight chill. By the time we closed the great circle of *Strange and Sacred Noise* with the snare drum music of . . . *and dust rising* . . . we had begun to sweat a little. The siren movement was a small moment of crisis but now we were back with our feet firmly in the familiar world of music—the world of rhythms, and cues nodded to one another, of smiling when a take went especially well. It was nearly nine in the morning when we played our last drum notes and made our weary ways to the Maclaren River Lodge for breakfast and a nap. We were back on the site by mid-afternoon, and after confirmation from Len that we were well and truly covered in the filming—minus some shots that were unusable because of insects swarms on the lenses—we quickly packed and finished loading the vans just as the rains began again.

My last view of our site through the sudden squall was of the lake. And I paused a moment in reflection. The dynamic relationship between noise and silence in John Luther Adams's music had been made clearer than ever. In our four performances outdoors from the desert to the tundra we had heard saturated noise break apart like spring ice on a northern lake. We listened as the broken shards of the noise were pushed aside to reveal incandescent silence. And we marveled as the small sounds of the forest and the desert wind came alive and filled those silences. But what we had *not* experienced was John's often-repeated assertions that hidden in noise are the sounds of voices. Noise for John is plasma, that is to say a substance of undefined shape and size in which all possible sounds can be found and through which they might be conducted to a listener. Art lies in the process of filtering the noise. Since noise is the perfected collection of all possible sounds, a sufficiently sophisticated filter could, theoretically at least, produce any sound you can imagine. Filter the noise just right and you can hear anything from the squeak of a screen door, to your mother singing, to the crack of the ball off Bobby Thompson's bat and the collective groan of Brooklyn as he rounded the bases. So when John says that hidden in the noise of *Strange and Sacred Noise* are the sounds of voices he does not mean this in a poetic or metaphorical way. They are there; we just had to find them.

Until the first plaintive siren notes I had not heard any voices. But at that moment of utter exhaustion around the lake I realized why we had come to the tundra. I found my answer to the question we had been posing: "What are we doing here?" We asked ourselves then, and we have repeated the question whenever we speak about that night. It's the same question that John whispered under his breath as we coiled cable at the marimba station, "What the hell are we doing here?" The answer has become clear for me: we had come to hear the voices. They appeared first as individual strands with each siren rising and falling separately until welling together as a single collected voice they spiraled inward toward the center of the lake, towards the heart of our labyrinth of percussion sound. At a distance from each other the voices were barely audible at first, their fragile lines threatening to disappear into the vastness around us. Suddenly our smallness overwhelmed me, and for a brief moment the enormity of the space around us seemed suffocating. But for a percussionist used to delivering lots of very loud sounds it also felt good to be chastened. And, importantly, in the small voices of the sirens I had found at least part of the answer to the nagging question of where nature was to be found in the percussion music of John Luther Adams. Nature, it seemed, might be heard in the metrics of scale—the accord between an act and the place it occurs. It might be heard as the small, singular zip of human performers standing alone in a large musical space, and in the refreshing smallness of that music heard within the ample embrace of a much larger world. The voices of the sirens were small indeed, but my impression was that they rang true. In the fullness of time this impression would be detailed as a set of ideas. The ideas would become themes for teaching and writing, and in turn the generative impulse for a new collaboration with John. But at that moment, under an enormous sky as a midsummer's dawn came to Alaska, I believed we had made at least one small, true thing. And in the midst of all the noise that was plenty.

Inuksuit: Music in the Second Person

Several months passed after we loaded out of the tundra before John and I spoke about that night in any detail. We had packed, eaten dinner at the Maclaren River Lodge—a remarkably similar menu to the breakfast offerings—and driven back. I had booked an early flight home so when we got back to Fairbanks at three in the morning, the sun already high in the sky, I went directly to the airport. I had been up for sixty hours on a two-hour nap and don't remember much about the flight home. Then one day walking in Toronto, killing some time before a solo concert, my phone rang and it was John. "What are we going to do next?" he asked. We talked for a while about the experience of *Strange and Sacred Noise*, of taking music meant for the indoors into the extreme outdoor conditions of the desert and tundra. And then we started to muse together about what a "true outdoor piece," a piece of percussion music conceived for and composed for outdoor performance, would sound like.[3] By the time I had walked up and down Queen Street and circled back towards the Music Gallery for the third time we had essentially sketched out plans for the piece that would become *Inuksuit*.

We started by detailing a list of what we had found in our outdoor performances of *Strange and Sacred Noise*. We learned:

1 that the focus and perceptual acuity needed to listen to a piece of music was transposable to environmental sounds. Listening intently outdoors meant that the ambient sounds we heard during performances of *Strange and Sacred Noise* took on the vividness of musical events.
2 that space mattered. Performing complex music in open spaces meant that individual elements could be tracked with greater clarity. (I remember seeing Iannis Xenakis wandering on stage before a rehearsal of his *Thalleïn* moving the chairs farther apart to achieve just this sort of clarity.)
3 that percussion instruments, many of which had been designed explicitly for use outdoors, worked well in our outdoor performances. This was especially true of triangles, snare drums, noisy metallic instruments, and sirens.
4 that there was an intangible aspect to outdoor performance that was widely appealing for both players and listeners. People liked making and listening to music outside of a concert hall.
5 and, that performing outdoors reconfigured our sense of scale in a way that leveled a healthy critique on the machismo of percussion playing.

Beyond these observations there were the voices of other percussionists who had also begun to talk about commissioning a new piece from John. J. B. Smith, the percussion professor at Arizona State University, had explored the possibility of commissioning a new outdoor percussion piece via a consortium of percussionists. Al Otte, founding member of the Percussion Group Cincinnati, and one of the most inspiring performers of percussion chamber music that I know, had issued his own challenge. While not explicitly invoking an outdoor work, Al suggested to John that he think about "moving beyond the monochrome" of *Strange and Sacred Noise* and make a "seminal" percussion piece, an *Ionisation* for our time. My Toronto conversation with John freshly in mind, and with these distinguished voices raising the same questions, it became time to ask: Could we move beyond the exportation of indoor music to the outdoors and make a new percussion piece that was designed for an outdoor performance? The signs were hopeful.

Yet in spite of the many positive signals and the informative experiences we had had in the desert, forest, and tundra there were some problems. For starters, while concert halls are largely uniform, outdoor spaces are widely varied. How do you make a piece if you don't know whether it will be played in Central Park, a California beach, or at base camp on Mount Everest? Can a piece be flexible enough to work in a wide variety of settings without losing the focus that is necessary to a coherent work of art? This was new territory, but in fact one of the primary goals of a new outdoor piece was to challenge the uniformity of the concert hall. We aimed at making a musical experience that would derive value from variations among sites. This meant that *Inuksuit* would not be *site-specific* but rather *site-determined*, as John has often described it. A site-specific piece is made to suit its site and posits an unproblematized rapport between event and location. A site-determined work is meant to change according to the site in which it is played. It posits a dynamic, mutually informative rapport between a musical event and its performance site. Ideally, the site affects the music. And in ways that we are just beginning to come to terms with, the music also affects the site.

We already know a lot about site-specific pieces since the default site for nearly all of them is a concert hall. Music performed there is designed to conform to the aesthetic values of that space as well as, and perhaps more important, to its commercial values. A primary goal of most concert halls (outside of academia at least) is to define, control, and transmit music as a commodity. External walls keep outside noises out (otherwise one cannot sell a ticket because of the contamination of the listening experience), and they also keep the inside noises in (if you could hear the music from the outside you would not need a ticket.) Concert halls profess a kind of democracy since there is at least a nominal commitment to an equivalent experience for every listener. But one does not have to probe too deeply to see that hierarchies of orchestral, loge, and upper balcony seating have commercial and artistic consequences for both listener and concert hall alike.

Commerce in turn drives education. Since commercial success awaits any musician who plays regularly in concert halls, especially in the highly profiled halls of big cultural centers, musical education is aimed at producing performers who excel at performing in concert halls. If you extend the definition of a concert hall in the realm of commerce, if not art, to include clubs, pubs, salons, and arenas—in essence any controlled space where sound is optimized and tickets are sold—then it is not unusual to find musicians who have *never* played outside of a concert hall. Why would a music conservatory spend very much time training its students for performance anywhere else? And why would arts management devote any attention to musical presentations that take place outside of a concert hall? Why would music critics (in their customary roles as arbiters of whether an audience spent wisely by buying a ticket to a particular concert) devote column inches to such an open performance?

Of course the answer is they would not and do not. Yet this leaves percussionists in a tricky spot, since many if not most percussion instruments were made for outdoor performance—snare drums, gongs, cymbals, bass drums, are good examples. If outdoor performance were only the norm we percussionists would be, by default, historically vetted members of the musical aristocracy! However, since it's not, recent decades have seen a dubious project of rehabilitation—of trying to prove that percussionists are as worthy as other instrumentalists—which has led to a generation of percussionists who see their rightful place as on stage, next to if not in front of the violins.[4] As percussionists have increasingly made their reputations on concert stages rather than on horseback or on the field of battle, not only has the percussionist's identity changed, but along with it instrument design itself. Brighter, lighter, and more standardized versions of outdoor instruments have come into favor. Why, after all, should we produce large quantities of deep revolutionary-style field drums with gut snares—instruments designed to deliver messages across miles of uneven terrain between military encampments—when neither indoor spaces nor the indoor performance traditions of chamber and orchestral music can tolerate the booming sounds they make? A marimba is a far better choice of percussion instrument for indoor spaces. The uniformity of its design, the relative gentleness of its sound, and a full complement of pretensions to the refinements of classical music make it much more like the viola or bassoon than its spunkier cousins in the traditional percussion music of Guatemala, Africa, or Indonesia.

So John and I asked each other whether contemporary percussion instruments, and frankly contemporary percussionists themselves, were suited to outdoor performance. Would performers be interested in a presentation to which no tickets could be sold (and therefore no artist's fees could be paid), or where there would probably be no review or recording (and therefore no progress through the maze of professional musical life)? And if we could find percussionists, would contemporary percussion instruments, bred for a life on the stage rather than on the steppe, be satisfactory? When I described these questions to Barry Shiffman, the inventive director of the Music and Sound Programs at the Banff Centre for the Arts, he responded that commissioning John Luther Adams to compose a work intended for the wild might be a perfect way to inaugurate the "Roots and Rhizomes" percussion program that I de-

FIGURE 5.3

signed for the Banff Centre. *Inuksuit* progressed quickly from there and by May 2009, when John arrived in San Diego to attend a performance of his work for orchestra *Dark Waves* that I conducted with the La Jolla Symphony, he brought with him a nearly completed score.

Inuksuit is an Inuit word that means "in the capacity of the human," and is the plural of *inukshuk*, the name given to stone sentinels that ring the circumpolar ocean and have their most impressive flowering in the Canadian Arctic. *Inuksuit* are mysterious objects, part sculpture and part signpost, erected by humans for many possible reasons: to mark a particularly good hunting spot, as a demarcation of territory, or simply as a sign of well-being, that good things happened to a particular group of people at a particular place. These rock structures also marked the northernmost outposts of human civilization and likewise the start of the uninhabitable regions of polar ice. They have been, effectively, a point of demarcation between people and wilderness. Of course, with each passing year of warming the distance between the *inuksuit* and the retreating polar ice, and as a result between the Inuit people and their wilderness, grows greater. John Luther Adams senses the poignancy keenly. As the concrete signs of humanity, the *inuksuit* stand for a change, quite possibly a permanent one, between people and their place. He also sees beauty in the shapes of the stones and the way they are stacked in pyramids, or arches; in single and double windows.

To a composer fascinated with shape—in *Strange and Sacred Noise*, for example, by the infinitely mutable architectures of Cantor processes, or by the welling waves of sound in his works for large ensemble such as *The Light that Fills the World* and *Dark Waves*—these shapes quickly became a rich source of inspiration. Note Adams's musical version of the *inuksuit* (Figures 5.3 and 5.4). In the context of the piece these structures can be played in either ascending or descending versions. In the case of the former a percussionist first plays the bottom line, then the bottom two lines, then the bottom three lines, and so on

Tom-toms
and Bass Drum

Double Window 3

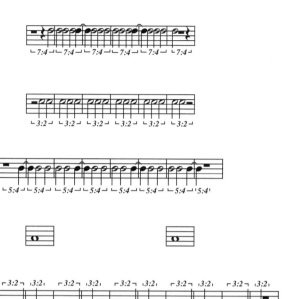

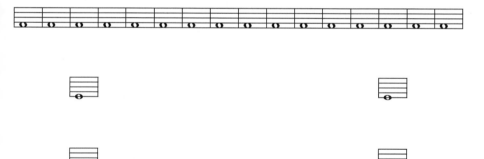

FIGURE 5.4

until all the parts are played simultaneously. The descending version reverses
the process and starts with all layers being played at the same time. Then with
each successive pass the percussionist peels one layer off the top of the structure until he or she is left with nothing.

Looking at the event map in Figure 5.5 one easily sees the formal shape of
Inuksuit.

Inuksuit: Event Map

GROUP 1	*Breathing*	*Calls*		*Waves*		*Clangs*		*Wind*	
	through megaphone (bullhorn, microphone, trumpet, or horn)	conch shell trumpet (Tibetan trumpet, airhorn, plastic horn, other horn or trumpet)		siren (timpano, wind machine (or water gong))		handbell (suspended bell, chime, temple bell, or Tibetan cymbals)		triangle (or small bell(s))	

GROUP 2		*Wind*	*Inuksuit (rising)*		*Waves*		*Inuksuit (falling)*		*Wind*
		rubbed stones (maracas, rattles, shakers, sandblocks, rice in drum, or other friction sounds)	tom-toms and bass drum		tom-toms and bass drum		tom-toms and bass drum		sizzle cymbal

GROUP 3		*Wind*	*Inuksuit (rising)*		*Waves*		*Inuksuit (falling)*		*Birdsongs*
		whirled tubes (blown tubes, bullroarer, or other Aeolian instruments)	suspended cymbals and tam-tam		suspended cymbals and tam-tam		suspended cymbals and tam-tam		orchestra bells (with optional piccolo parts)

TIMELINE	00:00	ca. 10:00	ca. 28:00	ca. 46:00	ca. 64:00	ca. 74:00

FIGURE 5.5

A percussion ensemble of between nine and ninety-nine players is divided into three equal groups. A supplementary group of piccolo players may be added for the performance of birdsong at the end of the piece. The piece begins with all players located at the center of a chosen outdoor site. Over the course of the piece the players radiate outward along equally separated paths, ultimately forming three concentric circles with Group One as the outermost, and Groups Two and Three, respectively, nearer the center. The trajectories of the outwards paths are determined by dividing the 360 degrees of the circle evenly by the number of players such that with nine players the pathways would be 40 degrees apart; with ninety-nine percussionists, each path would be separated by 3.64 degrees. Group One has the special function of controlling the pace of the piece and signaling the beginnings of new sections. This group leaves the center first and moves outward to its maximum distance, stopping at nine equidistant spots along the way. As with all of the music for all groups, each player acts independently, choosing his or her starting moment and the nine stopping points along the way without explicit coordination with the other performers. (Note: the outermost position of each group is to be predetermined as a part of the site evaluation, and it therefore constitutes a rare collective decision.) At each stopping spot a "breathing phrase" of between one and nine long breaths is performed. Normally the sounds of breathing will be amplified by means of a paper cone or megaphone. The breathing music of Group One is followed by the "wind music" of Group Two and then of Group Three. Wind music consists of friction sounds (sandpaper, rattles, and shakers) and whirled tubes (bullroarers, or other Aeolian devices). During their wind music the members of Groups Two and Three walk along predetermined pathways to their outermost positions, where sets of tomtoms and cymbals respectively have been preset.

The piece proceeds from there as a set of loosely coordinated events—in groups of three as you would expect—with each phase initiated by Group One. When Group One moves to "calls" (conch shell, plastic horn, or other such instrument) Group Two begins to play "Inuksuit rising" figures on a set of tomtoms, followed by Group Three playing its "Inuksuit rising" figures on sets of cymbals and tam-tams. When Group One switches (again, one-by-one in only loosely coordinated ways) to sirens, Groups Two and Three respond with "wave music." This consists of tomtom and bass drum rolls for Group Two, and cymbal and tam-tam rolls for Group Three. A set of "clangs" in Group One (cast iron skillets, temple bells, brake drums) initiates "Inuksuit Falling" figures in the skins and metals respectively. And finally the members of Group One start to walk back toward the center of the site, each playing a triangle or small bell. This marks the beginning of Group Two's shift to sizzle cymbals, and the transition of Group Three to birdsong played on glockenspiel. At this moment the supplementary group of piccolo players may join the birdcalls. The entire performance is to last between seventy-five and ninety minutes.

After having experienced three of only four performances of *Inuksuit* given to date—one as a performer in Group One—it may be too soon to draw real conclusions. What is remarkable at this early stage though is the way the piece defies standard categories of listening. In some ways a performance of *Inuksuit* sounds more like a sound installation than a concert. For example, unlike most concerts where the sonic experience is roughly similar for all listeners, experiences of *Inuksuit* may vary widely from listener to listener according to that person's position and movements over the course of the piece. In large sites it would not be unusual for many performers to be too far away to be heard by a given listener. And it's also quite likely that the musicians themselves might not hear each other for long sections of the piece. And if one does not need to hear the entirety of the piece in any given moment in order to have a valid experience, maybe one doesn't need to hear all of the moments of the piece either. It might be possible to have a valid experience of *Inuksuit* by listening to only part of the piece—the first third or last half for example. Most concerts would be ruined under such circumstances, but *Inuksuit* seems to flourish.

Perhaps then *Inuksuit* is a kind of a sound installation played by live performers. Not so fast. Much of the piece also seems concert-like. The players have a score; they have rehearsed; the performance begins at an established, perhaps publicized, time and date; there is a clear beginning and ending; and, there seems to be some reward for having heard all of it (or at least as much as possible given the characteristics of the site.) Upon examination the piece seems split: in the realm of sound, a performance of *Inuksuit* acts like an installation, and in the realm of behavior, especially on the part of the players, it acts like a concert. *Inuksuit* succeeds—and there is no doubt in my mind that it succeeds beautifully—in essence because John Luther Adams has attached the temporal and behavioral scheme of a concert to the open-ended listening experience of an installation. Many audience members reported to me that they had never encountered such a freeing and elastic listening experience. And one could easily imagine that an audience more used to sounding sculptures than concerts might easily have reported that they had never experienced such a disciplined and formally driven installation.

But what did the percussionists themselves think? They are, after all, the people who carried cymbals up the sides of hills and forded bass drums across ice-cold streams. *Inuksuit* demonstrates starkly that a performer who plays outside, leaves not just the pleasures of the optimized acoustic of a concert hall behind, but also its infrastructure—the assurance of freight elevators and stage crew, a green room and dry feet at a post-concert reception. Given the enormity of performers' efforts on behalf of the piece, was there a commensurate pay-off?

The question itself signals that percussionists are taking the creative, and not merely the re-creative, reins in the creation of new art. *Re-taking* the reins one should say, since arguably the two great sources for the western contemporary percussion repertoire were the noise experiments of the 1930s by Cage, Harrison, and Varèse (which, not coincidentally, took place largely outside of conventional concert spaces) and, a few decades later, the open-form works by European composers in the vein of Karlheinz Stockhausen's *Zyklus* or Iannis Xenakis's *Psappha*. But the thirty-five years since the composition of *Psappha* has seen a slow leaching of the spirit of sonic inventiveness and creative engagement on the part of percussionists. Instead we have been increasingly favored in recent years by a set of recital pieces that have more in common with a clarinet sonata or piano concerto than a Cage "Construction" or Alvin Lucier's *Silver Streetcar for the Orchestra*. Under the worst of circumstances in the new, percussive bland-ism, a percussionist reverts to being a mere executant—a performer in the model of the late romantic virtuoso, who contributes little more to a performance than simple manual expertise, and as a result sees as separable the questions of artistic merit in a composition and the level on which it is presented in performance.

But I believe that in *Inuksuit* John Luther Adams—in league with composers like Michael Pisaro and inventive percussionists like Vanessa Tomlinson (see *Spill*, her amazing performance of a collaborative composition with Erik Griswold)—signals a re-growth of the experimental impulse within mainstream percussion playing. And what is truly heartening, even at this early stage, is that *Inuksuit* has captured the imagination of no small number of young percussionists. The eighteen performers at Banff have grown in number to more than fifty at a recent performance at Furman University in South Carolina and to the maximum of ninety-nine in a performance in Texas. Most of these percussionists traveled at their own expense, some from considerable distances, to perform the work, and all played without a fee. If it is treated with respect by young performers who care deeply about it *Inuksuit* may eventually be to them what Karlheinz Stockhausen's *Kontakte* or Herbert Brün's *Touch and Go* were to the now middle-aged percussionists of my generation: a chance to create not just a new piece but a new set of roles and relationships. And make no mistake: *Inuksuit* has already added to the possibilities of exchange between composers, performers, and listeners. When the arduous circumstances of an outdoor performance mean that the majority of persons in attendance are also performers of the piece—as was the case with the world premiere of *Inuksuit* at Goat Creek near Banff—then the question of separate agendas between players and listeners disappears. And when a composer of a notated piece of music in attendance at a performance of his or her work cannot hear or even see all of the players; and, by extension, cannot control or vouch for the accuracy or artistic qualities of the performance; and, as a result, entrusts the control of a strictly notated piece of his or her music to a group of performers to the extraordinary extent that John Luther Adams has trusted performers of his *Inuksuit*, then have the roles of composer, performer, and listener not radically been rethought? Is a performer of *Inuksuit* not exercising the rights of a creator, and has the composer, as only one part of a music-making collective, not become a kind of performer?

Certainly these and other questions can only be answered in due time. But already we have some answers. We know that there are young percussionists who are willing to take on the quixotic challenges of *Inuksuit*, and are able to perform it on a convincingly high level. As for the question of whether or not standard percussion instruments, especially those developed for indoor performance, might be suitable outdoors, the answer is much less clear. To my ear many of the drum sounds seem too small, and the cymbals, while individually beautiful, have seemed too similar to one another when they were arranged in sets—too refined and homogeneous sounding—to function effectively outside. When percussionists have used "outdoor instruments," in particular plastic-headed drums meant for marching bands, the result has seemed coarse and unconvincing. On the other hand, there have been lovely surprises: the triangle sounds, tam-tams, and sirens (again) are winning. Not surprisingly these instruments are also the closest relatives to true outdoor percussion instruments: in the case of the triangles and tam-tams to the military instruments of the Janissary tradition, and in the case of the sirens to the noisemakers of the urban soundscape.

Most important of all, *Inuksuit* is a piece about the equilibrium between its human participants and the natural world in which they find themselves, between *it and us*. Faced with the enormity of the natural world, and the enormity of its current problems, the challenges of equilibrium are substantial. A performance of *Inuksuit* must not be simply the occupation of an outdoor space for purposes of playing a concert. In order to live up to its name, "to act in the capacity of the human," *Inuksuit* must stake a claim in the service of a balance between the intimacy of human contact with nature and the communality of human contact with other humans. On the surface that might sound like the kind of pantheistic formula Mahler or Goethe would love. But *Inuksuit* is no romantic screed. The intimate, found in the modest beauty of momentary coincidence with the natural world, ought not to be tainted by the designs of ownership, and the collective stands not for the anonymous power of the mob but for the communal multiplication of singular energies. In *Inuksuit* we are released from the heroic (and exhausting) stance of the first person singular. But while this music is not romantic, neither is it the dry product of game theory or stochastic strategies; in other words, it is not the academic music of the third person from Darmstadt or IRCAM. As neither the subjective tapestry of heroic narrative nor the blunt object of impersonal experimentation, *Inuksuit* is the truly rare music of the second person—an exquisite, hortatory state where a collusion of energies between humans and the natural world creates a music that no single person can make in a space that no single person can hear. In the second person magical things are willed into existence: from the first cascading wave of conch shells echoing off cliff faces in the invisible distance, to the whirling of tubes mixed with the wind in the leaves of nearby trees, to the moment the glockenspiels play bird song and local birds begin to sing along.

Zoom in on John Luther Adams. He is sitting at the center of a shallow amphitheater on the campus of Furman University. His eyes are closed as he listens to the soft dawning of bells and birdsong in the final moments of a performance of *Inuksuit*. A sudden breeze sends thousands of light "helicopter seeds" aloft, and as they whirl and eventually flutter to the ground their wooden chattering intensifies the sweet sounds of the triangle rolls, glockenspiels, and piccolos. It is a golden moment, the acoustical equivalent of being inside of a snow globe.

Now zoom out.

Zoom out beyond John and the swirl of helicopter seeds. Zoom out until the performers have become mere specks and the small lake beyond the amphitheater is a gray-green dot. Zoom out as far you can, far enough to see everything—every bit of this gorgeous blue planet. And the most magical thing of all is that you can still hear the music.

Notes

1. . . . *having never written a note for percussion* (1971) was composed by James Tenney for percussionist John Bergamo and consists of a single sustained or rolled note that starts as soft as possible, grows to maximum loudness and then recedes. Performances usually last between ten and fifteen minutes.

2. A notable exception to this is John Cage's *ASLSP (As Slow aS Possible)*, which in a current rendering in Halberstadt, Germany is scheduled to last 639 years. The piece begins with a rest, which, parsed at this tempo, produced eighteen months of silence.

3. My conversations with John Luther Adams were focused on making a new outdoor percussion piece. John has an earlier piece meant to be played outdoors, *Nunatsiaq* (The Beautiful Land).

4. See Allan Kozinn's December 27, 2009, article in the *New York Times* in which he claimed, as proof of a newfound legitimacy among percussionists: "If you think about it, drums are the new violins."

Work Cited

Adams, John Luther. *Strange and Sacred Noise*. Fairbanks: Taiga Press, 1997.

David Rothenberg

6 * Go There to Listen
How Music Based on Nature Might
Not Need Natural Sounds

John Luther Adams once told us where music came from. He wrote an essay called "The Place Where You Go to Listen" and explained how you need to first hear the music of the Earth before you will have any need to make your own music. It all started with an Iñupiaq shaman who came to this place, Naalagiagvik, and this is what she heard: "As she listened, she came to hear the breath of each place—how the snow falls here, how the ice melts—how, when everything is still—the air breathes. The drums of her ears throbbed with the heartbeat of this place, a particular rhythm that can be heard in no other place . . . She stands, motionless, listening to the resonant stillness. Then, slowly, she draws a new breath. In a voice not her own, yet somehow strangely familiar, she begins to sing . . ."

You do not start with your own music until you have truly heard the sounds of where you are—that may be his credo. Each place makes its own music, and yet it is a true effort of perception to learn to hear it. The idea that the sounds of the environment, the "echology," or the soundscape, is a form of music has been with us since Thoreau, since John Cage, since R. Murray Schafer, and it has long been a fragile message which few of us truly hear. Adams has heard it much more strongly than most composers because listening to his place has truly led him to change his own music. More than any other composer working today, Adams works carefully to learn so much from the rhythms, tones, and shapes of the environment that he has changed his music into something that usual human instruments can no longer play. Is it ironic that his most nature-derived composition can now only be performed by a machine?

Any composer who decides to construct her music out of direct inspiration from nature has to make a choice: shall I compose right from natural sound as raw musical material, or shall I emulate, evoke, be inspired by nature, as Cage spoke, "in its manner of operation," an idea that goes back to Aristotle? In many ways this is a safer, more artistic route. It is why George Crumb's *Voice of the Whale* is a greater musical work than Alan Hovhaness's *And God Created Great Whales*. Both composers wrote in the same year, 1970. Hovhaness took recorded whale song and played it behind a live orchestra, while Crumb, though he had listened closely to humpback whale recordings, thought it was more interesting to work with the longstanding musical culture of orchestral instruments and have his musicians learn from the whale, rather than using the actual sound of nature.

I have personally made plenty of use of recorded natural sound in my work, from birds, whales, water, and insects, and I can tell you there is a real peril in doing this. Quite simply, the sounds of nature do not need us. They have their place, their purpose, their sense, their certainty. What right have we to use them for our purposes? Putting them forward in themselves as music can easily be ridiculous, presumptuous, pretentious. The poet A. R. Ammons may have said it best, when he wrote, "Spare me Man's redundancy." We work so hard to fit in, but how could nature ever need us? It will outlast us no matter how much damage we do. We will never be more than a footnote to its vast music that began millions of years before we were conceived and will still be singing, in whale song, mockingbird song, river song, wind song—long after our own odd evolutionary strategy has played itself out. No species ever dominates natural history for very long.

Don't think I'm cynical here, or even pessimistic. I'm just stating the facts. We can do little for nature beyond appreciating how its beauty has come to pass through being and changing for a time too long to be counted. We will never figure natural sounds out, why they work, how they have evolved. They are greater and more necessary than any artifact of our quickly changing culture can ever be. The hermit thrush will outlast us, the cicada, the howl of the wolf. Nature needs these sounds, as much as it needs an eternity to evolve them. Besides, what do interesting sounds have to do with music? My friend the composer Eric Sawyer told me years ago the reason he has always written music for the piano before all other instruments. "The sound of the piano," he told me in school years ago, "is not an interesting sound. That's why so much interesting music can be made out of it." Come across one interesting sound and your ears may be floored. A noisy pitta. A gecko's cry. Snapping shrimp. Whistlers from distant galaxies. These are the sounds of nature; they are enough as they are.

Why would a composer ever say music should be an amalgamation of uninteresting sounds? The genius of the composer is to work out a system that combines simple enough sounds into a greater whole, sounds simple enough to need to be combined with other simple sounds. The history of music could thus be said to be a simplification of the pure wild noise of the world into refined pure tones, ready to be assembled into melodies and scales, based on order, system, consistency, something in human sound that nature cares little for.

With this view in mind, one could say John Luther Adams's music has gotten more normal, more traditional, over time. Earlier in his career he was stretching the behavior of string, wind, and percussion instruments to sound more like the sounds of the natural world. Detuning string quartets, re-counting rhythms, transcribing bird songs. But with *The Place Where You Go to Listen* he has removed the musician, and returned to the realm of simple sounds. This is not a criticism, but just the way he tells it. Sine tones, white noise, pink noise, this is where he begins, part of the long tradition of classical composers writing electronic music. There are rules, systems, methods to create the sound that do not begin with a notion of what the music should sound like. The methodology suggests how it must be constructed.

Yet early in the conception of this piece Adams decided sound would not be enough. He would make an installation using basic colors made out of light, no shapes, nothing too mimetic, no images of mountains or the dance of the northern lights. This work (I have not personally witnessed it) goes beyond compositional tradition to become a fixed artwork, an installation in a minimalist vein, akin to the light-frame interventions of James Turrell or Dan Flavin, a permanent fixture in the Museum of the North, though I could certainly imagine it appearing in the Dia: Beacon Museum up the road from my home place, a famous temple of extreme minimalist art, actually the biggest contemporary art museum in America. Pure shapes, stark simple forms, bold but subtle statements: that is what the Dia collects and Adams would easily fit in.

It may be a smart move for a composer to nod toward visual art if he wants to do something genuinely different, markedly abstract. David Stubbs wrote a short book recently dealing with the paradox that while modern art—from Impressionism and Cubism on to abstract expressionism and minimalism—is roundly accepted by mainstream culture as great and important, modern music, from Schoenberg and Stravinsky on to Cage and Stockhausen, is often reviled by classical audiences and even by musicians in orchestras. Pollock and Kandinsky retrospectives will be mobbed for months, while contemporary music is still considered inaccessible by too many cultured people. Why this disparity?

Some look to the history that argues that musicians made a conscious decision to turn against their public. Schoenberg wrote in his *Harmonielehre* that part of his atonal project was to turn against precisely what people expected from music, the whole history of tonality, structure, and its exploration that built up an entire culture's aesthetics of music. He spoke of being one of "the elect who refuse their mission," turning against the world and into the realm of the pure mathematics of sound. The early twentieth-century composers strove to delve deep into the end of music, something based not on any rich love of tone but a need to turn all that is solid into air, part of the whole twentieth century's explosion of art and all culture through doubt, hopefully in the end to possibility.

A hundred years later and we've now acclimatized to all possible sounds, but still the more abstract directions of music have not interpolated their ways into the mainstream of culture the way abstraction in art and design have. We still long for a song, for something to recognize, maybe because music was never designed to be representational of nature: we built then a long history of how to hold tones together into something we can dance to or sing to. People may surely appreciate the depth that may come with more involved, carefully structured and composed music, be it for small ensembles or great orchestras, but too many of us have been uncomfortable with that great composers' dream that has been realized in the last half century, the ability to make art directly out of sound. In any music made purely electronically, it is hard to imagine differently the live from the recorded performance. If no one is playing it, it exists only in the ethereal realm of sound that comes only from nowhere, without the physical presence of the musician. This can give it a holy, meditative aspect, or just make it impossible to pin down or to hold onto.

Adams is wise to ally his purest work with a visual component, because that is where our culture has had most acceptance of the strangest sounds. In film, in theater, we have been able to make artistic use of all manner of noises, and we in the audience can make sense of it. In visual art, where abstraction has ruled, sound has entered in recent decades but one of the problems in the acceptance of "sound art" is that the way sound is used is often too far from music. The fact of the sound being there can take priority over the quality of the particular sounds present. Art installations that use sound can learn a lot from the generations that have experimented in music, just as performance art is often best when it doesn't pretend to be totally different from theater!

Yet Adams knows well that when music, however daring or experimental, is paired with something visual it can have a tendency to step into the background. His installation of delicately changing colors and only soft light may have more akin with Scriabin's color organ (as used in a 2007 Omsk video recording of *Prometheus* available on YouTube, to give one instance) than with the strange behemoths making odd noises that appear more and more in art museums today. There are a handful of works that share Adams's aesthetic, several which appeared in the landmark Smithsonian / LA MOCA exhibit "Visual Music" in 2005, such as Pierre Huyghe's *L'Expedition Scintillante* and Cindy Bernard's and Joseph Hammer's *projections+sound*. Both of these works, together with Scriabin, explore the possibilities of single bold lighting in color as a way to form a multimedia temporal experience together with music. All, though, were made before we had fast enough computer processing to come up with a system to carefully sift color and sound out of numbers, the way Adams has done.

The Place Where You Go to Listen reflects nature by abstracting nature into pure sonic components, rather than trying to represent anything obviously visible in the landscape. Where can you place the work? What is it? It is a wall of light and a roomful of sound. It is a corner all to itself in the Museum of the North. It is a computer program, a complex series of instructions that reads empirical data from the geological, astronomical, and climatic changes in the Earth and translates them into sound, something technology can do more easily than humans.

It is important that Adams uses pure sine tones, white noise, and pink noise (which is white noise with the high frequencies filtered out). He wants to begin with very pure kinds of sound, to emphasize that his music is an abstraction, not a direct representation of what one might hear being out in the wilderness, at that original Iñupiat place where the shamans went out to listen, or out in your backyard, or out in a city street or in cabin by a mountain stream where the water rushes by in a complex choir of noise that is mesmerizing enough to listen to as it is. Music that is constructed right out of natural sounds has an immediate tendency to be more representational than an ensemble of pure, technological sounds. It might be too close to experience, too remote from idea.

When John was installing this unique project in its own room in the Museum, a member of the museum staff wondered if he would mind if they hung a nice photograph of the aurora borealis in the space, you know, to help the audience realize that some of the sounds heard were being generated by data tracking the radiation in the high atmosphere that made auroras visible. Adams was shocked—didn't they realize that his work was a complete aural and visual experience unto itself? And that, although it derives from information streaming from data recorders of the natural world, it explicitly does not resemble the appearance of that natural world, because it is composed, programmed, and constructed in the spirit of abstraction, out of the history of music, this least representational art, using pure human-defined sounds, and human defined pure colors of light, so it doesn't fall into the tired trope of music backing up real images of things out there in the world that we are so used to seeing in art, science, and nature museums? He felt disheartened, it really seemed that people were not going to get what he was after: an experience of pure tones and colors that reveals a place not by resembling a place, but by evoking a place, imitative only of nature perhaps in that Cagean "manner of operation," as its rhythms come from seismic data, the changing facts of weather, the motion of the moon. You'll never be able to "read" the data from the work, but feel that you're in the midst of it, in a whole new way.

And why is this way any less realistic than the immediate poise of a camera snapping a sudden fragment of time? Think of photographs of the aurora borealis—they cannot really capture what it is like to witness this moving, flickering phenomenon in near darkness. The aurora borealis is a beautiful piece of natural performance art that cannot be filmed or photographed. A time-lapse photo reveals only fuzzy colors, and a moving image cannot get enough light to capture the dynamic strangeness of it all. The northern lights have been painted as hanging, shimmering curtains of multicolored fire, and old engravings show an imaginary fierce luminosity that wants to leap from the page into our minds. Even films of the northern lights are not accurate, because of the lighting conditions. Perhaps computer simulations of this beautiful mystery look the most like what we actually see.

Is this ironic? No, just a peculiarity of the latest technology, something about us that may actually help us remember how we see something at the edges of our senses and our ability to explain. Adams's work with pure tones and noise may do the same. He does not need to worry about his music being too imitative of nature, because the sounds he starts with are relentlessly artificial, on purpose, right from the history of electronic music. He writes in the book that accompanies *The Place*, "noise imparts a kind of richness, from a random number generator, giving an internal life to the sound that you couldn't get any other way." Rather than using the rich, living, fractal qualities of natural sound that electronic tones often seem to lack, Adams brings life to his composition and its realization by translating data from the natural world into control information to alter the sound and color of his work. The numbers coming from one arena translate into something completely different: new sounds and colors not inherently connected to where the original data comes from.

So seismic rumblings need not be listened to directly, but their movement can trigger sounds and colors that the composer has chosen. The weather changes the music, the phase of the moon changes this music, the rhythm of day and night, the presence of fires and clouds. All of this information streams into the work and changes how it sounds and how it looks, all the while reflecting a consistent kind of minimalist purity. The work is clearly an exact composition, with none of the uneven, woolly trappings of someone like myself, who likes to improvise with the natural world, to play along with birds, bugs, and whales, and is tempted more by the rich rough sounds of nature itself than by its availability to the mathematics of instruction and control used by Adams and his team of programmers.

Paul Winter once complained to me, "Why aren't there *thousands* of musicians working with natural sounds, they are the greatest inspiration there is?" There really is very little framework for any critical discourse for dealing with

the connection between contemporary music, whether composed or improvised, with nature. How does such a connection matter? Is it just a hook to
make abstract music easier to talk about? How does rigorous planning and the
presence of the unexpected combine in 'natural' music?

In a way, the exact and brilliant programming behind *The Place Where You
Go to Listen* is one way to turn a composition into an improvisation. This is a
piece with no performers save the data that streams into it from the natural
world. You can never tell what nature is going to do. Adams as the composer
can sit back and be endlessly surprised by what his piece is going to come up
with, he's done the near impossible by creating a work that is never going to
bore him because it will never repeat itself. It is a world of rules that reflects the
improbable order of the world.

Is this the way all music is going to move in the game of technology that
is overtaking us? A new genre called 'reactive music' is now emerging to be
performed on smart phones and iPods. The composer sets up the parameters
for the music, but the listener can transform it in specific ways by shaking the
player in different ways. Random elements are introduced; the work is never
exactly the same. Music becomes software, works in parallel with our rest-
lessness and fear of the exactly repetitious. Performance has always brought
uncertainty to music but now technology can program this uncertainty to help
emulate aliveness.

Improvisers have always been afraid of endlessly sounding the same, and
that's why we have always thought of compositions merely as the starting point
for our performances. You only succeed as an improviser if you trust the sudden creativity of the performer more than the total plan of the wise composer.
But the keepers of tradition tend to believe that such audacity is always less
serious than the rigorous plan of the composition. Something about setting
the performer loose this way is just not as legitimate, as it depends too much
on spontaneous creativity and less on the grand, encoded vision.

Are they right? Which approach is closest to nature? They are both, of course,
artifice. Music is an abstract art, no? Just sound, structures of sound all about
itself, or so the old philosopher said. If you want to listen to nature, go out to
the original place where you go to listen. Bring it inside and we are like those
Japanese aficionados of the nightingale who would put a bird in a cage with
a cloak on the top of it and demand that he sing incessantly in the darkness.
Natural sounds in the confinement of human urban spaces are songs of sad-
ness, no? Paeans for a pure outdoor life gone by?

This may be why Adams stays away from this. Every natural history museum
and museum of the Arctic has rushing river noises, loon calls, evocative sounds.
His work is a composition, a pure arrangement of sounds based on exact

structural ideas. I wonder, though, what the viewer and listener would take away if we did not know the whole story about how and where the alteration of the sounds and colors comes from. The explanation of the system is part of the artwork. Is it accurately contained within the artwork? I am not really qualified to say because I am ashamed to admit I have not personally experienced it. I have been listening to fragments of it, reading up on it, watching on my own computer the digital flash presentation that accompanies the work in the actual museum. None of these is the real work. I am thus an imposter, with no qualifications to say anything accurate about the thing in itself.

But I have followed John's work for years, and also studied carefully what he has said about music and how it may affect the way we perceive the natural world. It is this concern that he and I share, which few musicians speak of. He has been trying to stretch traditional instruments beyond their boundaries for years, and in *The Place* he has realized a goal he has been edging towards for years, a pure music of the environment, made out of changes in the environment but not the sounds of the environment. If that is the goal, then does it matter what it sounds like?

I imagine the visitor leaving *The Place* with a portable image in her mind, of softly fading colors and washes of pure, technological sound, blended with the message she's been told on how it all comes from the rhythms of the natural world. Maybe not the rhythms, more accurately the machinations. The data stream, not the river stream. The pure visual and aural diagram of natural processes that is our pure abstraction from what is out there happening. And what might the world of nature think if presented with such sounds, if we were to bring these tones back out to the world in the portable iPod or iPad version someday, to take it out to the wilderness in that way the poet Ammons warned so against?

Even Thoreau was not upset by the *sound* of those newfangled telegraph wires strung up by the railroad track next to Walden Pond. Wasn't the thrumming of the wind on the wires kind of cool, nothing more than a giant Aeolian harp of the kind that so entranced Wordsworth, Keats, and Coleridge? There is a far romance in the resonance of strange sounds. There was electronic-sounding music in those transcendentalist days long before lightning had totally electrified our culture. As Bernd Herzogenrath quotes Thoreau's journals in this very volume, "What must the birds and beasts think where it passes through woods, who heard only the squeaking of trees before! I should think that these strains would get into their music at last. Will not the mockingbird be heard one day inserting this strain in his medley?"

I have to laugh at that one. Who *knows* where the mockingbird gets his ideas? People think the birds make use of ringtones, microwave oven sounds, and especially car alarms, but those sounds may very well have been based on the tones of mockingbirds to begin with. Sine waves and white noise are out there in nature, too, once we have the sense to consider these pure tones worth listening for. Same with pure color, and pure shape.

There is no doubt Adams's pure aesthetic experience can fit in anywhere. It came from Alaska, but it can change the way we listen, all over the world.

Bibliography

Adams, John Luther. *The Place Where You Go to Listen: In Search of an Ecology of Music*. Middletown: Wesleyan University Press, 2009.

Ammons, A. R. *Selected Poems*. New York: Norton, 1979.

Brougher, Kerry et al. *Visual Music: Synaesthesia in Art and Music Since 1900*. New York: Thames & Hudson, 2005.

Cage, John. *Silence*. Middletown: Wesleyan University Press, 1964.

Rothenberg, David. *Thousand Mile Song: Whale Music in a Sea of Sound*. New York: Basic Books, 2008.

Schafer, R. Murray. *The Tuning of the World*. New York: Knopf, 1977.

Schoenberg, Arnold. *Theory of Harmony*. Berkeley: University of California Press, 2010 [1910].

Scriabin, Alexander. *Prometheus*. http://www.youtube.com/watch?v=Dd66b4GXouw &feature=related Recorded in Omsk, Ukraine, 2007.

Stubbs, David. *Fear of Music: Why People Get Rothko But Don't Get Stockhausen*. London: Zero Books, 2009.

7 * The Thunder That Smokes

I'm obsessed with rhythm. Traditionally, melody and harmony have long reigned supreme in the historical appreciation and analysis of art music, but rhythm remains the most natural of musical expressions and oddly enough, also the last and least to be intensely explored. This began to change dramatically in the first part of the last century when a new generation of composers saw the limitless potential of this often overlooked aspect of music, art, and nature. They saw rhythm and, more specifically, the percussion family as a rich source for future investigation and musical possibility, while redefining the traditional notions of harmony and melody in the process. Nearly every important musical breakthrough since then has relied on rhythm as a chief component of its identity. Swing, rock, minimalism, electronic music, and hiphop all owe their infectiousness to the rhythmic qualities that make them unique.

The music of John Luther Adams shares that quality as well. A great example is the drum quartets that play such an integral part in his seminal work *Earth and The Great Weather: A Sonic Geography of the Arctic*. Adams started as a drummer in a rock band. Although most critical analyses cite different qualities regarding his unique contribution to contemporary music, I feel his relationship to rhythm is at the core of his achievement of what every musician and composer aspires to—finding one's own sound. It is frequently said that his music evokes the sounds and elemental qualities of nature, with an affinity for Alaska's cultures and landscape. Some of Adams's early compositions were partially inspired by the melodies inherent in nature (such as *songbirdsongs*). But it was through the rhythmic qualities of his music that new realms of discovery opened up for this composer—replete with a new set of unanswered questions to pursue. He followed these questions, and the results landed him in a unique place that he can call his own.

John Luther Adams utilizes rhythm and harmony in such a profound and unique way that many recognize his contribution as a starting point—the beginning of a new chapter in contemporary music. The rolling, dramatic sweeps of intersecting events and the serene stillness that are inherent in his music are both reasons so many equate it with the natural world in which Adams chooses to live and work. I agree. And I love those characteristics of his music.

I also, however, find a particular fondness for his active, compact, and fervent rhythmic writing. The drum quartets in *Earth and The Great Weather* can stand independent of the whole as fresh and exhilarating sonic places that also provide a foundation by which his subsequent work has been and continues to be influenced. These pieces are, in my opinion, a creative trailhead for the path that John Luther Adams continues following today.

Instead of offering meticulous, mechanical insights into the fascinating musical world that John Luther Adams has created, I'll address the mystery that's inherent in his music. To me, the elusiveness of his music offers a sense of hope, wonder, and possibility. I won't even write about the inherent bravery of this music; its freshness is enough for me. I don't want to get too involved with the details of Adams's formal influences either. Most readers of this book will by now know his affinity for painting and visual art. You will also be aware of the impact that composers such as John Cage, Harry Partch, Edgar Varese, Henry Cowell, Conlon Nancarrow, James Tenney, Lou Harrison, and Morton Feldman have had on him. We also know that his home—Alaska—and its native cultures have had a profound effect on his development and thereby his creative output.

I learned after becoming a fan of his music that Mr. Adams and I happen to have many parallel influences and interests, one of which is an appreciation of the rhythm and music inherent in nature. This includes the practice of making field recordings. We have both learned a great deal from the drumming of other cultures and the synthesis of these with our respective musical experiences. And of course, we both have rock-and-roll drumming in common as well. Therefore, the points that I'm about to discuss may be less analytical and more personal than some: my experiences undoubtedly reflect how I interpret his.

I am never more attuned to my rhythmic obsession than when alone out in the world. Whether it's on a long rural hike or a quick walk in the midst of a bustling urban center, rhythm pervades every instance. It is at the essence of our human experience. Most of us will never take note of this or even care. The fact remains, though, that we have an intense relationship with the rhythms of the world. I realize that it's easy to make grandiose statements about a word—a concept—as vague as this. Rhythm can imply everything from the cycles of the heavens or those of the seasons to the collage of incidental noises of society down to molecular processes. We are surrounded by and immersed in rhythm more than any other musical element just by being alive. More specifically, I believe that rhythm is the remaining frontier in contemporary music and will be the catalyst for many future chapters in the ever-dissolving stylistic distinction of popular and art music.

Earth and the Great Weather

I see the percussion quartets of *Earth and The Great Weather* as an important bridge in Adams's music; their origins are similar to the inspiration that Adams has mined up to then, but they also act as a point of departure. Although they stem from formalism, process, and, most important, ritual, they touch upon what's to come in *Strange and Sacred Noise* and *Mathematics of Resonant Bodies*. Moreover, they are the very reason that what proceeds from them takes a new direction: one filled with discoveries for Adams as he seeks the essence of experience for the performer and the listener. They go beyond the aural experience and create a new place—an environment. These works give us a sense of the trajectory of Adams's music: where it has been and where it's going. This is a pivotal time of transition and discovery for the composer. Certain key questions arise out of these pieces and their stand-alone arrangements for percussion ensemble, fueling several of his subsequent works.

Begun in 1989, *Earth and the Great Weather: A Sonic Geography of the Arctic* began as a thirty-minute piece commissioned by New American Radio for public radio. This work was inspired by the Arctic National Wildlife Refuge (a place that Adams helped protect through his efforts in expanding the Alaska National Interest Lands Conservation Act in 1980). It encompasses several different expressions of the landscapes—both literal and metaphorical—in a celebration of this place that has been sacred to the indigenous peoples of the region well before contact with North American settlers. This is a spiritual place for Adams, and he allows us to experience it through his sonic landscapes (Adams, *Earth and the Great Weather*). The piece was originally comprised of Aeolian harp recordings with Iñupiaq and Gwich'in-derived drumming and multilingual text (English, Iñupiaq, Gwich'in, and Latin) constituting lists of names, including those of animals, plants, places, and seasons. The way the text is presented with translations, subtle intonation, and slow pacing enables the listener to have their own experience as well as to imagine the experience of the peoples of this land. This is Adams's successful exploration of what he terms Sonic Geography: "a region that exists somewhere between place and culture, between human imagination and the world around us" (*Earth and the Great Weather*).

The composition quickly grew into an evening-length theater piece. The drumming grew in scope and duration and the Aeolian harp became a string quartet with layers of digital delay added to increase the fullness. The piece ended up a brilliant juxtaposition of powerful rhythms, ethereal strings, and evocative language that successfully gives the listener a poignant window into this spiritual place.

The drum quartets essentially act as sonic landmarks in *Earth and the Great*

Weather. They provide contrast but also keep the work grounded in a sense of place. Even more than place, however, the quartets help to provide the sensation of a setting. A setting here is the intersection of place and time. A narrative doesn't exist in this work. There is no overt action or direction in the music. The quartets aren't events with lead-ups and consequences but rather aspects of a whole experience. Expansion and contraction or convergence and divergence are words that consistently correlate with the aural experience of this music. These are natural events happening naturally—both in concert and opposition—throughout the course of the work.

At first, a general listening gives the impression that pieces with names such as *Drums of Winter, Deep and Distant Thunder*, and *Drums of Fire, Drums of Stone* were exclusively inspired by natural events—a collision of time and place in the Arctic National Wildlife Refuge. Excluding the sound design of prerecorded natural sounds, within these quartets it's relatively easy to imagine hearing the sound of thunder, hail and rain, river ice melting and breaking up, and gigantic seismic events. Closer listening, however, reveals the inner building blocks of a majority of the quartets as tactfully arranged rhythmic cells.

Simply defined, rhythmic cells are short rhythms of two or three notes that additively comprise a string of composite rhythmic events. The combination of these short cells creates meter that is steeped in the even (2) with the odd (3) (Rudolph, *Pure Rhythm*). This concept is the basis for music found in cultures from virtually every corner of the world. Cells are also something that we drummers are very familiar with since they are the common formula in which odd time signatures in Western music are counted and understood.

In most cultures, the rhythms that constitute the drumming are inextricably intertwined with the rhythms of dance and language. They are one. The rhythmic cells actually result from the rhythms of the text and ritual dance. The beat is a result of the language and melody; it's not abstract—rather, it's providing the groove. The elements of beat and language are not mutually exclusive. Adams's separate inclusion of both native text and native-inspired drumming cleverly acknowledge their connection but also put each in a setting where their minute subtleties and nuances, mellifluous or aggressive, can be more fully illustrated and thus more profoundly appreciated by the audience.

The *Earth Quartets* are constructed by mining the rhythmic cells from the drumming of dances and ceremonies of the indigenous Alaskan Iñupiaq and Gwich'in people. Instead of transcribing them, however, Adams sculpts them into new expressions. There's a degree of homage without imitation or parody. These cells converge and diverge with phrases growing additively into increasingly longer cycles. The arrangement and development of these cells constitute the melody of these pieces. Adams studied this drumming. He knows it well and appreciates the importance that it serves in Inuit and Athabascan life. Adams also knows the music of Cage and Cowell very well. He understands Cage's idea that time instead of harmony can be the determinant of formal structure. He's also knowledgeable concerning Cowell's extended rhythmic cycles and rhythmic scales, as evidenced by his references to Cowell's book *New Musical Resources*. Examination of the stream of shifting meters, tempos, and overlapping phrase lengths, including the perception of competing foreground and background rhythmic events in the *Earth Quartets*, suggest a process likely inspired in some part by Cowell (Nicholls, *The Whole World of Music: A Henry Cowell Symposium*).

Cowell, Cage, Harrison, and another early percussion champion, William Russell (as well as their contemporaries), were highly influenced by the music of other cultures as well. It is Adams's appreciation of these composers and the percussion music from the 1930s and 1940s that helped shape his earlier *Coyote Builds North America* percussion quartets, which were a steppingstone of sorts to the *Earth Quartets*. Additionally, the acquisition and interpretation of rhythmic notions from African, Indian, and Indonesian cultures by these composers led directly to the conception of many of the seminal minimalist musical compositions later in the century (such as rhythm cells and the Reich pieces *Drumming* and *Clapping Music*). These are some of the same compositions that have had at least a partial influence on Adams. I find a commonality between the drumming in the *Earth Quartets* and native drumming the world over, where higher voices usually provide faster rhythmic movement resulting in a type of chattering, middle voices provide the melody and "meat" of the piece, and lower voices typically play at a slower rate, grounding the music and reinforcing the middle voices.

Adams's interpretation of native drumming in the *Earth Quartets* sees the ever-present unison accents dissolve, with individual voices breaking away and providing counterpoint only to converge again and separate in an undulating, periodic tug-of-war between rhythmic consonance and dissonance. The trajectory between unity and seeming chaos give the impression of peaks and troughs—evoking an image given by Adams: "Rising like mountain ranges above the Aeolian plains are the three pieces for four drummers" (Adams, *Winter Music* 25). The sequence of this accordion-like dance is inconsequential. It's not the point. The emotional push and pull, and the sensation of experience in which the performer and listener are immersed, is what matters.

The constant interplay of the rising and falling of rhythmic consonance and dissonance is akin to a scene described in Adams's book *Winter Music*. He recalls witnessing the Iñupiaq ceremony Kalukak or the Box Drum Dance. Adams writes that this ritual is "grounded in the myth of the Eagle Mother, who gave the gift of music and dancing to the People." The ceremony is the highlight of the final night of the Iñupiaq Kivgiq celebration. As Adams describes it, "the frame drummers begin playing full force, until the box drummer cuts them off with a wildly irregular beat." This is a great illustration of the unity and chaos inherent in the Box Drum Dance. He later recounts the moment when "He [the box drummer] finally strikes the drum, in a sudden unison with the frame drums, the sound is stunning" (Adams, *Earth and the Great Weather*). The essence of the rhythmic contrast inherent in the *Earth Quartets* lies in Adams's experiences with the Iñupiaq as well as in the "elemental power of natural forces in the Arctic" (Adams, *Earth and the Great Weather*).

It is when these drum quartets are taken out of the context of the larger work that they serve as a hint of what's to come. Adams arranged the drum quartets for the Percussion Group Cincinnati by the request of and with assistance by Allen Otte. When the quartets, which act as pillars in the theater work, are removed and listened to as one continuous sonic experience, something else happens—namely the creation of an environment for both the audience and performer (Adams and Otte, *Strange and Sacred Noise*). Due to sheer volume and force the listener has no choice but to be fully and attentively immersed in the music. One pivotal aspect to also consider is that Adams in now in the audience. For the original performances of *Earth and The Great Weather* he was one of the drummers—he was inside of the music. But being an audience member for the PGC performance allowed Adams to experience a different aspect of the cumulative experience. He was able to hear some of the side effects within the elemental sound from a new perspective. That began the process of Adams asking the question of where a further exploration of these side effects—the hallucinatory phantom voices resulting from the written music—might lead him.

As opposed to the earlier *Green Corn Dance* percussion ensemble and the quartets from *Coyote Builds North America*, the *Earth Quartets* are not only longer but are also not telling a story (Adams, *Coyote Builds North America*). They create an experience rather than relating one. Through immersion in the elemental power and sheer intensity of this music, Adams hears the essence of drumming. Moreover, this leads him to the question of how to get closer to the heart of that sonic experience and the crux of the intersection of sound and time (drumming). The answer he discovers is to more fully explore the elemental sound of the instruments—not the drumming itself—but the very idea of the drum (Schick, liner notes for Adams's *Strange and Sacred Noise*). He explores the full breadth of sounds that the instruments are capable of producing. It's within the full engrossment of this core sound experience that the listener is transported to a more sensual place. It's not about formalism or the mathematics anymore (although mathematical theory does provide Adams the means with which to conduct some of his future experiments, such as *Strange and Sacred Noise* and the use of fractals from chaos theory as inspiration for formal structure). *The Earth Quartets* provide a bridge to the sensual by overwhelming the listener with the physicality and power of the sound. The physical attributes in this music arise out of its explosive and violent qualities.

It's interesting to note that these pieces come full circle when performed as a separate entity and without a conductor. During a performance it can be advantageous for the players to use movement or eurhythmics in order to play together and get through the work, thus reconnecting and keeping the music grounded in the sphere of its Alaskan dance and ritualistic roots. Of teaching the music to his students, Professor James Campbell of the University of Kentucky told me: "It's a powerful work where energy is key. It's easy to think of the piece only in terms of vertical alignment. But you have to always play with a sense of momentum and 'melodic' movement forward (horizontal motion). The performers have to go beyond the notation to bring a performance style to the rhythmic cells. The piece has to 'dance' and reflect the inspirational roots of the Alaskan Native ceremony."

Adams's music had long been connected to the serene beauty of the Arctic, as evidenced in his pieces *In the White Silence* and *Dream in White on White*, among others. There is an affinity with static beauty and ethereal spaciousness that pervades many of his works. In the *Earth Quartets* we hear the opposite. Through immersion into extreme animalistic power, Adams finds a balance in his music that reflects the seasonal conditions of his physical environment. The quartets unlock the counterbalance in his oeuvre, as well as revealing insight into the essential reality of sound. Through this discovery, the *Earth Quartets* become the starting point for a whole new side of Adams's output. These begin the lineage that results in *Strange and Sacred Noise* and *The Mathematics of Resonant Bodies* and *Inuksuit*: three pieces that are thoroughly absorbed in noise, the power of the music and the sounds themselves. The *Earth Quartets* bring him to a place where audible formal considerations are abandoned for a complete surrender to the sound. No doubt the influence by one of his mentors, James Tenney, comes into play at this point, with Tenney's thoughts on implicit and explicit rhythm and ergodic form being applicable considerations in composing these new percussion works (Tenney). The psychoacoustic properties inherent in these works are a probable instigator for Adams's continued use of the percussion medium. To Adams, these phantom voices are intriguing and welcome, albeit initially uninvited, sonic guests. Somewhat similar aleatoric properties are not uncommon in the music of the minimalism progenitor LaMonte Young (who studied with Leonard Stein, as did Adams) in his works *Trio For Strings* (1958), *The Well-Tuned Piano* (1964), and his *Dream House* installations. The music of another composer where more is heard than is written on the page is that of Alvin Lucier, including, among others, *Silver Streetcar for the Orchestra* (1988, for solo amplified triangle) and music from his recording *Still Lives* (2001). Glenn Branca, an Adams contemporary, whose music the composer appreciates, explores similar phenomena in his symphonies for electric guitar orchestra, as did Lou Reed in his foray into pure noise and psychoacoustic phenomena *Metal Machine Music* (1975) (Bangs). Rhys Chatham also is immersed in music with extra-acoustical properties in pieces such as *Two Gongs* (1971). I'd like to note that these composers all basically pursued their investigations independently of each other, even though there are similarities in their discoveries conceptually rather than stylistically.

Adams initially stumbles upon a similar—although again, unique in its own right—sonic reification in the *Earth Quartets* which leads him to leave self-expression and exploration of creativity behind in lieu of attentiveness to the essence of sound itself. Robert Black told me that during one rehearsal for the drum quartets in *Earth and the Great Weather* (for which he was one of the four original percussionists), he thought he heard someone yelling. Assuming it one of his fellow drummers calling out to address an issue, he stopped playing but quickly realized that no one had said anything. The drumming had elicited other voices that weren't on the page! These aleatoric voices were likely the by-product of sensory perception being tricked by the interactions of unintended overtones arising from the music. One simple definition of psychoacoustic properties as pertaining to this music could be the subjective human perception of sounds.

This phenomenon was a sort of epiphany for Adams, in my opinion. What was happening in the *Earth Quartets* was something that was natural and unplanned and therefore in complete agreement with nature as well as Adams's personal philosophy. More specifically, it aids the perception of a time-place confluence (experience) which was, after all, what Adams was after in the first place through his pursuit of creating a sonic geography in *Earth and the Great Weather*. Adams is the composer of his generation that is most fully dedicated to the potential of drawing out these phenomena in the realm of percussion. This is another reason to say that Adams adds a fresh dimension and renewed energy to the legacy of the percussion tradition of the American experimentalists of the last century.

It all starts with Nature. I travel with small recorders wherever I tour in search of new sounds and in an attempt to capture inspiring natural sound collages. Unlike the lions of early mobile recording such as Alan Lomax, Paul Berliner, Hugh Tracey and dozens of other key figures who rescued for us a treasure chest of folk music from around the globe, my focus has always been on sounds—

not performances. In my duo, On Fillmore, Darin Gray and I utilize our field-recorded sounds as an imaginary third member of the band who provides the shadowy illusions of place and time intersecting. When discovering *Earth and The Great Weather*, I knew I had a kindred spirit in John Luther Adams. However, this is the only piece, thus far, into which Adams has incorporated actual sound recordings of natural events. These sound recordings provide the glue in the work and act as enablers of connectivity. They also give the literal impression of place and experience. In my opinion, Adams has abandoned the use of field recordings because he's found a way to create experience and an environment—both serene and violent—exclusively through composition. Perhaps his fondness for these recordings hasn't waned but his perceived need to use them to this end has dissipated.

What I've learned through recording and listening to natural environments has deeply affected both the way I play and how I compose music. I've gained a greater appreciation and understanding of the dynamic relationships between sounds (a lesson of great value to one who plays drumkit). For anyone who has been obsessed with rhythm, the patterns (or lack thereof) in nature and society are a wellspring for the deeper understanding of the congress of sound events. John Luther Adams eloquently gets to the kernel of this notion in *Winter Music* when he writes: "Listening attentively to the music of the natural world, we encounter a different sense of time than in most human music. The rhythms are more subtle and complex. The tempos can be extreme—very much faster and very much slower than most of our music. And ultimately the music of nature leads us away from notions of tempo and rhythm to a more direct experience of the larger flow of time" (Adams, *Winter Music* 17).

I agree there are valuable lessons to be learned from listening to the world around us. Just the other night I took a break from writing this essay and sat on my back deck on an uncharacteristically temperate night for Chicago in February. I was struck by how the rhythmic qualities here in this city can so closely resemble a sonic scene from a rural location. The roar from the passing planes audible to anyone living under a landing pattern for O'Hare Airport are reminiscent of thunder, collapsing heaps of ice, or a rumbling waterfall. A closer listening to the macro hum of traffic on nearby bustling Lawrence Avenue reveals the inner content to be fast individual micro rhythms of a stream of autos passing each other, just as attentive listening to the drone of the ocean or static of a river reveals the individual characteristics of the surf crashing or the crackling of water running over distinct obstacles. Neighboring wind chimes and a plastic bag snagged on a high barren tree branch in the yard reveal the patterns of the wind. There's as much music inherent in this urban landscape as in any natural one. The difference is that in Chicago it's mostly the sound of man and society—whose rhythms I've learned to appreciate just as much as naturally occurring sound. The point is that at this intersection of time and place—in this setting—an experience is born.

This notion is something that Adams has always embraced in his life as a composer. Undoubtedly, not only his own life experience has aroused this but also the lasting influence of John Cage in his "aspiration 'to imitate Nature in her manner of operation'" (Adams, *Winter Music* 28). Adams beautifully encapsulated his thoughts on nature when he wrote: "The natural world is the most fundamental source of human intelligence, creativity, and culture. We don't create anything except answers to creation. And we're an inseparable part of nature" (Adams, *Winter Music* 127). He has successfully embraced the natural world and has artistically and meticulously reinterpreted and crafted his relationship with it. He evokes the sensation of it in his music and reinvents it without blatantly imitating it sonically (Adams, *Winter Music* 123).

Rock Drumming and JLA

John Luther Adams really started his musical life as a rock-and-roll drummer. He did have experience with trumpet, piano, and singing in choirs, but it was rock drumming that stoked his enthusiasm for music. He learned the music of the Byrds, Rolling Stones, Beach Boys, and Beatles in garage cover bands. He once told me that "at age 13 [he] emulated Ringo's drumming—its heavy, steady simplicity, with minimal fills." Adams's inspiration later came from the sensitive, lyrical drumming of Robert Wyatt of the Soft Machine and eventually many of the giants of jazz music and drumming. As his bands became more interested in writing their own music, their tastes started broadening too. Jimi Hendrix, Captain Beefheart, and Frank Zappa have all been named as influences at that time in his life. It was a Zappa album with the Varese quote, "The present-day composer refuses to die!" written on the back cover that continued to fuel the search for more adventurous music (Ross). The path to Varese eventually led to a whole crop of twentieth-century experimental composers, including many who have had a lasting influence and helped to shape Adams as a composer as well as a man.

Along with his bandmates, he started composing for his groups and eventually began to study composition. To a young Adams, his aspirations to compose seemed at odds with his rock drumming roots. The drumkit was left behind for staff paper and pencil. However, it's my opinion that his experience of performing on that instrument (including one gig opening for the Beach Boys with his band Pocket Fuzz) has had a lasting effect on his music. His early percussion pieces such as those from *Coyote Builds North America* find inspiration not only from the classic percussion literature of the 1930s and 1940s and the tribal drumming of the Nez Perce but also from his rock drumming days. Adams says of the work: "I wanted to combine the energy of rock drumming with the rhythmic complexity of 'art' music" (Adams, *Winter Music* 21).

That desire to draw energy from rock drumming is something that seems to have stayed with Adams's percussion writing. There's an innate intensity in this music resulting in an enrapturing psychological experience for both audience and performer. I'm extremely fortunate to make a good part of my living traveling and recording as the drummer in the rock band Wilco. It's a dream job that humbles me. There's nothing quite like the feeling of playing the drums. Doing it in front of many people simply adds a whole other psychological and physiological dimension (reaching far beyond an adrenaline rush). Because of the size of certain venues and spaces, amplification for all of the instruments is a must. I'd venture to say that the sheer physicality of performing on drumkit in a heavily amplified situation is largely unique in Western music performance. There are some similarities with the drumming of other cultures that come to mind, such as Taiko drumming from Japan, Bata drumming of Cuba or one of my major influences—the Samul Nori drumming of Korea, all of which put a heavy physical responsibility on the player. I think it's safe to surmise that performance of the *Earth Quartets* requires a very similar physicality and mental acumen. One might argue that the volatile natural forces that Adams is exposed to in the Arctic might be the primary influence in these quartets or that the native drumming traditions there are the real seeds for this music. Both of these are indeed major influences on these pieces. However, I wonder if Adams would have really had the courage to go as far as he did in respect to the volume, speed, and duration of the drumming if he hadn't experienced time behind the drumkit as a part of his primary musical cultivation.

We shouldn't discount the effect of his drumkit experience in his realization of the melody inherent within purely percussion pieces either. Steve Schick writes in his brilliant book *The Percussionist's Art* about drumkit being "by far the best example of the melodic potential of noise percussion instruments" and adds, "listen to Max Roach for melodic elegance, to Elvin Jones for sailing melodic vectors and crosscurrents, or to Ringo Starr for perfectly crafted melodic counter subjects. To me, drum set playing is storytelling and at the root of this most rhythmic of instruments, it is pure melody" (Schick, *The Percussionist's Art*). I think these truths are subconsciously ingrained in Adams, who is able to pull the melody out of a less diverse set of percussion instruments (as compared to drumkit) in the drum quartets of *Earth and the Great Weather*.

Adams credits Cage for showing him "that it was possible to compose complex and sophisticated music for percussion—smart music that also rocked" (Adams, *Winter Music* 78). I think that the *Earth Quartets* are the first true example of this credo for Adams and also the manifestation of Adams, the drummer. They are as much or more about feeling (for the performer and listener) as they are about composerly imagination or self-expression. They sound like the ultimate extension of his rock band days in that they truly rock and they must come close to feeling like that type of playing too (Adams was one of the four original drummers in *Earth and the Great Weather*). This is not music merely for entertainment and it goes beyond music for art's sake in that it successfully embodies the very catalyst for this music: native Alaskan drumming. It's a picture of the larger fabric of life and it transforms into ritual (Adams, *Winter Music* 70).

I don't think it's a stretch to draw the conclusion that Adams's connection to rock drumming was firmly lodged in his psyche when he composed the *Earth Quartets*—especially since these pieces are longer and louder and demand more of the performer than his previous percussion music. I want to make a clear distinction between power and volume, though. It's perfectly normal, while playing a drumkit, to play with an exacting intensity without bashing away and flailing one's arms like you're drowning. It's a skill—both physical and mental—that is attained after years of honing experience in a variety of playing situations. To put full concentration behind every note and every stroke, to be fully engaged in each exacting musical moment, is an elusive quality not easily attained by any musician. It comes down to intent. A really good rock drummer must put his or her full being into every part of a performance. Of course this isn't exclusive to the drumkit or even the drums—but the degree of muscle coordination and endurance among all four limbs is unique to the drumkit. To be a really great drummer in a rock band is by no means simple. I've been called upon to do things that I'd rate as challenging and difficult as anything that I've come across in contemporary concert multiple percussion literature. I believe that since Adams is versed in this knowledge, he's been able to employ that feeling, that sensation of really laying into the drums, with full commitment, and translate that to the modern classical arena.

I believe that these "rocking" elements in his percussion music appeal to a younger audience as well. The current generation of composers and performers all grew up with rock music and its myriad offshoots as the soundtracks to their lives. In today's cultural and economic climate, quality music that has a broader range of appeal has a bright future in the minds of programmers, record labels, and curators. Serious music that is able to bridge perceived generational and stylistic gaps in audiences will most likely find an equal place alongside the stalwart classics (the "greatest hits" of classical music) that are guaranteed to fill seats. Adams might have some similarities to the group of composers sometimes labeled totalists, who, as described by Kyle Gann, are composers who "write music that has the rhythmic energy of rock and the intellectual substance of 'classical' music." Even though Adams doesn't typically compose for the standard rock and jazz instrumentation that many composers who are categorized as totalists incorporate into their music, he certainly doesn't shy away from pounding drums (a sound common from *Sing, Sing, Sing* to *In-A-Gadda-Da-Vida* and beyond). I think it's fair to say that the timbres used in his percussion writing have more in common with contemporary popular music than one might initially think. These are sounds familiar to anyone who's heard the deep, throaty, tomtom dominated drumkit tones of Maureen Tucker of the Velvet Underground, Cream's Ginger Baker, Levon Helm of the Band, Ringo Starr, or even Mick Fleetwood; or conversely to anyone who's heard the explosive, resonant drum sounds of Elvin Jones, John Bonham, Tony Williams, or Keith Moon. Several years after his abandonment of rock-and-roll drumming, Adams's (through his own investigations) hits at the core of why the drum kit has reigned supreme in the realm of percussion for the last half century—sound, energy, and groove.

The timbres that are called for in Adams's percussion music are wisely chosen. I've heard many recordings infected with bad sounds that as a result quickly become dated. In an effort to stay current, many artists jump on the technological bandwagon and incorporate into their music the instrument *du jour* or the popular software of the moment. This is often a chief factor in many records being trivialized due to sound alone (or abuse of sound, depending on how you view it!), sometimes shortly after a recording is released. Timeless records are not only comprised of classic songs or compositions but are also usually filled with just plain good sounds. I think much of the music for which we reserve the term "timeless" also relies on recording techniques and instrument timbres that have held up through decades of critical listening. Adams has consistently utilized great sounds and specifically great drum tones in his music. Even in circumstances when other performers are choosing specific instruments, the instrumentation called for in the score coupled with the scored rhythms alone carry enough specificity to ensure impeccable sounds. Bass drums and tomtoms have been a part of the human landscape for millennia. Snare drums, tam-tams and air-raid sirens, though not on everyone's list of favorite sounds, are nonetheless common enough in modern society and consistent enough in construction to guarantee the breadth of tonal color and dynamic response called for in Adams's compositions. As a big fan of field recordings of African drumming from the 1930s and 1940s, I can attest that the archaic tones of those drums are often in most respects superior to the sound of most ultra-engineered and overly constructed modern drums. Even though Adams's pieces are likely to be performed on modern instruments, the range of tone and playing style harkens back to a much older, enduring sound.

Thunder and Smoke

In choosing to write about this seminal work for Adams and the three drum quartets that are such an integral part of the piece, the sonic image of thunder couldn't be too far from my thoughts, as anyone who's enjoyed these pieces can attest to. But I also think that smoke is a deceptively accurate term when used to describe the mysterious rolling, swelling, swirling, and undulating rhythmic qualities of much of Mr. Adams's best music.

I originally chose the title *The Thunder That Smokes* as a variation on the title *The Smoke That Thunders*, a brazen solo drumkit piece by the legendary drummer, composer, and cultural icon Max Roach. This cut appeared on his solo record *Survivors*; Roach is credited on it with playing the multiple percussion set. The title is the native name of Victoria Falls (Roach). It's comprised of an unwavering bass drum and hi-hat ostinato with chaotic outbursts on tomtoms, snare drum, and cymbals over the top and features several instances of cyclical, spacious silence sprinkled throughout. This is one of the least structured of Roach's solo pieces. There are some recurring motifs and a juggling of feel enhanced with pushes and pulls. Elements converge with the steady pulse, only to diverge into a storm of activity without a clear audible rhythmic relationship to the feet keeping the pulse underneath. Although they sound nothing alike, many of these characteristics are shared with the *Earth Quartets*. Both composers have had a profound impact on the evolution of percussion music. Max Roach most famously did this through his exploration of solo drumkit composition. John Luther Adams is opening up the possibilities of percussion as well, focusing in his case on pure sound.

This focus is redefining how percussion will be received by future generations. Adams has created a more sensual and physical world with his recent percussion music. He addresses the essence of drumming—sound and time—and does so with dedication and a degree of bravery not experienced in our generation. At the same time he is showing the tremendous spectrum of sound—both real and imagined—within the percussion family. In his recent percussion music, formalism is diminished to its most primal stratum. Audible processes are absent. This part of his creative output has more in common with noise artists such as Merzbow or the drone pieces of Tony Conrad or Jim O'Rourke than it does with many of his new music contemporaries. It delves into psychoacoustic properties with the performance space playing an integral role in the overall experience of the works. I'm especially excited to see how his recent forays into outdoor performances of his percussion music will influence his future work.

On a trip to Fairbanks we spoke about our mutual desires to investigate percussion performance out-of-doors and the *Inuksuit* project that Adams had already begun. I related how many of my favorite percussion records (most of which are field recordings consisting of tribal drumming) were recorded outside and the effect that must have had on the sound quality of the recordings. There's a deeper warmth of tone and a naturalness of sustain and decay that often get overlooked in a recording studio or performance stage, where clarity and purity are usually the primary goals. In my opinion, drums just blend better outside.

Of course it's the music and not just the sound that causes Adams's music to be lasting. His contributions to the development and growth of contemporary percussion literature continue to demonstrate his eminence in the field of modern composition. Not often does a composer tackle so many different areas of music in the explorations of his or her art. From lush and languid orchestral music to driving percussion music, from investigations into psychoacoustic events and pure sound to the use of technology and science-based media, and from his writing for small chamber ensembles to full multimedia theater productions, John Luther Adams continues to create a body of work full of discovery, substantive innovation, and purity of spirit that will inspire and steer generations to come.

Bibliography

Adams, John Luther. *Coyote Builds North America*. Composer's notes on *Five Percussion Quartets*. Taiga Press, 1980.

———. *Earth and the Great Weather*. Composer's notes. Taiga Press 1993.

———. *Winter Music*. Wesleyan University Press, 2004.

Adams, John Luther and Alan Otte. *Strange and Sacred Noise* (DVD). Conversation. Mode, 1997.

Bangs, Lester. *Psychotic Reactions and Carburetor Dung*. Vintage Books, 1988.

Cowell, Henry. *New Musical Resources*. Contributor: David Nicholls. Cambridge University Press, 1996.

Gann, Kyle. *Minimalism Gets Complex: Totalism*. NewMusicBox. November 1, 3, 2001.

Nicholls, David (ed.). *The Whole World of Music: A Henry Cowell Symposium*. Harwood, 1997.

Roach, Max. Conversation with John Schaefer. *New Sounds Live: Max Roach, Uptown String Quartet*, Program #1018. WNYU, February 17, 1994.

Ross, Alex. "Song of the Earth." *The New Yorker*. May 12, 2008.

Rudolph, Adam. *Pure Rhythm*. Advance Music, 2006.

Schick, Steve. Liner notes for John Luther Adams's *Strange and Sacred Noise*. Mode, 1997.

Schick, Steve. *The Percussionist's Art: Same Bed, Different Dreams*. University of Rochester Press, 2006.

Tenney, James. *Meta-Hodos and Meta Meta-Hodos: A Phenomenology of 20th Century Musical Materials and an Approach to the Study of Form*. Frog Peak Music. 1986.

Robert Esler

8 * How Do You *Play* with an Aura?
The Mathematics of Resonant Bodies

In 2003, I heard the premier performance of *The Mathematics of Resonant Bodies* in a small studio at the University in California, San Diego. It was not the "official" premiere but it certainly was the first-ever performance of this work. Steven Schick performed the seventy-minute work and I had the unique and surprisingly challenging task of operating the CD player, which was playing back the recorded auras. My initial reaction was that this was a piece for percussion and tape. Essentially, I thought you hit "play" and a bunch of electronic sounds engulf the instruments. I could not have been more mistaken. What I heard that evening changed my entire process of interpreting music. It did not happen at the precise moment of hearing the music, but I can trace back to that experience as a point where I realized that I was thinking about music all wrong.

The music of *Mathematics* is dense and practically material-less. The catalog of numbers, or math, used to create the piece is by no means reflected as antiseptic music, or dry and meaningless. It is seventy minutes of rolling waves of energy transposed onto a series of percussion instrument arrays. Accompanying this energy is a series of well-crafted auras, in this case electronically produced by complexly filtering the noise of the percussion instruments. Collectively, the performance of *Mathematics* is a unique and dynamic experience.

The piece consists of eight movements respectively: *burst* for two snare drums and two tenor drums, *rumble* for bass drum, *shimmer* for eight triangles, *roar* for large tam-tam, *thunder* for eight tomtoms and two pedal bass drums, *wail* for large siren, *crash* for eight cymbals, and *stutter* for two snare drums and two tenor drums. Each movement contains an aura that is played simultaneously with the acoustic instruments. For the first and last movements, the auras are performed in unison with the drums; the remaining movements progress in counterpoint to the solo instrument. The auras are intricately composed of filtered noises extracted from the same instruments being performed. Most of the raw recordings for the auras were performed by Steven Schick, to whom the piece is dedicated, at the University of Alaska, Fairbanks, and recorded by Scott Fraser. A couple of others were extracted from the Percussion Group Cincinnati's recordings of *Strange and Sacred Noise*.

Mathematics can be staged in a variety of ways. Adams and Schick have experimented with quad surround sound (four channel live mix, or dual stereo) but normally a simple stereo field is perfectly acceptable. The overlying task is to envelop the listener with a dense texture of both electronic and acoustic sound, ultimately allowing for more complex harmonies and voices to be heard. Adams makes a poignant statement about the auras for this piece: "All noise contains pure tone. And the complex sonorities of percussion instruments conceal choirs of inner voices. In *The Mathematics of Resonant Bodies* my search is to find and reveal those voices" (Adams, *Mathematics*).

It is important to make abundantly clear in *Mathematics* that the percussion instruments and the auras work together, they are one object and not two separate bodies. The description of the piece is often noted as "for Percussion and electronically generated auras," "solo percussion and processed sounds" or more inappropriately, "for percussion and electronics." Despite the lack of nomenclature for music of this kind, the best description for a piece of this nature is "for percussion instruments and their auras." The "and" is the most troubling linguistic hurdle, as it demotes the auras to a simple objective entity, the "choir" as Adams alludes to above. The collective attribution of both instrument and aura serves as the ultimate "revealer" of beauty in sound.

Interpreting an Aura

This discussion sows the seed of an underlying problem that I struggled with when initially interpreting the piece. How do you play with an aura? The word "aura" is a mystery. It stems from the Greek meaning, "breath, or breeze" and in Latin refers to "wind and air." Later in the nineteenth century the term is borrowed by metaphysics to imply a "subtle emanation from and enveloping living persons and things" (Oxford). Through these opaque references it is clear that at the very least, an aura is something entirely intangible.

The auras in *Mathematics* are tangible, however. They are prerecorded and fixed. How is this any different from an instrument-and-tape piece? The common technical functionality is still present, more or less. The performer can make a CD of the auras, and perform with each track through numerous hours of rehearsal. Though this format would exclude the well-designed click-track. A more appropriate rendering of the auras would be in a computer program that can simultaneously play three independent tracks. Whatever format one chooses (ADAT, magnetic tape, CD, computer, etc.) there is still an issue of performing with the media.

Performing aside any semi-autonomous media is an estranging process. We must submit to media as they are often blind to our presence. Compromises are usually made in order to preserve the unity between self and machine.

Mathematics initially would suggest that a precise execution between performer and aura is necessary to achieve such careful integration. Each recorded aura is accompanied with a click-track, which would imply the performer is meant to accurately align their part with each aura. Moreover, if performed in this manner one could completely ignore their corresponding auras in favor of the incessant "tick-tock" that invades the performer's psyche. So far, with score and CD in hand, there is absolutely no difference between *Mathematics* and a "_____ and tape" piece.

At first you may think that I am being a harsh critic of Adams's use of technology. I could easily pretend to be a pretentious music critic and claim that an interactive computer application (like Max/MSP or Pure Data) would have truly given the auras justice. Technology of this kind could literally create auras derived from the performance of each instrument in real time. This would ultimately accomplish what Adams *really* intended. That type of statement would be easily said and I could stop writing my article at this very moment.

Despite *Mathematics* feeling like a piece for tape the similarity only exists for purposes of dissemination and feasibility. In my experience, works for a complex arrangement of technology have more difficulty getting played. More important, there is no need for such an array of digital wizardry. The appearance and execution of the media have nothing to do with how the piece is interpreted. In fact it is the provocation of the word "aura" that inspires a different treatment of the piece. The word lends itself to something great or majestic. An aura is special (see Ellen Dissanayake's *Homo Aestheticus* for more on the concept of "making-special" in art).

The Role of Play in the Interpretation, Rehearsal, and Performance of Music Scores

I was convinced early on, through Schick's performances and my early conversations with Adams, that *Mathematics* is not just a piece, but a process. It embraces emanations of ritual and metaphor. It is clear that for Adams the placid and magnificent "auras" of the northern regions are special both artistically and personally. How does a simple performer with simple drums and metals revive the frozen attitudes of a place that is host to glacial plains, dark winters, light-filled summers, and land reaching as far as one's imagination?

Interpreting music and realizing its performance can be a complex flirtation between creativity and play. For me personally interpretation moves far beyond the written score and performance practice into the realm of experiential construction. A performance is an experience; one of which utilizes music, sound, theater and place. It is a creative experience and subsequently can be subject to creative realizations. "How do you *play* with an aura?" This was a question

I asked over many weeks of rehearsing *Mathematics* and led toward the challenging search for an experience that could encompasses the qualities of such a work.

Writer, theorist, and performer Stephen Nachmanovitch believes play is the root of creativity in the arts and sciences. I sustain Nachmanovitch's assertion. For me play has served as an essential part of music making and interpretation. Play, as a concept, is a social construct. It exists as a quality, a state, or perhaps even a boundary. We move in and out of this place freely and it is ensconced in our daily behavior. There are many theories that exist on the relevance and significance of play in our lives. Johan Huizinga writes, "we might call it a free activity standing quite consciously outside 'ordinary' life as being 'not serious' . . ." and it "stress[es] the difference from the common world by disguise or other means" (Huizinga 13). Performance theorist, Richard Schechner, positions play on his "fan," which organizes his inclusive model of performance on a sliding spectrum of structural freedom and restriction. The higher points on the fan—ritual, ceremony, and shamanism—include more orderly structures. The lower points—ritualization, art-making, and play—include freer and more disorderly processes. He asserts, "Performances are make-believe, in play, for fun" and continues by citing Victor Turner's well-known aphorism, "as if" equals "is" (Schechner xvi–xix). By looking at these and other notions of play in both everyday life and art making it becomes increasingly clear that play sinuously moves within states of reality, imagination, and something in between. It is illusory.

Play has been used actively as a process in a variety of situations. The National Institute for Play engages in numerous research projects that substantiate play in learning, thinking, relaxing, creativity, and problem solving. The NIFP's slogan published on their website is: "Play + Science = Transformation." Huizinga observes play as a state that lays aside "serious" everyday situations; the NIFP perhaps engages this same notion but flavors it within the auspices of the empirical processes of science and experimentation: both elicit distinct strata of behavior. We are essentially different when we are playing or in a state of play. Play, according to Huizinga, is not serious, thus it provides a parallel construct to *real* life and a place where we can abandon our *otherness*. Moreover, when we are at play we are subjective and open to our environment. As the NIFP website says: "What is Play? It is a state of being that is intensely pleasurable. It energizes and enlivens us. It eases our burdens, renews a natural sense of optimism and opens us up to new possibilities . . . play sculpts our brain; it makes us smarter and more adaptable" (http://www.nifplay.org/front_door .html). The language is provocative: play energizes, enlivens, eases, renews, opens, sculpts, and makes. Play is progressive. Nachmanovitch writes, "improvisation, composition, writing, painting, theater, invention, all creative acts are forms of play, the starting place of creativity in the human growth cycle, and one of the great primal life functions" (Nachmanovitch 42).

As performers we often travel to this state, though we may not call it "play." We do not perform our instruments; we play. It is plausible, after reading the above descriptions of the activity, to say that musicians are often *at play*. What is so serious about music? If we take Huizinga at his word, all of the performing arts "stress the difference from the common world by disguise or other means." Playing the drums is not much different from hammering nails into my new roof. It is the "serious" aspect that clouds the understanding between states of play and non-play in music. Interpreting a piece is both a process and act. We "play around." We try things "just for fun." We explore, naïvely perhaps, to find viable solutions, essentially allowing new possibilities to reveal themselves. There is no lack of "seriousness," nor are we fooling around. Play is not childish, nor is it child-like; rather, it is how we travel toward innovation.

Interpretation and performance are creative endeavors. We as performers have creative license to perform the repertoire we choose in the manner we desire. Play is essential for arriving at our creative goals. Rehearsal is a type of play state. We come to a rehearsal with a serious objective—the performance—but with a playful attitude on how to create an experience. Decisions get made and there may be a few "What if . . .?" or "Let's try this . . ." An overarching serious and nonserious activity takes place. We all know it is not the real performance, though we try to simulate that performance. Meanwhile, progress must be made toward a holistic interpretation that will ultimately lead to a meaningful performance. As Victor Turner once wrote: "Play can be everywhere and nowhere, imitate anything, yet be identified with nothing" (Turner, 233–34). During a rehearsal there may have never been any *playful* actions, no fooling around, disengagement, or roller coasters, yet we still have engaged in *play*. Turner writes further, "although 'spinning loose' as it were, the wheel of play reveals to us . . . the possibility of changing our goals and, therefore, the restructuring of what our culture states to be reality." As musicians, could it be that play is everywhere whether we use it, notice it or not?

There is no rubric for creativity. We cannot arrive at creative ideas through logic, empiricism or determinism. It is spontaneous and free. A friend and fellow percussionist in Arizona, Doug Nottingham, once described his performance of John Cage's *Variations III* and *Child of Tree*, which through the instructions of the score happened simultaneously. Essentially, if something during the performance happened that was ancillary to *Child of Tree* it by proxy became part of *Variations III*. One example Nottingham gave was his presentation of *Child of Tree*, for amplified plant materials. At one moment during the piece he put a bag of popcorn in the microwave for the given time period of that section. The popcorn was the plant material, and of course the popping was the sound element. The microwave was part of *Variations III*, and it was obvious that the two worked quite well together. It was a piece inside a piece and an instrument inside an instrument.

Arriving at an interpretation like this is not part of any performance practice or logical behavior. The popcorn was both fun and interesting. It satisfied criteria from the score and was highly creative. I am certain that Nottingham was quite a *playful* interpreter at this time in his life, and even more certain that the idea for this gesture was entirely inspired by everything and nothing. It was most likely pure spontaneous, genuine creativity.

If we say interpreting and rehearsing embody modes of play, then is the act of performance not play? To take Huizinga literally, performance would be the "serious" notion of reality, *real life*. The creativity, interpretation, and playfulness are over and the actual objective experience begins. This is, however, probably not the case. We are still at play. As I said earlier: "What is so serious about music?" What about the experience of playing? During acts of play many people and scholars document what is called a state of flow. Mihalyi Csikszentmihalyi describes flow as "the state in which people are so involved in an activity that nothing else seems to matter; the experience itself is so enjoyable that people will do it even at great cost, for the sheer sake of doing it" (Csikszentmihalyi, *Flow* 4). A performance is a type of flow state. During a performance one can lose awareness of one's interior self and one's performed activity. Bodies and minds can dissolve into an experience where "there is little distinction between self and environment, between stimulus and response or between past, present and future" (Csikszentmihalyi, *Beyond Boredom and Anxiety* 35–36).

Flow in contemporary music performance is something I have termed super-corporeality, a state of being aside from one's self during performance (Esler, Dissertation). We are aware of our *self*, the person we are away from the stage; yet we engender a different self through the experience of playing, the self beside ourselves. We are above (super-) our bodies and minds in the state of performance (-corporeality). Moreover, there is no apparent pragmatic reason for performing music: it will not feed people, create jobs, nor end wars and we do it "for the sheer sake of doing it." Flow is a conduit toward meaning. For a performer of *Mathematics* this may mean something much greater than it appears to the listener. The performer may become deeply engaged in the ebbing patterns of each movement, or the intricate peculiarities of the auras as they bounce off each acoustic surface of the space. For the listener these details may never be realized; there exists a different reality. Flow is intrinsically personal and provides the performative construct for meaningful experiences. Flow is a place of both comfort and estrangement, though it is perhaps one of the underlying reasons why any of us do what we do.

I can only guess as to the both excitement and frustration Schick was going through in the early process of learning *Mathematics*. The piece was not completely finished, and was changing at times on a daily basis. In fact the premier performance at Los Angeles County Museum of Art (LACMA) was not the same piece as is published today. The last snare drum movement, then called *Buzz*, was completely different. Moreover, the auras were going through multiple realizations; the piece was like a puzzle. I would assume that the initial phase of the piece at this stage was navigating the geography of instruments: eight triangles, four snare drums, or eight cymbals. During the first informal performance, I specifically remember Schick comporting his arms within a row of triangles, crossing and uncrossing into unusual angles and statuesque poses, to sustain a consistency between the two voices as they overlapped. The same was true for several of the other movements, as the limitations of percussion hardware can often create unexpected structural compromises, which can lead to fascinating physical displays in performance. Such technical phenomena appear throughout the repertoire in pieces like Maki Ishii's *Thirteen Drums* or Chinary Ung's *Spiral*, along with countless others. Essentially, the sculptural component of the instrumentation was being played by Schick and playing Schick simultaneously. To play is to be played (for more detail into Schick's interpretation of *Mathematics* see Schick, *The Percussionist's Art: same bed, different dreams*).

There is no easy way to communicate what play is. It is "everything and nothing." We encounter it passively and actively. It provides the fodder for creativity and a structure for meaning. It is the genesis of experience and the exodus of thought. It inspires and confuses. Whatever it is, we are certain that it is entirely complex, yet inherently simple. As musicians we should not be afraid to greet play as it enters our world. It will inevitably provoke many great interpretations and even greater performances. As performers we are given the task of creating reality, something over which we have almost total control while simultaneously no control whatsoever. It is truly one of the great privileges in life.

Beyond the Horizon

The question remains, "How do you play with an aura?" Contemporary music performance, it has seemed to me, invites critical thinking, hyper-embodiment, and hypo-awareness through its constructed experiences. Music performance is often a selfish endeavor—self-imposed or self-centric might be better terms, as music performance is not negative. For a long time, however, I chose to perform music that was physically demanding, technically challenging, and showcased a high level of mental dexterity. These choices were not wrong but they were definitely selfish. I believed in the music but I also enjoyed the athletic and studious values that these pieces projected for me.

This disposition changed when I began interpreting *Mathematics*. I quickly became consumed by the Arctic abstractions of Adams's music and the awareness it gave me of the sanctity of nature. Reading *Winter Music* (Adams's self-reflective book) inspired me to try to communicate Adams's idea of "place as music, music as place" (Adams 130). Putting this simple idea into practice was difficult.

I have been performing works with technology for some time. In 2003, I created a realization for Philippe Boesmans's *Daydreams* for marimba and computer, which I programmed myself. This led me to conclude that the "electronics," "tape" or "computer" components are just as fundamental in interpretation as the score itself (Esler, *Daydreams*). Every aspect of a piece should be considered in order to construct a cohesive performance. My mini-treatise was inspired by a number of performances I had seen where the electronic/computer portion was treated as ancillary to the performers themselves. It often appeared as though the performers never even thought about how the technological component integrated with their own performances. These experiences spawned my personal polemic for the treatment of technology in music interpretation.

For *Mathematics* the auras, as a concept, were the central object of my interpretation; I did not perceive this aspect as "technology." My original concept was for each movement to be perceived through a circular series of colors, both visually and aurally, with the first and last movements being identical. I would create a unique lighting palette and a carefully designed sound system for each movement that would accentuate and extend the qualities of the auras. I thought of incorporating images of Alaska around the performance space, but rejected the idea as kitsch. There were a few problems with my first draft at experiential construction. The idea was nice, and would probably have been very interesting, but it was completely void of any connection to place. Instead it was a theatrical production that would further distance the listener from the specialness of the aura.

After having played around with a variety of sonic and theatrical ideas I realized that sound was not necessarily my first point of entry any more. This may seem strange, but sound can be a distraction at times. I was well aware that Adams had conceived *Mathematics* as an exploration of sound and noise but I could not see how sound alone solved the issue of place. I was not content with performing the piece as normal; I felt there was something hidden that I needed to discover.

As another playful experiment, place superseded sound in my continuing

Mathematics adventure. Steven Schick had premiered *Mathematics* in theaters at LACMA, the Winter Garden Plaza in Manhattan, and the Subtropics Festival in Miami. I wanted approach this differently; I began to entertain the notion of performing the movements in a variety of physical structures that would extend the potency of each aura. This included foyers, lobbies, rooftops, and other spaces within grand and majestic structures. I played around with a number of locations in Southern California, such as the Neurosciences Institute in La Jolla, the Getty Center in Los Angeles, Camp Pendleton Marine Corps Base near Oceanside, and the historic battleship Star of India in the San Diego Bay, to name only a few. At one point I had the most absurd idea of performing *burst* and *stutter* at the firing range in Camp Pendleton (as though the military would have even let me near there), *shimmer* and *rumble* at the Getty Center, *roar* and *thunder* on the Star of India, and *crash* and *wail* at the Neurosciences Institute. All this in one day! It was far from logical, even silly, but it did bring me closer to the type of experience I was looking to construct.

After discarding this trans-California production I was stymied by the grand narrative I was exploring. The manifestation of "play" in my interpretive quest was confusing and I was beginning to consider just playing the piece "normally." Despite what Nachmanovitch says about play and creativity, play can be frustrating. The NIFP never states that there may be times when play leads you towards a dead end. "Playing with an aura" was becoming more than a speed bump: it was beginning to look like an endless wall. What was I looking to accomplish? I had two very simple objects in front of me: place and aura. Yet I was lost in their simplicity.

Around this time I was involved with a performance of Alvin Lucier's *Chambers*, a piece for small sound chambers carried through larger spaces. The basic premise is for the players to find interesting sonic chambers that can be observed in a large environment as well in their own micro-environment. The players can experience their environments through their smaller chambers as well as in the greater space (Lucier, 60). *Chambers* begins with everyone close together playing or activating their chambers (mine was a large almglocken, or Alpine bell, with a marble inside) and as the piece progresses each individual slowly drifts apart until no other players in the group can be heard. It is a beautiful piece and an inspiring activity. For this particular performance I scouted several locations around La Jolla, California, that were large enough to accommodate approximately twenty students. I looked at several locations, including Black's Beach, the La Jolla cliffs, the eucalyptus forest on the UCSD campus, and a large soccer field overlooking the Pacific Ocean. Each had their relative beauty and convenience, but the soccer field was my final selection, mostly for practical purposes.

The performance was absolutely stunning. The air was quite still that day so the performance lasted much longer than if it were windy. Despite my students finding the activity/piece silly (but fun and stimulating) the experience provided me a new perspective. During the location scouting I had a fleeting thought: "What if I performed *Mathematics* right here on the La Jolla cliffs?" Is the piece really that different from *Chambers*? It is usually assumed that the various conventions of theatrical infrastructure are a universal component to any performance. There are exceptions to this assumption, such as the music of David Dunn, Michael Pisaro, Alvin Lucier, and various types of folk and traditional music, to name a few. But what is stopping someone from putting drums into a car and driving to the Parthenon in Greece to play Iannis Xenakis's *Psappha*? The score does not say: "Please only perform within standard concert infrastructure." Pink Floyd recorded an album in the ruins of Pompeii; why could I not play *Mathematics* on a giant cliff?

Honestly, the idea still seemed a bit ridiculous. A few months before this hazy epiphany I had discussed the idea of performing the movements of *Mathematics* in different spaces with Adams. We both seemed optimistic, but it was clear there was an amount of intrigue mixed with a little confusion. Graduating to the wide open outdoors was perhaps even more vexing. I later discussed my idea with Schick, who had already performed the piece several times throughout the country. We played around with several different ideas for natural environments in which to play each movement. We imagined the snare drums (*burst* and *stutter*) in the ocean surf or underneath a highway overpass, the triangles (*shimmer*) deep in an ice cave, the siren (*wail*) in a giant canyon, the tam-tam (*roar*) in the middle of the desert and the cymbals (*crash*) next to a construction site. A lot of ideas were thrown around, some were just fun, and others were quite serious.

Though it was a very poetic notion, the thought of producing such a performance was more than a nightmare and not much different than my trans-California catastrophe. I had to simplify. The next version of this idea was much more practical. For a while I had settled on organizing the piece around six locations in a small area of La Jolla, beginning and ending at the beach. It seemed logistically challenging but definitely not impossible. The performance would begin with everyone congregating at Black's Beach and after each movement we would all walk to the next location. A novel concept, but again it lacked cohesive substance in my overall interpretation. For me, the central figure of this piece was still the aura. The concept was hollow. I was not *playing* hard enough.

It was not until I visited the Anza-Borrego Desert State Park (just for pure enjoyment) that I realized from where the auras of *Mathematics* are derived.

The music of Adams is more than just fleeting descriptions of "the frozen landscapes of the North," or "a sonic geography of the Arctic." Out there in the desert I finally understood that the auras were right there in front of me. The aura was not the sound, but the place. How then do I put the place in the aura? About a week later I met with Schick again and after a brief conversation about my realization he said, paraphrased: "What if you just played the piece in the desert?" The thought did not immediately register but the more I digested the idea the more it settled.

The music of Adams is inspired by experiences far away from contemporary infrastructure. The sound of a calving glacier and the waxing and waning of the Northern sun are experiences; they cannot be recorded and played back. These experiences only exist if we seek them, breathe them in. *Mathematics* to me is an experience. The open landscape of the arid desert transplants the very essence of an aura to the experience of just being there. No roads, no wires or buildings, just the rest of the world surrounding you. That is where the music lives.

The end of the story is quite simple. My loyal friends, colleagues, a few lucky passers-by and I went out to Box Canyon in the Anza-Borrego Desert during February of 2006 and performed *Mathematics* for the first time at that place. It was truly an experience, from ritual to metaphor, from play to place. Later that same day we all performed (including Steve Schick and his percussion group in residence at the University of California, San Diego, red fish blue fish) *Strange and Sacred Noise* overlooking the Carrizo Badlands about ten miles away, which eventually inspired a series of subsequent performances in vast and open land-scapes across the continent (see Schick's chapter in this anthology).

Looking back I can only say that the conceptual framework of *play* brought me toward this dramatic experience. I was never consciously *playing* and was certainly not trying to cultivate such a concept. It was completely natural, "everywhere and nowhere." The entire process was creative and evolutionary. In the field of experimental music we can take ourselves too seriously. We are no different from children in a sandbox. We play every day just for the sake of doing what we do. If I did not continue to play with ideas that were to me silly or impossible then I would have most likely settled with performing *Mathematics* more conventionally. There is nothing wrong with either interpretation (inside or outside) but experimenting and playing is how we progress as musicians and in our greater cultural context.

To answer my own question: "How do you play with an aura?" You take it as far as you can go before you fall, you lift it as high as you can until your knees weaken, and you listen to it as long as you can until it no longer speaks. I have yet to encounter a composer who inspires more interpretive and creative depth in their music than Adams. As a performer, this entire process has completely changed how I approach music. I have since focused my professional output as a performer toward projects that affect awareness of cultural, social, and community issues. I have changed my expectations and begun to use music as an agent for approaching everyday situations in education, critical thinking, and dynamic experiential construction. Most important, working on this project has made me a better person; it has humbled me in many ways. But in the end, I still just play.

Bibliography

Adams, John Luther. *Winter Music*. Middletown, Conn.: Wesleyan University Press, 2004, 130.

Adams, John Luther. *The Mathematics of Resonant Bodies*. Fairbanks: Taiga Press, 2003.

"*Aura*" Oxford English Dictionary, 2nd edition. Oxford: Oxford University Press, 1989.

Csikszentmihalyi, Mihalyi. *Flow: The Psychology of Optimal Experience*. New York: Harper & Row, 1990, 4.

Csikszentmihalyi, Mihalyi. *Beyond Boredom and Anxiety*. San Francisco: Jossey-Bass Publishers, 1975, 35–36.

Dissanayake, Ellen. *Homo Aestheticus*. Seattle: University of Washington Press, 1995.

Esler, Robert. *A Phenomenological Approach to Contemporary Music Performance*. Dissertation, University of California, San Diego, 2007.

Esler, Robert. "Re-realizing Philippe Boesmans' Daydreams: A Performative Approach to Live Electro-Acoustic Music." *The Proceedings of the International Computer Music Association*. Miami, 2004.

Huizinga, Johan. *Homo Ludens: A Study of Play-Element in Culture*. London: Routledge, 2000, 13.

Lucier, Alvin. "Chambers." In *Reflections: Interviews, Scores, Writings 1965–1994*. Cologne: Musik-Texte, 2005, 60.

Nachmanovitch, Stephen. *Free Play: Improvisation in Life and Art*. Los Angeles: J. P. Tarcher, Inc., 1990, 42.

National Institute for Play. http://www.nifplay.org (accessed Feb. 1, 2009).

National Institute for Play. "What Is Play?" http://www.nifplay.org/front_door.html, (accessed Feb. 7, 2009).

Schechner, Richard. *Performance Theory*. New York: Routledge, 2003, xvi–xix.

Schick, Steven. *The Percussionist's Art: Same Bed, Different Dream*. Rochester: University of Rochester Press, 2006.

Turner, Victor. "Body, Brain and Culture." (Paper presented at the symposium on Ritual and Human Adaptation, November 11–12, 1982 in Chicago, Illinois), 233–34.

9 * Qilyaun

The shaman drums. He goes into trance.
His soul moves free . . . His spirit goes down.
He dives through the tundra.
It is hard to get through.
It is cold and dangerous.
He enters. He is gone . . .
  * From *Ancient Land: Sacred Whale*, by TOM LOWENSTEIN

Qilyaun is the Iñupiaq word for the shaman's drum. Translated
literally, it means "device of power." The drum is the shaman's vehicle
for spirit journeys. The shaman rides the sound of the drum to and
from the spirit world.
  * Introduction to the score of *Qilyaun*, by JOHN LUTHER ADAMS

In 1995 I accepted a position as an Assistant Professor of Music at the University of Alaska Fairbanks. I had recently completed my studies at the University of Miami, where I first encountered the music of John Luther Adams, listening to a CD recording of *Earth and the Great Weather*. As a result of that experience, while preparing for the adventure of moving to the far north, I resolved to meet him.

Resettling in Alaska was an amazing experience. In addition to the thrill of my first tenure-track university position, I was living in a strange and captivating place. Alaska is wild, potent, gigantic and empty, seemingly devoid of roads or other manifestations of humanity. That emptiness is replaced with towering mountains, snow-filled forests, vast plains, great rivers, and everywhere, wildlife. In comings and goings, I saw more animals in their natural surroundings than the rest of my life all together: grizzlies, polar bears, whales, king salmon, great horned owls, bald eagles, moose, wolves, and caribou. The weather was equally striking, with bone-dry air, and winter seasons that span October to May, at times as cold as minus 50 degrees Fahrenheit. The subarctic sky is all daylight June to August, and almost continuously dark November to January. The Arctic night possesses a vivid light, filled with the aurora borealis, snow reflections, and extended sunrise/sunsets, casting hues of pink, orange and red upon a cold, clear sky.

I had many vivid experiences that first year, two of which are mentioned here. The first occurred en route to Alaska via the *Columbia*, a ferry sailing from Bellingham, Washington. One afternoon we steamed into the proximity of a large group of humpback whales, gathering for migration to waters near Hawaii. Pods, or small groups of whales, appeared all around the ship as far as the eye could see, leaping out of the water, as well as vigorously smacking the surface with their tails, at times repeating in regular pulse, hitting the water hard . . . really hard. Everyone onboard was mesmerized, and some people mentioned they had heard of, but never witnessed the spectacle. It was an electrifying moment.

The second was my first experience with live Alaska Native music and dance at the Alaska Festival of Native Arts. Dance ensembles from throughout the subarctic travel to Fairbanks annually to perform at the three-day festival. A dance group will have anywhere from five to fifteen drummers, with as many dancers, and everyone sings. Of particular interest to me was their drum, called a *qilyaun* in the Iñupiat language. The *qilyaun* is a large frame drum with a handle, held in one hand while the drummer, seated, either lightly taps or plays with terrific loudness. It has no shell, but is simply a round wooden frame with a skin stretched tautly across. When the drummers are playing intensely, the noise is impressive and distinct. Their drumming is visceral, played seated, but leaning forward, intent. Much of the music is comprised of 5/8 and 7/8 phrases, such as 2-3, or 2-2-3. They performed all night, one hour at a time, group after group, hailing from tiny villages throughout Alaska, Canada, and Siberia.

As good fortune would have it, John lived in Fairbanks, and in a short time we became friends. We used to meet at the local favorite restaurant Thai House, or at his studio, outside of Fairbanks on Moose Mountain where we would talk late into the night. Occasionally we'd meet for a sauna and dinner with friends of his that included the conductor Gordon Wright, Fairbanks physician Leif Thompson, and the poet John Haines, to name a few. Having both grown up as drummers, we had similar musical influences and experiences. John had performed timpani in the Fairbanks Symphony, which became part of my job duties at UAF. And my newfound enthusiasm for Inuit drumming was a source of much discussion, as John holds a special love for, and impressive knowledge of, Native Alaskan culture. Another connection was that when we met, he was completing *Strange and Sacred Noise* for the Percussion Group Cincinnati, a professional trio whom I studied with at the University of Cincinnati College-Conservatory of Music in the 1980s.

We conversed extensively about music, poring over scores and listening to pieces together. From those conversations several ideas stand out as relevant to *Qilyaun*. As he was then completing *Strange and Sacred Noise*, his ideas were very close to that work, and his essay of the same title accurately captures what was in his mind. One important concept was the idea that his music would create a sense of place in which to experience sound. This place is where every part touched by the sound becomes the piece: the acoustics of the sounding instruments, "the acoustics of the performance space, and the psycho-acoustics of our own hearing" (1998). John also discussed the fact that he sought singularity as a pure musical vehicle. He sought to create music that is devoid of expectation or resolution, and that invites one into a "deeper experience of the sound." "My concern is not with musical 'ideas' and the rhetoric of composition, but with the singular sonority—that sound which stands for nothing other than itself, filling time and space with the vivid, physical presence of a place. Immersed in the enveloping presence of elemental noise, in the fullness of the present moment, we just may begin to hear, with the whole of the self, something of the inaudible totality of sound."

In 1997 I received funding to award a commission for a percussion solo through the Fairbanks Symphony Association, and I approached John about the project. At the time John was considering creating an Inuit Alaskan opera, so we began discussions with the idea of a 7–10 minute piece that would become a solo segment of the larger work, dealing with the subject of the shaman-drummer. During our deliberations, we considered using a *qilyaun*, experimenting with various ways to perform with it. Ultimately, there was difficulty in perceiving it as a solo instrument in part because playing with one hand limits its versatility, and since it has no shell, its resonant character had limitations. Instead John selected a concert bass drum because it produces a huge, deeply sonorous sound. And, like the *qilyaun*, the bass drum is *singular*.

Another area of discussion pertained to the inclusion of an electronic component to the piece. I had been engaged with combining percussion and electronics for a number of years and was keen to continue this path. Since their textures are primarily comprised of unpitched noise, the integrative possibilities are fertile, and their combined use has produced landmark musical literature. John Cage's *Imaginary Landscapes* (1939–42), and *Cartridge Music* (1960); as well as Karlheinz Stockhausen's *Kontakte* (1960) and *Microphonie I* (1964), are representative of classic works that blend the salient aspects of both mediums into compelling musical experiences. In our very early discussions, John was skeptical about creating an electronic work as he had always steered clear of the sounds associated with it. He had incorporated electro-acoustic processes in some of his work, but was always careful to use only acoustic sounds created live by the performers of his works. For example, certain segments of *Earth and the Great Weather* employ a series of delays among the string parts as part of the compositional structure. However, one additional factor made using electronics for the piece attractive: we had a world-class concert hall for the premiere.

The Charles W. Davis Concert Hall at the University of Alaska Fairbanks is a place that musicians love to perform in. It was built in the late 1970s during the heyday of the Trans-Alaska Pipeline, when the state was flush with money and intent on developing infrastructure. The home of the Fairbanks Symphony and the Arctic Chamber Orchestra, it is a beautiful hall both sonically and visually, yielding a rich sound with a sustained, yet subtle resonance. The design of the 900-seat hall creates an open ambiance that is spacious, yet intimate. John knew it well, having performed and also recorded several of his works there. We had access to the hall in order to work out ideas and we also had solid beginnings of an inventory of audio resources. This led us to conclude that before us lay the opportunity to create something really spectacular with electronics. Quickly the discussion turned to a longer work, of concert length. As our discussions ensued, John conceived the idea of using a modified delay system to fully exploit not only the resonance of a large drum, but the entire space. In other words, during the premiere I would play bass drum (and much more), but the hall would become the *qilyaun*.

With the addition of electronics, we decided to bring a sound designer into the project to create a multi-delay/feedback system that would give treatment for three delay lines, one on each side, and one in the rear. John asked Nathaniel Reichman to be part of the project. Nathaniel was a former student of John's at Bennington College who was raised in Alaska, but now lived on the East Coast. We worked on the system Nat designed for the Davis Hall in November 1997 and during April 1998, in a lead-up to the premiere. We also enlisted the help of Michael Henchman, a local telecommunications engineer and musician. He helped us wire the hall and manage the many audio issues that arose through the work. We constructed a system that included large speakers mounted behind the screen facades on the sidewalls above the audience. Microphones were seated approximately six feet in front of three speakers (two on the side and one in the rear), in order to pick up the delay lines and re-feed them into the system.

Eventually John conceived a three-movement work for solo percussion, digital delay, and spatial resonance. The first movement, scored for bass drum, became the final published piece. The second movement was scored for six cymbals, two tam-tams, and crotales; and the third, eight tomtoms, eight cymbals, and a kick drum. Each of the movements utilized the customized digital delay and resonance spatialization system. They also all used similar linear-mirror musical structures, meaning that each movement progresses

TABLE 9.1. Overall Compositional Structure.

Section 1 Begin through H mm. 1–72	Section 2 Letter I through Q mm. 73–144	Section 3 Letter Q through Z mm. 145–215	Section 4 Letter R through Ll mm. 216–309
Fast (32nd notes at quarter note = 80) with incrementally decreasing sizes of crescendo-decrescendo waves.	Rhythmic deacceleration	Rhythmic acceleration	Fast (32nd notes at quarter note = 80) with incrementally increasing sizes of crescendo-decrescendo waves.

to completion of a specific process deemed a halfway point. The second half is the exact music in reverse, to the first note of the work, thus two mirrored halves. The working title for the premiere performance was *The Immeasurable Space of Tones*. We performed the seventy-minute work twice, once in Alaska in 1998, and then at Oberlin Conservatory the following year, where it was titled *Ilimaq (Spirit Journeys)*. Shortly afterwards, John published the first movement as a single work, naming it *Qilyaun*.

Structural Considerations

What follows is an analysis of *Qilyaun* from structural, audio, and performance perspectives. This is not so much a comprehensive overview of the piece as it is a narrative that sheds light on preparations for the work. It represents notes that Nathaniel and I made prior to the premiere and subsequent performances, and it illuminates what we were concentrating on during the performances.

The score used for this analysis is the current edition of *Qilyaun*, for either single drummer with digital delay or bass drum quartet. The full score for four players perfectly creates the digital delay feeds, with part four as the solo line. The second and third movements are discussed, but not analyzed, as that goes beyond the scope of this article. Their structure is quite similar to the first movement, hence much of the content of this section applies to them as well. Those movements should figure well in a broader study of John's unpublished work.

The piece is a set of rhythmic constructs performed in strict four-part canon. Layers of bass drum rolls produce sonic waves that deaccelerate, than accelerate to a unison conclusion. The tempo marking is quarter note = 80 throughout. The two halves precisely mirror each other, and the piece divides into four sections (Table 9.1).

TABLE 9.2. Number of Crescendo Waves per Eight Measures, Section 1.

	Begin	A	B	C	D	E	F	G	H	I	J
Drum 1				1	2	3	4	5	6	7	8
Drum 2			1	2	3	4	5	6	7	8	18
Drum 3		1	2	3	4	5	6	7	8	18	-----
Drum 4	1	2	3	4	5	6	7	8	18	-----	-----

TABLE 9.3. Letter L (numbers represent strikes per measure).

32	30	28	26	24	22	20	18
16	15	14	13	12	11	10	9
8	8	7	7	6	6	5	5
4	4	7/2	----	3	3	5/2	----

In sections 1 and 4, the thirty-second note remains constant throughout. Rhythmic and textural interest is created with the use of crescendo-decrescendo waves that shorten in duration every eight measures. Table 9.2 outlines the number of waves per eight bars from measure A to H.

At letter H, the swells increase to eight over four bars, then eight over two bars (one each quarter note), then accents on the upbeat over thirty-second notes for two bars, then odd thirty-second notes accented over two bars (Figure 9.1).

The contraction of the crescendos in the first section create a sense of buildup in the music, leading to a heightened intensity that morphs into a plateau of fff volume while rhythmically beginning the deacceleration process.

Sections 2 and 3 constitute a gradual deacceleration, then acceleration, respectively. This is accomplished by reducing the number of notes by two each measure.

Placed on a graph (Table 9.3), one can see how the number of strikes in each measure line up, so that the performer is constantly phasing in and out of a unison with the other voices.

At letter N the sonic deacceleration continues, but in a different texture. Fortississimo accented strikes in combination with pianisissimo rolls occur at steadily expanding time intervals, one per number of quarter note beats listed (Figure 9.2).

Table 9.4 shows how the four parts are lining up from letter Q. At letter R, the mirrored reverse process begins, leading to a return to the opening of the piece.

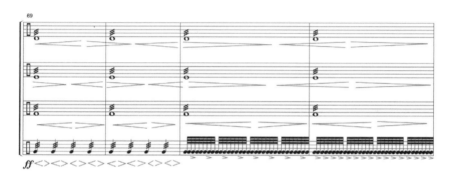

FIGURE 9.1

In Section 3 (letter Aa, m. 216), the construct of crescendo waves returns, this time decreasing in numbers per eight bars (Table 9.5).

In the original premiere, the end of the piece was followed by the digital delay/feedback aura that lasted approximately an additional ten minutes.

Sound Design

Since the digital delay and spatialization was such an important aspect of the work, I asked Nathaniel Reichman to contribute his recollection of the sound design, which follows:

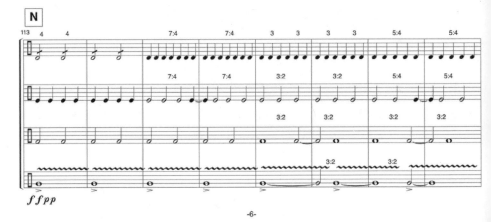

ƒƒpp

-6-

FIGURE 9.2

TABLE 9.4. Letters Q through T:
Each space represents four bars; numbers represent strikes per four-bar phrase.

Letter	Q		R		S		T	
Drum 4	4	3	2	2	1	1	1-------	0--------
Drum 3	2	2	1	1	1-------	0--------	1-------	0--------
Drum 2	1	1	1--------	0--------	1--------	0--------	1	1
Drum 1	1------	0--------	1--------	0--------	1	1	2	2

TABLE 9.5. Number of Crescendo Waves per Eight Measures, Section 4.

	Aa	Bb	Cc	Dd	Ee	Ff	Gg	Hh	Ii	Jj	Kk	Ll
Drum 1				10	8	7	6	5	4	3	2	1
Drum 2			10	8	7	6	5	4	3	2	1	1
Drum 3		10	8	7	6	5	4	3	2	1	1	1
Drum 4	10	8	7	6	5	4	3	2	1	1	1	1

The musical goal of the electronic processing in *Qilyaun* was to accentuate and amplify the naturally occurring resonances in the performance space. In broad terms, we mic'ed the percussion instruments, amplified them, and sent them through a series of delay lines that would feed loudspeakers and our carefully controlled feedback matrix.

The first loudspeaker was placed directly in front of the performer, facing the audience, and we amplified the performer's direct sound by mic'ing the bass drum fairly closely. The performer was fed a click track that was calculated to coincide with our delay lines. The direct sound was fed into a twenty-four-second delay line, the output of which fed another loudspeaker at the back of the hall, facing the back of the audience. We made every effort to make the delayed sound of the bass drum sound as close as possible to the original, live sound. The direct (electronic line-level) output of the thirty-second delay line was also mult'ed and sent to a second thirty-second delay line, which in turn fed a loudspeaker at the left of the audience. This was also mult'ed and sent to the third (and last) thirty-second delay line, which fed a loudspeaker facing the audience's right. The overall effect was that one would hear a phrase coming from the bass drum, and subsequently hear exactly the same phrase at the rear, left, and right with thirty-second intervals. This was the easy part.

We then placed microphones roughly six feet away (and sometimes more) from each loudspeaker, and mixed their output into the delay matrix. Without the delays in place, there would have been instant and near-deafening feedback. But with the delays, we avoided direct feedback. We made every effort to mix the mic'ed sound of the loudspeakers back into the delay matrix at the same level as the direct sound from the bass drum. But the mics were far enough away from the loudspeakers to pick up naturally occurring resonances in the room, and these resonances were doubled, tripled, quadrupled, etc. as the sound moved around the room. We became keenly aware of the most likely resonant frequencies (which also were the ones that would occur during direct feedback), and notched the first two or three out using very narrow parametric eq's. After these first two or three were removed, a small orchestra of quieter resonating frequencies in the room presented themselves.

During rehearsal, we would tune the system of delays and feedback as closely to the space as we could, and the infinitely re-processed sound of the percussion instruments would turn into big beautiful washes of abstract sound moving around the hall. In Fairbanks, Alaska, at the Charles W. Davis Concert Hall, we had great success managing these sounds. These rehearsals gave us the confidence to perform *Qilyaun* in other halls, and as soon as we did, we realized just how difficult and tenuous it was to recreate the first experience.

At the subsequent performance at Oberlin College, with less preparation time and unfamiliar equipment, the process proved even more challenging, and the consequent sonic results were not as satisfying. Difficulties notwithstanding, JLA's desire to extrapolate an "aura" out of the resonance was central to the project, and it seeded notions of what could be done for future works. Again, Nathaniel writes: "The very delicate nature of this feedback system and the tremendous effort needed to initiate it caused John Luther Adams to look elsewhere for the same musical result. His concept of the electronic 'aura' in the pieces following *Qilyaun* came from this experience. The creation of these auras (*Red Arc/Blue Veil*, *Dark Waves*) was quite similar to the process used in *Qilyaun*, but instead executed in the more highly controlled studio environment."

Performance Considerations

We held discussions regarding coloristic considerations for the piece, including tuning of the drums, types of heads, selection of mallets, microphone placement, and so on. John favored as large a bass drum as possible, pitched as low as possible for good sound. He also favored large, general-articulation mallets, but we both knew that the spectrum of colors and sounds called for a truly versatile stick. For this performance, I used a pair of Andrew Feldman staccato timpani mallets with bamboo handles. These succeeded in pulling out the drum's lower fundamentals while vividly sounding thirty-second notes at quarter note = 80.

With heavy use, bass drums are prone to rattle, and eliminating every rattle became a mammoth project itself. All of the spring-loaded lug mounts were removed, the springs were wrapped in Teflon and the spaces stuffed. We mic'ed the bass drum with a pair of Neumann U-87s running through a Manley pre-amp. The cymbals, gongs, and drums were mic'ed with a variety of devices, ranging from Sure SM57s for the drums to an array of condenser microphones for the metallic instruments.

Qilyaun has two primary challenges for the performer. The first is sustaining an energetic yet accurate pace of thirty-second notes throughout the first and fourth sections. Playing a large bass drum with a loose head and big mallets, a performer requires significant energy to sustain the thirty-second-note waves of crescendos-decrescendos, especially in reaching the dynamic levels the music calls for. I used to shift from one set of muscles to another as I went through the piece, in order to rest some while others were working. I could

FIGURE 9.3

drum with my back, shoulder, and elbow muscles, and also wrists. There was also a matter of pacing, much like in running a race, in order to deliver an even amount of intensity throughout.

In the fast sections, during the crest of a wave (fortissimo), the drum is responsive to the thirty-second-note strikes. But when going down to pianissimo the already excited head flops about, which in turn creates a considerable stick rebound variance, challenging the performer to be vigilant in order to keep all notes sounding consistently.

Sections 2 and 3 pose the second challenge for the performer. While not as physically demanding, the timing of the playing must clearly articulate the metric process, convincingly sounding the various numerical pairings in the canon (Figure 9.3).

Even though both John and myself refer to the deacceleration/acceleration using those words, it is important for the performer *not* to not think of the music as such, but rather as a number of notes per measure (or per two measures), while strictly observing mm. = 80. In short, the tempo never wavers. In JLA's work, there is a need for taut rhythmic applications on the part of the performers. I practiced each metric value repeatedly, so that wherever I was in the music, the notes values were not only correct, but (to say in slang) "they rocked." This was also really important in our deliberations. The rhythms had to have a sense of momentum, however irregular.

Learning the piece this way provided me the best opportunity to line up the four parts throughout when playing with three other versions of myself via the digital delay system. When I was able to practice with the delay system going, I listened to the click as softly as I could in order to hear as the sound from the speakers circled the house before sweeping back onto the stage. JLA wanted to avoid what he considered "romantic era" crescendos, employed in countless dramatic orchestral works, which go long on the build and then initiate a steep ascent in the last few beats. John's crescendos are geometric, with a straight, gradual climb to the top, a very brief moment, and then a deep, steady descent.

World Premiere

In the days leading up to the performance, we frequented the Davis Hall a number of times late at night, as that was the only time we could work in the space without interruption. We had a terrific dress rehearsal of the now-seventy-minute work before a small invited audience of about twelve friends. It was then we first were able to step back, experience the work in full, and realize we had created a unique and powerful event.

There was a big crowd in Davis Hall on the evening of Saturday, April 18. John has a solid following of enthusiasts in Fairbanks, and they came out in force. The evening began with *Burst*, a movement for percussion quartet from *Strange and Sacred Noise*, performed by my students. Then John took to the stage for remarks about the piece. Much of what he spoke about was related to the program and notes, which follow:

THE IMMEASURABLE SPACE OF TONES (1998)**
for solo percussion, recirculating feedback and spatial resonance

    I. Time, the Drum, and Tone Emerging
    II. Spectral Waves
    III. . . . And Swirling Thunder
Scott Deal, Percussion

**Premiere Performance*
Commissioned by the Fairbanks Symphony Association
Sound design by Nathaniel Reichman, Michael Henchman and John Luther
    Adams
Lighting design by Dale Kormitz
    "Even where there is nothing to be seen, nothing to be touched,
    nothing to be measured,
    where bodies do not move from place to place, there is still space,
    and it is not empty spaces; it is space filled to the brim,
    space becomes alive,
    the space that tones disclose to us."

                             Victor Zuckerkandl

"John Cage defined 'experimental music' as 'music, the outcome of which is unpredictable.' By that definition, this new work is easily the most experimental music I've ever made. The score is through composed and conventionally notated. But the essence of this music arises in the spaces between the notes, and in the resonant spaces of the performance space. All of the sounds are acoustical in origin, and produced 'live' by the percussionist. No synthesizers, samplers or prerecorded sounds are employed. The only electronic processing is amplification and time-delayed recirculation of the percussion sounds, which are slowly transformed by the natural acoustical resonances of the Davis Concert Hall."

John Luther Adams

The first movement is the most substantial, and the most difficult, by far. That night it was a swirling cyclone that gradually deaccelerated to a low rumble interspersed with great blows of sound. I struck the drum really hard. As the music sped up again the hall was energized by the thundering drum delays that gradually transformed into multilayered washes of sonic aura. The metallic second movement was serene and ethereal, performed with soft rolls and chime-like strikes. It seemed to float weightlessly inside the space, producing high-frequency melodies that John later described as "angel voices." The second movement has several huge crescendos on a large tam-tam that are simply unbelievable. The third movement, performed on the large drumkit, was an electrifying return to the intensity of the bass drum movement with an explosive mix of skin and metal. Commenting on the final movement, John's wife Cindy told me it was like sitting in the middle of a firestorm. The piece required athletic and intellectual rigor that brought me to the brink of exhaustion. Yet there was something transformative about being pushed to the limit while counting madly, as delayed drums swirled around my ears like speeding freight trains.

The audience response was most enthusiastic and sustained over numerous curtain calls. On a certain level, I believe they considered the music successful, and they enjoyed my drumming. However, there was more in Davis Hall that evening. Many solos elicit audience reaction based on the performer's ability to give a dynamic rendering, and certainly this music invites that energy. However, John doesn't really compose solos possessing the traditional classical music aesthetic. With his music, there is no rendition, nor drama, and there is no individual. Rather, he composes in commitment to the moment itself, empty of all save time and sound. If not even one person had applauded I would have felt just as strongly about the performance. We all felt strongly, and we also understood. We had gone to the place of ecstatic, elemental noise.

Works Cited

Adams, John Luther. *Qilyaun*. Fairbanks, Alaska: Taiga Press, 1998.

Adams, John Luther. "Strange and Sacred Noise." In *Winter Music: Composing the North*. Middletown, Conn.: Wesleyan University Press, 2004, 130.

Lowenstein, Tom. *Ancient Land, Sacred Whale*. New York: North Point Press, 1995.

Zuckerkandl, Viktor. From *Sound and Symbol: Music and the External World*, in Bollingen Series 44. Princeton, N.J.: Princeton University Press, 1956.

Todd Tarantino

10 * The Color Field Music of John Luther Adams

G enerally speaking, the music of John Luther Adams can be classed into four interrelated categories that I will call Alaskan, color field, abstract, and hybrid. As the name implies, the Alaskan works, such as *Five Athabascan Dances, Sauyatugvik: The Time of Drumming* (both 1996) and parts of *Make Prayers to the Raven* (1998), are grounded in the culture and musical traditions of Alaska's indigenous peoples. While defined by their use of Alaskan traditional melodies and techniques, these works exist within a relatively traditional twentieth-century tonal world articulated by clearly delineated phrases and sections. The abstract works, for instance *Strange and Sacred Noise* (1997), most of *The Mathematics of Resonant Bodies* (2002), and parts of *Dream in White on White* (1992) are more experimental; often their moment-to-moment surface results from the illustration or representation, in musical notation, of mathematic or scientific processes: for instance, the slowly unfolding Shepard tones of the opening of *Dream in White on White*. The hybrid works seem transitional, while at times grounded in "Alaskan" scenes, they may or may not have a tonal narrative. These compositions stand apart from Adams's other works and have an almost dramatic narrative sense—many of them consist of small vignettes or melodies juxtaposed; *Earth and the Great Weather* (1990–93) is probably the most important work in this category; *Night Peace* (1977) and *Forest Without Leaves* (1984) are other good examples.

Since 1999, the bulk of Adams's output are color field compositions. In these works the overall sonority changes little from beginning to end; there is no real narrative of phrases and harmonies, and movement within or through a saturated gamut replaces harmonic motion. In their overall sound, color field works present a slowly shifting singularity enlivened by surface disturbances.

While Adams's hand is evident in his Alaskan and hybrid works, it is (perhaps intentionally) obscured in his color field and abstract works. Consequently, over the years, criticism of these pieces has tended toward the poetic and is often limited to generalities about the "timeless" nature of the "sound," the depth of the "mood" or the "Arctic" colors and "peaceful" harmonies.[1] If we assume that the critics themselves are not at fault—reviewers, perhaps understandably, are not writing technically and no one else has—it would seem

TABLE 10.1. Color Field Works of John Luther Adams.

1992	*Dream in White on White*
1995	*Clouds of Forgetting, Clouds of Unknowing*
1998	*In the White Silence*
1999	*In a Treeless Place, Only Snow*
1999	*Time Undisturbed*
2000	*The Light That Fills the World*
2001	*Dark Wind*
2001	*After the Light*
2001	*The Farthest Place*
2001	*The Immeasurable Space of Tones*
2001	*Among Red Mountains*
2002	*Red Arc / Blue Veil*
2003	*for Lou Harrison*
2005	*. . . and bells remembered . . .*
2005	*Veils*
2005	*Vesper*
1986/2006	*for Jim (rising)*
2006	*The Place Where You Go to Listen*
2007	*Dark Waves*
2007/2010	*The Light Within*
2007	*Nunataks*
2007	*Three High Places*
1973/2007	*Always Very Soft*
2008	*Sky with Four Suns / Sky with Four Moons*
2010	*Four Thousand Holes*

that there is no language for understanding this "Arctic" surface, describing its narrative progress, or identifying deviations and regularities within a form. In the absence of an analytical language, critics resort to clichés; performers and conductors, rudderless, can only play the notes; and analysts must reinvent the wheel with each composition. Adams loses his agency as a creator: becoming a mystic channeling the Arctic North rather than a composer working within a musico-cultural surround.[2] This paper attempts to remedy this situation by outlining some of the normative techniques found in Adams's color field works, while in the process developing a framework for understanding, evaluating, and assessing creative choices.

On a formal level, Adams's color field pieces tend to enact multiple coexisting algorithms; once processes are put in motion, there are few deviations. Pitch choice within a work or section is limited to a particular continuum, or gamut, and pitch change is systematized. Often the complete gamut sounds continuously and pitches outside of the gamut are not employed. Adams's gamuts lack pitch hierarchy; consequently, there is no simple way to measure consonance and dissonance or directed motion within a work. Thus, in this regard, beyond enumerating their mechanics, there *is* limited language to assess or analyze these works. Nonetheless, Adams's surfaces are the result of an enormous amount of precompositional planning, there *are* "dissonant" pitches and, in reality, the compositions do not emerge fully formed from an algorithm. Like any other genre of music, constraints guide compositional choices, decisions are made, and revisions are undertaken before the work reaches its final form and, in some instances, this process continues even after a work's premiere.

Layers

The surface of these compositions consists of different musical entities layered atop each other. As in Bruckner, individual strata are defined primarily by their rhythmic profile.

Figure 10.1a, chosen randomly as representative of the color field works, is from the 2006 revision of *for Jim (rising)*, scored for three trumpets and three trombones.[3] At first glance, the score shows what appear to be arpeggiations at different speeds: reading from the top, the first trumpet arpeggiates a B♭-major triad in septuplet half notes; the second a G-major triad in half-note triplets; the third an E-major triad in half-note quintuplets. The trombones also arpeggiate: the first, a C-major triad in half notes; the second, a G-major triad in whole-note triplets; and the third, a C-major triad in whole notes. Each pitch of the arpeggio has the same duration; the final pitch of the arpeggio is held longer. Together, the vertical relations do not yield any sort of a standard progression; instead it appears as if several overtone series unfold simultaneously: vertical sonorities should be understood as incidental simultaneities, not as chords.

Using linear harmonic content or tuplet / non-tuplet-type, the instrument(s) can be grouped into four strata: Trumpet 1; Trumpet 3; Trumpet 2 and Trombone 2; Trombone 1 and Trombone 3. Of the strata consisting of more than one member, Trombone 3 is at half the speed of Trombone 1 and Trombone 2 is at half the speed of Trumpet 2. A common meter, 4/4, and coordinating tempo, 80 bpm, unite the various layers. These unifying factors are only notational conveniences, however; as with harmony, the rhythmic elements are separate, placed atop one another.

Rather than being understood in relation to an unmarked quarter note (at 80 bpm), these tuplets are shorthand notation for proportionally related tempi. Specifically, in this excerpt a triplet quarter note is not meant to articulate a duration equal to two-thirds that of an unmarked quarter note. Instead, the large triplet is a notational convenience for a tempo that is one and one-half

FIGURE 10.1A

FIGURE 10.1B

times as fast as the tempo articulated by the unmarked quarter note. Thus in Figure 10.1a, the various tuplets articulate tempos, united by a coordinating tempo (that conducted by the conductor), rather than a common meter. The metronomic regularity of pitch change emphasizes these tempo relationships: within a coordinating tempo of quarter note = 80, the individual lines articulate (reading from the bottom of the score upwards) the tempos 20, 30, 40, 50, 60, and 70 beats per minute respectively. Inspired perhaps by Cowell's suggestion in *New Musical Resources*,[4] Adams uses tempo relationships as an analogue for harmonic relationships, here: 2:3:4:5:6:7 (Figure 10.1b). With this in mind we can see that what really unites the layers is not a 4/4 meter or a tempo of 80 bpm, but an unsounded "fundamental" tempo of 10 bpm (the equivalent of the double whole note); each individual layer relates to this fundamental tempo.[5]

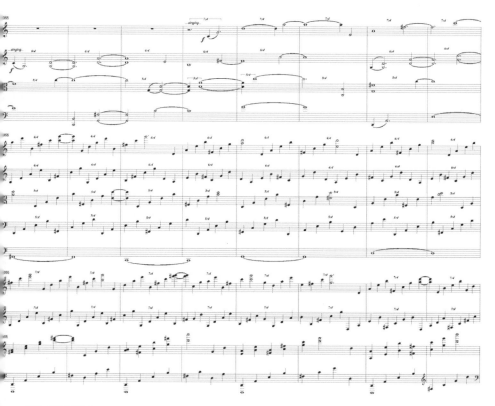

FIGURE 10.2

In Adams's other color field works harmonically related tempo schemes are similarly employed; to date, the most complex realizations are found in the installation works: *Veils*, in particular.

Playing Types

Beyond the rhythmic regularity and layering of tempo, there is a further characteristic of the strata. First, the line of the phrases is unidirectional: they arpeggiate upwards, reaching a high point before beginning again at the bottom. Second, pitches change with a metronomic regularity. These two characteristics are essential components of the arpeggiated style, one of four textures / playing types used in the color field works. Compare Figure 10.1a with Figure 10.2, from 2003's *for Lou Harrison* for solo string quartet, string orchestra, and two pianos.

Again layers are defined by tuplet relation, that is, speed: septuplets in the first piano; sextuplets in the orchestral violins; quintuplets in the orchestral violas and celli; quarter notes in the second piano and double whole notes in

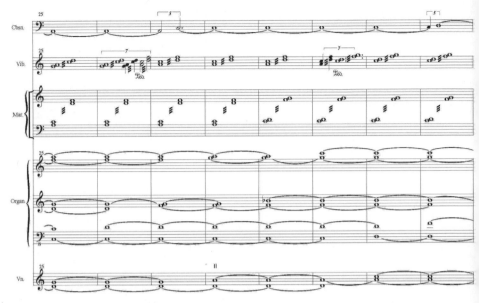

FIGURE 10.3. *The Light That Fills the World* (chamber version), mm. 25–32.

the orchestral bass. The solo strings, while utilizing normative quarter and tuplet species, have a mix of note values as do, to a lesser extent, the other instruments. (Note the half note tuplets at the culmination of the repeated figure in the right hand of the first piano). The shape of the melodies is also different from those of *for Jim (rising)*. Instead of repeated "(rising)" vectors, these tend to be repeated "tilde" (~) shapes. (See, for instance, the second solo violin line from 355–60.) These two subtle differences—a change in shape and a slackening of metronomic regularity in individual rhythms—are the hallmark of the second playing style used in the color field works: the singing style. Note as well the playing direction in the two violin parts at the top of the score: "… singing … ."

Figure 10.3 demonstrates the third playing style: the sustaining style, here in all instruments; again layers are individuated by tempi. As in the arpeggiated style, pitch change is metronomic and melodic shape tends to be unidirectional. The difference between the arpeggiated and sustained styles is that in the sustained style individual pitches tend to be held for longer periods and arpeggiations tend be of bands of pitches rather than individual pitches—an analogue would be slowly moving a cluster of pitches up an organ keyboard. Because of its dependence on pitch bands, the sustaining style is usually found in chordal and sustaining instruments: organs, string ensembles, mallet percussion, and tremolo piano.

When the sustaining style is assigned to an instrument that does not traditionally sustain (such as the piano), a fourth mode of playing, the "hammered" or "drumming" style, is sometimes used. In *Among Red Mountains*, rather than using tremolo, Adams rearticulates each piano chord several times in order to sustain pitches for a longer period than is physically possible: as each attack decays, the chord is restruck.[6] This "drumming" style is indebted to the indigenous drumming techniques referenced in many of Adams's "Alaskan" works, notably both versions of *Saugyatugvik: The Time of Drumming* (orchestral version: 1995; chamber version: 1996) and the multiple bass drum composition *Qilyaun* (1998).

Tempo layers are a priori and continuous throughout the color field pieces. When playing style changes, it tends to enhance the structure of a work. Lengthier compositions, especially those pieces that Adams refers to as "landscapes,"[7] sometimes alternate sections that privilege an arpeggiated style with those that privilege a singing style. Tying these two styles together is the sustaining ground. Instruments are often assigned to a particular playing style for the entirety of a piece or section of music.

Pitch

The primary colors of these pieces result from the saturation of a fixed collection of pitches, or gamut. Sometimes a single gamut will sound for the entirety of a piece, in other instances gamuts change with each section to provide a sort of narrative development. Adams's gamuts are of three types: gamuts built from the bottom up and made up of interval sequences duplicated at a particular distance, usually the octave ("spectral gamuts"); gamuts built from the bottom up without octave duplication of groups of pitches; and gamuts built from the center outward; the composer calls the last of these "butterflies."[8] Usually, gamuts are derived from a series of alternating intervals (for example: minor second, major third, minor second, major third, etc.) above a particular pitch. Gamuts can be twisted or modified to fit presumably more important musical parameters, such as pentatonic, hexatonic, or septatonic limits in *for Lou Harrison*; a desire to begin on the pitch "D" in *The Immeasurable Space of Tones*; or a wish to avoid a particularly potent and/or discordant interval or sound.[9] By limiting his gamuts in these ways, Adams is able to avoid monotonous and predictable pitch choice.

On the large scale, *for Lou Harrison* is structured as the alternation of arpeggiating sections and singing sections. Each section uses a different, though nonexclusive, gamut and both methods of bottom-up gamut formulation are evident. Unlike *Clouds of Forgiving, Clouds of Unknowing*, whose gamuts expand their interval content from seconds to octaves as the piece progresses, the

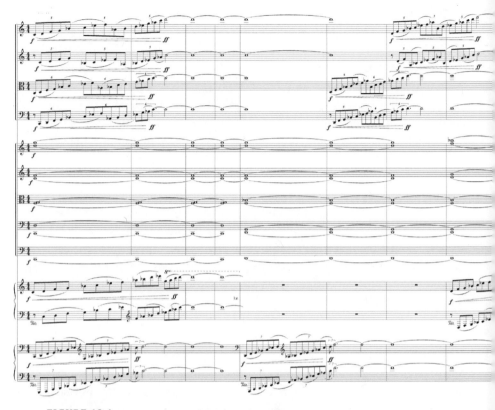

FIGURE 10.4

gamuts of *for Lou Harrison* do not themselves create a directed motion from beginning to end.

Figure 10.4 shows the opening of *for Lou Harrison*. We see the rhythmic strata and can note the arpeggiated style in the solo strings and pianos; at this point, the orchestral strings use the sustaining style.[10] Each of the strata plays the pitch series [C, D, F, G, B♭, C, E♭, F, A♭, B♭, D, E♭, G, A♭, C, D] in metronomic rhythms and proportionally related tempi.[11] This is the gamut for the opening section of the work and it is heard, essentially every pitch always, for the full duration of this section: nearly ten minutes.

Although the gamut of A1 utilizes the pitches of a C natural minor or E♭ major scale, classing it as one or the other forces it into a suit that doesn't fit. Compressing the pitch material within an octave ignores the way these pitch sets are used: the gamuts are relatively fixed in register based on the tessiturae of individual instruments. To get a sense of the richness of the whole, imagine an ensemble of harps of varying sizes whose non-gamut strings have been removed.

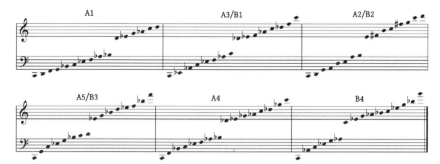

FIGURE 10.5. Gamuts in *for Lou Harrison*.

for Lou Harrison utilizes both spectral gamuts and simple gamuts. Both types are constructed from intervallic series and altered as necessary to keep them within a five, six, or seven-pitch collection. Thus, gamut A1 seems to be built from chains of fourths a whole step distant, with Db altered to D in order to fit a seven-tone collection:

TABLE 10.2

	D		G		C		F		Bb		Eb		Ab		D
C		F		Bb		Eb		Ab		D		G		C	
C	D	F	G	Bb	C	Eb	F	Ab	Bb	D	Eb	G	Ab	C	D

Linearly it is understood as the alternation of species of seconds and thirds:

TABLE 10.3

M2		M2		M2		M2		M2		m2		m2		M2	
C	D	F	G	Bb	C	Eb	F	Ab	Bb	D	Eb	G	Ab	C	D
	m3		m3		m3		m3		M3		M3		M3		

The spectral gamut B3/A5 is different. It is composed of an intervallic sequence—alternating fifths and minor sixths—duplicated at the octave, twelfth, double octave, and double octave plus a fifth:

TABLE 10.4

									G		D			Bb	F
						C			G			Eb		Bb	
				G			D			Bb			F		
		C		G				Eb		Bb					
C	G		Eb		Bb										
C	G	C	Eb	G	Bb	C	D	Eb	G	Bb	D	Eb	F	Bb	F

FIGURE 10.6a and b. *Nunataks*: (a) m. 19; (b) m. 27.

This second mode of constructing bottom-up gamuts is related to the idea of rhythmic layers: as a "fundamental" with overtones. In gamut B3/A5 the "fundamental" is the sonority C-G-E♭-B♭ (or more abstractly, the intervallic pattern P5-m6-P5) duplicated at four of the first five harmonic partials; in essence, outlining a harmonic spectrum of this composite fundamental.

The remarkable solo piano work *Nunataks* of 2007 uses "butterfly" gamuts in its intermittent arpeggiations. Essentially, these gamuts are symmetrical chord formations around a particular pitch or dyad. Figure 10.6a spreads the interval sequence M2-m3-M2-P4 spreading from both sides of A♭; while 10.6b spreads the sequence P5-P5 from both sides of the dyad A♭/A. If spectral gamuts are a pitch analogue of tempo-harmonic strata, then butterfly gamuts are a pitch analogue for an axial formal-structural concept.

Narrative

Adams's melodic devices range from the more ordered techniques of arpeggiation, band shifting, chord inversion and its corollary, rotation, to more esoteric processes, such as melodicles and number games. Similar procedures inform his approach to rhythm.

As its name implies, arpeggiation is the presentation of the individual pitches of the gamut in sequence. Often this is the sole means of melodic writing for slow melodic bass instruments in the sustaining mode of playing. Among instruments at a quicker tempo, such as the pianos and solo strings of Figure 10.4, arpeggiation of the gamut can be combined with pitch rotation. Thus, piano 2 plays the entire sequence of pitches: 1–14; 1, 2 before rotating one step and playing the sequence again: 2–14; 1, 2, 3. This process continues throughout the opening section of *for Lou Harrison*.

Arpeggiation and rotation can also be seen in sustaining instruments, such

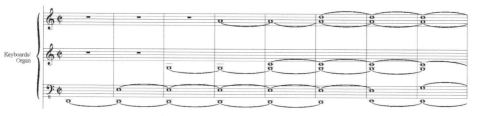

FIGURE 10.7

FIGURE 10.8

as the organ of *The Light that Fills the World*. The gamut of its opening strophe consists of alternating seconds and thirds restarting in the highest octave.

TABLE 10.5

D	E	G	A	C	D	F	G	Bb	C	D	E
1	2	3	4	5	6	7	8	9	10	1	2

Figure 10.7 demonstrates, in the six layers of the organ, a combination of arpeggiation and rotation of the gamut at a slow sustaining tempo. Figure 10.8 reduces the organ part of the entire first strophe of *The Light That Fills the World*. Separating the six layers and considering only their pitch classes demonstrates that each layer (with the exception of the uppermost) plays the gamut in sequence before reiterating its initial pitches.[12] Thus the left foot plays the pitch sequence 1–10, 1, 2; one measure later, the right foot begins the sequence 2–10, 1, 2, 3; the lower left hand plays 3–10, 1, 2, 3, 4 and so forth.

Adams also often uses a process related to rotation: gamut inversion. In this method, the gamut is treated like a triad and presented in a series of inversions, akin to turning an object around in one's hand to contemplate it from different perspectives. Unlike rotation, which begins the gamut on each pitch of the sequence, inversion begins the gamut at particular starting points. A good example is found in the celesta parts at Letter C of *In the White Silence*. From this point in the score, the gamut is first presented from its first pitch before being restated on its third, fifth, seventh, ninth, eleventh, and thirteenth pitches, respectively.

A melodic technique that Adams seems to have a special fondness for is

FIGURE 10.9. Gamut inversions: *In the White Silence*, celeste (mm. 116–27, rests removed).

FIGURE 10.10. *The Immeasurable Space of Tones*, piano pitches (mm. 471–524).

band shifting. In this technique, Adams takes the pitch gamut and filters out pitches above and below a certain segment; the segment is then shifted in a particular direction. This shifting can be within a frozen pitch palette or else a shift through the pitch-classes of the gamut. Often band shifting is used in mallet and tremolo instruments.

Gamut 4 of *The Immeasurable Space of Tones*, shown most clearly in the changing notes of the organ beginning at measure 439, alternates species of sixths with perfect fifths built on D; the contrabass instrument plays every other pitch of the series.

TABLE 10.6. *The Immeasurable Space of Tones*, Gamut 4 (first half).

D	B	F#	D	A	F#	C#	A	E	C#	G#	E	B	G#	D#	B	F#	D#	A#	F#	C#	A#	E♯

The piano in this section demonstrates band-shifting through the pitch classes of the gamut. Figure 10.10 shows the first eleven chords of the piano part beginning at measure 471.

Two aspects of this reduction are worth highlighting; they show Adams altering his system. First, the pitch D♯ in the second chord is outside of the gamut and represents a choice based on sound: the composer wished to avoid a clash with other sustaining instruments.[13] Second, the piano presents shifting segments of the full gamut: pitches 1–4 built as a chord are followed by pitches 3–7, 5–9 and so forth. This continues slowly rising through segments of the gamut until the full gamut has been presented. The choice of when to drop an

FIGURE 10.11

FIGURE 10.12. *Dream in White on White*, solo strings (mm. 53–58).

octave is determined primarily by piano/pianist limitations even though it may also have harmonic implications.

Band shifting through a fixed harmonic field can be seen in the percussion part of *The Light That Fills the World*, the pitches of which have been reduced in figure 10.11.

Conceiving of the gamut as a verticality, the percussion parts here move slowly upwards through the sequence (1–4; 2–5; 3–6 . . .) leaving off the lowest pitch with each new chord.

A more free technique of melodic development can be seen in the "Lost Chorale" sections of *Dream in White on White* (Figure 10.12). The entire section makes exclusive use of the seven pitch classes of the D-dorian mode: D-E-F-G-A-B-C. Repeated melodic fragments in expanding parallel intervals are combined in a mosaic canon, their pitches chosen by a game of numbers that however parsed appears as analytically capricious as it is compositionally intuitive. Using ordinal numbers for pitches of D-dorian, the Lost Chorales of measures 53–86 can be translated as follows:

TABLE 10.7

	3471		127134		5761		51345
	1256		564571		1324		62471
3471		127134		5761		51345	
1256		564571		1324		62471	

FIGURE 10.13. *Time Undisturbed*, flute (mm. 9–18).

FIGURE 10.14. *for Lou Harrison*, viola/cello (mm. 121–30).

The singing sections of *In the White Silence* are similarly inscrutable. Both seem to be clear examples of Adams composing.

While individual rhythms are usually metronomic, Adams also uses arpeggiation, algorithms, and arbitrary devices to determine rhythmic values. In the singing sections of *In the White Silence*, *Time Undisturbed*, and *Make Prayers to the Raven*, rhythmic values are determined by an additive series that is "arpeggiated" up and down.

Figure 10.13, from the Western instrument version of *Time Undisturbed*, shows an additive and subtractive series [1, 2, 3, 4, 5, 6, 5, 4, 3, 2, 1] of multiples of the normative duration (quintuplet-quarter) determining the rhythmic profile of the flute's arpeggiation of the pitch gamut.

In the singing sections of *for Lou Harrison*, the individual rhythms are controlled by a numeric series derived from taking the characteristic melodic tilde, stacking it vertically, numbering the pitches and "playing" the sequence in multiples of the normative duration (Table 10.8).

Adams exerts as much control on the macrocosmic level as he does on the microcosmic level, structuring time through two methods: either time is cordoned off and portioned, objects placed within it as in a mosaic, or time is cordoned off and divided, with objects hanging from a central axis. The first method owes a large debt to the work of John Cage. The second may be related to the fact that the quantity of overtones of a sound increases and then decreases with a swell in volume, but more likely is a consequence of Adams's predilection for symmetry. The first can be understood to represent objects in a bounded landscape, while the second is a more contemplative, ritually ordered space.[14] Examples of the Cage mosaic structure include the "A" sections of *for Lou Harrison*, the Lost Chorales of *Dream in White on White* and *In the White Silence* and the curious percussion trio *Always Very Soft*.

In this last work, three groups of undefined graduated percussion — metal,

TABLE 10.8

		F	8
		Db	7
6	C		
4	Ab	Ab	5
		F	3
2	Eb		
1	C		

TABLE 10.9. *Always Very Soft*, Time Segmentation (in measures).

1 — 36	37 — 72	73 — 108	109 — 144	145 — 180
1 — 45	46 — 90	91 — 135	136 — 180	
1 — 60	61 — 120	120 — 180		

glass or wood, and membrane—individually enact notated accelerations over the course of nine minutes, gradually rising in pitch as they accelerate. Table 10.9 shows the way in which the 180 measures of the composition are segmented in complementary ratios.

After deciding on the premise for the composition—three simultaneous proportionally related accelerations—a likely chronology for the construction of the piece would be as follows. First, Adams determined a number of measures that would yield the ratio desired (3:4:5), choosing, thus, from multiples of sixty measures. Likely the choice of 180 is a practical one; choosing either sixty or 120 measures would yield less friendly rhythmic values within the individual accelerations or else a shorter duration for the composition: three or six minutes, instead of nine. Once the division into 180 measures is set, the duration is segmented as in Table 10.9. From there Adams must plot out acceleration levels within the time spans. He chooses an acceleration based on note values, beginning at a double whole note, eliminating quarters linearly before reaching the whole note (7-6-5-4). He then eliminates eighth notes to reach the half note (again 7-6-5-4) before increasing the number of impulses per measure from two to thirty. The corresponding tempo acceleration is from 10 bpm to 600 bpm. The accelerations are slightly different in each part though their beginnings (10 bpm) and ends (600 bpm) are the same.

In choosing at which points to move to another level, the composer's hand is evident; certain levels are held onto slightly longer than others (perhaps to ease in coordination) and in the uppermost layer, the stages between double whole note and whole note are eliminated entirely. From the standpoint of establishing Adams's approach to structure, this piece evidences the ways that time is

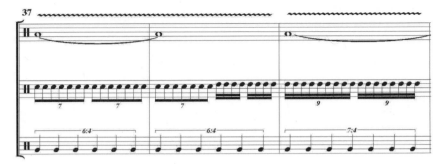

FIGURE 10.15. *Always Very Soft*, mm. 37–39.

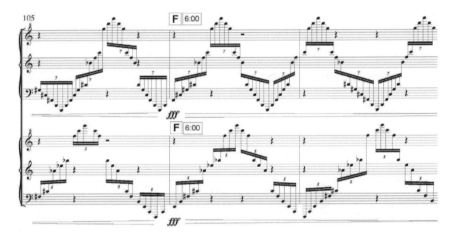

FIGURE 10.16. *Dark Waves* (two-piano version), central axis (mm. 105–7).

segmented and segmented again in order to place individual events within bounded spans.

Axial form also involves the segmenting of time. While mosaic structures place items within a duration, axial structures place items around a central moment. In some cases these central points are not one explicit timepoint, but rather an entire section of music. When axial forms are found within a section, we can point to a particular moment from which the entire ensemble hangs. Clear instances of axial forms can be found in the B sections of *for Lou Harrison* as well as in, among others, the orchestral and two piano versions of *Dark Waves*.

The structural foundation of *Dark Waves* is two simultaneous series of amplitude waves. The twelve-minute work is built around a central axis at which point both waves crest at the dynamic *fff* (measure 106).

TABLE 10.10

Timepoint	1			88	144				424				704	760	
Piano 1	64	24		56	70	42	62	106	106	62	42	70	56	24	64
Piano 2	88			56	40	60	60	50	70	70	50	60	60	40	56	88

Around this axis Adams builds a symmetrical duration series articulated by amplitude envelopes. Table 10.10 demonstrates this symmetry by noting the intervals between timepoints (in quarter notes) of the high and low points of each amplitude wave.

The central structural axis of *Dark Waves* is at timepoint 424 (measure 106: 6:00) with subsidiary structural pillars found at timepoints 88 (measure 22: 1:12), 144 (measure 36: 2:00), 704 (measure 176: 10:00) and 760 (measure 190: 10:48). Of these the structural dissonance is strongest at timepoints 144 and 760, owing to the great discrepancy between the dynamic levels (*f* and *ppp*, respectively) of the layers. With one exception these amplitude envelopes also determine the change of tuplet division of the beat: a sequence that is also symmetrical around the central axis.[15]

Large Scale Form and Working Within It

With these structural principles enumerated, we can see how Adams organizes his color field pieces on the largest scale. Here again symmetry plays an enormous role, whether in a symmetrical alternation of individual elements and/or sections, or else through large-scale interval expansion within the gamuts: given a belief in inversion, this, too, is symmetrical.

The overall structure of the seventy-minute *In the White Silence* (1993) is the alternation of three different types of music: harmonic clouds with scales (sustaining-arpeggiating: A), chorales (singing: B), and wave-like lyrical sections (singing: C). These are arranged as follows:

TABLE 10.11

ABA	C	ABA	C	ABA	C	ABA	C	ABA

The structure creates a nice symmetry around the central chorale (measure 557–612), as well as an alternation of sustaining and singing textures.

The section of *In the White Silence* beginning at Letter D of the score (corresponding to the first C section of Table 10.11) demonstrates how Adams plays with his structure to maintain the forward momentum of the work. Within the lyrical C sections each solo instrument enters in turn, joins in song, and leaves. The continuous ascending/descending arpeggios that begin in the

FIGURE 10.17. *In the White Silence*, mm. 205–12.

unaccompanied celesta and spread to the full ensemble further emphasize this symmetry. Throughout the section, the ensemble is divided into four strata, each consisting of a singing instrument and an arpeggiating instrument and differentiated by their tempi: quarters, quintuplets, sextuplets, and septuplets at 80 bpm, a 4:5:6:7 tempo ratio related to a fundamental tempo of 20 bpm. Given the pervasive symmetry, it is likely that the entire section would be centered on an axis. In reality, the individual parts seem to employ more of a mosaic structure. On a subconscious level, this tension between axial form and mosaic form signals to the listener the necessity of continuation; the symmetry may be restored on the larger level.

Looking closer, the arpeggiating instruments (vibraphones 1 and 2, celesta and harp) play the expanding gamut in metronomic rhythm, while the singing instruments (the solo quartet) play the same up-and-down arpeggiating pitch

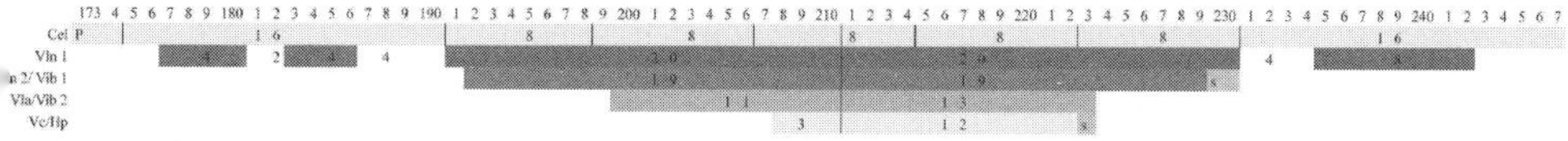

FIGURE 10.18

sequence to a rhythm derived from variants of the additive series [1 + 2 + 3 + 4 + 5 + 6 + 7]: 56, two times the perfect number 28, the sum of the series, is the magic number for this section.[16]

The foundation of this section is the duo celesta/violin 1; the other duos are built atop it to create a sense of incomplete symmetry. Figure 10.18 shows the points of entry and exit within the section.

After a two-measure presentation of the gamut, the celesta begins at measure 175; it will play for seventy-two measures. In this light the central point of this section is located between measures 210 and 211; both violins hang from this measure (violin 2 like the cello ends with a measure of notated sustain). In this context, then, the viola/vibraphone 2 and cello/harp layers enter late. The symmetry is further subverted with the closing bookend violin melody beginning at measure 235, which does not match the opening bookend violin melody at 177. On a larger scale, the broken symmetry of this section creates an expectancy in the listener that symmetry may be restored in the final C section of the work.

The second movement of 2007's *Three High Places* also shows the composer's hand at work subverting a strict axial form. Structurally, this movement for solo violin centers on a repeated figure that swells to fortissimo at measure 14. From this point six-note figures branch in both directions in a palindrome of groups, not pitches. The groups themselves come from exploration of the gamut of fifths built on G, duplicated at the octave. While the pitch outline follows a formal algorithm, the dynamics, particularly in the measures following the climax, are asymmetrical. Comparing measure 11 with its structural complement at measure 17 shows this disjunction (Figure 10.19).

The genesis of *The Light That Fills the World* provides a telling insight into Adams's compositional priorities and decisions. The work went through two versions before reaching its published form. After its premiere Adams changed the gamut, feeling that the original gamut was "too predictable." In revision, Adams would stumble on the idea of superimposing a seven-pitch collection over the chromatic field, an idea he would explore further in *The Immeasurable Space of Tones.*[17]

Version two differs from the published version in many ways, most tellingly in its length: it is shorter by 78 measures. Both version two and the published version are in six sections, each defined by its gamut and tempo relationships,

FIGURE 10.19A

FIGURE 10.19B

and both are built around a destabilized central axis. Although the intervals used to create the gamuts expand from seconds through sevenths before culminating in octaves, the tempo relationships are symmetrical around the axis. Tables 10.12a and 10.12b show the relationship of tempo layers in this version of the work and the published version.

The major difference is the duration and entry of the violin and contrabassoon in the opening and closing sections as well as details of the destabilized center. With the revision of the length of the opening and closing sections (in the second version, each is half the duration of the published version) the sustaining organ part was reconceived. In the second version, rather than treating its gamut as six separate canonic layers, as described above, it is understood as a shifting series of pitches (i.e. 1, 2, 3, 4, 5, 6; 3, 4, 5, 6, 7, 8; 5, 6, 7, 8, 9, 10; . . .).

I mention this revision as a way of getting at several of Adams's compositional priorities that have been evident in my analysis throughout. First, on a structural level, the revision changes from a pyramidal form, symmetrical around a central axis—ABC|CBA—to a corbelled form, symmetrical around a central axis and with two subsidiary axes: ABA|ABA. Second, as in *In The White Silence* there is both a hierarchy of and roles for the instruments. In this light, instrumental roles and hierarchies are more important than the placement of the instruments in time: in both versions, the organ is a sustaining ground and it is to it that all other instruments are related. Finally, Adams is trying to achieve a specific sound: the gamut was changed from a more predictable gamut to a more complicated gamut and pitch-classes were limited to a subset of the chromatic field.

Many composers of the post–World War II generation have tried to remove

TABLE 10.12a. Duration Relationships: *The Light That Fills the World*, Second Version.

Contrabassoon	12/5	32/5	24/5			24/5	32/5	12/5
Violin	6/4	16/4	12/4	Destabilized		12/4	16/4	6/4
Marimba	12/3	16/3	12/3	Center		12/3	16/3	12/3
Vibraphone	24/7	32/7	24/7			24/7	32/7	24/7

TABLE 10.12b. Published Version.

Contrabassoon	24/5	32/5	24/5			24/5	32/5	24/5
Violin	12/4	16/4	12/4	Destabilized		12/4	16/4	12/4
Marimba	12/3	16/3	12/3	Center		12/3	16/3	12/3
Vibraphone	24/7	32/7	24/7			24/7	32/7	24/7

themselves from the compositional process, whether through relying on performers' intuition, chance, algorithm, or serial techniques. No matter what is used, however, as long as there is something composed, whether verbal instruction or pitch instruction, on paper or orally, the composer is still involved, from choosing the materials to prioritizing certain parameters over others. In cases where the musical language is personal, it takes concerted effort to find meaning in that language. By exploring the elements that together combine to form his environments and the ways they bond into greater wholes, I have attempted to open up the grammar of Adams's particular musical language. John Luther Adams has worked to perfect his Arctic soundscapes for more than a decade, seeking to create a music that reflects the place it comes from and that, in its sensuous concretion of number, aims to limit the role of the composer and recreate the very conditions that govern placeness. This trend might cause us to look at Adams as a non-composer—perhaps, more mystically, as a "channeller"—but looking carefully at his compositions reveals his creative hand at work.

Notes

1. ". . . a contemplative evocation of the vast, stark landscape of the Great North" in "Review of Clouds of Forgetting, Clouds of Unknowing," *Billboard* (February 21, 1998); "long, sustained harmonies, with puffs of Arctic winds blowing the sound one way or another" in Alan Rich, "The Adams Family" *L.A. Weekly* (November 14, 2002). For better or for worse, Adams's website (http://www.johnlutheradams.com) quotes any number of other such reviews: "a translucent ecstasy," Mike Dunham, *Anchorage Daily News*; "Adams' music sounds like it has nothing to accomplish. It simply exists, hanging in mid-air, waiting to be listened to," *The All Music Guide*; "amazingly beautiful, peaceful, and reflective," *Chamber Music Magazine*; there are many others.

2. I take a similar approach in my analysis of *for Lou Harrison*: "Wayfinding in John

Luther Adams's *for Lou Harrison"* Perspectives of New Music 47, no. 2 (Summer 2009) 196–227.

3. The original version (subsequently withdrawn) of *for Jim (rising)* appeared in *Perspectives of New Music* 25, no. 1/2 (Summer 1987) 447–54.

4. In a forthcoming article I take up the process of exploring harmonic progressions through tempo in certain of Adams's works. On Cowell, see Henry Cowell, *New Musical Resources*, with notes and an accompanying essay by David Nicholls (Cambridge, New York: Cambridge University Press, 1996), 49ff.

5. There is perhaps a relation here to Rameau's theory of the fundamental bass, which suggests that every interval is generated by some fundamental sound that may or may not coincide with its lowest pitch. For a clear explanation see Thomas Christensen, *Rameau and Musical Thought in the Enlightenment* (Cambridge: Cambridge University Press 1993), 90ff.

6. A similar playing style is found in Adams's recent *Four Thousand Holes* (2010). Although both these works feature the piano, the "drumming" style is not limited to this instrument.

7. *Night Peace* (1977); *A Northern Suite* (1979–80/2004); *The Far Country of Sleep* (1988); *Dream in White on White* (1992); *Clouds of Forgetting, Clouds of Unknowing* (1991–95); *In the White Silence* (1998); *In a Treeless Place, Only Snow* (1999); *Time Undisturbed* (1999) and *for Lou Harrison* (2003). Conversation with author, February 2, 2009. Adams's categorization seems to correspond to works that have distinct sections.

8. Email to author: August 6, 2008. "Years ago I made sketches for gamuts expanding from a central tone. I called them 'butterflies.'"

9. See Gamut 5 of *Immeasurable Space* (beginning at measure 647) for the replacement of two pitches at the bottom of a gamut: the organ plays the proper gamut while the contrabass instrument replaces the lowest two pitches; another example is the use of D♯ and A♯ in the violin and vibraphone in Gamut 4 of the same work. (See measure 480 and others.)

10. One might ask why the solo strings are understood to be in the arpeggiating style rather than the singing given their octave drops within arpeggios. Here, Adams bends to instrument reality: if the strings were able to play the full range of pitches in the arpeggiated gamut without an octave shift, there would be no octave drops. The held notes at the end of each sweep are notated sustains.

11. Here there are five, reading from the bottom of the score up: Piano 2; Piano 1; Orchestral Strings; Solo Cello and Viola; Solo Violins.

12. The uppermost layer is, in fact, playing the pitches of the gamut as they exist in that octave. That is to say, in this highest octave the gamut continues to duplicate the fundamental of the gamut: here, D-E-G-A-C-D.

13. Adams recalls that he wanted a more diatonic sound within the chromatic complement and so limited pitch choice after a certain limit. Email to author: February 16, 2009. "Although I wanted the piece as a whole to encompass the full chromatic field, I wanted each individual section (and each moment to moment sound) to be diatonic."

14. Some works seem to display a third method of formal structure, like a mobile, though it is likely that this appearance is deceptive, instead masking a form similar to

one of the two previously described. In some cases, for instance *Nunataks*, without seeing the composer's sketches it may prove very difficult to unravel the underlying structure. It appears to consist of several structures laid atop each other; like the mountains
of its title, these structures poke through each other at certain points.

15. In Piano I the central envelope bookends septuplets with sextuplets; the final
measure of the work is a part of the scheme although the diminuendo does not reach to
its final beat.

16. While it is perhaps coincidental, 56 is also the magic number of Dufay's ceremo-
nial isorhythmic motet *Nuper Rosarum Flores* (1436). Likely, the idea of a perfect number
appealed to both composers.

17. Email to author: February 28, 2009. "After hearing the first performances of 'The
Light,' I realized it was too predictable, that I needed to break the symmetry. So I decided
to limit myself to seven-tone gamuts. This gave me the idea of superimposing a seven-
tone limit over [a] chromatic field, which I explored for the first time in 'The Immeasurable Space of Tones.'"

11 * The Light Within

On a crisp autumn day sitting inside Meeting—[James] Turrell's
skyspace at PS1 in Queens, New York—I experienced my own epiphany
of light. From mid-afternoon through sunset into night, I was transfixed
by the magical interplay of light and color, above and within.

* JOHN LUTHER ADAMS, from notes to the
  orchestral score of *The Light Within*

He is sitting in a room that has had most of the ceiling cut away, watching the play of artificial lighting on the gallery wall against the subtly changing color of the sky. Out of this period of quiet observation, a process probably only ever fully understood by the composer is set in motion, and from this encounter with light will come an impression in sound: *The Light Within*.

John Luther Adams has long taken the time to sit and listen and wait for the music in his surroundings. The songs of birds, the weight of ice, and the richness and power of the aurora borealis across the night sky feed his imagination. Though his home state of Alaska may provide the most iconic and frequent source material, Adams's work is not landscape painting but an aural expression of a very personal experience of place.

For *The Light Within*, scored for a small ensemble or full orchestra (depending on the version) and an electronic "aura" track, Adams takes the visual interplay between two migrating sources of light and transforms it into moving harmonic fields. The live performers are also amplified so that the full range of sounds can fully meld and envelop the audience in a saturated aural experience.

When the music begins, it is an exhalation. The clarinet, bassoon, and brass launch a drone of solid color, accented by the rolling glimmer of the percussion. This is no overwhelming wave of sound threatening to unmoor the listener, however, but a total embrace of vibration. The drone is not static, but a breathing mix of live performers and electronically processed sounds. It feels solid, like a strong wind that holds your weight when you lean into it. The various instrumental lines move within this cloud of sound, occasionally brushing the surface, ornamented by the piano's freely arpeggiated material which plays around and through it. The horizon changes ever so incrementally without flagging in intensity for just shy of twelve solid minutes. And then, with a final pitch sounding from the percussion, piano, and lower strings, everything that has been displayed is sharply inhaled and swallowed away again, leaving behind only the aural memory of tones. It's as if it isn't the music that has entered and left the frame but that the listener's ear has simply raised and lowered the volume on a never-ending sonic event.

In a sense, much of Adams's work blends into a sort of metaphorical stream of continuous sound, though he sees particularly strong links between *The Light Within* and previous compositions such as *The Light That Fills the World*, *Dark Waves*, and *Red Arc/Blue Veil*. He spoke about these pieces, how they fit into his larger catalog, and addressed some of the deeper motivations behind his output during a conversation we had on a warm spring evening in Central Park (transcribed below).

It would be easy to get lost in the romance of the backstory that has grown up around Adams, a composer inextricably tied up in postcard-ready images of the powerful natural beauty that surrounds him. And in a way he has embraced that, writing publicly about his experiences hiking through remote areas of Alaska and advocating passionately to protect them from the ever-increasing onslaught of environmental threats. But remarkably, this awe-inspiring landscape does not overwhelm his own voice; instead, it always delivers him back to what he knows is his primary work—the quite solitary, introspective task of putting notes on paper. It's actually while standing on a busy Manhattan street corner that he finally distills our hours of conversation and a lifetime of experience down to this core fact. "I can't even imagine not doing it," he says. "Music is the thing that gives my life meaning."

*   *   *

April 2, 2010—5 p.m.
Central Park, New York City
Condensed and edited by Molly Sheridan

MOLLY SHERIDAN: Before we look more carefully at how you built *The Light Within*, can we go back to the more personal moments when the idea for the work first took root? When you think now about the genesis of the piece, what images and stories come to mind?

JOHN LUTHER ADAMS: Sure. That's easy. It was fall, maybe October of 2006. I was visiting here in New York City and went over to P.S. 1 to experience a piece by an artist I really admire, James Turrell. This is one of his sky spaces. The piece is titled *Meeting*, after the Quaker meeting houses. Turrell himself is a Quaker, and he's designed several meeting houses for Quaker congregations.

I had never been in one of these sky spaces, so I just spent the afternoon in this place. It's a small room with a hole in the ceiling straight through to the sky. When you walk in, there's kind of a pale yellow ambient light around the room, benches all the way around the perimeter, and this opening to the sky . . . a window with no glass in it. And you just sort of settle in and steep yourself in the light. And over the course of the hours, the light within and the light without change their relationship. The colors change, and the intensities of the light change. The day I was there, it was particularly magical around sunset. The artificial light in the room and the changing light of the sky came into perfect equipoise and just fused into this single field of floating color that you feel as though you could reach out and touch. But of course you can't. You can't tell where it is. It's a really magical space. Out of that experience came *The Light Within*.

I didn't realize it at the time, but it turns out to be the introverted twin of an earlier piece called *The Light that Fills the World*. The original instrumentation for *The Light Within* was just six instruments and electronic tracks, but just this last month I've completed a version of it for a chamber orchestra with electronic tracks.

MS: How does it change the philosophy or the psychology of the piece, then, when it starts out as such a small, intimate thing and then you sort of blow it up?

JLA: The truthful answer is—it doesn't change because it was an orchestral piece in my mind from the get-go. The original version of the *The Light Within* was commissioned by the Seattle Chamber Players and the California E.A.R. Unit. The Chamber Players is a quartet—they have flute, clarinet, violin, and cello. And I tried and tried and just couldn't wrap my mind around that instrumentation. I wanted a bigger sound. So I asked them, "Would it be okay if I included electronic tracks?," which I've been doing in a lot in my recent pieces—mixing acoustic instruments with electronic sounds. And they said sure, that would be fine. I started to work, and then I asked them, "Would it be okay if I added percussion and piano?" And they said, "Well, you know, that's not really what we had in mind, but okay." And that fit the E.A.R. Unit's instrumentation, so the E.A.R. Unit signed onto the project.

That was the original form of the piece: six instruments and electronic sounds. But even so, it's orchestral in conception. So when I had an invitation from the American Composers Orchestra to do an orchestration of the piece, I leaped at it and really composed the piece that I was trying to compose in the first place.

MS: Can you *ever* resist adding percussion?

JLA: Have I done anything without percussion? Or have I done anything worthy without percussion? It's hard to resist! You know, I guess it's kind of my piano. I rely on it a lot, in part because I understand it more physically than I do any other instrument or set of instruments because I was a percussionist. But I think it's also because percussion is such a rich and varied medium. Are we talking about a drum set, or a marimba, or guiro and slapstick? You know, there are just so many percussion instruments that it's a very rich palette. I often find that I can't resist it because it's just so useful.

MS: When you think, "Man, that's useful!" In what way? For what?

JLA: Color. That would be one answer. I tend to think of sounds in terms of color, whether it's harmonic colors or timbres—instrumental colors, as we often say—or some more elusive sense of color or texture or tactile surface. The physicality of the sound really appeals to me. That doesn't necessarily mean loud, or big even, although a lot of my music is full. It saturates the tonal space. I've also done very quiet, very delicate pieces. But there's something about the physicality of not just percussion, but the physicality of music itself that I love.

MS: So much of your work can be traced to this experience of physically being in a place, probably most often somewhere in your home state of Alaska. When it comes to *The Light Within*, however, we're talking about inspiration stemming not from the scope and power of that landscape, but of light as experienced in this New York City gallery space. But again, you mark the *place* as the starting point. When you need to begin work on a new piece, do you look for a place like that to begin? Or does it just happen?

JLA: I guess it just happens, and I don't know how or why. I'm probably looking without knowing that I'm looking. It's so much a part of the way I experience the world that I can't get around it. But I think that's true for all of us.

MS: When you're in that space, what are you really processing at that point? In the end, the music is not a narrative, but it's not strictly an ambient piece, either, in the traditional sense of the term.

JLA: Yeah, it's a deeper response to a very specific experience. I'm provoked by something—by a work of art, by something I read, by the death of someone I love, by camping in an extraordinarily beautiful place. Something happens, and it's powerful. And then, after it's over, I try to figure out what that experience meant—or what it *might* mean—and music is the best way I know to do that.

You know, I carry a little notebook that has musical staves in it, and so I'm always jotting notes down. Oftentimes, I'll start with a drawing. I'm a terrible sketcher, but a lot of my work aspires to what Kyle Gann and, before him, Aaron Copland called the sounding image. I can almost hear the whole piece at once, somewhere in my peripheral hearing. Or I imagine I can, like it's just over there on the other side of that hill, and I can almost hear it. And sometimes part of trying to get in touch with that is trying to draw it. Trying to make a picture of it on paper.

MS: We've already spoken briefly about how *The Light Within* is connected inversely to *The Light That Fills the World*, but you mentioned to me in an email, and I wrote this down so I wouldn't forget, that *Dark Waves* and *Red Arc/Blue Veil* are also "clearly related, at least to me."

And I want to dig around in that "at least to me," because listeners find their own connections in your music—often, it seems, some variation on the phrase "shimmering and impressionistic landscapes"—but how do *you* characterize the connection?

JLA: You know, that's my favorite thing—when a listener hears something that I haven't heard, that I didn't know was in the music. Ultimately, that's what we hope for: That someone else takes the music and makes it their own and that there's more to discover in the music than the composer understands.

But from my perspective, I think with all those pieces I was after a kind of immersion in a saturation of color and texture and the physical presence of the sound. They're all immersion experiences. And I'm also interested in turning that inside out. Rather than concentrating the sound and concentrating the listener's awareness right here, dispersing the sound and focusing the listener's awareness outwards.

All of the pieces you've mentioned began almost like Rothko paintings—just these big forms, these colors, these juxtapositions, these sizes and weights. *The Light Within* is essentially two harmonic fields: one that you might say represents the interior light, the light within; the other represents the exterior light, the light that fills the world. The interior light is composed of perfect fourths and the exterior is perfect fifths, and the whole piece is just this rising and falling of those two harmonic fields and the ebbing and flowing of their dynamic levels: their relationships to one another and those moments, when they come, when they fuse into a more complex chromatic field.

MS: Is there then a relationship not just in philosophy between *The Light that Fills the World* and *The Light Within*, but in terms of things you might point out in the score?

JLA: No, the forms of the two pieces are different, though they both use similar harmonic material.

MS: The recordings had me flipping back and forth on that point, and my ears were telling me yes, but then no.

JLA: They're similar harmonic worlds, but they're not formally the same. In a way *Red Arc/Blue Veil* works a little more like *The Light Within*. And then there's *Dark Waves*. *The Light Within* is two harmonic fields, perfect fourths, perfect fifths, converging, diverging. *Dark Waves* is three harmonic waves, all perfect fifths, rising and falling in and out of phase, and then in the middle of the piece, cresting into this one huge tsunami. *Red Arc/Blue Veil* is two harmonic fields, but they're a little bit more complex. They rise and fall and converge in the middle. All these pieces share that. The harmonies are similar. The textures are similar, and the pieces are essentially single shapes. Each of those pieces I think of as one big complex sound.

One way that *The Light Within* and *Dark Waves* relate is that if you hear the orchestration of *The Light Within*, or if you look at the score of that orchestration side-by-side with the orchestral score of *Dark Waves*, they really look alike on the level of texture. It's a sound that I've been working toward in the orchestra for many years. But I don't get that many opportunities to work with orchestra. Not many of us do these days. And I think that's why I spent a year writing *Dark Waves*, because I thought, "How many opportunities am I going to get to write a piece for triple woodwinds symphony orchestra?" So I wanted to get that sound right. And I think I did find it in *Dark Waves*. But as I said, when I wrote the chamber version of *The Light Within*, I didn't really fulfill the commission. In essence I wrote a sketch for an orchestra piece.

MS: Are you satisfied with the recordings of these pieces, not in terms of the quality of the performances, but in terms of the actual experience—the spatialization of the sound and the visual cues of watching bows move and people breathe when it's done live?

JLA: I grew up with recordings, and that's how I learned music and how I discovered most of the music that I still love. There are things we can hear on recordings that we miss in live performance. So, you know, I don't strike any kind of philosophical stance on the issue of recordings versus live performance. Even so, particularly with a piece like *Dark Waves*—as good as, say, the recording of the Radio Netherlands Philharmonic Orchestra is—hearing it live is better because of exactly what you said. It's all around you. That piece, as much as anything I've done, is about being completely overwhelmed by the sound—being immersed in it and having it come crashing down on you, being lost at sea. And, like you said, getting the visual cues of seeing the bows move and watching players take breaths and seeing percussion mallets moving. I think that helps the listener hear more of the fine details. There's a lot going on in that piece that can sound like just a wash in a recording. But then in a piece like *Red Arc/Blue Veil*, there are wonderful things that happen acoustically and psycho-acoustically with difference tones and interference between the crotales and the piano and the electronic tracks that are intense in performance, but can be even more so listening to a recording through headphones.

So I think they're just different experiences, ultimately, and different aspects of the music come out. I like making recordings, even when they're flawed, which they always are. And with pieces like the ones we're talking about, I don't feel that a recording is in any way a pale copy of the thing itself.

MS: Actually, I was kind of surprised when I sat down to listen to all of these pieces again before this interview. I thought this was going to be an epic four-hour exercise, but they were each only about thirteen minutes long. For me, the pieces generated a false memory of time through their character.

JLA: I like that observation. They are brief, but large. That was something that I was exploring in these pieces after *Clouds*, *White Silence*, and *for Lou Harrison*. Those pieces for small orchestra are long. I wanted to try and do something short that at least suggested that scale, that weight.

You know, *Dark Waves* is only twelve minutes and I worked on it for a year — many, many drafts! And I think it and *The Light Within* are the two pieces in which I've most fully realized an aspiration that I keep talking about: to make a piece that is one sound. And so when someone says, "Oh, that was great, but it was too short!," it makes me think they got the one sound and that somehow the scale of the thing, the weight, the pacing, if you will, made sense and what I thought would be this overwhelming and maybe incomprehensible mass of sound, actually made some kind of sense to the ear. It works at some level. And that's really what I'm into these days. Not "Is it an elegant realization of my brilliant conception?," but "Does it work? Does it sound?"

MS: The gut analysis.

JLA: Yeah. Even though I'm still very much a formalist, and I like my drawings and my little sketches and schemes and processes, more and more I actually don't want you to hear that. Years ago, we were rehearsing *Earth and the Great Weather*. The rhythms are pretty complicated, and I'd grouped the notes in a certain way that reflected my thinking, but that really wasn't the clearest notation for the performers. And Amy Knoles, my good buddy who doesn't mince words, just said, "You know John, I don't want to see your process! Just tell me what to play." That was a great lesson. So it's no longer about the performers seeing my process, or the listener hearing my process. That's my responsibility, and I can enjoy solving the problems and take pride when I get it right, but that's not what music is about. The performers have enough to do without having to contend with how clever the composer is; listeners aren't there to be impressed with how clever the composer is. Listeners want to hear music that socks them in the gut.

MS: It seems like you take a lot of time building each piece.

JLA: Yeah, I'm slow. I'm slow.

MS: What is the tenor of that process? Is it a battle, a meditation? Is it anxiety inducing?

JLA: Yes. I think any question you could ask, the answer would be yes because it's so many different things. Is it obsessive behavior? Yes. Am I just slow? Yes. Am I a perfectionist? Yes.

MS: Do you have a fear of finishing?

JLA: No. But I like the continuing discovery. I like being surprised. I like realizing that, "Oh, I haven't really solved that. There's more. There's another layer." I especially like it when, as I am right now, I'm doing what I call foundation work on a new piece, which is the most difficult and the most crucial time in the process. So I think it's not so much fear of completion as it is a fear of not working.

MS: When you consider your work collectively, does it feel like one long piece in a sense?

JLA: Totally. I keep looking at ways to make a whole piece as one sound, as one breath. It almost feels like this whole life's work is one piece. I like that. It feels as though, without knowing it, when I started this with that first garage band rehearsal, I got lucky because this is something you can do for a whole lifetime and still never reach the end.

MS: Still, I feel like your natural curiosity could have pulled you in so many directions. So why make music the core of your life's work?

JLA: Fair question. I guess the short answer is it's my life's path; it's the central thing in my life. Music is what has given my life meaning and coherence and direction for the last, oh, forty-five years. Trying to figure out how to play the drum set when I was twelve feels like an awakening of something that has carried me ever since.

There are certainly other threads in my life that I could have followed. And I wouldn't even mind somehow working myself out of a job as a composer. It seems like maybe that's implicit in the direction of the work. But not too soon! Maybe, like, the day after I die I could stop being a composer.

Dave Herr

12 * Timbral Listening in *Dark Waves*

> *The melding of rhythm, pitch and timbre creates unified fields of*
> *sound. My objective is to leave these fields as untouched as possible,*
> *letting them fill time and space with forms and colors as simple and*
> *beautiful as they can be.*
>
> * JOHN LUTHER ADAMS, *The Place Where You Go to Listen* 3

Background

During the summer solstice in Fairbanks, Alaska, the day lasts nineteen hours and twenty-five minutes; during the winter solstice it lasts just three hours and forty-one minutes. Over the past decade, evocations of this dramatic contrast between light and darkness have become pervasive in the music of John Luther Adams, as evidenced by the titles of some of the composer's recent pieces: *The Light That Fills the World* (1999/2001), *After the Light* (2001), *Dark Wind* (2001), *The Light Within* (2007), *Sky with Four Suns and Sky with Four Moons* (2008). In his book *Winter Music*, Adams quotes Canadian composer and musicologist R. Murray Schafer as observing that, "In the special darkness of the northern winter . . . the ear is super-sensitized and the air stands poised to beat with the subtle vibrations of a strange tale or ethereal music." "I listen for that music," says Adams (*Winter Music* 9). "The light in the northern latitudes embodies colors and feelings that I've experienced in no other place. After living in Alaska for many years, I came to wonder whether I could somehow convey these colors and feelings in music. Beginning with *The Light That Fills the World* (1999/2001), in a series of works including *Dark Wind* (2001), *The Farthest Place* (2001–2), *the Immeasurable Space of Tones* (2002) and *Red Arc/Blue Veil* (2002), I pursued a music composed entirely of floating fields of color" (*The Place Where You Go to Listen* 2).

Indeed, *The Light That Fills the World*, *Dark Wind*, *The Farthest Place*, and *the Immeasurable Space of Tones* can all be seen as "lightscape" compositions—sonic equivalents of the natural cycles of light that occur in the atmosphere of Alaska, and universal characteristics of light itself. While these pieces share certain sonic similarities to earlier Adams works, they are unique in their conscious avoidance of obviously melodic content in exchange for the "color fields" of timbral composition.

In an analysis of one of Adams's earlier large-scale works, *Dream In White On White*, the musicologist Mitchell Morris makes a case for that piece's more melodic sections as representations of a subjective individual against the backdrop of a "natural" world: "The formal and affective structure of *Dream In White On White* reveals an oscillation between 'objective' evocations of the cold, sublime landscape and 'subjective' moments in which emotional reactions take the foreground of the music" (134). The composer is clearly aware of this "subjective" aspect of his music, and how, by eliminating melodic content, he is able to remove the notion of the individual from it: "If in the past, the melodic elements of the music have somehow spoken of my own subjective presence in the landscape, in the newer music there are no lines left—only slowly changing light on a timeless white field" (*Winter Music* 138). In place of melodic material, Adams achieves this effect of "slowly changing light" through the use of gradually evolving timbres and harmonies across a fixed structural backdrop.

Adams's choice to associate light with timbre seems completely natural, as the link between the two concepts is almost axiomatic throughout human societies. Just as we speak with unfounded certainty of pitches as existing on a vertical plane—of being "higher" or "lower" than one another—we also speak of timbres as existing on a gradient of lightness—with tones heavy in lower harmonics being "dark" and tones heavy in higher harmonics being "bright." This concept of timbre/light association is not peculiar to Western ears, either. In a discussion of Tuvan instruments and listening habits, ethnomusicologist Valentina Süzükei recalls, "We'd be sitting outside and [Tuvan musician Idamchap] would say, 'Look over there at those mountains. Look at the shadows. There's a spot from the sun, shadows from the clouds . . . Now it's changed. A shadow has suddenly appeared where only a second before, there was light.' Idamchap was trying to point to the way that visual images have depth and volume. And the analogy he wanted to make was with sound—that sound works the same way" (Levin 47). What is distinguishable from Western music, however, is the way the Tuvans employ what Süzükei refers to as "timbral listening"—a kind of gestalt form of aural perception whereby single pitches are not distinguished from one another and the entire sound of the music is heard as the formation of a single complex sound mass. Although melodic music does exist in Tuva, timbral listening, Süzükei claims, is an inborn trait for the people of the region: "You can't destroy the timbre-centered system, even if there is a lapse of a whole generation, because the sounds are lodged in the cultural memory of nomads. Timbral sound-making and timbral listening will survive as long as herders live in nature and listen to the sounds of the taiga and the steppe, birds and animals, water and wind" (58).

It is perfectly logical, then, that the music of John Luther Adams should become similarly timbre-oriented. After all, interior Alaska is as much a part of the taiga as is Tuva. In the process of trying to compose the light and darkness of the Alaskan "lightscape" in his recent music, Adams could find no better method than that of timbre-based composition.

In 2006, Adams created a timbral composition that took the subjective presence of the composer even further away from the music, designing a space in which sounds are empathetic to the natural proportions of daylight and darkness, the levels of seismic activity, the fluctuations of the earth's magnetic field, in the atmosphere in and around Fairbanks. The lighting in the space is empathetic in color to the location of the sun in the horizon. In this sound and light installation, *The Place Where You Go to Listen* (2004–6), two harmonic fields, one called the "Day Choir," the other the "Night Choir," vary in register, strength, and spatial location according to the position of the sun above, below, and around the horizon. In addition, extremely high-frequency sounds that Adams calls the "aurora bells" respond to changes in the magnetic fields of different locations in Alaska that are associated with the northern lights, and seismic activity beneath the surface of Alaska is echoed in bass tones referred to as "earth drums."

Despite the rigorous association of sounds to natural phenomena in *The Place*, there is still some element of Adams's subjectivity in the piece. As Alex Ross notes, "on the one hand, it lacks a will of its own; it is at the mercy of its data streams, the humors of the earth. On the other hand, it is a deeply personal work, whose material reflects Adams's long-standing preoccupation with multiple systems of tuning, his fascination with slow-motion formal processes, his love of foggy masses of sound in which many events unfold at different tempos" (*The Place Where You Go to Listen* x). This contradiction does exist to an extent, but these slow-motion formal processes and foggy masses of polyrhythmic sound are themselves the product of Adams's immersion in the region. They are personal only in that they must come through the composer (in any composition, after all, a composer must at *some* level choose the sounds within the piece). But their point of origin is clearly external. By letting nature "perform" the music using these pre-composed sounds, and by eliminating the subjective presence of human performers through the use of computer-generated sounds, Adams was successfully able to achieve the effect of a timbral "sound of light" as devoid of human subjectivity as possible while still being a musical composition: "*The Place* resonates with nature. But this nature is filtered through my ears. For the listener I hope this music sounds and feels natural, as though it comes directly from the earth and the sky. Yet the decisions about the timbres, tunings, harmonies and melodic curves, the dynamics, rhythms, counterpoint and musical textures were mine . . . Although I tried to minimize the evidence of my hand, I remain the composer" (*The Place Where You Go to Listen* 8).

But *The Place Where You Go to Listen* is something of an anomaly. Even after its composition Adams remains primarily a composer of instrumental works for "live" performance, with the sound installation *Veils* and *Vesper*, and the electro-acoustic soundscapes of *the place we began* being the composer's only other works without human performers. If Adams's goal is to remove self-expression from his music, why utilize other people, each with their own expressive interpretations, in the realization of his pieces? Is listening to and watching an orchestral performance not an inherently anthropocentric activity? It seems clear that Adams's notion of composing a natural setting does not necessarily conflict with a human presence: "In art and music, landscape is usually portrayed as an objective presence, a setting within which subjective human emotions are experienced and expressed. But can we find other ways of listening in which the landscape itself—rather than our feelings about it— becomes the subject? Better yet: Can the listener and the landscape become one?" (*Winter Music* 63). Thinking in terms of this idealized fusion between landscape and individual, it becomes clear why many of Adams's more recent works utilize *both* "objective" electronic elements and "subjective" human elements simultaneously, forming a unified whole.

Dark Waves, written in 2007, is exemplary of this fusion between live and electronic elements. The timbres, harmonies, and dynamics of both are derived from the same material and coordinated throughout the piece's entirety, and through clever spatial deployment of sounds, the composer succeeds in combining the two forces at the physical points at which the listener hears them. In addition Adams uses a formal structure that places the piece in a series of works that follow the symmetrical path of a so-called "solitary wave." Through the use of a series, and through the use of symmetry within the series, Adams calls attention away from the structure itself and onto the audible experience of the piece.

Adams cites three points of reference in the piece's composition, all visual artists: J. M. W. Turner, James Turrell, and Mark Rothko (e-mail message to author, June 17, 2010). The use of the natural lightscape in the works of Turner and Turrell are self-evident. But Adams sees the same evocation of nature in the blurred edges of Rothko's paintings. While composing *The Immeasurable Space of Tones*, Adams made this entry in his journal: "Writing about Rothko, Brian O'Doherty asks, rhetorically: 'Why all this blurring of edges?' I'm asking myself the same question about the new piece. It might well be called *Colors on a Diatonic Ground*, or *Light on Snow*. Both light and snow have soft edges"

(*Winter Music* 65). These "soft edges" also abound in *Dark Waves*. There is a minimum of clear delineation between the different live instruments of the ensemble, between live and electronic elements, even between different orchestrations of the same piece.

Despite its use of a unified timbre in the manner of *The Immeasurable Space of Tones* and other lightscape compositions, *Dark Waves* was intended to be heard as something other than the aural equivalent of the lightscape of interior Alaska. "As I composed *Dark Waves* I pondered the ominous events of our times: terrorism and war, intensifying storms and wildfires, the melting of the polar ice and the rising of the seas," writes Adams. "Yet even in the presence of our deepening fears, we find ourselves immersed in the mysterious beauty of this world. Amid the turbulent waves we may still find the light, the wisdom and the courage we need to pass through this darkness of our own making" (*Dark Waves* iii). The light of the piece is not that of the heavens of Alaska, but that of a human optimism. Extremely dark timbres of environmental and political crisis are interwoven with bright evocations of hope to form a unified whole.

Timbral and Harmonic Unity in *Dark Waves*

Dark Waves exists in two scorings—an original version for orchestra and electronics and a subsequent version for two pianos and electronics. In both scorings of the piece, the composer first created the electronic sounds (which he calls the "aura") and then scored the live instrumental material based on that, adding figurations natural to the playing techniques of the instruments (*Dark Waves* iii). But the sounds of the auras themselves are in fact built from samples of the very live instruments used in either piece. This creates a sort of chicken-and-egg scenario in which neither the electronic music nor the live instrumental music could be said to preexist or overshadow the other.

Despite being ostensibly two orchestrations of the same piece, the piano version is markedly different from the orchestral version, offering the question of whether the two versions can be truly viewed as one. "Because of the very different sonorities of the aura, not to mention the very different figurations in the pianos, the two-piano version is really a different piece," says Adams. "I sometimes think I should have given it a different title" (e-mail message to author, May 25, 2010). Although there certainly is enough sonic difference between the two versions to warrant them being heard as two discrete pieces, there are aspects that inseparably join them. First, they have the same basic structure; each piece is exactly twelve minutes long and follows a symmetrical form based on an approach toward a central climax followed by a retreat from it. Second, although the auras of either piece are different due to the timbres of their sources, their effects go hand-in-hand with one another. Adams writes,

"Sibelius observed that, unlike the piano, the orchestra has no pedal. But in *Dark Waves* I wanted to create one [through the creation of the aura]" (e-mail message to author, May 24, 2010). Ironically, the reverse effect is true in the piano version of the piece. By removing portions of attack and combining forward and reverse piano samples, Adams actually manages to create a "piano" which—like the string and wind instruments of the orchestra—is able to achieve dynamic swells and notes sustained with flat amplitude. The differences in the timbral qualities of the auras and the inherent differences between the live instruments in both versions serve to complement one another and not to disassociate the pieces.

In the performance notes to the orchestral version of the piece, the composer states: "The electronic sounds are generic and impersonal. The sounds of the orchestra are specific and human. The musicians of the real orchestra impart depth and texture, shimmer and substance to the electronic sounds. They give the music life. Their instruments speak in different ways. They change bow directions. They breathe. They play at different speeds. They ride the waves" (*Dark Waves* iii). Adams even instructs the string players to bow freely, adding another layer of choice, of subjectivity, to the live portion of the piece. But unlike the "subjective" harp melodies and vibrato strings that lay atop the landscape of *Dream in White On White*, the live and electronic parts in *Dark Waves* are unified to form a single, complex timbral unit.

In a prescient 1982 article discussing the history of works that utilize both electronics and live stringed instruments, David Neubert writes, "Imitative processes involving both electronic effects and string effects resulted in attempts to establish a common timbre. With the advent of computer technology, perhaps a perfect fusion will someday be achieved. When that fusion occurs, the instrumental/electronic medium will no longer be a hybrid form—it will be a new and unified one" (550). It is clear that Adams has a similar notion regarding this so-called "unified form" in *Dark Waves*: "I conceived of the entire piece as a single sonority, a vast sea of sound in which everything flows into everything else" (e-mail message to author, May 24, 2010). By creating a common timbre between live and sampled instruments, the composer disintegrates the barrier between subjective human forces and objective electronic ones. Adams further confuses the difference between the two through microphone and panning of the sounds in the loudspeakers. In the orchestral version the composer mikes the orchestra and routes the players' live sounds through the same loudspeakers as the aura. In the piano version he does the reverse, placing the loudspeakers near enough to the players to blend the two sound sources. These spatial arrangements again suggest a mirror between the two versions of the piece. In both cases the goal of the composer is to blend the human and electronic sounds into one homogeneous unit, or, as Adams says, "I wanted the aura to expand and deepen the tonal space of the orchestra. But I didn't want the listener to be able to distinguish live from Memorex!" (e-mail message to author, May 25, 2010).

The next method Adams uses to homogenize timbre in *Dark Waves* is through the use of harmony. The live instruments are always matched in timbre to their "aural" counterparts in harmonic content. "Timbral listening is very familiar to me," Adams affirms. "For years now I've approached harmony and timbre as pretty much the same thing. It's all one continuum" (e-mail message to author, June 9, 2010). Indeed, as Joseph Fourier discovered, the timbre of every sound is in fact a musical harmony, a combination of sine waves derived from harmonic and inharmonic overtones of one or multiple fundamental frequencies. In *Dark Waves*, Adams uses a similar strategy, treating individual tones as harmonic building blocks toward a timbre consisting of all twelve tones of the chromatic scale spread to almost seven octaves.

Adams creates a series of harmonies, based on stacks of perfect fifths that thicken the timbre of the piece as it develops towards a central climax, the piece's point of greatest timbral and harmonic depth. These stacks emanate from three "points of germination," (henceforth referred to as "PG"), the pitches of C1, D1, and E1. The extreme low register of these notes serves to evoke the namesake "darkness" in timbral terms. The interval of the fifth allows for timbral and harmonic developments that begin as open consonances but become more complex as the piece progresses. This development starts (in the orchestral version) with a trichord of E-B-F♯, played on the first double basses, first cellos, piano, and contrabassoon. Soon, the two other PG enter in the bass instruments—D in the second double basses and tuba, and C in the third double basses. These notes extend up a fifth in each of the double basses, adding the pitches of A and G to the harmony. The timbre of the whole is enriched both in tone and register by the addition of the second cellos, violas, bassoons, and trombones, which all play notes of the original E-B-F♯ trichord, transposed up either one or two octaves (Figure 12.1). Throughout the piece, the addition of new instruments and new passages within preexisting instruments always occurs in this "upward" motion until violin section 1a is playing artificial harmonics sounding the note of A7 during the central portion of the piece. This note is the natural termination point of the PG starting on E1, the result of a vertical stack of eleven perfect fifths from that pitch.

As a result of the extension of these stacks of perfect fifths, the listener hears clear harmonic developments coordinated across the entire ensemble at two points during either half of the piece. During *Dark Waves*'s opening measures, just over half of the pitches of the chromatic scale are accounted for. In scale

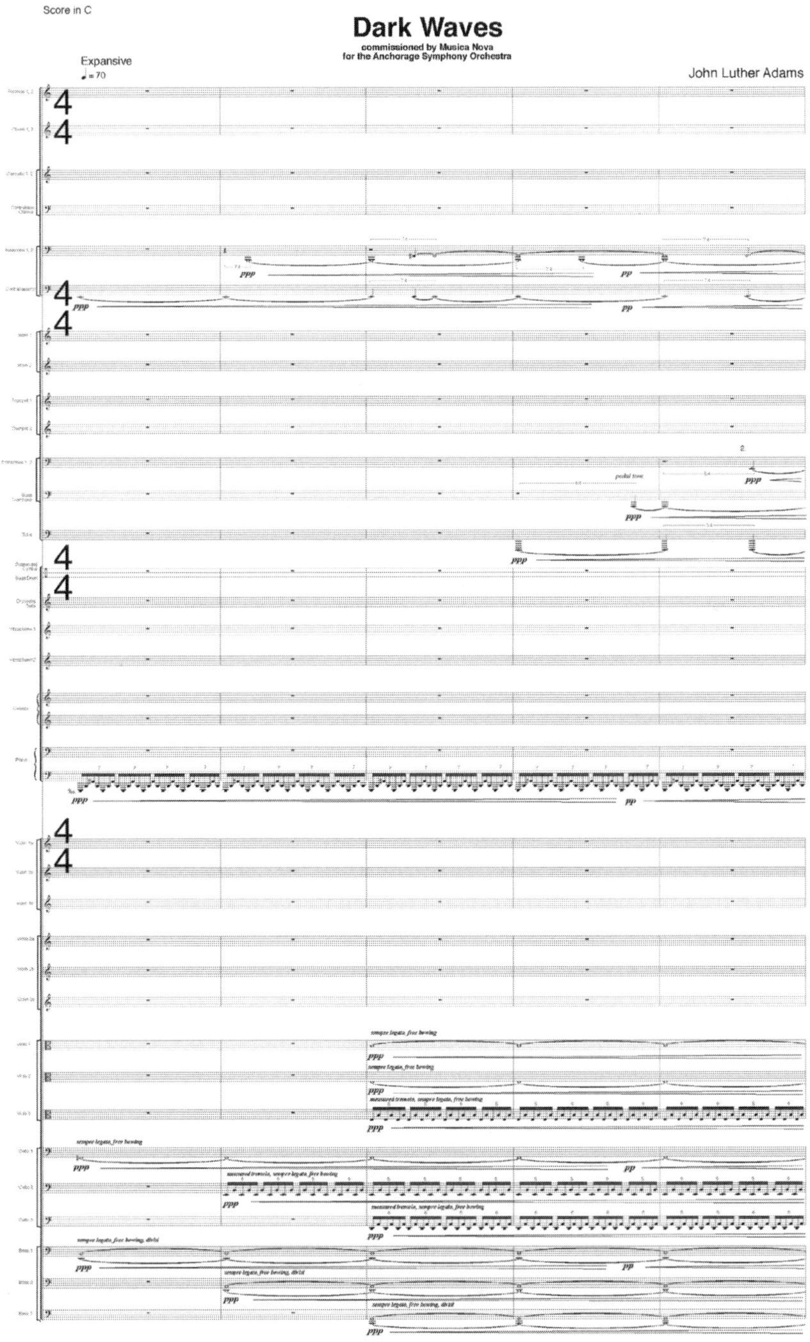

© Taiga Press 2007 - used with permission

FIGURE 12.1

	C	G	D	A	E	B	F#	C#	Ab	Eb	Bb	F
Actual clusters (M2)	C	G	D	A	E	B	F#	C#	Ab	Eb	Bb	F
	D	A	E	B	F#	C#	Ab	Eb	Bb	F	C	G
	E	B	F#	C#	Ab	Eb	Bb	F	C	G	D	A

→

Point at which all twelve pitches have entered piece

←

	C	G	D	A	E	B	F#	C#	Ab	Eb	Bb	F
Theoretical clusters (m2)	C	G	D	A	E	B	F#	C#	Ab	Eb	Bb	F
	C#	Ab	Eb	Bb	F	C	G	D	A	E	B	F#
	D	A	E	B	F#	C#	Ab	Eb	Bb	F	C	G

FIGURE 12.2

order, they are C, D, E, G, A, B, and F#. Over the next six minutes, as the piece builds toward its central climax, Adams expands the original chords, allowing pitches from the different PG to overlap with one another. The piano, for example, changes from figurations playing three-note groupings of E-B-F# to figurations playing four-note groupings of D-A-E-B at the piece's one-minute mark. Although the PG for this chord is clearly D, as the figuration starts on D1, its upper notes form a hybrid with the lower notes whose point of germination is E. The first instance of this harmonic development occurs in measure 33, when the original E-B-F# trichord is expanded to C# and G# in the third cellos and third violas. The second and final development occurs in measure 63, when the first violins complete the chromatic scale with the addition of Bb and F. Although these developments occur first in the strings, they immediately appear in the other sections of the orchestra, making these moments sound with full timbral changes across the entire ensemble. The selection of PG with distances of major seconds between them turns the resultant harmonies into the expansion of a giant tone cluster. Adams could have used minor seconds for an even denser harmonic motion, but the overlapping pitches would have been quite far from one another, forcing the piece to reveal the entire chromatic scale quite early in its development (Figure 12.2).

The sound of a fortissimo swell of all the instruments of the orchestra at the piece's axis is quite impressive. It is as close as the medium can come to achieving the effect of white noise—the equal distribution of tones across a bandwidth at equal amplitude—in an equally tempered tuning system of twelve notes. The "whiteness" of this noise is, of course, a metaphor derived from the actual whiteness (that is, the colorlessness) of white light—the equal distribution of wavelengths across a visual spectrum. But this is just one of the many color associations used to describe the timbres of noise. Pink noise, for example, is the product of an inverse proportion between frequency and intensity. Pink noise becomes less powerful as frequency rises, so that all octaves are heard with equal force.[1] Noise may also be filtered to bring out certain frequencies, altering its timbre enough to imply a fundamental pitch.

The use of filtered noise has become an important element in Adams's recent works, starting with *Strange and Sacred Noise* (1991–98) — an extended cycle for percussion quartet. In the first and last pieces of the cycle Adams directs the players to change playing position on their snare drums to incorporate more or less noise in their tone, reflecting a natural phenomenon in which noise and signal patterns inherent in electronic transmissions follow the forms of certain fractal figures. Adams's use of the "color" of noise has only increased in the years following this piece: "Even after the discoveries of *Strange and Sacred Noise* and *The Mathematics of Resonant Bodies* [2002], I couldn't have imagined what a profuse spectrum of colors is hidden in a band of noise" (*The Place Where You Go to Listen* 48).

In *The Place Where You Go to Listen* Adams uses synthetic noise generators and filters to achieve the timbral sonorities of the lightscape and other geographical aspects of Alaska. Each of the sounds is the result of filtered pink noise: the phases of the moon are heard in the slow sweep of a narrow band-pass filter across a relatively large frequency spectrum; the subterranean earthquakes of Alaska are heard in noise tuned to a range of 24.47Hz[2] to 48.42Hz (*The Place Where You Go to Listen* 208); the electromagnetic fields associated with the aurora borealis are tuned to the highest parts in the noise spectrum, reaching an apex of 6825Hz (*The Place Where You Go to Listen* 199). Although harmonic fields are present in the Aurora Bells, the multiple-band tuning of the Day and Night Choirs are essential for their existence. The noise of the Day Choir is tuned to the seven notes within the bottom four octaves of the harmonic series, which rise as more light is in the atmosphere, and expand in bandwidth as cloud formations allow for a clearer image of the sun. The noise of the Night Choir is tuned to the Day Choir's inversion. Although the choirs are based on the harmonic series, Adams actually tunes their pitches to equal temperament in order to avoid unwanted reinforcement between the harmonics.

The harmonic filtration of noise through an equal-tempered prism is also the defining method by which Adams treats the timbres of *Dark Waves*. If we consider the "white noise" climax as the point of origin for all the timbres within the piece, it becomes apparent how Adams uses a technique of subtraction on the sounds of the orchestra that is akin to the literal subtractive synthesis used in *The Place*. The darkest harmonies of *Dark Waves* — the piece's raison d'être — are the result of a careful "low-pass" filtration of the overall noise one hears when all instruments of the orchestra are playing in all available registers.

Dark Waveforms

An important and heretofore unexamined element of *Dark Waves* is its chiastic structure. "Symmetry is predictable," writes Adams. "It neutralizes questions about where the music is 'going' or what will happen next. If the next sound is inevitable, then it's free to stand only for itself. Without the expectations of narrative development or 'the element of surprise,' both the composer and listener are free simply to listen to the music" (*Winter Music* 132). In *Dark Waves* this symmetry allows for a redirection of focus away from the piece's structure and toward its use of timbre.

We find symmetrical forms throughout Adams's music. Adams's entire *Strange and Sacred Noise* cycle, for example, has a kind of large-scale symmetry across its constituent pieces, with even more definitive symmetry found within the individual pieces themselves. Like the lightscape compositions, those pieces are also based on natural phenomena—the forms of infinitely repeating, fractal figures and other symmetrical forms that occur in the natural world. There is, however, still the subjective presence of the composer in these symmetries, since they are significantly and intentionally altered at times. Regarding the avoidance of strict symmetry in and its implication of the composer's personal presence in those pieces, Adams wrote: "Although I feel free to break the symmetry at any time, I try to do so primarily in response to the physical characteristics of the instruments, or to practical realities of performance and notation, rather than to my own ideas of what should happen next. Morton Feldman did this with an exquisite touch. He called his forms 'crippled symmetry'" (*Winter Music* 134). This quote makes it clear that Adams intends a minimum of his presence in *Strange and Sacred Noise*, and indeed several pieces in the *Noise* cycle do not break their underlying forms at all. However when Adams does depart from the forms, the effect is apparent. In *Dark Waves* the form is intact throughout. Every moment in the first half of the piece is accounted for by a moment in the second half, allowing it to end exactly where it starts and implying a kind of infinitely repeating process.

Dark Waves has yet another important resemblance to *Strange and Sacred Noise* through its use of a formal structure derived from what is known in chaos theory as a "solition," or "solitary wave." Solitary waves retain their shape and velocity over long distances. This structural model was explicitly stated as a point of reference in the performance notes of *solitary and time-breaking waves*, a piece from the *Strange and Sacred Noise* cycle: the piece, writes Adams, "echoes the natural phenomenon in which waves of varying periods converge to form a single, massive solition or solitary wave" (*Strange and Sacred Noise—solitary and time-breaking waves* i). The same is true for *Dark Waves*, Adams notes: "*Dark Waves* is essentially the same form as *solitary and time-breaking waves*. I used this very consciously and quite rigorously in *Dark Waves*, as well as several other pieces . . . In my solition pieces, each of the tempo layers (1/3/5/7) can be heard as a stream of solitary waves. And the piece as a whole might also be considered as a kind of tsunami or solition" (e-mail message to author, June 3, 2010).

This technique of using the same formal structure across several pieces was explained by Adams in describing the compositional process of another piece: "By freezing a particular motive the artist is free to concentrate on deeper nuances in other dimensions of the work . . . some of the sounds [of the piece] are similar, even identical to earlier works. But this is very different music. Even within itself, the new piece embraces a series of sorts. Identical formal structures recur from section to section. The temporal relationships between sounds remain the same. Only the sounds themselves change. Rather than moving on a journey through a musical landscape, the experience is more like sitting in the same place as light and shadows slowly change" (*Winter Music* 62). By using essentially an identical formal structure between *Dark Waves*, *solitary and time-breaking waves*, and a number of other pieces, Adams is able to highlight the new elements of each piece. In the case of *Dark Waves* this new element is the use of constantly and subtly shifting timbres emanating from a uniform, homogenous sound source: "The underlying form of the music provides me with a discipline in composing. It also gives the music a coherence that I hope the listener can sense. But the form and process is no longer the object of attention. It operates (so to speak) beneath the surface of the waves. The only 'it' that I want to hear is the sound itself" (e-mail message to author, June 17, 2010).

In examining the formal elements of *Dark Waves*, it is important to once again compare and contrast the orchestra version of the piece[3] with *solitary and time-breaking waves*. In both pieces dynamics are used as the metaphor for the rise and fall of naturally occurring waves. Waves almost always start from the quietest possible sounds of the instruments that play them, and then rise to a single peak before returning to their starting position. Also, the amplitudes of the climaxes of the constituent waves build with proximity to the central climax (i.e. in either piece, one might find a single instrument with a wave cycle climaxing at the successive dynamic markings of *f*, *ff*, *fff*, *ff*, *f*). Although the central climax would already be significantly louder than the peaks of any of the individual waves due to their combination at that moment, this technique of building in a pyramid formation toward and away from the center reinforces the crescendo/diminuendo structure present in each of the individual waves.

The waves of *solitary and time-breaking waves* are completely unaltered in form. The four tam-tams for which the piece is scored play perfectly symmetrical crescendos and diminuendos in temporal ratios of 1/3/5/7 (Figure 12.3).

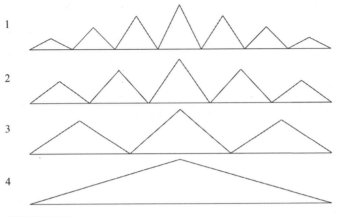

FIGURE 12.3

The choice of prime numbers for these ratios allows the waves to exist without conflicting with one another (waves of ninths, for example, would have peaks that coincide with the waves of thirds, diminishing the importance of the central climax). The same temporal ratios exist in *Dark Waves*, with the exception of an explicitly-composed "1" wave—dynamic peaks occur at every third, fifth, and seventh of the piece, with lengths of seventy, forty-two, and thirty measures apiece—but their treatment is somewhat different, accounting for the subtle changes in timbre that define the piece. Instead of dividing the orchestra into sections that play through each of the dynamic waves in full (as in *solitary and time-breaking waves*) Adams places the waves "beneath" the instruments of the orchestra. As the composer explains, this choice to break the instruments up across the waves was done out of practical consideration: "Without three full orchestras there just aren't enough instruments to fully sound all the waves. If you stack twelve perfect fifths on the fundamentals C, D and E, I think you'll see why there aren't enough instruments in the orchestra to do this in a way that would sound effectively. To keep all those tones going in the lowest octave I would have needed five contrabassoons and five bassoons, five tubas, six piccolos, and similarly Wagnerian forces. And even so, those instruments would have been playing constantly—which wouldn't have been humanly possible . . . So I had to ride the surface of the waves (the most prominent moment to moment sounds), distributing the sounds throughout the orchestra. To make things more difficult I wanted to make the whole piece sound like one large complex sonority with no solos, nothing standing out" (e-mail message to author, June 16, 2010). The aura is a boon in the realization of this unified sound. By composing an electronic track that contains an essentially infinite number of players, all free from the human limitations of breath, bow length, and limited stamina,

Adams achieves his effect of three simultaneous orchestras (in addition to the live orchestra) capable of playing constantly. In fact, the aura itself is composed for three orchestras, playing separately the three large-scale waves Adams would have needed to create in his live instrumental sections (Figure 12.4).

In the orchestral scoring of the piece, Adams achieves this effect of the instruments "riding" the waves by dividing the orchestra into six major groups—woodwinds, brass and pitched percussion, piano and celesta, first strings, second strings, and third strings—which are linked by dynamic. These groups trade between one another which of the three wave patterns they are playing at any given time, leaving only the implication of the larger forms of the waves underneath the smaller waves of the individual instruments (Figure 12.5). It should be noted that these dynamic groups do not *always* contain their namesake instruments. The relationship of the instruments within a given group is especially complex in the strings. For example, all of the violas start by riding the wave of the third string section, switching to the wave of the first string section at measure 22 (the peak of a large-scale wave of fifths), the wave of the second string section at measure 36 (the peak of a large-scale wave of thirds), and the wave of the third string section at measure 46 (the peak of the large-scale wave of sevenths). With each successive shift, however, the violas of the different sections are matched with the strings of their appropriate sections, so that by measure 46, all three violas are aligned with their correct instrumental waves. The same process holds true for the violin sections, which enter even later than the violas in the same upwards shift of registers previously discussed.

Embedded within these large-scale waves are smaller ones, as well. These miniature waves are represented within their larger waves by tempo layers consisting of sextuplets, quintuplets, and septuplets. These rhythmic divisions occur at the level of the quarter note, half note, and whole note. Although the piece is written in 4/4, there is never a division of the beat that is actually in a grouping of four. Instead Adams uses this meter as a sort of tempo grid, a neutral division of the beat that gives preference to none of the tempo layers over the others. As these tempo layers play simultaneously in the different instrumental sections they represent, at a micro level, the waves that divide the piece at the macro level. In addition, the envelope, the attack and release, of every instrumental articulation mirrors the crescendos and diminuendos of the instrumental sections as they "ride" the large-scale waves.

Conclusion

In the years following the turn of the twenty-first century, the music of John Luther Adams has increasingly become a sonic evocation of light, and in particular the "lightscapes" of Alaska—the dramatic contrast between lightness

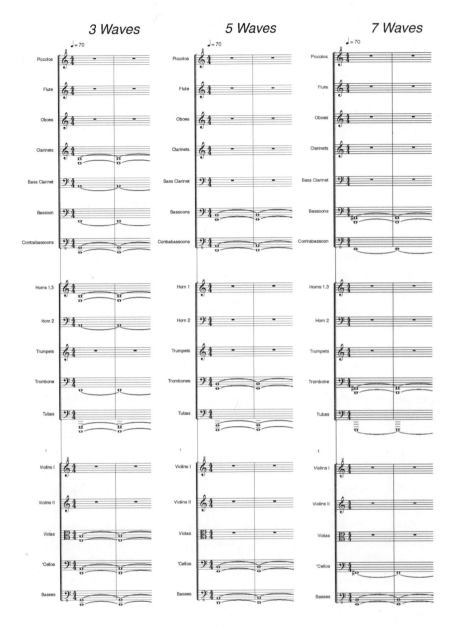

© Taiga Press 2007 - used with permission

Opening measures of each of the three orchestral auras
(dynamics not written in)

FIGURE 12.4

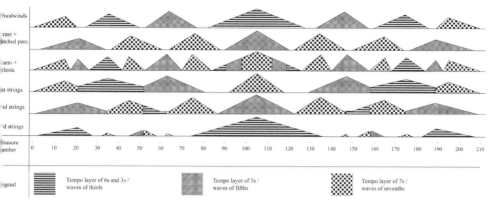

FIGURE 12.5

and darkness that occurs throughout the latitude of 64°51'N. Long gone are the sonic allusions of *songbirdsongs* (1974–1979) and the landscape compositions of *Night Peace* (1977), *A Northern Suite* (1979–1981) and *The Far Country of Sleep* (1988). Also missing from Adams's recent pieces are elements that serve to act as the human presence in the music as anything but part of the natural environment. In place of the lush melodic lines that float above the impassive backdrop of *In the White Silence* and other pieces that seek to evoke the human feeling of being in a place, Adams uses fields of harmony and timbre — unified throughout all the instruments in a given piece — to be heard as sonic equivalents of the lightscape.

In *Dark Waves*, Adams uses this notion of light not to create the sonic equivalent of the natural lightscape of Fairbanks, but as the evocation of human optimism. To achieve this, Adams starts by unifying the sounds of live instruments and a prepared electronic "aura" — matching them in timbre and spatial location. The sounds of the electronics in both the orchestra scoring and two-piano scoring exist as mirrors to one another: in the orchestra version, the aura allows for the instruments to maintain a constant resonance in the manner of a piano's damper pedal, while in practicality the players must change bows, breathe, and rest; in the case of the two-piano version, the aura allows for gradual swells devoid of attack common to instruments of the orchestra, but impossible on a piano. The harmonies of the piece are used as a means by which to create timbres that progressively thicken and then thin over the course of its twelve minutes. Simple chords based on three extremely low notes, C1, D1, and E1, expand in register and condense in harmonic distance until a complete twelve-note tone cluster has been built atop those three points of germination at the piece's central climax.

If we take the opposite approach to understanding the timbres and harmonies of the piece, treating the full field of sound during the central climax as a form of noise—the equal distribution of tones across the full "bandwidth" of the instruments—we notice how Adams uses a type of subtractive "filtration" to create the piece's other harmonies and timbres. This same filtration of noise through a twelve-tone equal-tempered prism is used to create the sonic equivalent of light in Adams's empathetic light-and-sound installation, *The Place Where You Go to Listen*. And the use of filtered noise in general has become an essential element in Adams's timbral compositions.

Finally, Adams uses a chiastic formal structure based on the naturally occurring "solition," or "solitary wave." This form, which Adams has used in several pieces over the past decade, involves multiple simultaneous tempo layers which peak at different moments and converge to form a climax at a piece's center. By using a fixed form across many pieces, Adams is essentially working in series, which allows him to focus on the most important elements within a given piece. In *Dark Waves* the focus is on the creation of complex harmonies and textures, and the provocation of "timbral listening."

Notes

1. The octave from 100 to 200Hz, for example, would have the same power as the octave from 10,000 to 20,000Hz. In order to achieve this, each successive octave is attenuated by three decibels along a linear slope.

2. This frequency, the harmonic basis for the piece, is a multiple of the cycles per second, the literal frequency, of the Earth's rotation.

3. The same formal elements exist in the two-piano version, but the orchestral scoring provides a more complete picture of these elements, as the many sections of the orchestra allow for more simultaneous wave-forms than could exist in the piano score.

Bibliography

Adams, John Luther. *Strange and Sacred Noise*. Fairbanks: Taiga Press, 1991–1997.

Adams, John Luther. *Dark Waves*. Fairbanks: Taiga Press, 2007.

Adams, John Luther, and Kyle Gann. *Winter Music: Composing the North*. Middletown, Conn.: Wesleyan University Press, 2004.

Adams, John Luther, and Alex Ross. *The Place Where You Go to Listen: In Search of an Ecology of Music*. Middletown, Conn.: Wesleyan University Press, 2009.

Levin, Theodore, and Valentina Süzükei. *Where Rivers and Mountains Sing: Sound, Music, and Nomadism in Tuva and Beyond*. Bloomington: Indiana University Press, 2006.

Morris, Mitchell. "Ectopian Sound or The Music of John Luther Adams and Strong Environmentalism." In *Crosscurrents and Counterpoints: Offerings in Honor of*

Berngt Hambraeus at 70, ed. P. F. Broman, N. A. Engebretnen, and B. Alphonce. Göthenburg: University of Sweden Press, 1998, 129–41.

Neubert, David. "Electronic Bowed String Works: Some Observations on Trends and Developments in the Instrumental/Electronic Medium." *Perspectives of New Music* 21 (1982–83), 540–66.

13 * **Place and Space**
The Vision of John Luther Adams
in the Ultramodernist Tradition

John Luther Adams is often identified as a leading contemporary representative of the American experimental tradition, and with good reason. But
in this essay I'd like to suggest that "experimentalism" may be too narrow a
word to encompass his art, in part because it tends to suggest that the *means*
by which music is produced is at least as important as, or even more important
than, the ultimate product or its motivating ambition. Following the classic
definition by Michael Nyman in his *Experimental Music, Cage and Beyond*, experimentalism finds its rationale in the very act of exploration, and the originality of said process is the guiding factor for judging its worth; the results are
in a sense incidental (1–26). And so Cage's chance procedures, Nancarrow's
work with the player piano, Partch's orchestra of self-designed instruments,
Cowell's interior piano techniques and clusters—all these are markers of experimentalism, prized for their freshness and exceptionalism.

This description is certainly true of Adams's sonic explorations. His music *is*
motivated by investigations of sound and process, not dependent on any pre-
existent aesthetic, dramatic, or metaphysical program. Yet while experimentalism as defined above is a valid component of an anti-establishmentarian
practice, it strikes me as insufficient to explain in depth what makes Adams's
work (and those of his predecessors) so original and profound. Instead I'd like
to propose that we examine the composer from the perspective of an "American
maverick," a term which opens up other avenues of exploration and definition.
"Maverick" is a difficult term to define in terms of aesthetics, though its implications are nevertheless clear. The actual term is defined (in *Webster's 7th Collegiate Dictionary*) as "an individual who refuses to conform to his group," and
originated from the Texas rancher Samuel Maverick, who declined to brand his
cattle. Thus a "maverick" cannot be easily categorized; its identity does not rest
on conventional taxonomies. In music, the term has been applied to a diverse
group of composers, whose affiliation results less from either technical or aesthetic similarities between their music, than from a common attitude toward
other traditions, and the manner in which their creative ideas were inspired
and realized. Adams himself is directly tied to this historical stream, not just

because of the nature of his work, but also because of his close personal ties with two of its important members, James Tenney and Lou Harrison (the former a teacher, the latter a friend and mentor, both "descendants" of the initial generation comprising such composers as Ives, Ruggles, Cowell, and Seeger).

The first generation of these composers was self-proclaimed as "ultramodernists." While Charles Ives had written the majority of his *oeuvre* before World War I, the circle in which he became known as a kind of *paterfamilias* really did not begin to assert itself as such until the 1920s. For a brief period, led by the Pan-American Association concerts directed by Edgard Varèse, and by the pioneering New Music Edition publications of Henry Cowell, this group promoted a form of American modernism that was very different from its European counterpart (Gann 27–28). Though highly dissonant, it tended not to share the interest in Central European Expressionism (associated with the Second Viennese School). Its language tended to be astringent and bracing, but with suggestions more of an extroverted, visionary stance, rather than introverted investigation of the unconscious. Likewise, the ethnographic research of Bartok and the renascent primitivism of Stravinsky seemed of little interest to these more radically-minded composers; Dvorak's admittedly open attitude towards black music, and the American "Indianists" of the immediately preceding generation had explored this realm in a manner that remained deeply conservative in its musical means, and probably discredited this approach in their eyes.[1]

Indeed, if other non-Western musical traditions were interesting to these composers, it was because they were an alternative to the ruling European aesthetic of the time. Ives is the classic sad case of a composer yearning to write a truly American music, stymied (as he saw it) by philistine performers, conductors, critics, and patrons slavishly following a Continental *diktat*. His contemporaries, supporters, and like-minded colleagues believed strongly that the American quality of *invention* would bring forth this original, national music. And this spirit animates a host of documents and practices that define the movement: Charles Seeger's "dissonant counterpoint" and its supreme application in the music of Carl Ruggles; Henry Cowell's promotion in *New Musical Resources* of a musical "unified field theory" that connects harmony, rhythm, and color via the common thread of the overtone series; Varèse's evocation of the machine age in a counterpoint of sonic blocks and static harmonic complexes; and Ives's extensive experiments in every imaginable technique: ranging from the extreme sound collages in *Putnam's Camp* of the First Orchestral Set and *The Fourth of July* of the *Holidays Symphony*, to concise and focused explorations of polystylism and spatial arrangements in *The Unanswered Question*, and even to serialism in *Chromatimelodtune*.

So far this rejection of Eurocentric tradition, and embrace of technical invention, would seem completely in tune with the definition of experimentalism we presented at the start of this essay. But there is yet another aspect just as critical to the essence of this music: a belief in its visionary potential. Of course, music has always claimed a spiritual component, and from the outset has been tied to the sacred. The great music of the Middle Ages and Renaissance is predominantly liturgical, and in the ironclad intricacies of Bach's practice one senses a metaphor for a sort of heavenly order. Later, Beethoven's Romantic sensibility bespeaks an ecumenical and humanistic spirituality. But the music of the pioneering American generation of modernist composers takes this impulse and gives it a distinct inflection. The core impulse comes from American Transcendentalism, in particular of Emerson and Thoreau, and finds its first strong manifestation in the music of Ives. It is grounded on beliefs that: (1) the surface of existence is a scrim under which lies a deeper and truer reality, waiting to be revealed, (2) the surest way to this reality is through close observation of nature, and (3) this revelation is democratically available to all. Ives certainly is the first and most vocal proponent of this musical attitude. In his *Essays Before a Sonata*, he writes, "music is beyond any word analogy, and we believe that the time is coming, but not in our lifetime, when it will develop possibilities inconceivable now—a language so transcendent, that its heights and depths will be common to all mankind" (8) and "if he (this composer, poet, or laborer) . . . is open to all the over-values within his reach . . . if he accepts and sympathizes with all, is influenced by all, whether consciously or subconsciously, audibly or inaudibly . . . *then* it may be that the value of his substance, and its value to himself, to his art, to all art, even to the Common Soul is growing and approaching nearer and nearer to perfect truths—whatever they are and wherever they may be" (92).

One sees this stance not only in Ives, but in many of his successors, above all Cage (though *his* spirituality is far less grandiose, relying on the almost deadpan attitude of Zen for its expressive tone).

What one begins to realize is that this American visionary voice ties music to a *place*, albeit an idealized one. Music is not its own, self-contained justification, but rather a *gateway* to some heightened space. It's not that surprising that one of Ives's earliest works, still in his conservative tonal style, was a cantata titled *The Celestial Country*. His orchestral major works cited above all have moments of hallucinatory revelation, where the present moment melts away to reveal events transpiring over broad ranges of time and space (such as the child's dream of the Revolutionary War soldiers in the program for *Putnam's Camp*). Likewise, Carl Ruggles, while a far more abstract composer, nevertheless evidences a similar belief in a transcendent reality that is illuminated via musical means. His *Men and Mountains* bears the inscription by William Blake, "Great things are done when / Men and Mountains meet; / This is not done by / Jostling in the Street." Another work of his is even titled *Portals*.

In short, much music from this movement seems to be the result of composers constructing, or more precisely, *discovering* a new landscape both deeply embedded within and simultaneously beyond the everyday. In a facile way, this impulse could be called an attraction to the "cosmic," but I think a more precise description is to say it involves the development of a *cosmography* ("a general description of the world or of the universe . . . the science that deals with the constitution of the whole order of nature," Webster's Seventh New Collegiate Dictionary). Through music, a map slowly emerges of this realm, one both autonomous and yet inextricably tied to the physical world. Paradoxically, it often evokes the infinite with a discourse that can be laconic, even verging on boring in its materials or unfolding (at least to some). It can eschew romantic drama. It often presents the sonic event as its own justification, even as it subtly strives to amplify us and lead us to a different psychic space. It is simultaneously immanent and transcendent. And as such, its willingness to acknowledge the mundane, while still pursuing a higher reality through it, seems a particularly American combination, a natural spiritual response to the scale, diversity, grandeur, and enduring *reality* of the land.

John Luther Adams's music has a number of obvious connections to this aesthetic and practice. To begin with, almost every writer on his music, as well as the composer himself, have commented on his fundamental rootedness to Alaska as a physical and spiritual home. Of course, this is obvious and true, yet also there has never been anything overtly "pictorial" about the music's relation to its inspirational landscape. A work such as *In the White Silence* may suggest in its title vast snowy expanses, but there's not any concrete, programmatic connection to specific topography or phenomena. Adams himself has said he considers his works "not so much as musical compositions or pieces, but as *places* . . . places for listening, places in which to experience the elemental mystery of noise" ("Strange and Sacred Noise" 146). He describes the distinction between the influence of physical geography and the idealized realization of a musical counterpart as, "I like to say that the music is no longer *about* place, but has in a sense *become* place" (*Winter Music* 57).

Above all the expansiveness of Alaska has granted Adams a vision of *space* that is particularly intense and vivid. He has written of the way that the vast natural processes one witnesses in this landscape cause the egotistical component of artistic creation to shrink, and to draw one into the position of a close observer of something already present, rather than a maker of a previously unimagined object: "The awesome and indifferent forces of nature are stark reminders of the insignificance of our personal dramas and passions. They offer us undeniable reassurance that whatever we may inflict upon ourselves and upon one another, there are processes at work in the world far larger, older and more complex than we can understand" ("Strange and Sacred Noise" 143).

Looking closer at Adams's actual music, we see this stance playing out in specific musical techniques and approaches. Three seem particularly strong and essential to his practice.

First, over the course of his career there has been a continuous expansion of *scale* in the dimensions of his works. This plays out particularly in the realm of time. A piece such as *Strange and Sacred Noise* presages this trend, as it lasts about an hour, but it is made up of nine separate movements. *In the White Silence* and *for Lou Harrison* are each about an hour long, each in single movements. The electroacoustic *Veils* (to be discussed below) is six hours, and *The Place Where You Go to Listen* is theoretically endless, as it collects realtime geophysical data from throughout Alaska and translates it into sonic-visual gesture. Adams has commented on the importance of Morton Feldman to his work, and in particular that composer's distinction between duration and scale as a factor in altering the very nature of the creative act (*The Place Where You Go to Listen* 59–60). Such immensity is one way in which to draw the listener into a work that becomes a *place* rather than an *event*.

Second, in order to fill this space, Adams has always been interested in *process* as a way to generate his music. This approach has the benefit of creating large swaths of sound, guaranteed to have a particular general character, but dispensing with the agonizing note-by-note choice that can plague a composer working in unfamiliar harmonic territory (and ultimately clog the music's flow). It also moves creative choice into a realm beyond the composer's personal tastes and control. In this, Adams shares common ground with Cage, though his music has (at least up to his extraordinary installation *The Place Where You Go to Listen*) mostly involved the making of scores whose notated events are precise and replicable.[2] Adams's approach is often *algorithmic*; he sets up processes that spin themselves out according to a strict rule-set, regardless of the time taken, or the momentary aesthetic implications of the result. This approach is reminiscent of the elaborate processes of rhythmic transformation in Conlon Nancarrow's player piano studies, and to certain process-oriented works of James Tenney, which are notable for the elegance and economy of their algorithms (a favorite of mine being *Koan* for solo violin from the *Postal Pieces*.) In Adams's 1997 percussion ensemble suite *Strange and Sacred Noise*, there are moments when the music seems to be petering out into an ever-sparer texture, in which one might assume the piece is ending. But then, at the moment of greatest possible fragility, it begins to slowly pick itself up and return to a dense, throbbing soundfield (an example being the *". . . dust into dust . . ."* opening movement for two snare and two field drums). Here processes of addition and subtraction are in dynamic contest with one another, and contradict the traditional formal and narrative discourse.

Finally, Adams has embraced an aesthetic stance very close to the combination of immanent and transcendent described above. His music is often full of activity, and there *is* a sense of directed motion, but it tends to be strophic or cyclic, rather than a single narrative thread from the beginning to end of the piece. Its teleology is more cyclic than directional. He has written that he was helped to develop this aspect of his practice from Tenney's concept of "ergodic form," "in which any moment of the music is statistically equivalent to any other moment. Ergodic form is self-similar at all levels, from macrostructure to micro-topology. An entire piece of music is conceived, composed and experienced as a single complex, evolving sonority. In my own music I try to combine a similar singularity of sound and form with an equally intense sensuality (the legacy of Feldman), and an integration of pitch and rhythm (the theoretical legacy of Cowell)" ("Remembering James Tenney" 7).

Tenney, in his extended theoretical essay *Meta+Hodos*, presents the concept of iconic musical events, "*klangs*," which can be analyzed as blends of different parametric elements, so as to create a striking aural profile that is similar in nature to what has been called "thematic" in earlier periods, but in fact is more complex and less easily reducible. Paradoxically, the very richness of the sound event creates an impression that can satisfy without any extramusical content, even though it may open up previously unanticipated experiential vistas for the listener. Again, Adams writes, "[Tenney's music] stands for nothing other than itself. It conceals nothing. It simply *sounds*. Form, harmony, compositional techniques and processes—everything is out in the open, within immediate reach of our ears. Paradoxically, this only increases its mystery. The primacy of sound gives . . . a special magic that penetrates directly to the core of the attentive listener's consciousness. With no surprises or dramatic distractions, we surrender our expectations. We simply listen" (8).

It is clear that while the composer is paying tribute to the work of a teacher, he is also outlining a key element of his own practice.

This leads us to Adams's *Veils*, an immense yet evanescent electroacoustic work. I regard it as transitional, and as such critical in the composer's development, in that it develops a technological practice which will come to even greater and more radical fruition soon thereafter in *The Place Where You Go to Listen*. It continues the progression toward ever-greater duration (six hours), at least for any piece of his with a fixed duration. And it establishes this sense of a very real yet simultaneously ideal sonic *place* into which the listener enters, experiencing both constant variety and transformation, *and* yet also a fundamental, "eternally" unchanging character.

Veils was completed in April 2005, with programming assistance from Jim Altieri. The basic concept of the piece is that pink noise is filtered through a series of "scrims," which are tuned to prime partials of the overtone series, starting from 11 (11, 13, 17, 19, 23, 29, 31). (See Figure 13.1a–d.) The scrims are band-pass filters, constructed in MaxMSP, an interactive/algorithmic program that is also used to determine the rate at which each filter is opened and closed to create a "sweep" through the entire range of the filtered noise. In turn, each sweep is defined as a "voice," and the different versions of *Veils* contain different numbers of these voices.[3]

Falling Veils is, as the title indicates, a series of descending voices (thirty-five total). *Rising Veils* contains twenty-five voices. *Crossing Veil* uses both rising and falling voices, for a total of thirty.

It becomes clear that:

Falling Veil moves through a seven-note justly tuned scale within the octave: C, D♭, E♭, F, G, A♭, B♭.

Rising Veil moves through a 5-note justly tuned scale within the octave: C, D♭, E♭, F, A♭.

Crossing Veil features two different 5-note scales in its upper and lower registers. The former is F-A♭-B♭-C-E♭, and latter F-A♭-C-D♭-E♭. The overall collection results in six pitch classes, four in common to both scales.

Each pitch is derived from the prime number harmonics off a low D fundamental tuned to −23c (18.1074 Hz). The resultant pairings of pitch class and tunings are as follows:[4]

TABLE 13.1

Harmonic (from 12-tone equal temperament)	Pitch Name	Cents Deviation
11	G	+27
13	B-Flat	+17
17	E-Flat	−18
19	F	−25
23	A-Flat	+4
29	C	+6
31	D-Flat	+21

Adams fell into writing the piece as a byproduct of the sketching he was doing for *The Place Where You Go to Listen*. It provided a way for him to begin to test the sort of soundworld which would ultimately color that piece, and it

Falling Veil

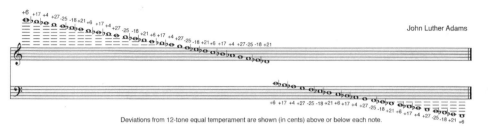

John Luther Adams

Deviations from 12-tone equal temperament are shown (in cents) above or below each note.

FIGURE 13.1A

Crossing Veil

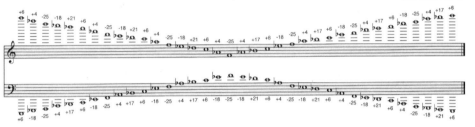

John Luther Adams

FIGURE 13.1B

Rising Veil

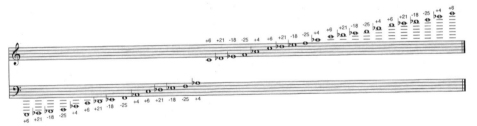

John Luther Adams

FIGURE 13.1C

Vesper

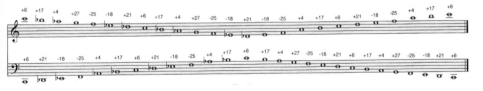

John Luther Adams

FIGURE 13.1D

so excited him that he turned it (rather quickly) into a work in its own right. He had started working with its materials in summer 2004, but it was only in April 2005 (in a span of roughly three weeks) that the piece took off. Part of the stimulus was an extended visit by Altieri, a former student and accomplished programmer, who developed a MaxMSP patch that allowed Adams to alter the structure and usage of the harmonic scrims in real time. As a consequence, Adams was able to "sketch" *Veils* at the computer in a manner similar to that of his acoustic composition at the piano (*The Place Where You Go to Listen*, 55).

After the determination of the harmonic scrims, the other major decision in the piece involved the rate at which the sweeps would occur. Adams writes in his composer's journal: "I audition different time scales for the *Veils*, ranging from thirty-five minutes to one year. At such widely varied speeds, the same sounds require very different treatment. It seems that the slower the speed, the denser the fields want to be, both in terms of number of voices and bandwidth of the single tones. But regardless of the speed, there's a delicate balance between saturating the tonal space and maintaining a degree of clarity and transparency to the textures" (*The Place Where You Go to Listen* 59).

As already noted, the composer ultimately chose a temporal scale that determines the piece's six-hour duration. The rhythmic structure within that time frame is as follows. Each *Veil* has a certain number of layers, which in turn are composed of voices (sweeps). The tempo of the overall harmonic sweep for each layer is in a ratio to every other layer based on the prime harmonic numbers used to tune the pitches. For *Falling Veil*, the proportions are 11/13/17/19/23/29/31 (seven layers). For *Rising Veil*, they are 17/19/23/29/31. For *Crossing Veil*, they are 13/17/19/23/29 for rising voices and 17/19/23/29/31 for falling ones. Within each layer, each individual voice enters at regular, evenly spaced time intervals. On the macro-rhythmic level, then, the structure is that of a mensuration canon. Within the layers, on a more "micro" level, it is that of a traditional ("staggered") canon. This combination makes for a particularly rich contrapuntal web, and if one is reminded of fifteenth/sixteenth century Renaissance music, that's on track. Adams has commented to me that, "*Veils* [is] my homage to renaissance polyphony. While I was composing . . . I was listening to Ockeghem's *Missa Prolationum*, and Lassus's *Prophetiae Sibyllarum*."

The *Veils* each have instructions for lighting progressions that make gradual transitions from one color to another. To take one example, *Falling Veil* moves from violet to green to blue to yellow, and then returns to violet via retrograde. The sensory connection of sound and sight here reminds one of Scriabin.

Finally, there is an element of "macro-modularity" to the work, in that each of the three *Veils* can be performed separately, or they can be combined for simultaneous performance. A six-channel realization is preferred, though a stereo mixdown is allowed.[5]

And now from the analytic to the phenomenological: What does *Veils* sound like?

There are several distinct impressions left by the work. First, its shimmering timbral palette is varied and seductive. While composed entirely from filtered pink noise, the music projects a radiant, constantly mutating "orchestration." One (thinks one) hears winds, brass, organs, voices, strings. Specific colors will vary from listener to listener, but the overall impact is genuinely symphonic.

Second, the music seems to constantly change without changing at all. Part of the reason is that with layer-sweeps repeatedly beginning at regular intervals from both the highest and lowest registers, these registral "bookends" are always present.[6] But within this framework, there are constantly changing harmonies emerging. One can hear them as chords, but even a little close attention reveals separate new pitches emerging from the texture every few seconds. It is fascinating to hear music which is strongly *progressional*, but to which it's basically impossible to assign any particular *direction*.[7]

Third, when the different tempos of the layers (themselves in counterpoint to the regular deployment of voices within them) are combined with the variable interval distances that emerge from just intonation tuning, the progressions are always unpredictable in their content, and their exact rate of emergence. As a result, even though this in one sense is "still point" music, it is rich in ever-engaging, surprising detail. Thoroughly modal, it doesn't seem redundant because of its "recombinancy": familiar pitches continue to return, but their harmonic role changes and interacts with different emerging frequencies.

Fourth, while ravishingly beautiful, the music is hard to call "pretty." In this sense, despite a certain surface connection to New Age, *Veils* is a resolutely abstract and challenging concert piece, even though most will experience it as an installation. I believe this results because all events are equal within it; none are highlighted for special attention, and hence none are precious.

Finally, *Veils* is spacious. One feels an enormous sense of deep breath motivating it. Adams's scrupulous concern with finding the correct dimensions for the work manifests itself in the way that we can hear details at a (never mechanical) rate that allows us to perceive them, and lets them resonate. It is slow enough to allow contemplation, but it does not plod, or bore us with too limited a palette too predictably recycled. In the visionary sense, it suggests an opening into an endlessly expanding and mutating landscape, open to discoveries that will be surprising and engaging, but not violent or shocking.

Since we have spoken of cosmography, space, and place throughout this essay, it's worth risking one more concrete analogy. I have never been fortunate enough to see the northern lights, but I cannot help—after having experienced *Veils* in a concert/installation setting, and in my home—thinking that it is in some way a parallel to viewing that natural phenomenon.[8] The sense of open-ended wonder the lights inspire seems closely tied to the experience Adams wishes for the listener.

By now it should be evident how Adams represents yet another step in the maverick tradition that unites a deep love of the acoustic *reality* of sound with a visionary spirit, which sees music as means to a higher order. On the side of the "real," Adams's embrace of the overtone series as his harmonic template, and his extension of the ratios of just tuning into the world of tempo and rhythmic development, are a natural extension of the "unified field" proposed now almost a century ago by Cowell in *New Musical Resources*.[9] On the other hand, the vast celestial choir that is *Veils*, and its evocation of a transcendent landscape, recalls Ives with his "Universe Symphony," which he wrote would consist of two simultaneous layers, lower and upper register instruments, reflecting the Earth, and "the skies and the Heavens," respectively (*Memos* 106).[10] Between these two, the real (but with a grandiose plan of scientific union of elements) and the ideal (but with its rootedness in nature), the connective tissue is *invention*. Here Adams continues an American tradition, embodied in Nancarrow's player pianos and rhythmic canons; La Monte Young's intonation theory and well-tuned piano; Cage's prepared piano, gamuts, and recursive time-block structures; Harrison's homegrown gamelan and embrace of its music's colotomic structure. Adams is a composer who is poised, through a series of fortuitous life choices (for many of which he couldn't possibly see the eventual resolution), that have allowed him to combine his personal temperament with resources of the twenty-first century to advance the experimental and transcendental tradition. A composer who has both a rigorous bent and a mind sympathetic to overarching structure and strict process, he is also deeply respectful of the "beautiful accidents" of nature, and willing to accept surprises along the creative routes he follows. In *Veils* (and *The Place Where You Go to Listen*), he is a composer with clear ideas and the right mindset to use advanced technology creatively. This is possible because, for all its complexity, an application such as MaxMSP makes a certain sort of "constructivist" composition on an enormous scale feasible in a far more "natural" manner than ever before possible. Despite its abstraction, Adams's approach and use of this resource is "musical" in the sense that it still allows for taste and intuition. In this sense, he's the right person at the right moment to take what has been bequeathed him by his ancestors, and honor them by advancing it into a new realm.

Notes

1. Of course, any such generalization opens one up to correction. In the initial ultramodernist generation, John J. Becker's *The Abongo* evoked both African drumming traditions, as well as exploring rhythmic complexity. The later Cowell became entranced with a host of world music traditions. And of more recent mavericks after their initial heyday, Lou Harrison of course championed the Indonesian gamelan as a contemporary ensemble and alternative to European classical instruments, and Harry Partch sought to re-create an archaic music that predated the entire Western European canon. Nevertheless, in the 1920s these tendencies were far less evident.

2. In some cases, there are accidental byproducts of the fixed score that are integral to the piece, as in the combination tones that emerge from the textures of his percussion music, such as *Strange and Sacred Noise* and *the Mathematics of Resonant Bodies*. But while not entirely predictable, the existence is anticipated in the score, and their occurrence is not a shock, nor a contradiction of the works' basic premises.

3. The following analysis is deeply indebted to the assistance of the composer, who engaged the author in an extended email correspondence in June 2010, answering a wide range of technical questions and providing documentation for the work, which could never have been otherwise obtained.

4. Some may wonder why, with a fundamental labeled D, the eleventh partial should be a G instead of a G♯. The reason is that the D is substantially lowered from its equal-temperament tuning, which in turn causes a downward shift of the higher partials. Adams names his notes based on the equal temperament pitch to which they are closest (though he of course always shows the exact deviation from ET in cents).

5. There is a companion piece to *Veils*, titled *Vesper*. Its pitch field is confined to the 4-octave human vocal range. Its total scalar set is seven pitches, and combines simultaneously rising and falling scales, using C-D♭-E♭-F-G-A♭-B♭; G, however, is omitted in its rising form, so that there is always a 7:6 pitch-class ratio between descending and rising scales. It has ninety voices, and uses all the prime number tempo ratios for its layers.

From a personal perspective, I don't find *Vesper* as compelling as *Veils*. Such judgment may be inappropriate for a scholarly article, but one of my several lives is as a critic, and I don't want to mute it too severely. *Vesper* seems a little too constrained by its register, and so many processes moving within a more limited range may in fact start to muddy the acoustic waters. Ironically, *Veils* to me sounds more "choral," in that individual pitches as they emerge have more room to resonate.

At the same time, I think Adams may be correct in his instincts, and *Vesper* should in fact be a "real" choral piece. While the demands on stamina would be phenomenal, if a score were to be realized from its algorithms, and a willing ensemble found, the results might be equally extraordinary. Even dividing the work into sections that could be performed separately, then spliced together in an omnibus recording, might do the trick.

6. At the midpoint and endpoint of the piece they make a dramatic statement, when the sweeps through the middle registers have finished, and leave them sounding alone.

7. Though if one has the files on one's computer and can play "drop the needle" via moving the time cursor on the playback application, the differences between harmonic fields, say ten minutes apart, are dramatic. They are, however, like the differences of

voicings of a single giant chord (different inversions) rather than mutually exclusive pitch collections, a fruit of the background modal structure of each *Veil*.

8. Indeed, Adams seems to make the connection even closer with his directions for lighting of the piece.

9. "For more than thirty-five years I've aspired to the ideal of a unified field of pitch and rhythm that Cowell proposes in New Musical Resources. In *Veils* and *Vesper* I finally achieved it" (e-mail communication of the composer to author).

10. And also performed by orchestras scattered on mountaintops along a river valley.

Bibliography

Adams, John Luther. "Strange and Sacred Noise." *Yearbook of Soundscape Studies. Vol. 1: Northern Soundscapes*. Eds. R. Murray Schafer and Helmi Järviluoma. Tampere 1998, 143–46.

———. "Remembering James Tenney." *Musicworks*, no. 98 (summer 2007).

———. *The Place Where You Go to Listen*. Middletown, Connecticut: Wesleyan University Press, 2009.

———. *Winter Music: Composing the North*. Middletown, Connecticut: Wesleyan University Press, 2004.

Cowell, Henry. *New Musical Resources*. Cambridge & New York: Cambridge University Press, 1930.

Gann, Kyle. *American Music in the Twentieth Century*. New York: Schirmer, 1997.

Ives, Charles. *Essays Before a Sonata, The Majority, and Other Writings*. New York: W. W. Norton, 1961, 1962.

———. *Memos*. New York, W. W. Norton, 1972.

Nyman, Michael. *Experimental Music: Cage and Beyond*. Cambridge & New York: Cambridge University Press, 1999.

Tenney, James. *Meta + Hodos* and *META Meta + Hodos*. Oakland, California: Frog Peak Music, 1986.

Bernd Herzogenrath

14 * The Weather of Music
Sounding Nature in the Twentieth
and Twenty-first Centuries

Climate is what you expect. Weather is what you get.

* ROBERT HEINLEIN, *Time Enough for Love*

*Music as I conceive it is ecological. You could go further
and say that it IS ecology.*

* JOHN CAGE, *For the Birds*

What is the weather of music? In seminal works of classical music which refer to the seasons (Schumann's Symphony No. 1, "Frühling [Spring]"; Gershwin's "Summertime"; or Vivaldi's *The Four Seasons*), or to the weather, such as Beethoven's Symphony No. 6 ("Pastorale"), with its fourth movement, "Thunderstorm," composers were primarily concerned with an *acoustic/musical translation* of *subjective sense perceptions*, that is, with a *representation* of nature and natural forces. Sometimes, the representation even threatens to *erase* nature itself—Gustav Mahler, when his friend, the conductor Bruno Walter, visited the composer in Steinbach at Attersee in the mountainous region in Upper Austria and was impressed by the spectacular vista of the Höllengebirge, is reported to have commented: "You won't have to watch it anymore—I have already composed it away . . ." (Walter 30).

This essay, however, is interested in the question of whether there is another connection between nature, weather, and music beyond representation, if weather phenomena themselves can be music, and if music itself can be "meteorological." I argue that whereas the composers of the eighteenth and nineteenth centuries were mainly interested in the *representation* of the subjective effects of weather phenomena, the avant-garde more and more focuses on the *reproduction* of the processes and dynamics of the weather as a system on the edge of chaos. I will illustrate this by the additional claim that a particular American modernist tradition in music from Charles Ives via John Cage to John Luther Adams starts with the writings of Henry David Thoreau—who provides an aesthetics of music, the radicalism of which is only followed up upon today and culminates in John Luther Adams's search for an "ecology of music."[1]

Let me first point out the particularity of Thoreau's musical aesthetics and "musical ecology." In 1851, Thoreau notes an acoustic experience in his journals that reveals his particular sensibility to his sonic environment—"Yesterday and to-day the stronger winds of autumn have begun to blow, and the telegraph harp has sounded loudly ... the tone varying with the tension of different parts of the wire. The sound proceeds from near the posts, where the vibration is apparently more rapid" (*Journal* III: 11). This was not an isolated case: Thoreau focuses on the "sound of nature"—and in particular the "sound of the weather"—in various other entries in his journals: "Nature makes no noise. The howling storm, the rustling leaf, the pattering rain are no disturbance, there is an essential and unexplored harmony in them" (I: 12). Thoreau is exploring the audible world like a sound-archaeologist, carefully distinguishing "sound" from "music":[2] "now I see the beauty and full meaning of that word 'sound.' Nature always possesses a certain sonorousness, as in the hum of insects, the booming of ice ... which indicates her sound state" (I: 226–27). What Thoreau is pointing at is the fact that nature itself produces what one might call ambient sound. Thoreau's sensitivity for environmental sounds heralds an avant-garde aesthetics in music that begins with the work of Charles Ives. That Ives, and Cage and Adams as well, were effectively influenced by Thoreau is beyond question. I am interested more in which *particular* inspirations these composers draw from Thoreau's aesthetics, and how they made these inspirations fruitful for their own ecology of music. Thus, let me begin with Ives's reading of Thoreau.

Charles Ives
The Weather of Music as Representation
Far from the madding crowds, metropolises and music centers of the world, awry to every "trend" in the classical music of the declining nineteenth century, Ives was composing his music in Danbury, Connecticut, a music that was intimately related to New England Transcendentalism, a literary-philosophical movement that can be understood both as a secular brand of American Puritanism, and as American Romanticism, since it drew its inspiration from that of which America had in abundance—Nature (with a capital N). American Transcendentalism is inextricably intertwined with the names Ralph Waldo Emerson and Thoreau. While Emerson's metaphysical and idealistic (in the sense of a Hegelian Idealism) brand of Transcendentalism made him the philosophical spokesman of the movement, his disciple Thoreau followed a much more materialist and physical philosophy, without however completely casting off Emersonian Metaphysics. This seemingly small difference in the initial conditions will have important effects, since Thoreau's ambivalence in this matter will result in the contrasting readings of his work by Ives and Cage respectively.

Ives is a dyed-in-the-wool Transcendentalist, and Thoreau is promoted to the role of private patron saint for his own conception of music. In an essay on Thoreau, Ives emphasizes that "if there shall be a program for our music, let it follow [Thoreau's] thought on an autumn day of Indian summer at Walden . . ." (*Essays* 67). In these 1920 *Essays Before a Sonata*, which Ives conceived as a literary counterpart to his Piano Sonata No 2 ("Concord"), Ives summarizes his understanding of the central idea of Emersonian Transcendentalism, which is also the guiding tenet of his own work — "Is it not this courageous universalism that gives conviction to [Emerson's] prophecy, and that makes his symphonies of revelation begin and end with nothing but the strength and beauty of innate goodness in man, in Nature and in God — the greatest and most inspiring theme of Concord Transcendental philosophy?" (*Essays* 35).

If Ives's phrase "symphonies of revelation" obviously refers to both Emerson's visionary power and the musicality of his oratorical prose, Ives also finds these very qualities in Thoreau's writings — "Thoreau was a great musician, not because he played the flute but because he did not have to go to Boston to hear 'The Symphony.' The rhythm of his prose . . . would determine his value as a composer. He was divinely conscious of the enthusiasm of Nature, the emotion of her rhythms, and the harmony of her solitude" (51).

The reason for Ives's reference to both Emerson and Thoreau can be found in the observation that Ives reads Thoreau's materialist sound-aesthetics on the foil of Emerson's Idealism, according to which nature is the expression (and effect) of reason — "the whole of nature is a metaphor of the human mind" ("Nature" 24). As has been pointed out, in Emerson's work, the subject's triumph over nature takes center stage (Schulz 117). Defining intuition and imagination as primary sources of a creative comprehension of Truth, for Emerson, the creative subject attains a divine status — "Whoever creates is God" (*Journals* V: 341).

To Emerson mind, not matter, is of prime importance — matter is only a manifestation of the mind. Thoreau, in contrast, stresses the material and sensual aspects of nature — "We need pray for no higher heaven than the pure senses can furnish, a *purely* sensuous life . . . Is not Nature . . . that of which she is commonly taken to be a symbol merely?" (*A Week* 307). Thoreau does not *read* nature like, does not interpret nature according to a spiritual principle external to it — such a principle, because of nature's manifoldness, is immanent to it. For Thoreau, nature and its music are not only "God's voice, the divine breath audible" (*Journal* I: 154), but also — and maybe even first and foremost — "the sound of circulation in nature's veins" (I: 251). It is in this stress on nature as sensuous experience and materiality that Thoreau deviates from Emerson. Thoreau focuses on (the music of) nature as a material, physical process, not as an Emersonian emblem of reason—"The very globe *continually transcends and translates itself* . . . The whole tree itself is but one leaf, and rivers are still vaster leaves whose pulp is intervening earth" (*Walden* 306–7). Transcendentalism is understood by Thoreau to be completely physical—the natural, dynamic process of metamorphosis, of continuous change . . . transcendence becomes immanence . . .

Gilles Deleuze rarely mentions Thoreau in his writings. Yet, in a prominent passage where he actually does, he refers precisely to Thoreau's "affirmation of a world *in process*, an *archipelago*. Not even a puzzle, whose pieces when fitted together would constitute a whole, but rather a wall of loose, uncemented stones, where every element has a value in itself but also in relation to others; isolated and floating relations, islands and straits, immobile points and sinuous lines" (*Critical and Clinical* 86).

For Emerson, in contrast, nature is the manifestation of the spirit, of reason, and the "music of nature" is spirit/reason expressing itself, is thus pure transcendence, pure metaphysics.[3]

Even if Ives is following Thoreau in his music aesthetics and makes the sonority of the world his main principle, he is mainly interested in the sonority of the human world, which he does not reproduce, but *represents*, and which he generates from various quotations and samples taken from European classical music, American popular tunes, and liturgical music, as well as from the compositorial transformation of sounds of everyday human life. Thus, Ives does not only compose nature, but complex cityscapes/soundscapes, impressions of man's urban "second nature"—thus, in *Over the Pavements*, he layers the irregular movements, speeds, and rhythms of people, carts, and horse-carriages into a polyrhythmic, albeit controlled, ensemble: "In the early morning, the sounds of people going to and fro, all different Steps, and sometimes all the same . . . I was struck with how many different and changing kinds of beats, time, rhythms, etc. went on together—but quite naturally, or at least not unnaturally when you get used to it" (*Memos* 62).

In a similar vein, his *Holidays Symphony*, according to Ives, paints "pictures in music of common events in the lives of common people" (*Memos* 97–98), and his hymns "*represent* the sternness and strength and austerity of the Puritan character" (*Memos* 39, emphasis added). With Ives transferring the Emersonian Transcendentalism's "correspondence" of spirit and nature to the realm of music,[4] his "weather of music" always coagulates into a *representation*, that is, a sonic picture of the weather—for instance, in the *Holidays Symphony*, an acoustic "picture of the dismal, bleak, cold weather of a February night near Fairfield" (*Memos* 96), with the weather itself in turn "reflecting the sternness of the Puritan's fibre" (*Memos* 96n1). If, according to Emerson, "language clothes nature as the air clothes the earth" (*Journals* V: 246), and if the use of "compositorial languages," such as tonality or atonality, according to Ives, depend "a good deal—as clothes depend on the thermometer—on what one is trying to do" (*Essays* 117), which representational effect one is aiming at, then, quite obviously, bad weather (or weather at all) does not really seem to exist for Ives—only inappropriate outdoor gear.

Thus, even if Ives explicitly refers to Thoreau, his relation to Thoreau, with all of Ives's interest in experimental soundscapes, is a one-sided and single-minded affair at most. For Ives, listener and composer are aural equivalents to Emerson's almighty and visual *me*—as with Emerson, music for Ives is not only "purely a symbol of a mental concept" ("Correspondence" 115),[5] but the almost mystical revelation of the Emersonian Over-Soul, with the composer's role matching the one of Emerson's Poet: "For Poetry was all written before time was, and whenever we are so finely organized that we can penetrate into that region where the air is music, we hear those primal warblings . . . The men of more delicate ear write down these cadences more faithfully, and these transcripts though imperfect, become the songs of the nations" ("The Poet" 449).

Like Emerson, Ives stresses the need for the representation and translation of those "primal warblings," since he, notwithstanding his acceptance of "sounds," always emphasizes the need of a "subjective corrective" to bring out/about the sounds' "ethereal quality" ("Music and Its Future" 192). For Thoreau, however, the "music of nature" needs and requires no translation—"This earth was the most glorious musical instrument, and I was audience to its strains" (*Journal* II: 307). Thoreau lets the sounds rest and dwell in their semantic indeterminacy, focusing on "the language which all things and events speak without metaphor" (*Walden* 11) instead, a language of the real that, beyond the seemingly stable and fixed realm of representation, is an open, dynamic system that is "permeated by unformed, unstable matters, by flows in all directions, by free intensities" (Deleuze/Guattari *Thousand Plateaus* 40), a real that, because of its machinic set-up, in fact "is the abolition of all metaphor" (69).

Ives, in his privileging of the idea over the senses, does not follow Thoreau in his deviation from (and perhaps re-conceptualization of) Emerson's idealistic Transcendentalism, and is thus closer to Emerson than to Thoreau.[6] When Ives takes over from Thoreau the development of a conception of art that is indifferent to the source of its materials, however, and also to more traditional aspects of form, he begins a turn in music that proceeded to become an aesthetic dictum with avant-gardists such as John Cage.

John Cage

The Weather of Music as Mapping

"Is not all music program music? Is not . . . music . . . representative in its essence?" (*Essays* 4). Cage would have definitively answered Ives's rhetorical question with a firm "No!" Cage deviates from Ives in that he precisely puts Thoreau's shift of emphasis toward nature's materiality center stage in his own aesthetics. Cage came across Thoreau's *Journals* for the first time in 1967, and has since made Thoreau not only the addressee of numerous compositions, but his "[retroactive] muse": "Reading Thoreau's *Journal*, I discover any idea I've ever had worth its salt" ("Diary" 18). One of the challenging ideas that Cage saw already "prefigured" in Thoreau is the nondualistic conception of the world that counters Emerson's doctrine of the "metaphoricity of nature" and the partitioning of the world into *me* and *not-me* with a fundamental co-existence of both spheres—according to Thoreau, "all beauty, all music, all delight springs from apparent dualism but real unity" (*Journal* I: 340). Beauty (and music) for Thoreau and Cage are explicitly *not* Hegel's "idea made real in the sensuous" (284)—and Emerson and Ives would certainly have embraced the Hegelian concept. Nature, for Thoreau and Cage, is not a function of the idea: perceptions are not interpretations of the world, but part of that world. This notion completely contradicts both the Idealism inherent to Emerson's Transcendentalism and its claim that the subject imposes its power on matter. If Emerson claims that "the poet conforms things to his thoughts . . . and impresses his being thereon" ("Nature" 34), that the creative subject in-forms matter in the first place, then for Thoreau, in contrast, "the earth I tread on . . . is not a dead inert mass. It is a body, has a spirit" (*Journal* II: 165). With regard to the telegraph harp being played by the weather, the resulting music of which he claimed to be "the most glorious music I ever heard" (*Journal* III: 219), Thoreau states: "the finest uses of things are accidental. Mr. Morse did not invent this music" (*Journal* III: 220).[7] Cage finds in Thoreau thus both the focus on materiality of nature, which Ives still had "subjectified" into human and symbolic music, and the accidental, which Ives always had attempted to control. It is exactly these parameters that Cage turns into the center of his compositions. Against the traditional composer's attempt at control, Cage envisions "a composing of sounds within a universe predicated upon the sounds themselves rather than the mind which can envisage their coming into being" (*Silence* 27–28). For Deleuze and Guattari, this focus on "pure sounds" and random processes "is a question of freeing times . . . a nonpulsed time for a floating music . . . It is undoubtedly John Cage who first and most perfectly deployed this fixed sound plane, which affirms a process against all structure and genesis, a floating time against pulsed time or tempo, experimentation against any kind of interpretation, and in which silence as sonorous rest also marks the absolute state of movement" (*Thousand Plateaus* 267).

In his absolute reduction of subjective control and his valorization of sound Cage combines two other maxims of Thoreau—"the music is not in the tune; it is in the sound" (*Journal* IV: 144), and "the peculiarity of a work of genius is the absence of the speaker from his speech. He is but the medium" (III: 236). The radical difference in Ives's and Cage's reference to Thoreau can be illustrated by recourse to a passage from *Walden*: "Sometimes, on Sundays, I heard the bells, the Lincoln, Acton, Bedford, or Concord bell, when the wind was favorable . . . At a sufficient distance over the woods this sound acquires a certain vibratory hum, as if the pine needles in the horizon were the strings of a harp which it swept" (*Walden* 123).

Ives repeatedly quotes this passage and always emphasizes the "spiritualizing effect" of the sound described by Thoreau—the symbolic meaning of the distant church bells, a "transcendental tune" (*Essays* 69), a mere echo of a more divine "sphere music." Cage, in contrast, combines Thoreau's auditory observation with his remark on the accidental Aeolian music of the telegraph harp. This merging of sound and indeterminacy becomes his "Music for Carillon," a composition for chimes, which for Cage "translates" nature "without metaphor," by transferring the natural patterns of the wood's grain into musical notation. By drawing stave-lines onto the wood, Cage lets the musician 'read' the knotholes and grain patterns as notes—in a similar way, in "Music for Piano," Cage uses the material irregularities of a sheet of paper to determine the position of notes.

Thoreau's preference for sounds and for the accidental makes him a progenitor of a decidedly avant-garde musical practice in Cage's eyes, a practice that does away with the individual as locus and agency of control. This also means that this aesthetics is not dealing with the *representation* of affectations and sensations anymore, but with the *reproduction* of the dynamics of natural processes. Thus Cage not only states the importance of sounds (and silence) for him as a composer, but claims much more fundamentally that "the function of the artist is to imitate nature in her manner of operation" (*Silence* 194). Here, I argue, music becomes "meteorological," since nature operates according to extremely complex dynamics, probabilities and improbabilities . . . like the weather! What's fascinating about the weather thus is not just the power of its atmospheric special effects, the combined LucasArts™ of thunder and lightning, but even more the fact that the weather is a highly complex, dynamic, open (and thus in the long run unpredictable and uncontrollable) system of forces and intensities. For Cage's aesthetics and compositional practice, this means that they reveal a line of flight, a vector "away from ideas of order towards no ideas of order" (*Silence*

20), with the stress being on *ideas* of order, that is, a *mental* order as against a "natural order" with its own "manners of operation" and self-organization. This introduction of indeterminacy and chance into the compositional process molecularizes it, frees it from the molar regime of representation and makes it form rhizomatic connections with the virtualities of the environment. Cage's swerve in his compositional plan away from ideas of order toward chance can be read parallel to Deleuze's distinction between the (molar) plan of organization and the (molecular) "plan of composition" (*Spinoza* 128), in which "there is no longer a form, but only relations of velocity between infinitesimal particles of an unformed material. There is no longer a subject, but only individuating affective states of an anonymous force. Here the plan is concerned only with motions and rests, with dynamic affective charges" (*Spinoza* 128).

Against the Emersonian stress on the representation (and control) of nature by the individual, Thoreau and Cage emphasize *perception* as a practice in both art and life. According to Chris Shultis, Cage and Ives posit "the two poles of self (. . . the coexisting and controlling) in American experimental music, connecting contemporary concerns to a nineteenth-century past" (xviii), two poles already prefigured in Thoreau and Emerson. The compositional complexity of Ives's work is due to an *intertextual* interweaving of "samples of culture" that are ultimately (re)inscribed in a higher (transcendent) unity. The modernist Ives folds cultural quotations, including cultural quotations of nature, nature *as* a cultural quotation, into each other and thus implicitly refers to a "supplementary dimension" underlying these quotes—and, as Deleuze and Guattari remark with regard to the cut-ups of William S. Burroughs, "in this supplementary dimension, unity continues its spiritual labor" (*Thousand Plateaus* 6). Like the work of Joyce, Ives's work "affirm[s] a properly angelic and superior unity" (6)—"this is to say the fascicular system does not really break with dualism, with the complementary between a subject and an object, a natural reality, and a spiritual reality" (6). With regard to that "higher unity" in Ives, David Nicholls has poignantly referred to it as an "organized chaos" (67). For Cage, it is a "purposeless play," an *against organization/control* that is (at) the heart of life and art: "This play . . . is an affirmation of life—not an attempt to bring order out of chaos nor to suggest improvements in creation, but simply a way to wake up to the very life we're living, which is so excellent once one gets one's mind and desires out the way and lets it act of its own accord" (*Silence* 12).

It is that attitude in Thoreau to "the very life we're living" that makes him such an inspiration for Cage—"Thoreau only wanted one thing: to see and hear the world around him . . . he lets things speak and write as they are" (*For the Birds* 233–34). Instead of painting symbolic sonic pictures, Cage's compositions rather construct maps and charts, that is, *topographies* of natural processes. It is thus more than a coincidence that the motif of the map is so important in Cage's work—see on the one hand his many compositions based on atlases or celestial charts, such as *Atlas Eclipticalis*, or the *Etudes Australes* and the *Etudes Boreales*, and on the other hand Cage's various graphic notations . . . maps, not tracings, in that they are "entirely oriented toward an experimentation in contact with the real" (*Thousand Plateaus* 12).

Cage's *mapping* of the weather of music finds its maybe most direct and literal reflection/precipitation in his *Lecture on the Weather*. In this composition, passages from Thoreau's journals (determined by chance operations) read simultaneously by various speakers in tempi of their own choice, and field recordings of wind, rain, and thunder condense into a commentary on the political climate of the USA in the mid-1970s. In a performance of *Lecture on the Weather* at the Cage-Fest in Strathmore, Maryland, on May 5, 1989, "doors were open to the outside where a storm began to be audible and visible . . . this had the interesting effect of eradicating the distinction between 'inside' and 'outside'—the meteorological display over Strathmore Hall was continuous with what was going on in the room where Cage's more gentle storm included the weather of predetermined and coincidental conjunctions of sound and voice variables" (Retallack 248)—"the performance in fact "is not *about* weather; it *is* weather" (Perloff 25).

Cage's weather of music thus can be understood as an assemblage of sonic intensities and natural processes—the compositions become "meteorological systems" themselves. These systems, however, are, as Cage himself admits and regrets, still "framed"—even silence has the precise temporal coordinates of 4:33. This is one of the decisive differences between Cage and the sound installations of John Luther Adams that aim at reproducing the weather of music as a dynamic *ecosystem*.

John Luther Adams
The Weather of Music as Ecosystem

As Gigliola Nocera has emphasized, the living and working conditions of Ives and Cage were comparable to Thoreau's isolation at Walden Pond—Ives was working far away from the art centers in Danbury, Connecticut, and Cage in Stony Point, in New York State (see Nocera 356). Isolation is an even bigger issue with John Luther Adams,[8] who lives and works in Fairbanks, Alaska, approximately 125 miles south of the Arctic. Adams's work is highly influenced by his environment, this Arctic, "hyperborean zone, far from the temperate regions" (Deleuze, *Critical and Clinical* 82), far from equilibrium.

And like Cage and Ives before him, Adams sees himself connected to the Transcendentalist position as well—in particular that of Thoreau:

I feel my music is part of a tradition of independent composers from Ives, Varese and Cowell, through Cage, Harrison, Feldman, Nancarrow and Tenney. Thoreau was an early source of inspiration for me. *Walden* is one of the few books that actually changed my life. There is a certain aspiration to transcendence in my work. But, as with Thoreau, it's a transcendence that rises not from religion, rather from deep within the Earth. (John Luther Adams, personal email to the author, Sept. 26, 2007)

From his early works onwards he has always pointed out that he wants his music to be understood as an interaction with nature—as a site-specific contact with the environment that he calls "sonic geography" ("Resonance of Place" 8).

Adams's sonic geography can be found in a cycle called *songbirdsongs* (1974–80), consisting of various imitations of Alaskan birds reminiscent of Olivier Messiaen's *Catalogues d'oiseaux*. Although Adams in the compositional process and the transcription brings birdsong into a human scale in terms of tempo, modulation, pitch, and other qualities, he conceptualizes the different melodies—or "refrains"—as a "toolkit," so that during the performance, an ever-new aggregation of phrases and motifs comes into existence, an open system, indeterminate in combination, length, intonation, tempi, and so on. *Earth and the Great Weather* (1990–93), an evening-long piece, a kind of opera consisting of field recordings of wind, melting glaciers, thunder, in combination with ritual drummings and chants of the Alaskan indigenous people, was "conceived as a journey through the physical, cultural and spiritual landscapes of the Arctic" ("Sonic Geography"), a traversing of smooth "Eskimo space" (Deleuze and Guattari, *Thousand Plateaus* 494).[9]

In a further step, Adams combined his "sonic geography" with the concept of what he calls "sonic geometry" ("Strange and Sacred Noise" 143). Adams is more and more interested in the "noisier" sounds of nature and refers to findings of Chaos Theory and Fractal Geometry in order to find sonic equivalents for nature's *modus operandi*—*Strange and Sacred Noise* (1991–97) is an example of this approach.[10]

To date, the culmination of Adams's sonic geography/geometry has been his recent project *The Place Where You Go to Listen*, the title of which refers to an Inuit legend according to which the shamans hear the wisdom of the world in the whisper of the wind and the murmur of the waves, being sensitive to what Deleuze, with reference to Leibniz, calls "little perceptions" (*Difference and Repetition* 213).[11]

Adams aims at the realization of a "musical ecosystem, . . . A work of art . . . that is directly connected to the real world in which we live and resonates sympathetically with that world and with the forces of nature" (Mayer, "Northern Exposure"). Adams not only *imitates* nature in its manner of operation, as does Cage; he taps into nature's dynamic processes themselves for the generation of sound and light. Adams developed this project in close collaboration with geologists and physicists—as Adams stated in an interview, "at a certain level, it was like . . . they were the boys in the band" (Mayer, *Living on Earth*).

In Adams's installation, real-time data from meteorological stations all over Alaska and from the five stations of the Alaska Earthquake Information Center are collected, coordinated, and made audible through pink noise filters. As Curt Szuberla, one of the physicists involved in the project, explains, "the strings and bells and drumheads are plucked, bashed and banged based on the geophysical data streams. And the geophysical data streams . . . are the fingers and mallets and bells that hit things and make things sound" (Mayer, *Living on Earth*). *The Place Where You Go to Listen* is a permanent installation at the Museum of the North in Fairbanks, where sound and light are generated in real time through data processing of the day and night rhythms, the rhythm of the seasons, of the moon phases, the weather conditions, and the seismic flows of the magnetic field of the Earth—nature itself, as well as the music it produces, operates according to its own times and speeds (and slownesses). Hours, even days, and more might pass between perceivable seismic changes or changes in the magnetic field of the Earth. *The Place* is an open system, a machinic aggregation operating according to what Deleuze calls "differences of level, temperature, pressure, tension, potential, *difference of intensity*" (*Difference and Repetition* 222)—just like the weather. Adams's noise-filter-machine is plugged into the sun-machine, and also into the wind-machine, rain-machine, and so on; these in turn couple together to form the weather-machine. Digital machines cut into the flows of nature, but within a machine/nature ecology/ontology which is not based on the strict separation of these two spheres in which nature is either a fixed, unchanging essence or the mere retro-effect of culture and representation. It is based rather on an ecology/ontology of dynamics and production. Adams's installation thus presents "modes of individuation beyond those of things, persons or subjects: the individuation, say, of a time of day, of a region, a climate" (Deleuze, *Negotiations* 26).

The Place Where You Go to Listen focuses on nature as process and event—in an almost Stoic emphasis on *becoming* versus *being*, Adams privileges time-sensitive dynamics, not clear-cut states. In his study *La théorie des incorporels dans l'ancien stoicisme*, to which Deleuze refers in *Logic of Sense*, Emile Bréhier states that, according to Stoic thought, "one should not say, 'the tree is green,' but 'the tree greens' . . . what is expressed in this proposition is not a property, such as 'a body is hot,' but an event, such as 'a body becomes hot' " (Bréhier 20–

21).[12] This *becoming*, writes Deleuze, passes the line "between the sensible and the intelligible, or between the soul and the body" (*Dialogues* 63)—or nature and culture—and places itself "between things and events" (*Dialogues* 63). By getting rid of the *is* of representational thought, where an object's quality is at least potentially related to a subject that expresses this quality as an attribute, by replacing fixity with process as both the subject's and the world's manner of operation, these infinitive-becomings have no subject: they refer only to an "'it' of the event" (*Dialogues* 64). Adams's installation goes further in the direction of the event than Ives and even Cage—although these two composers had also already pondered the conflict between the processuality of nature, and the means of art. Ives asked himself: "A painter paints a sunset—can he paint the setting sun? . . . [Is there] . . . an analogy . . . between both the state and power of artistic perceptions and the law of perpetual change, that ever-flowing stream, partly biological, partly cosmic, ever going on in ourselves, in nature, in all life?" (*Essays* 71).

Ives tried to master this problematics by increasing the complexity of his compositional means. Cage also emphasized that he did not think it correct to say "the world as it *is*"—"it *is* not, it becomes! It moves, it changes! It doesn't wait for us to change . . . it is more mobile than you can imagine. You're getting closer to this reality when you say as it 'presents itself'; that means that it is not there, existing as an object. The world, the real is not an object. It is a process" (*For the Birds* 80).

But—Ives was still the subject in control of chaos, and Cage, in spite of all indeterminacy, regretted that he was still creating "clear-cut" objects. Adam solves this problem by leaving the executing/processing energy to the processual forces of nature itself. Music and environment thus become an ecosystem of a dynamics of acoustic and optic resonances interacting in and with an environment in constant flux. "Music" in this sense thus for Adams becomes something entirely different than a means of human communication about an external world: "If music grounded in tone is a means of sending messages to the world, then music grounded in noise is a means of receiving messages *from* the world. . . . As we listen carefully to noise, the whole world becomes music. Rather than a vehicle for self-expression, music becomes a mode of awareness" ("Ecology of Music").

Thus, *The Place Where You Go to Listen* leaves behind the idea of a music *about* nature, of music as a means of the *representation* of nature and landscape, on which Ives, for example, still relied, and creates music as a part of nature, as coextensive with the environment: "Through attentive and sustained listening to the resonances of this place, I hope to make music which belongs here, somewhat like the plants and the birds" (Adams, "Resonance of Place" 8). Even more direct than Cage, Adams emphasizes nature's manners of operation in not only taking them as a model, but by directly accessing such means and relating them to the becoming of a site-specific environment, creating works that *are* this relation—a music of place, of a place where you go to listen.

Even if Adams does not explicitly refer to Thoreau, his work is indebted to Thoreau's sound aesthetics—even more so, I argue, than Ives's or even Cage's work. As it is for Adams, music already for Thoreau is part of the environment—nature has no need to be translated or represented, nature and the environment already sound, already *express themselves*. In *Walden*, Thoreau writes that "making the yellow soil express its summer thought in bean leaves and blossoms rather than in wormwood and piper and millet grass, making the earth say beans instead of grass—this was my daily work" (*Walden* 157). If Thoreau calls this natural expression by the name of "saying," he is evoking a correspondence between the expression and production of nature—a correspondence that goes far beyond the level of representation. The expression of nature on the side of production arrives in the subject as impression, so that from the perspective of culture, what we call representation is already rooted in nature—"every word is rooted in the soil, is indeed flowery and verduous" (*Journal* I: 386).

"A history of music would be like . . . the history of gravitation"—with regard to Adams's physico-musical ecosystem, this sentence perfectly makes sense as a postmodern credo of New Music . . . however, this sentence is Thoreau's (*Journal* I: 325), and here we have come full circle, to Walden Pond, where Thoreau was hearing an ecology of music that only today is being realized.

Notes

1. And it should be noted that this radicalism makes Thoreau a patron saint not only of music, but also of ecology.

2. See also Thoreau's essay "Walking" and its concept of "wildness"—"sound" can be read as "wildness" with regard to music (as sound organized by a traditional composer) . . . the unformed, unintended, untamed in comparison to John Sullivan Dwight's canonization in Thoreau's time of European Classical Music (and in particular the compositions of Beethoven) as *the* paradigm for a future American Music.

3. In the above quotation from *Essays Critical and Clinical*, Deleuze explicitly refers to Thoreau and Emerson, and does not discriminate between their respective brands of Transcendentalism. For reasons that I hope become clear in this essay, I see the need for a more precise distinction between the two.

4. For the theory of correspondence, see, for example, Emerson's "Nature."

5. See also: " 'the music' as being the character of the idea or spirit, quite apart from its embodiment in sound" (John Kirkpatrick's footnote in *Memos* 242).

6. Betty E. Chmaj calls Ives the "Emerson of American music" (396). On the relation Ives/Emerson, see also Shultis.

7. Thoreau goes even further and envisions the coexistence of the telegraph harp with the greater cycle of nature—"What must the birds and beasts think where it passes through woods, who heard only the squeaking of trees before! I should think that these strains would get into their music at last. Will not the mockingbird be heard one day inserting this strain in his medley?" (*Journal* III: 219). There is a loud and clear "Yes!" to Thoreau's question—today's birds have integrated radio jingles and cell phone ring tones in their song . . .

8. Adams, it has to be noted, is also an environmental activist and founder of Alaska's Green Party. Mitchell Morris thus dubs Adams a " 'Green' composer" (131), referring, however, to the notion of ecology as in *Deep* Ecology, whereas I would suggest placing Adams firmly within a Deleuzian ecology that is based on a nondualist ontology.

9. In fact, the first movement of *Earth and the Great Weather* is already named "The Place Where You Go to Listen."

10. *Strange and Sacred Noise* is a concert-length cycle of six movements for percussion quartet. Its first and last movements (". . . dust into dust . . ." and ". . . and dust rising . . .") are based on the Cantor set and Cantor dust (the two-dimensional version of the Cantor set). These fractals model the behavior of electrical noise, which Adams takes as a diagram for the percussion set to explore "the dynamic form of the Cantor dust, whereby in an infinite process, line segments are divided into two segments by the removal of their middle third" (Feisst, "Music as Place"). See also Sabine M. Feisst, "Klanggeographie—Klanggeometrie. Der US-amerikanische Komponist John Luther Adams." *MusikTexte* 91 (November 2001): 4–14.

11. A direct Leibnizian reference can be found in his *New Essays on Human Understanding*: "To hear this noise as we do, we must hear the parts which make up this whole, that is the noise of each wave, although each of these little noises makes itself known only when combined confusedly with all the others, and would not be noticed if the wave which made it were by itself . . . we must have some perception of each of these noises, however faint they may be; otherwise there would be no perception of a hundred thousand waves, since a hundred thousand nothings cannot make something" (55). Such a "sonorous ocean," it can be argued, the becoming-perceptible of micro-sounds "underneath the [human] radar," also provides a more materialist version of the Pythagorean idea of "sphere music": contrary to a the harmonious universe rotating according to well-tempered intervals, it would refer to the multiplicity of sounds of the world—nature changes constantly, everything moves, and everything that moves oscillates according to a certain frequency, the total result of which would be white noise (the murmur of the universe). Such a concept, I argue, also defines much of today's electronic music (see, for example, Murphy, in particular 161–62).

12. My translation of: "On ne doit pas dire, pensaient-ils: 'L'arbre est vert,' mais: 'L'arbre verdoie' . . . Ce qui s'exprime dans le jugement, ce n'est pas une propriété comme: un corps est chaud, mais une évènement comme: un corps s'échauffe."

Bibliography

Adams, John Luther. "Resonance of Place." *The North American Review* 279: 1 (Jan/Feb 1994), 8–18.

———. "Sonic Geography of the Arctic. An Interview with Gayle Young." (1998) http://www.johnlutheradams.com/interview/gayleyoung.html (last accessed July 8, 2010).

———. "Strange and Sacred Noise." *Yearbook of Soundscape Studies. Vol. 1: "Northern Soundscapes."* Ed. R. Murray Schafer and Helmi Järviluoma. Tampere 1998, 143–6.

———. "In Search of An Ecology of Music." (2006) http://www.johnlutheradams.com/writings/ecology.html (last accessed July 8, 2010).

———. Quoted in Amy Mayer. "Northern Exposure: A museum exhibit converts activity in the Alaskan environment into an ever changing sound show." *Boston Globe* April 16, 2006.

———. Quoted in *Living On Earth*. Radio Interview with Amy Mayer, see www.loe.org/shows/segments.htm?programID=06-P13–00016&segmentID=5 (last accessed July 8, 2010).

Bréhier, Emile. *La théorie des incorporels dans l'ancien stoicisme*. Paris: Librairie Philosophique J. Vrin, 1970.

Cage, John. *Silence*. Hanover, New Hampshire: Wesleyan University Press, 1973.

———. *For the Birds: John Cage in Conversation with Daniel Charles*. Boston and London: Marion Boyars, 1981.

Chmaj, Betty E. "The Journey and the Mirror: Emerson and the American Arts." *Prospects* 10 (1985): 353–408.

Deleuze, Gilles. *Spinoza: Practical Philosophy*. Trans. Robert Hurley. San Francisco: City Lights Books, 1988.

———. *Difference and Repetition*. Trans. Paul Patton. New York: Columbia University Press, 1994.

———. *Negotiations*. Trans. Martin Joughin. New York: Columbia University Press, 1995.

———. *Essays Critical and Clinical*. Trans. Daniel W. Smith and Michael A. Greco. Minneapolis: University of Minnesota Press, 1997.

Deleuze, Gilles, and Guattari, Felix. *A Thousand Plateaus: Capitalism and Schizophrenia*. Trans. B. Massumi. Minneapolis: University of Minnesota Press, 1987.

———. *What Is Philosophy?* Trans. H. Tomlinson and G. Burchell. New York: Columbia University Press, 1994.

Emerson, Ralph Waldo. "Nature." *Ralph Waldo Emerson. Essays and Lectures*. Ed. Joel Porte. New York: Library of America, 1983, 5–49.

———. *Ralph Waldo Emerson. Essays and Lectures*. Ed. Joel Porte. New York: Library of America, 1983, 445–68.

———. *The Journals and Miscellaneous Notebooks of Ralph Waldo Emerson*. 16 Vols. Ed. William H. Gilman et al. Cambridge, Mass.: Harvard University Press, 1960–83.

Feisst, Sabine M. "Klanggeographie—Klanggeometrie. Der US-amerikanische Komponist John Luther Adams." *MusikTexte* 91 (November 2001): 4–14.

———. "Music as Place, Place as Music. The Sonic Geography of John Luther Adams." (unpublished manuscript).

Hegel, G. W. F. *Aesthetics: Lectures on Fine Art, Vol. I*. Trans. T.M. Know. Oxford: Oxford University Press, 1998.

Ives, Charles. *Essays Before a Sonata, The Majority, and Other Writings*. Ed. Howard Boatwright. New York and London: W. W. Norton & Company, 1999.

———. *Memos*. Ed. John Kirkpatrick. London: Calder & Boyars, 1973.

———. "Music and Its Future." *American Composers on American Music. A Symposium*. Ed. Henry Cowell. Palo Alto: Stanford University Press, 1933, 191–8.

———. "Correspondence with Clifton Joseph Furness, July 24 1923." Ives Collection, Yale University. qtd. in Charles W. Ward 'Charles Ives's Concept of Music.' *Current Musicology* 18 (1974): 114–9.

Leibniz, G. W. *New Essays on Human Understanding*. Ed. and trans. Peter Remnant and Jonathan Bennett. New York: Cambridge University Press, 2nd Edition 1996.

Morris, Mitchell. "Ectopian Sound or The Music of John Luther Adams and Strong Environmentalism." *Crosscurrents and Counterpoints*. Ed. Per F. Broman et al. Göteborg: 1998, 129–41.

Murphy, Timothy S. "What I Hear Is Thinking Too: The Deleuze Tribute Recordings." *Deleuze and Music*. Ed. Ian Buchanan and Marcel Swiboda. Edinburgh: Edinburgh University Press, 2004, 159–75.

Nicholls, David. *American Experimental Music, 1890–1940*. Cambridge: Cambridge University Press, 1990.

Nocera, Gigliola. "Henry David Thoreau et le neo-transcendentalisme de John Cage." *Revue d'Estetique* (1987–88): 351–69.

Perloff, Marjorie. *Radical Artifice. Writing Poetry in the Age of Media*. Chicago and London: University of Chicago Press, 1991.

Retallack, Joan. "Poethics of a Complex Realism." *John Cage: Composed in America*. Ed. Marjorie Perloff and Charles Junckerman. Chicago: University of Chicago Press, 1994.

Schulz, Dieter. *Amerikanischer Transzendentalismus: Ralph Waldo Emerson, Henry David Thoreau, Margaret Fuller*. Darmstadt: Wissenschaftliche Buchgesellschaft, 1997.

Shultis, Chris. *Silencing the Sounding Self: John Cage and the Experimental Tradition in Twentieth-Century American Poetry and Music*. Boston: 1998.

Szuberla, Curt. Quoted in *Living On Earth*. Radio interview with Amy Mayer, see www.loe .org/shows/segments.htm?programID=06-P13–00016&segmentID=5 (last accessed July 8, 2010).

Thoreau, Henry David. *The Journal of Henry David Thoreau*. Ed. Bradford Torrey and Francis H. Allen. In fourteen volumes (bound as two). New York: Dover Publications, 1962.

———. *The Illustrated Walden*. Ed. J. Lyndon Shanley. Princeton: Princeton University Press, 1973.

———. *A Week on the Concord and Merrimack Rivers*. Harmondsworth: Penguin, 1998.

Walter, Bruno. *Gustav Mahler. Ein Portrait*. Berlin und Frankfurt: Fischer, 1957. (First Edition: 1936).

David Shimoni

15 * *songbirdsongs* and *Inuksuit*
Creating an Ecocentric Music

C an music be ecocentric? Can it communicate a view of the natural world that, instead of assuming a preeminent role for human beings, inherently values the entire biosphere? It is a question well worth asking, as growing environmental crises threaten both human and nonhuman life on the planet.

People have sought to reflect on their connection to the rest of the natural world through music for a very long time, but many pieces of music inspired by the nonhuman natural world actually say more about the humans who composed them than about their source of inspiration. Beethoven's "Pastoral" Symphony, for instance, musically describes scenes in the country, but Beethoven himself said it was "more a matter of feeling than of painting."[1] In other words, Beethoven was more concerned with expressing a human, subjective experience than composing a physical description. Or take the innumerable songs about nightingales:[2] typically they reveal a lot about the poet who identifies his nighttime thoughts with the nightingale's song, but they illuminate little about the bird's song itself. In fact, very few of the nightingales represented in these pieces exhibit any of the vocal complexity of actual nightingales. In contrast to the communion with nature that exists on the surface of these pieces, the radical simplification of birdsong in a piece that focuses on a human experience communicates an underlying anthropocentric perspective.

Since the turn of the twentieth century, some composers have attempted to represent nature more "authentically." Olivier Messiaen, for example, spent hours listening to and notating birdsongs before using them in compositions. In Messiaen's preface to the score of *Réveil des oiseaux* for chamber orchestra and solo piano, he wrote, "There is nothing but birdsongs in this work. All were heard in the forest and are perfectly authentic." The advent of recording technology seemed to further increase the potential for authentic representations of the natural world. In Ottorino Respighi's *Pini di Roma*, Einojuhani Rautavaara's *Cantus Arcticus*, or Alan Hovhaness's *And God Created Great Whales*, the recorded sounds of birds and whales singing create a startling effect within orchestral pieces.

It seems to me that the drive to authentically represent other musical beings in our music stems from the desire to integrate humans into the greater web of life through sound. We might ask, do these kinds of "authentic" representations communicate an ecocentric perspective any more than the earlier works focused on the human experience of nature?

Let us focus on Messiaen briefly because he is closely associated with the representation of birdsongs. Certainly, Messiaen's notations come closer to conveying the rhythmic and frequency contours of birdsongs than did the efforts of most composers before him. Additionally, when he uses birdsongs he often tries to keep them in their contexts, quoting not one song or species but several.[3] In an interview with Antoine Goléa, Messiaen explained his use of birdsongs this way: "It is in a spirit of no confidence in myself, since I belong to this species (I mean the human species), that I have taken birdsongs as a model. If you want symbols, we can further say that the bird is the symbol of freedom . . . Despite my deep admiration for the folklore of the world, I doubt that one can find in any human music, however inspired, melodies and rhythms that have the sovereign freedom of birdsong" (234).

Messiaen clearly values birdsongs greatly. He says that he is attracted by their "sovereign freedom." But can the freedom that he describes be preserved in a musical work that tries to capture it? Is it possible that pieces that imitate the nonhuman natural world "authentically" often undermine what they try to extol?

In his book *Aesthetic Theory*, Theodor Adorno writes that nature and art are fundamentally opposed and that when we take a studied, or objectifying, approach to nature—whether in a natural park or an artwork—we rob it of its essence: "The concept of natural beauty rubs on a wound, and little is needed to prompt one to associate this wound with the violence that the artwork—a pure artifact—inflicts on nature. Wholly artifactual, the artwork seems to be the opposite of what is not made, nature . . . Through its duplication in art, what appears in nature is robbed of its being-in-itself, in which the experience of nature is fulfilled . . . Planned visits to famous views, to the landmarks of natural beauty, are mostly futile. Nature's eloquence is damaged by the objectification that is the result of studied observation, and ultimately something of this holds true as well for artworks" (81–90).

Moreover, Adorno writes, any attempt to reconnect to nature through naturalistic art is doomed to fail, because it appropriates that which it attempts to celebrate: "All naturalistic art is only deceptively close to nature, because, analogous to industry, it relegates nature to raw material" (86). Thus, when a composer uses birdsong in a composition, he risks communicating a characteristically anthropocentric sense of control over the source, no matter how authentically he replicates it. It is analogous to what we do to a landscape by turning it into a natural park crossed with scenic byways and overlooks: in the words of Alison Byerly, we have "removed it from the realm of nature and designated it a legitimate object of artistic consumption" (53). All of this may be unintentional, but it is communicated nonetheless.

Imitating nature may also produce inferior music. In *The World as Will and Idea*, Arthur Schopenhauer discusses the metaphysics of music and why it should not be imitative of physical things. He suggests that music and the phenomenal world, or nature, are "two different expressions of the same thing" (169) but that music "gives the inmost kernel which precedes all form, or the heart of things" (170). Its expressive power and its universality depend on it expressing this inmost nature of things: "The unutterable depth of all music—by virtue of which it drifts over and beyond us as a paradise familiar yet ever remote, comprehensible and yet so inexplicable—rests on its echoing all the emotions of our inmost nature, but entirely without reality and far removed from its pain" (171). Therefore, he continues, if a piece of music expresses the nature of something that also has a physical manifestation in the world (such as a bird or a tree), the expression "must have proceeded from the direct knowledge of the nature of the world . . . and must not be an imitation produced with conscious intention by means of concepts; otherwise the music does not express the inner nature, the will itself, but merely imitates its phenomenon inadequately" (171). Schopenhauer singles out Haydn's *Seasons* and *Creation* for criticism and most likely would have also criticized Messiaen, Rautavaara, and others for imitating rather than expressing "the inner nature" of their inspirations.

It would seem that any attempt to represent nature in music fails both nature (Adorno) and music (Schopenhauer). Is it possible for a composer to incorporate the music of the nonhuman natural world authentically while preserving the freedom of that world and music's expressive potential? Instead of making music *from* nature, in which nature is treated as a resource, can we make music *with* nature, in such a way that both humans (composer, performers, listeners) and the rest of the natural world retain at least a sense of autonomy and creativity in the process?

In this essay, I want to propose that two pieces by John Luther Adams achieve this state of co-creation with the nonhuman natural world: *songbirdsongs* (1974–79), one of Adams's earliest pieces, and *Inuksuit* (2009), one of his most recent. Adams went in several different directions in the years between these two pieces, yet in *Inuksuit* he brings to fruition a seed that he planted in *songbirdsongs*. The pieces share much in their musical materials, compositional approach, and ecological philosophy. Both reflect Adams's view that "the challenge for artists today is to move beyond self-expression and beyond anthropocentric views of history, to re-imagine and re-create our relationships with this planet and all those (human and other-than-human) with whom we share it" (*Winter Music* 128).

*   *   *

Songbirdsongs consists of nine pieces for piccolos and percussion that incorporate the songs and sounds of nineteen different birds. Adams began each piece in this set by making field transcriptions of birdsongs in Georgia and Alaska. As Messiaen has explained (Samuel 94–95), transcribing birdsongs is a difficult endeavor. Birds use notes located between those that are found in Western scales. Birds are rhythmical but do not necessarily follow a consistent beat. It is difficult to know for which instrument to notate their songs, since they often sing faster and higher than any human instrument can play. Additionally, the sounds they produce vary considerably in timbre, since birds have two voiceboxes that they use both separately and together.

Adams chose to score most of the birdsongs for piccolo, since, among Western instruments, it most closely resembles birds' timbre and register. The technique of flutter-tonguing also allows Adams to approximate the sound of certain bird trills, such as that which the wood thrush uses to end its songs. But the piccolo still has its limitations. The highest note playable on a piccolo is in the range of 4000 Hz, whereas the song of the hermit thrush can reach twice as high.[4] Nor can piccolo players play as quickly or as delicately as a hermit thrush sings in that range. Nor can Adams realistically ask for all of the microtonal pitches that birds use, except by means of *portamento* or pitch-bending. Adams, in fact, makes the ultimate disclaimer in the preface to the score of *songbirdsongs*: "This music is not literal transcription. It is translation. Not imitation, but evocation. My concern is not with precise details of pitch and meter, for too much precision can deafen us to such things as birds and music. I listen for other, less tangible nuances. These melodies and rhythms, then, are not so much constructed artifacts as they are spontaneous affirmations . . . No one has yet explained why the free songs of birds are so simply beautiful . . . Beyond the realm of ideas and emotions, language and sense, we just may hear something of their essence."

Like Messiaen, Adams refers to the "freedom" in birdsongs. He tells us, however, that his "translation" will be more spontaneous than fixed. Indeed, by employing musical indeterminacy to authentically evoke not only the birds' songs but also their singing behavior, Adams preserves both the beautiful details and the essential freedom in the birdsongs.

There is no score, per se, for *songbirdsongs*. Instead, the performance folio for the musicians contains the following: (a) performance notes that apply to

1. Wood Thrush

This was my first setting of birdsong. It dates from spring 1974. I was living in an old farmhouse in Georgia. Each morning before dawn, and again at dusk, haunting, liquid music reverberated through the cool air. As I walked among oaks, dogwoods, poplars and sycamores, now and then I would catch a glimpse of the singers, always deeper in the woods. I listened carefully to these phrases for weeks before trying to write them down. Even now, it's impossible to articulate the feelings that the song of the Wood Thrush stirs in me.

Bamboo Wind Chimes/Celesta
Begin the piece, playing Bamboo Wind Chimes, very gently. Anytime after Piccolo I has played two phrases, begin playing Celesta, with phrase #1. From then on, Celesta phrases and rests may be played in any order. A phrase may be repeated, but not immediately following itself. Between Celesta phrases, return to Wind Chimes. End anytime after Piccolo I.

Piccolo I
Begin 15 to 30 seconds after the Wind Chimes, playing phrase #1. From then on, phrases and rests may be played in any order. A phrase may be repeated, but not immediately following itself. End before the other players, with phrase #3.

Bamboo Wind Chimes/Xylophone
After Piccolo I enters, begin playing Bamboo Wind Chimes. After Piccolo II has played two phrases, begin playing Xylophone, with phrase #1. From then on, phrases and rests may be played in any order. A phrase may be repeated, but not immediately following itself. Between Xylophone phrases, return to Wind Chimes. After Piccolo II has finished, end the piece with phrase #1, followed by gently fading Wind Chimes.

Piccolo II
After the Celesta has played two phrases, enter playing phrase #1. From then on, phrases and rests may be played in any order. A phrase may be repeated, but not immediately following itself. End with phrase #3, anytime after the Celesta has finished.

FIGURE 15.1

the whole work; (b) an event map for each piece that shows the relative order of events among the different players; and (c) parts for each instrument, consisting of a collection of unordered phrases for each piece. To create each piece, the performers must interpret their parts according to the instructions that are given in the notes, maps, and parts—instructions that are carefully derived from each bird's singing behavior.

Figure 15.1 shows the event map for "Wood Thrush," the first piece. Only the most general parameters are given to the performers: the bamboo wind chimes should sound throughout the movement; the other instruments should enter and end in the order, piccolo I, celesta, piccolo II, and xylophone; each performer should start with the first phrase on his or her part after the preceding player has played two phrases; and no phrase should be repeated immediately after itself. Otherwise, Adams leaves it up to the players to determine the order and timing of their phrases.

Furthermore, in the general performance notes Adams instructs the players that "wherever possible," this music "should be performed surrounding the audience" or while the musicians "rove around and among the listeners." He also tells them not to be afraid of silences, to "play mindlessly, shaping the music as it unfolds," and to find a balance between "sensitively playing with

FIGURE 15.2. The first two phrases of each part in "Wood Thrush." Piccolo II is the inversion of Piccolo I. Celesta is the inversion of xylophone. Xylophone and celesta echo the contour of the piccolos. Missing phrases "2" in Piccolo II and xylophone are measured rests.

the other musicians and ignoring them." Thus, the performers of *songbird-songs* time their playing largely based on their internal rhythm and the acoustic context, as a bird would, rather than on a predetermined metric and contrapuntal structure. Moreover, the acoustic context resembles the natural world as closely as is possible in a concert hall.

Before looking at the individual phrases of "Wood Thrush," it is worth reviewing the real singing habits of wood thrushes, as described by Donald Kroodsma in *The Singing Life of Birds* (237–54). The wood thrush's song is nearly always in three parts: an introductory *bup-bup-bup* repeated on a single pitch, a whistle that often sounds like an arpeggiated chord, and a flourish involving a trill. Additionally, the wood thrush maximizes variety in its singing. Each individual has a repertoire of whistles and flourishes that he continually recombines, so that he never sings the same complete song back-to-back and only rarely sings the same whistle or flourish back-to-back. Moreover, when two neighboring wood thrushes that share song elements are singing back and forth, each actively avoids using any shared element that his neighbor just used.

Figure 15.2 shows the first two phrases of each part in "Wood Thrush." One can see that each phrase in the piccolo parts has the three-part structure of the wood thrush's song. The piccolo I phrases are transcriptions of songs that Adams heard. The piccolo II phrases are inversions of the piccolo I phrases. That is, for each interval that piccolo I ascends, piccolo II descends by the same interval, and vice-versa. This construction, combined with the instruction to the performers not to immediately repeat phrases (Figure 15.1), ensures that the two piccolo parts will sound like two wood thrushes, full of variety and never repeating themselves or each other. Of course, the piccolo II part by itself is derived and not purely "authentic," but it allows Adams to capture the singing *behavior* of the wood thrushes very authentically.

The celesta and xylophone parts are also derived from the wood thrush song, though not as obviously. The xylophone part shadows the up-down-up-down motion of the wood thrush phrases, but at a slower tempo and without the trills (see, for example, piccolo I, phrase 2 and xylophone, phrase 1). The celesta plays the inversion of the xylophone, just as piccolo II plays the inversion of piccolo I.[5] The timbre and the slow and steady rhythm of the percussion instruments make them like echoes of the birds.

As "Wood Thrush" begins, the sounds of bamboo wind chimes evoke a faraway land. When the other instruments enter, they speak a familiar, yet untranslatable, language. Most importantly, the songs of the wood thrush seem *alive*, because they are not frozen in one iteration. By making music in real time with these songs, the performers preserve the songs' natural freedom and ineffable beauty.

Each of the other pieces in *songbirdsongs* includes the songs of one to three species of birds. All of the pieces are indeterminate, but each contains different rules for the musicians, depending on the balance of variety and repetition in the featured birds' singing. Table 15.1 juxtaposes the natural history and ethology of the birds with the design of each piece. In general, the species with more variety in their singing—such as the wood thrush, hermit thrush, and red-eyed vireo—are represented with more different phrases, and the birds with a smaller repertoire—the red-winged blackbird, field sparrow, and mourning dove, for example—are represented with fewer phrases.

The second piece, "Morningfieldsong," features the song sparrow and field sparrow. In contrast to the wood thrush, both of these birds have a fixed repertoire of songs (Kroodsma 225–37, Nelson). Moreover, they may share songs with neighbors and may use these shared songs to match each other in duets.

TABLE 15.1. Life History, Ethology, and Musical Setting of Birds in *songbirdsongs*. Instruments are listed in order of appearance.

Movement / Instrumentation	Species (in order of appearance)	North American Breeding Area	Natural Song Structure	Ethology	Representation in *songbirdsongs*:	Setting / Rules of the Piece
WOOD THRUSH						
2 piccolos, bamboo wind chimes, celesta, xylophone	wood thrush	Eastern range	"soft *bup bup bup* at the song's beginning . . . the loud whistled prelude and the softer fluty flourish."[a]	Never sings the same song back-to-back; rarely repeats neighbor.[a]	Piccolo II plays the inverse of Piccolo I. Xylophone echoes the contour of Piccolo I. Celesta plays the inverse of xylophone.	17 phrases. A phrase may not be repeated directly after itself.
MORNINGFIELDSONG						
2 piccolos, 5 temple blocks, 4 high bongos	field sparrow	Eastern range. Open areas and edges.	"begin slowly and speed up towards the end . . . consisting of four parts."[a]	Fixed repertoire.[a]	Piccolo II and temple blocks	5 phrases. Identical parts for two instruments.
	song sparrow	Wide range.	"typically starts with abrupt, well-spaced notes . . . may add other trills with different tempo and quality . . . Patterns of songs vary over the species' enormous range."[b]	Fixed repertoire of songs, sometimes sharing songs with neighbors.[a]	Piccolo I and high bongos	12 phrases. Identical parts for two instruments.

MEADOWDANCE						
2 piccolos, maracas, sizzle cymbal	red-winged blackbird	Wide range. Open areas.	"The 1-second song starts with an abrupt note that turns into a musical trill."[b]	Fixed repertoire. Both males and females sing.[c]	Piccolo II	4 phrases. Each phrase played 2-5 times.
	eastern meadowlark	Eastern range. Open areas.	"consists of plaintive, clear whistles, slurred and nearly always descending at the end."[b]	Individuals may sing up to 100 different versions, often repeating one version many times.[c]	Piccolo I	9 phrases, each played 2-5 times.
AUGUST VOICES						
2 piccolos, orchestral bells, 2 xylophones, tam-tam, cymbals, vibraphone	pine warbler	Eastern pine forests.	"a musical trill."[b]	Possess more than one song; may alternate songs.[d]	Piccolo II and orchestral bells start with pine warbler.	2 phrases.
	red-eyed vireo	Wide range.	"a broken series of slurred notes. Each phrase usually ends in either a downslur or an upswing."[b]	Each male has 30-40 songs. Neighboring males don't share songs.[a]	Piccolo I starts with Red-eyed Vireo.	19 different phrases.

Movement / Instrumentation	Species (in order of appearance)	North American Breeding Area	Natural Song Structure	Ethology	Representation in *songbirdsongs*:	Setting / Rules of the Piece
	purple martin	Eastern and Central range. Prefers nesting in human-provided habitat.	"a series of musical chirps interspersed with raspy twitters."[b]	Possess 11 different kinds of calls, songs, and subsongs.[d]	Xylophone enters with Purple Martin. Towards the end all instruments are playing Purple Martin.	3 different kinds of phrases, some repeatable.
MOURNING DOVE 3 ocarinas, 2-3 marimbas	mourning dove	Wide range. Primarily open areas and edges.	"three-parted nest call . . . a *coo-OO-oo*, highest in the middle."[b]	Not well studied. Individuals may have multiple songs.[d]	All three differently tuned ocarinas.	3 phrases.
APPLE BLOSSOM ROUND At least 2 piccolos, 2 or more xylophones, 7 tom-toms	northern (Baltimore) oriole	Eastern and Central range.	"a series of rich whistled notes interspersed with rattles."[b]	Individuals sing several different versions of their song. Little sharing of identical songs.[c]	All players.	4 different phrases, repeated and played by all instruments.

NOTQUITESPRINGDAWN						
2 piccolos, 4 triangles, vibraphone	eastern towhee	Eastern range. Forest edges and dense shrubs.	"a loud *drink-your-teeee!* lasting about 1 second. The first note (*drink*) is sharp and metallic, and the final note (*tea*) is a musical trill."[b]	Size of repertoire and repetition of songs varies with geographic region and time of day.[a]	Piccolo I	12 phrases. May not repeat a phrase immediately.
	American robin	Wide habitat.	"a string of 10 or so clear whistles assembled from a few often-repeated syllables, and often described as *cheerily, cheer up, cheer up, cheerily, cheer up.* The syllables rise and fall in pitch but are delivered at a steady rhythm."[b]	10-20 syllables in repertoire. Will highlight one for a while, then another.[a]	Piccolo II	Free combination of 9 song fragments, as well as calls.
JOYFUL NOISE						
2 piccolos, low whip, high whip, timpani, crotales, bass drum	Carolina wren	Eastern range. Dense shrub.	"a loud, repeated series of several whistled notes: "tea-kettle, tea-kettle, tea-kettle."[b]	Sings one song repeatedly before switching to another. The song itself is reiterative. The female also sings.[a]	Piccolo I starts and ends with wren.	6 phrases. One phrase is repeated several times before switching to a new one.

Movement / Instrumentation	Species (in order of appearance)	North American Breeding Area	Natural Song Structure	Ethology	Representation in *songbirdsongs:*	Setting / Rules of the Piece
	tufted titmouse	Eastern range.	"a fast-repeated, clear whistle: *peter-peter-peter*. The birds repeat this up to 11 times in succession."[b]	Sings one song repeatedly before switching to another. The song itself is reiterative. The female also sings.[a]	Piccolo II starts with titmouse. Piccolo I plays titmouse in the middle.	7 different phrases. One phrase is repeated several times before switching to a new one.
	northern cardinal	Eastern range.	"a loud string of clear down-slurred or two-parted whistles, often speeding up and ending in a slow trill. The songs typically last 2 to 3 seconds."[b]	Sings one song repeatedly before switching to another. The song itself is reiterative. The female also sings.[a]	Timpani throughout. Crotales towards the end. Piccolo II moves to cardinal.	9 different phrases. One phrase is repeated several times before switching to a new one.
EVENSONG 2 piccolos, brass wind chimes, celesta, log drum, tubular bells, bowed crotales, optional violin and xylophone	varied thrush	Pacific Northwestern forests.	"Strong whistled tone on a single pitch, usually buzzy in quality."[b]	Successive songs are possibly organized for maximal contrast.[a]	Bowed crotales and optional xylophone	7 phrases.

Bird	Range	Song description	Notes	Instrument	Phrases
ruffed grouse	Northern range.	"Male drums with wings to produce a series of deep thumping sounds that increase in tempo."[b]	Not a songbird. It makes sounds by rapidly beating its wings as it takes off.	Log drum	1 phrase.
Swainson's thrush	Wide range. Nests in far northern coniferous forests.	"flute-like, spiraling upward."[b]	3–7 song types per individual. Song types often sung in a specific order during singing bouts.[d]	Piccolo II	5 phrases.
hermit thrush	Wide range. Nests in Northern and Western forests.	"a melodious, fluty warble, mostly on one pitch, starting with a clear whistled note."[b]	Successive songs are organized for maximal contrast. One of the last songbirds in the evening.[a]	Piccolo I and optional violin	9 phrases.

[a]Taken from Donald Kroodsma, The Singing Life of Birds.
[b]Taken from Cornell Lab of Ornithology, www.allaboutbirds.org (accessed 5/1/10).
[c]Taken from Alvaro Jaramillo and Peter Burke, New World Blackbirds: The Icterids.
[d]Taken from Cornell Lab of Ornithology, www.bna.birds.cornell.edu (accessed 11/11/10).

For this movement Adams assigns the songs of the song sparrow to both pic-colo I and high bongos and the songs of the field sparrow to both piccolo II and temple blocks. Each musician in a pair is free to order his phrases as he likes. In this way Adams creates the impression of spontaneous duets in each species.

The fifth piece, "Mourning Dove," is the only movement in which piccolos are not used. Adams replaces them with three ocarinas—ancient, (usually) ceramic wind instruments that closely approach the haunting sound of the mourning dove.[6]

In the seventh piece, "Notquitespringdawn," Adams captures the continual improvisation of the robin's song. American robins typically sing a string of "10 or so clear syllables," each of which has between two and four notes (Cornell Lab of Ornithology). Adams writes four different triplet sixteenth-note figures. Each triplet represents a syllable of a robin's song, and Adams indicates where these syllables may be repeated, connected, or broken off (Figure 15.3). He also notates robin *calls*—often single-note trills—for the same piccolo.

"Joyful Noise," the eighth piece, features the Carolina wren, northern cardi-nal, and tufted titmouse. These three species share two uncommon character-istics: both the males and females sing, and each of the males' songs consists of a single quickly repeated melodic cell. The males sing one of these repeti-tive songs several times before switching to another. To accommodate these singing traits Adams notates several melodic cells for each species, indicates that each should be repeated a certain number of times to create a song, and instructs the musicians to repeat one song "2 to 5 times" before switching to a new song (figure 15.4).

The combination of these three species together indeed creates an energetic cacophony, or "joyful noise."

When Adams pairs birds within a piece, he is careful to pair birds that share the same habitat. For instance, the red-winged blackbird is paired with the eastern meadowlark in the third piece, "Meadowdance," as both birds live in meadows and other open areas. "Evensong," the last piece, features the ruffed grouse (which makes drumming sounds with its wings), varied thrush, Swain-son's thrush, and hermit thrush, all of which nest in far Northern climates.

Adams calls the nine parts of *songbirdsongs* "pieces" rather than "move-ments" to indicate that they are not dependent on one another. They may be performed independently or in a different order from that which is in the score.[7] In this way the flexibility of the entire work is similar to the flexibility of each movement. The form in the score does follow a logic, however. "Wood Thrush," the first birdsong that Adams completed, was written when he was living in Georgia. In fact, the first eight songs are based on birds that nest in the American Southeast. "Evensong" uses birds that nest in the far North, which

notquitespringdawn

Laconic

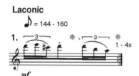

Phrases 1-4 may be freely combined in any sequence, without pauses between them, to form a variety of longer songs.
❋ = a point at which a phrase may be broken off.

FIGURE 15.3

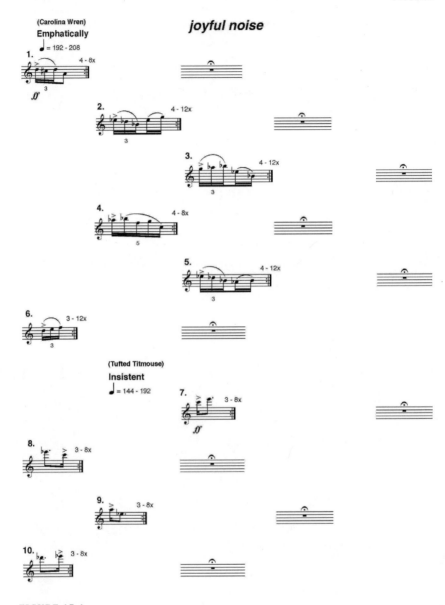

FIGURE 15.4

Adams only heard after he traveled to Alaska for the first time in 1975. "Evensong" also features the hermit thrush, one of the last songbirds to stop singing after sunset. As the songs are presented in the score, they therefore seem to follow the course of a day and the trajectory of Adams's life.

All of the music for piccolos in *songbirdsongs* is closely derived from birdsongs, with one exception: In "August Voices," the fourth piece, the purple martin is represented not only by its song but also by a quick figure that seems inspired by its motion. Adams marks it "like cascading spirals of flight." In addition, there is one birdsong setting that is not entirely authentic from an ethological perspective. In "Apple Blossom Round," the sixth piece, Adams's northern orioles seem to share songs between individuals, whereas Jaramillo and Burke write that few males in this species share an identical song (199).[8] Adams recalls that the character of the oriole phrases suggested to him the setting of an energetic canon, a musical possibility he could not resist (personal communication). The piece is effective musically, and even though the repetition between individuals is not authentic, Adams's indeterminate format still preserves the "autonomy" of the birds.

The birdsongs played by the piccolos and ocarinas are in the foreground throughout *songbirdsongs*. Sometimes the percussion instruments also play birdsongs; at other times they serve other functions, such as creating ambience or adding a nonmelodic, articulating, and energetic element. For instance, Adams starts "Wood Thrush" with bamboo wind chimes and ends "Evensong" with brass wind chimes, both of which create an aura of magic that gently eases the music out of and back into silence. The marimbas in "Mourning Dove" and the maracas and sizzle cymbals in "Meadowdance" play a similar ambient role. As the celesta and xylophone gently echoed the wood thrush in the first piece, the celesta and chimes echo the thrushes in "Evensong." The triangles and vibraphones in "Notquitespringdawn," the tam-tam and cymbals in "August Voices," and the bass drum and whips in "Joyful Noise" play a more emphatic, articulating role. The percussion plays melodic duets in "Wood Thrush," "Morningfieldsong," "August Voices," "Apple Blossom Spring Round," and "Joyful Noise." Only in "Evensong" is a bird species represented only by percussion—the varied thrush by crotales (and optional violin) and the nonsinging ruffed grouse by log drum.

These shifting roles for the percussion highlight the fact that *songbirdsongs* does, indeed, recreate our relationships with those with whom we share the planet. First, it alters the composer-source relationship. Unlike many earlier settings of birdsongs—for example, the third movement of Mahler's *Third Symphony* (subtitled "What the animals in the forest tell me") or Wagner's *Siegfried*, where the Forest Bird informs Siegfried of the ring and Tarnhelm in

Fafner's cave—Adams's birds do not function as part of a human drama. The title of the work, the acoustic layout of the performance, the authenticity of the birdsong representations, and the featured role the birdsongs are given throughout the work communicate that the drama is about what the birds actually do, as told in their language, rather than what they seem to be telling us.

Second, *songbirdsongs* alters the composer-performer relationship. Adams gives the performers considerable freedom in shaping the pieces by combining a mobile, or polyvalent, structure with the precept to "imitate nature in her manner of operation" (Cage, Coomaraswamy).[9] As Bernd Herzogenrath explains in his essay, Cage applied this precept to create pieces such as *Music for Carillon No. 5*, in which the performer reads the knot shifts and grain patterns from ten wooden boards as notes. With *songbirdsongs* Adams creates a more kinetic interpretation of the precept: a piece in which nature's "manner of operation" is the singing behavior of birds, which the performers use to create music in real time.[10]

Adams writes in the preface to the score that he may have "abdicated the position of the Composer." Indeed, he has in many ways surrendered control over the piece to both his source and to his performers, producing, in his words, no more or less than "answers to Creation." *Songbirdsongs* cultivates an appreciation for the creativity and spontaneity of the performers and the birds alike. The work's indeterminate structure allows us to feel that the birds and the performers have agency within its creation, and this feature, as much or more than its authenticity of pitches, rhythms, and timbres, makes the work both ecocentric and musically alive.

Songbirdsongs is ultimately an optimistic piece. Within the confines of the performance space, it presents a relationship between human beings and other beings that is more peaceful and respectful than what the ideology of anthropocentrism has produced. Whereas many pieces that incorporate the sounds of nature may merely remind us of our estrangement from the nonhuman natural world, *songbirdsongs* reintroduces listeners and performers alike to the biosphere and allows us to play with its other inhabitants. Into the music it gently invites what Messiaen called birds' "freedom," what Adorno called nature's "being-in-itself," and what others have simply called "wilderness." It protects what people have repeatedly destroyed by approaching too closely.

* * *

That destruction is what makes *Inuksuit*, Adams's only other indeterminate piece, less optimistic. *Inuksuit* is Adams's first piece intended specifically for outdoor performance. It is a meditation on permanence and impermanence and on how we relate to our world in space and sound. Adams writes in the preface to the score of *Inuksuit* that the piece is "haunted by the vision of the melting of the polar ice, the rising of the seas, and what may remain of humanity's presence after the waters recede." To Alex Ross of the *New Yorker* he said: "The piece is really site-determined. It's really all about finding the music *within* the place and exploring the music *of* the place."

The world premiere of *Inuksuit* took place in the summer of 2009 at the Banff Centre in the Canadian Rockies. The first performance in the United States occurred at Furman University in Greenville, South Carolina, in April 2010 and was followed immediately by a performance at the Round Top Festival Institute in Round Top, Texas. I had the pleasure of playing in the performance at Furman and attending the performance at Round Top.

In Canada, eighteen percussionists performed the piece twice—first in the outdoor amphitheatre at the Banff Centre and then in the mountains near Canmore, Alberta. In the latter performance, the musicians were spread over thirty acres on both banks of the rushing Goat Creek. At Furman forty-three percussionists and seven piccolo players were situated in meadows and woods over an area spanning about fifty-five acres and halfway encircling Furman's Swan Lake. The performance began and ended just in front of an amphitheatre situated on the north side of the lake. At Round Top, ninety-seven percussionists were distributed over about forty acres, in denser woods and gardens surrounding a still creek. The size of the ensemble and the acoustic separation caused by the dense woods led to a longer performance than at Furman, despite the smaller total area.

In his essay, Steven Schick gives a captivating description of the genesis of *Inuksuit*. I would like to describe its form in some detail and articulate what I find to be its underlying narrative.

The music of *Inuksuit* progresses as shifting and overlapping blocks of sound. As Schick has described, the performers are divided into three groups, and the piece is structurally divided into five sections. Each group of performers plays one of seven kinds of sounds within a section, as may be seen in the event map for the piece. Specifically, the performers in Group 1 perform, in order, "Breathing," "Calls," "Waves" (on a siren-like instrument), "Clangs," and "Wind" (on a triangle). Group 2 plays "Wind" (with a friction instrument like rubbed stones); "Inuksuit (rising)," "Waves," and "Inuksuit (falling)" (all on tom-toms and bass drum); and "Wind" (on sizzle cymbal). Group 3 plays "Wind" (on whirled tubes); "Inuksuit (rising)," "Waves," and "Inuksuit (falling)" (all on suspended cymbals and tam-tam); and "Birdsongs" (on orchestral bells). As indicated on the event map (see Figure 5.5), Adams suggests that

Group 3 may be supplemented with piccolos for "Birdsongs." He gives options for instrumentation in other sections as well, and in the performance notes, he encourages "varied and imaginative soundings of *Inuksuit*."

Although no group plays exactly the same music as any other, there is enough overlap between the music of the three groups to make them coherent. The event map shows that the three groups line up playing the same type of sound (though on different instruments) in "Waves," exactly at the midpoint of the piece. All three groups also play "Wind" at some point. Groups 2 and 3 have the same order of sections, except that Group 2 ends with "Wind" and Group 3 ends with "Birdsongs." Additionally, in the first, third, and fifth sections of the piece, Adams calls for undulating or oscillating sounds ("Breathing," "Waves," and "Wind") and in the second and fourth sections he calls for sounds with discrete attacks ("Calls," "Clangs," and "Inuksuit"). The one exception to this large, alternating pattern is that Group 3 plays "Birdsongs" with discrete (if gentle) attacks in the fifth section.

Each of the parts of *Inuksuit* except "Birdsongs" is constructed of a series of phrases in which either the rhythmic proportion of notes or the number of repetitions of a figure steadily contracts or expands from phrase to phrase. I will discuss how this is done in each section, beginning with the "Inuksuit" figures.

As Schick explains in his essay, real "inuksuit" are stone configurations created by native Arctic peoples from Alaska to Greenland. Adams ultimately composed a total of sixty-six different "Inuksuit" parts of four different types — stacks, windows, double windows, and pyramids (Figures 15.5–15.8) — matching the different types of real inuksuit that he observed in the Arctic. These sixty-six parts are divided evenly between Groups 2 and 3. Since no two players may double an "Inuksuit" part, and since the three groups are supposed to be equal in size, there may be up to thirty-three players per group and ninety-nine players in the ensemble. If there are fewer than ninety-nine players, some of the "Inuksuit" parts are not played.

The composition of *Inuksuit* began with the question of how to translate a three-dimensional form into audible time. To meet this challenge Adams relied on the idea (which he attributes to Henry Cowell's *New Musical Resources* and Conlon Nancarrow's *Studies for Player Piano*) that employing multiple simultaneous tempi gives music depth.

In Figure 15.8 one can see that Adams has stacked eight staves for this pyramid part, each containing sixteen iterations of a single note value. The measures of the staves line up with each other vertically. One way to express the length of the notes in each staff is in terms of fractional measures per note (ms/note). On the bottom staff are whole notes, whose length could be expressed as

Tom-toms
and Bass Drum   Stack 1

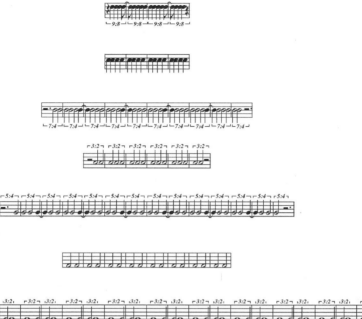

FIGURE 15.5

one ms/note. For the sake of comparison, let us express it as the equivalent 2/2 ms/note. The next higher staff contains triplet whole notes, each note lasting 2/3 ms/note. Above that are duple half notes, which last 2/4 ms/note. The pattern continues to the top, where the nonuplet quarters each last 2/9 ms/note. Thus, as one moves up the staves, the notes progressively quicken, though the beat remains the same.

The players in Groups 2 and 3 are instructed to play the "Inuksuit" parts "ascending" in the second section and "descending" in the fourth section. When the player is instructed to play a part ascending, she is to start by playing the bottom stave only, from left to right. When she has completed that, she is to play the bottom two staves together, again from left to right. The pattern continues until she is playing all nine staves simultaneously. As each staff is added, the quicker notes give the impression of a quicker tempo. When the musician is playing multiple staves, Adams thus creates the impression of multiple tempi.

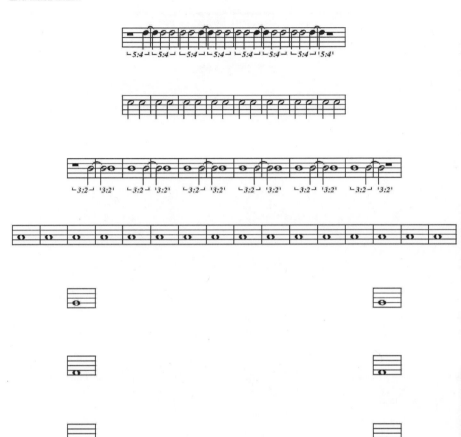

FIGURE 15.6

When the player is instructed to play the figure descending, she reverses the process, starting with all the staves and ending with the bottom staff alone.

Adams also plays with expanding and contracting rhythmic proportions and phrase lengths in the other sections of *Inuksuit*, such that during the first half of the piece, successive phrases add notes, and during the second half of the piece, they lose notes. As a result, *Inuksuit* has a dynamic structure of one enormous, seventy-minute wave.

Tom-toms
and Bass Drum

Double Window 1

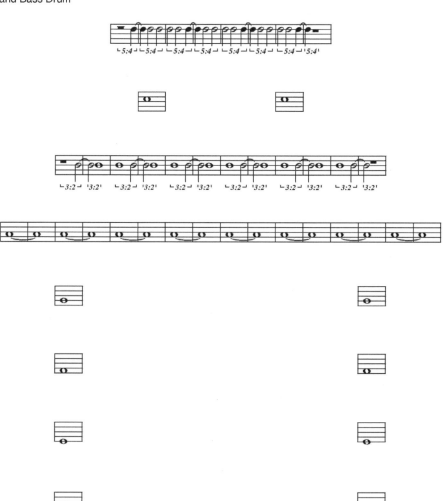

FIGURE 15.7

In the first section of music, the groups enter quietly in succession, one performer at a time. In "Breathing" (Group 1) and "Wind" (Groups 2 and 3), each motivic figure lasts for two measures, but the figures accumulate in successively longer phrases. In "Breathing," for instance, the players start by taking two long breaths, each lasting two measures, and then rest. They then take three breaths and rest. This process continues until they have taken ten breaths, in a phrase lasting twenty measures.

Tom-toms
and Bass Drum   *Pyramid 1*

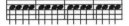

FIGURE 15.8

In the second section of music, the music continues to thicken. In "Calls"
(Group 1) each phrase lasts one measure, but Adams instructs the performers
to sound increasing numbers of calls on their conch shell trumpets in that time.
The first phrase asks for two calls in the rhythm of half notes. The next phrase
asks for three calls in the rhythm of triplet half notes. The pattern of quickening
rhythm continues until the players sound ten calls in the rhythm of eighth note

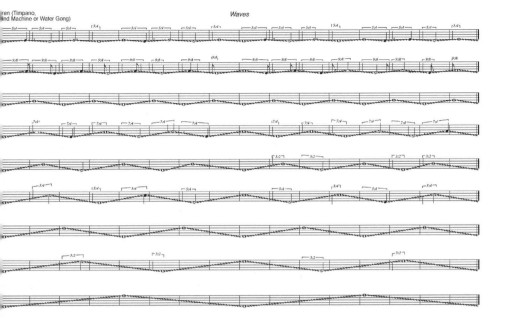

FIGURE 15.9

quintuplets. After they reach the end of the pattern, they are free to repeat any of the previous phrases for as long as Group 1 remains in "Calls." Meanwhile, Groups 2 and 3 add sound by adding rhythmical layers in "Inuksuit (rising)."

At the center of the work for all three groups is "Waves," in which numerous hairpins form a microcosm of the whole piece. Figure 15.9 shows a sample "Waves" part. Here the total phrase length again remains constant (sixteen measures), while the time given to each figure within the phrase changes. For the members of Group 1, the waves expand; for the members of Groups 2 and 3, the waves contract.

In the fourth section, the music starts to thin out. In Group 1 "Clangs" proceeds like "Calls" but with gradually slowing, rather than quickening, rhythms. Groups 2 and 3 shed one layer of sound after another in "Inuksuit (falling)."

In the final section of *Inuksuit*, all drums are gone. The "Wind" parts for Groups 1 and 2 resemble the earlier "Wind" parts, except that the phrases now begin with ten two-measure figures and gradually whittle down to two two-measure figures. Finally, the piece dissolves back into the performance site through the sound of birdsongs played by Group 3 on orchestral bells (with optional piccolos).

The "Birdsongs" are the only sounds not structured in the kind of rhythmic proportions described above. The performance notes state that notations of

FIGURE 15.10

birdsongs local to the performance site should be used. The performance folio of *Inuksuit* contains notations of birdsongs heard in Alberta, Canada, which were used in the premiere at Banff, but Adams notated different birdsong figures for the two subsequent performances. Adams was actually revising *songbirdsongs* when he wrote *Inuksuit* in 2008–09, and some of the birdsong notations in *Inuksuit* are taken right out of the score of the earlier piece. Thus, the Banff performance employed songs of the song sparrow, hermit thrush, western meadowlark, fox sparrow, Lapland longspur, and snow bunting, the first two having come out of *songbirdsongs*. The performances at Furman and Round Top used the songs of the wood thrush, song sparrow, field sparrow, eastern and western meadowlarks, red-winged blackbird, purple martin, red-eyed vireo, Baltimore oriole, eastern towhee, American robin, northern cardinal, Carolina wren, and tufted titmouse—all except the western meadowlark "borrowed" from *songbirdsongs*. Unlike *songbirdsongs*, where Adams includes rules for the performance of each bird's song that are derived from the bird's singing habits, the birdsongs in *Inuksuit* are written with no particular instructions other than to leave space between each phrase (Figure 15.10).

Does *Inuksuit*, in Adams's words, "move beyond self-expression" and "re-imagine and re-create our relationships with this planet and all those (human and other-than-human) with whom we share it"? Adams has left no doubt about his intentions: the performance notes clarify that he wants performers and listeners alike to engage their surroundings as a result of the work: "This work is intended to expand our awareness of the never-ending music of the world in which we live, transforming seemingly empty space into more fully experienced place . . . *Inuksuit* invites exploration and discovery of the relationship between music and the site, as well as the musicians' interactions with both. The musicians are encouraged to consider carefully the selection of instruments, the distribution of performers, and the acoustical properties of the performance site."

Furthermore, Adams's compositional process of transforming the Inuit inuksuit into sound involved neither the self-expression nor the use of connotations that went into other works inspired by the natural world, like Beethoven's "Pastoral" Symphony, Mahler's Third Symphony, or Ferde Grofé's *Grand Canyon Suite*. Adams's process required, rather, that he objectively create musical equivalents of unsounded forms. In this sense, Adams does certainly move beyond self-expression.

As already discussed, Adams yields decisions about the instrumentation, size of the ensemble, choice of *Inuksuit* parts, distribution of the ensemble, and individual pacing through the piece to the performers. By making the completion of the compositional process dependent on other musicians, Adams also re-creates relationships, as he did in *songbirdsongs*.

What about the music itself? Does it transform relationships? Let us start at the beginning. The standard *indoor* concert usually begins as follows: performers walk on stage, receive applause, pause for a brief moment, and then begin the music. In contrast, a performance of *Inuksuit* begins more discretely. The performers gradually gather at the performance site. Since there is no conductor to cue the beginning, the performers must sense the timing of the opening gesture, which is the sound of a single performer breathing outdoors with minimal amplification. To obtain the silence necessary for this sound to project, the performers are very quiet, and the audience responds to them with silence and attentiveness. In this human silence, all who are present notice the natural sounds of the performance site filling the air. In fact, the first sounds of *Inuksuit* are the sounds of the performance site itself. At Goat Creek, the sound of the gushing stream was most prominent. Elsewhere, the sounds of birds singing and wind rustling through trees were noticed. The music of the place is thus included in *Inuksuit* from before the first written "note." The place becomes not just where the performance is happening; it is the first performer in *Inuksuit*. By yielding some of the foreground to the place, the composer and performers draw our attention to the sounds of the outdoors, which listeners may notice and value. Though it cannot force a change, *Inuksuit* does make it possible for listeners to "re-create our relationship with the planet."

Let us go further. The first performer breathes through a tube. What is the sound of breathing? It is like the sound of the wind — so much so that when the first "Breathing" figure begins, it may go unnoticed by an inattentive listener. There is little individual expression in it. The performer does not "shape" notes to "project" an emotion; there is no pitch to be shaped, and there is no need for the performer to affect his breathing. The sound is simple, as is the pattern of breathing. Essentially the performer is projecting his *aliveness*, a sort of inner kinetic energy, in certain rhythmic patterns and at certain locations.

After "Breathing," the next sounds, in the order in which they are heard, are made by rubbed stones or other friction instruments (Group 2, "Wind"), whirled tubes, bullroarers, or other Aeolian instruments (Group 3, "Wind"), and conch shell trumpets (Group 1, "Calls"). These instruments are all "simple" in several ways. They are very old means of making sound. They can be produced with little modification of natural materials.[11] They offer variation of sound quality only along one dimension (volume). And, as explained earlier, the figures for which these sounds are used follow a simple development. As a result, little in the way of personal emotional expression can be communicated with them.

Most of the rest of the sounds of *Inuksuit* are made with constructed percussion instruments: tomtoms, bass drum, tam-tam, suspended cymbals, sirens, handbells, triangles, and sizzle cymbal. The patterns used in "Wind," "Waves," and "Clangs," however, are still simple, and the patterns of the "Inuksuit" sections, though complex, are still not "self-expressive."

Group 3 plays "Birdsongs" on orchestral bells, supplemented by piccolos. These are certainly "constructed" instruments. Additionally, this is the only section of the piece with a melodic pitch arrangement. The conch-shell trumpets and handbells heard earlier are monotone, the whirled tubes are limited to a few harmonics, and the sirens are predictable along a pitch spectrum. Although the birdsongs are complex melodically, however, they are not self-expressive. They are intended to be merely transcriptions of natural birdsongs.[12]

So how do all of these elements — the seventy-minute wave, the discrete and oscillating sounds, simple and complex sounds, birdsongs, and the sounds of the place — affect the listener? Is there a narrative that ties them together? Although Adams has not indicated one, I, perhaps naively, find a musical history of life on Earth in *Inuksuit*. The piece begins in a state of presence and potential. As the sound of breathing emerges from the wind, it seems to connect all members of the animate world to each other and to the surroundings. Soon the sounds of breathing, whirled tubes, and rubbed stones accumulate and swirl together, quickening the air. They seem like the first stirrings in the primordial soup four billion years ago. As the first section of the piece progresses, the sounds grow in volume and timbres and spread throughout the space of the performance site.

Then, suddenly, the first call of the conch shell trumpet pierces the air. It is the first sense of an individual standing out from a context within *Inuksuit*. It is also the first sound that only a human could make. Perhaps it is the first sign of humanity in this musical history of the world. Soon another conch trumpet is heard. Communication! Two individuals, each making their presence known, stake their claim while responding to one another.

The conch shell trumpets pile on to each other until the first strike of a bass drum commands attention. *Wham!* It is the sound of another individual, announcing the beginning of "Inuksuit (rising)." The volume and suddenness of the sound introduces an element of power. The drum seems to signal the phase of history in which human command over the natural world produces fire, agriculture, and steel. As rhythmic layers are added within "Inuksuit (rising)" and the rhythm of the "Calls" becomes faster, the music becomes more complicated and tumultuous. Now all the sounds are specifically human sounds. They do not blend with the surroundings. They are assertive and clangorous. Just like real-life inuksuit are physical assertions of a human presence in a landscape, these "Inuksuit" seem to be an aural assertion of our power to transform a landscape.

Then the "Waves" begin. It is as if the entire place starts to heave. The sirens, played by Group 1, bring their connotations of urgency to the music. The tomtoms, bass drums, suspended cymbals, and tam-tams thunder like earthquakes. If the heterogeneity of the second section created a sense of unease, now the growing homogeneity—the shaking and quaking of all the groups—is terrifying. The music seems to evoke a time (the present, perhaps) when the insults inflicted on the planet by humans finally make it quake in response.

After a brief period in which all three groups are swelling simultaneously, Group 1 starts the long descent with "Clangs." Do these represent death knells tolling for the ultimate self-destruction of humankind? They start rapidly, piercing the air like the "Calls" earlier. As they begin to expand and slow, the "Inuksuit" figures return where they left off, eight rhythmic layers thick. As the players of Groups 2 and 3 shed one layer after another, the chaos slowly dissipates. The discrete attacks—the stamps of individuality—slowly subside, like a giant beast that has been mortally wounded. The last section of music fades in. Groups 1 and 2, playing gentle swells on triangles and sizzle cymbals ("Wind"), return us to a quieter, swirling, undulating world. The changes in timbre and the gradual shortening of the "Wind" phrases create a long diminuendo.

Finally, Group 3 begins to play "Birdsongs," while real birds sing and call throughout the performance site. Although one might be tempted to say that the performers make music with the birds, I suspect the birds do not perceive it this way. What is clear is that, as in *songbirdsongs*, Adams cedes the musical *language* to the birds, here for the purpose of letting his music dissolve into the music of the place. And so long as there are birds, it works quite beautifully. *Inuksuit* fades into the world around it. Is this a view of "what may remain of humanity's presence after the waters recede"? If so, is it a world of humans blending in with their surroundings, or are the humans gone? Is humanity itself like Shakespeare's "poor player that struts and frets his hour upon the stage and then is heard no more"?[13]

In the preface to the score of *Inuksuit*, Adams suggests that certain questions may arise through its performance: "What does it mean to act creatively with and within our environment? Can we listen and hear more deeply the field of sound all around us? How does where we are define what we do and, ultimately, who we are? And how do we understand the brevity of our human presence in the immensity of geologic time?" Adams does not answer these questions himself. He leaves it to the piece to provide different answers for each listener.

Above I have outlined a narrative deriving purely from the aural experience of *Inuksuit*, but there is also a strong spatial dimension to the experience. Whereas *songbirdsongs* seems to lead us on an aural expedition to an imagined land, *Inuksuit* leads us to explore a real place.

As the first section of the piece proceeds, the performers move through the performance space, stopping at nine equidistant points on the way to their performance stations. In the act of gauging the distance between stops, the performers become aware of the physical space. As I walked to my performance site at one of the farthest edges of the lake at Furman, I was aware of the sounds of frogs hopping into the lake next to me, the way the path that I followed curved downwards from the starting location, and the height and moisture of the grass where I stood. When the listeners begin to move throughout the performance space, they, too, become aware of it.

Since every performer is situated in a different place and the audience members are free to explore the place as they wish, each performance of *Inuksuit* is a very individual experience for players and audience members alike. Each individual notices different details of the sounds, biota, and topology of the place and how they interact. One of the most memorable elements of the Furman performance for me was the resonance of conch-shell trumpets over the lake during "Calls." I also enjoyed the look that a brood of seemingly perplexed ducks gave me as I played a siren in "Waves." Clearly these experiences were prominent for me because I was stationed right at the lake. As I wandered through the woods at Round Top, the pleasure was very different; I had the feeling of walking through a magical forest, discovering hidden fairies playing percussion instruments! I noticed the stillness of the stream juxtaposed with the hustle-bustle of the music.

Because of this spatial dimension, I find *Inuksuit* to be a salve to the modern feelings of placelessness and alienation from the natural world. In Western urbanized societies, our contemporary lives involve the constant movement from one "controlled environment" to another, none of which bear a clear relationship to our core necessities. We are inextricably tied to the natural world through our needs for food, water, and shelter, but few of us make our own food, collect our water, or build our homes from natural materials that we collect. Instead they appear to us in packages at the grocery store, through a faucet coming from a wall, or as large, prefabricated conglomerations of wood, steel, brick, plastic, and paint. Moreover, we travel in minutes what used to take weeks, and with television and the internet, we can be "virtually" anywhere at any time. Though one may be awed by how easily we control and adapt to our surroundings, our groundlessness takes its toll in what is increasingly termed "environmental depression." Worse still, our attempts to reconnect to the natural world in specially designed places known as "natural parks" often do not succeed, since, as Byerly and Adorno have described, we bring to them an alienated attitude built on consumption.

Inuksuit, however, grounds us in a place. As I dug my feet into the earth to strike a prayer bowl in "Clangs" and then listened to it reverberate over the water, I felt my entire body connected to the performance site. Each experience of *Inuksuit* has been distinctly the experience of it *in a given place*. Adams's prefatory comments clearly indicate that the point of *Inuksuit* is not primarily the communication of the piece's narrative structure but rather the creation of an event in which music informs the experience of a place, and the place informs the music. As a result, performers and listeners are neither alienated from, nor consuming, the surroundings, but are aware of and connected to them. Ellen Dissanayake has written that art is the process of "making special." Through *Inuksuit* the performance site becomes "special" to us.

At the end of *Inuksuit*, players and listeners walk back to the starting location, giving up some of their individual experience to share in a sense of common origin and destiny. When we leave the site, either as performers or listeners, our relationship with "the place" and with our "place" in it has been transformed. We have listened to our surroundings and made music with them, but we have also become aware of how powerful we can be in collectively transforming a place.

In *Inuksuit* Adams is not trying to express "all the emotions of our inmost nature," as Schopenhauer thought music should do, but neither does he merely imitate the natural world. The sounds of *Inuksuit* are intended to join, inhabit, and fill the performance site. Furthermore, *Inuksuit* does not rob "what appears in nature" of its "being-in-itself," as Adorno wrote. It actually facilitates experience of the space in which it takes place.

It was Cage's intention in *4'33"* to open our ears to hearing the whole world as music. Adams takes *Inuksuit* one step further. *Inuksuit* treats the natural world as something to be heard *and engaged*. Adams integrates the natural world itself into the piece, making it a full partner in the act of music-making.[14] By shifting our attention away from ourselves in isolation to our place in a larger whole, *Inuksuit* becomes ecocentric music.

Ultimately *Inuksuit* inspires us to reflect on transience and permanence, as the inuksuit of the Arctic inspired Adams. Stone inuksuit may appear permanent relative to a human lifespan. Perhaps they will even remain after the rising seas recede. But they have lasted only a blink of the eye when compared to the age of the Earth itself. Likewise, Adams's *Inuksuit* may gain a permanent place in our musical culture, but each experience of it is transient. After all its raucousness permeates a site, the music dies away, and any trace of our presence on the site soon vanishes. What remains after *Inuksuit* is nothing more nor less than the change it creates in us. Whereas *songbirdsongs* helps us to experience the freedom of birdsongs, *Inuksuit* helps us to connect deeply to a place. What we do with that connection is left up to us.

Notes

1. The phrase "mehr Ausdruck der Empfindung als Malerei" appeared in the handbill for the concert of December 22, 1808, when the piece was premiered. It also appears in the autograph score. See David Wyn-Jones, *Beethoven: Pastoral Symphony* (Cambridge University Press: Cambridge, 1995), 1, and Wilhelm Altmann, Foreword to miniature score of Beethoven *Symphony no. 6* (London: Eulenberg, 1942).

2. Schubert, Brahms, Tchaikovsky, Alabiev, Granados, Berg, Faure, and Hahn are just a few of the composers who have composed nightingale songs.

3. See, for example, *Réveil des oiseaux* or *Catalogue d'oiseaux* for piano.

4. See hermit thrush sonograms in Kroodsma 258.

5. The first phrase of the xylophone is the only one that does not exactly invert the corresponding phrase in the piccolo, the first and last intervals having been altered.

6. One of the percussionists must play the third ocarina.

7. The instrumental requirements are also different for each piece, ranging from two piccolos and two percussionists in "Wood Thrush," to two piccolos, four percussionists, and optional violin and additional percussion in "Evensong." Adams's reasoning for this is again that the pieces do not need to be performed as a set. However, a complete performance of *songbirdsongs* requires at least two piccoloists and three percussionists. This arrangement requires the percussionists to redistribute the parts in "Evensong."

8. At the time that *songbirdsongs* was written, both Baltimore orioles and Bullock's orioles were called "northern orioles." The two actually have different coloration and singing patterns. Given that Adams was in the eastern United States, whereas Bullock's orioles are only found in the western part of the country, the birds Adams heard were most likely Baltimore orioles.

9. Cage made the phrase famous, but he got it from Coomaraswamy.

10. In his chapter for this book, Herzogenrath explains how in *The Place Where You Go to Listen*, Adams removes performers from this equation, using a computer to generate sounds that track nature's manner of operation in real time.

11. The performances of *Inuksuit* gave me my first encounter with whirled tubes, which produce a fundamental tone and harmonics by moving columns of air through a ridged tube. Granted, the plastic tubes are modern and required some manufacturing, but the principle is quite simple. Shortly after hearing *Inuksuit*, I was on a farm, where I heard nearly the same alternating series of harmonics coming from a steel gate on a windy afternoon. I believe that the steel supports of the gate were pierced by the lattice-work of the gate, making a hollow tube that resonated when the wind was blowing.

12. Adams's performance notes use "transcription," rather than "translation," which was used in *songbirdsongs*. To be precise, the piccolo parts seem to be single-voice transcriptions. The orchestral bells parts contain a sort of shadow line under the main line— perhaps a way to come closer to the sound of multiphonics of which birds are capable. The shadow line is similar to the celesta parts in "Wood Thrush" from *songbirdsongs*.

13. *Macbeth*, Act V, v.

14. Herzogenrath writes that *The Place Where You Go to Listen* "leaves behind the idea of music as a means of the *representation* of nature and landscape . . . and creates music as a part of nature, as coextensive with the environment." The difference in the pieces is that in *The Place*, normally unheard geophysical processes are made audible, whereas in *Inuksuit*, sounds actually made by the natural world are intertwined with human-made sounds.

Bibliography

Adams, John Luther. *Winter Music: Composing the North*. Middletown, Conn.: Wesleyan University Press, 2004.

———. *Inuksuit*. Performance folio. Fairbanks: Taiga Press, 2009.

———. *songbirdsongs* (revised edition). Performance folio. Fairbanks: Taiga Press, 2009.

Adorno, Theodor W. *Aesthetic theory*, ed. Gretel Adorno and Rolf Tiedemann, trans. Robert Hullot-Kentor. Minneapolis: University of Minnesota Press, 1997.

Byerly, Alison. "The Uses of Landscape: The Picturesque Aesthetic and the National Park System." In *The Ecocritical Reader*, ed. Cheryl Glotfelty and Harold Fromm. Athens: University of Georgia Press, 1996.

Cage, John. "Happy New Ears." In *A Year from Monday: New Lectures and Writings*. Middletown, Conn.: Wesleyan University Press, 1967.

Cornell Lab of Ornithology. www.allaboutbirds.org (accessed May 1, 2010).

———. www.bna.birds.cornell.edu (accessed November 11, 2010).

Coomaraswamy, Ananda. *The Transformation of Nature in Art*. Cambridge, Mass.: Harvard University Press, 1934.

Dissanayake, Ellen. *Homo Aestheticus: Where Art Comes From and Why*. New York: Free Press, 1992.

Goléa, Antoine. *Rencontres avec Olivier Messiaen*. Paris: Slatkine, 1984.

Jaramillo, Alvaro and Peter Burke. *New World Blackbirds: The Icterids*. Princeton, N.J.: Princeton University Press, 1999.

Kroodsma, Donald. *The Singing Life of Birds*. New York: Houghton Mifflin, 2005.

Messiaen, Olivier. *Reveil des oiseaux*. Score. Paris: Durand, 1955.

Nattiez, Jean-Jacques. *Music and Discourse: Toward a Semiology of Music*. Trans. Carolyn Abbate. Princeton: Princeton University Press, 1990.

Nelson, Douglas. "Song overproduction and selective attrition lead to song sharing in the field sparrow (*Spizella pusilla*)." *Behavioral Ecology and Sociobiology* 30 (1992): 415–24.

Ross, Alex, and Evan Hurd. "Video, John Luther Adams's *Inuksuit*." *The New Yorker* (online edition), September 2, 2009. http://www.newyorker.com/online/blogs/newsdesk/2009/09/video-john-luther-adams-Inuksuit.html (accessed May 1, 2010).

Samuel, Claude. *Olivier Messiaen: Music and Color*. Trans. E. Thomas Glasow. Portland, Ore.: Amadeus Press, 1994.

Schopenhauer, Arthur. *The World as Will and Idea*. 1818. Ed. David Berman, trans. Jill Berman. London: J. M. Dent, 1995.

Noah Pollaczek

A Catalogue of Works By and About John Luther Adams

The singular musical voice of John Luther Adams is embodied in over thirty years of creative output. This bibliography aims to explore the many facets of Adams's artistic life, through a survey of the composer's works, recordings, and writings, as well as the literary manifestations and audiovisual media that have been produced about Adams.

The works section—which encompasses compositions to sound and light installations—describes Adams's musical output in detail. It includes work creation and publication dates, instrumentation and duration, and premiere and commercial recording information. A discography inventorying Adams's recording history follows, with each entry denoting a published recording's label and release date, media type and length, work titles if multiple compositions are present, and recording history and performers involved. The writings section comes next, and has been subdivided into three parts—pieces written by Adams; other authors' writings about Adams; and previews and reviews of recordings, books, and performances of Adams's work. Concluding the bibliography, the composer's artistic presence in a wide range of audio and visual media, from radio and film to the web, is documented.

Numerous resources proved helpful in putting together this bibliography. Sabine Feisst's compilations[1] of Adams's work served as a valuable reference. In concert with the composer's personal website,[2] these two resources provided a foundation for many of the entries that follow. Additionally, LexisNexis[3] and IIMP[4] supplied data for the citations of authors' writings about Adams, with WorldCat[5] serving as a primary reference for locating information regarding the composer's musical scores (most published through the Fairbanks, Alaska-based *Taiga Press*). Liner notes from Adams's sound recordings, as well as the websites of the labels producing them—Cantaloupe,[6] Cold Blue,[7] Mode,[8] New Albion,[9] and New World Records[10]—were consulted for information concerning recording dates and performer names listed in the discography. Finally, the compiler gratefully acknowledges the personal assistance of John Luther Adams: for granting access to his musical archives and memory bank, and for verifying and enhancing the information gathered from the above sources.

Catalogue of Works

Listed alphabetically

Across Golden Distance

Composed October–November 1986. Revised December 1986. Unpublished (manuscript reproduction at the NYPL).

For eight horns (two horn quartets antiphonally placed). 8:45.

First performed 1986 by members of the Fairbanks Symphony, Fairbanks, AK.

Composed 1998. Unpublished.

For three trumpets, three trombones, tuba, timpani, three percussionists.

First performed November 1997 by Maj. Philip Chevallard and the U.S. Air Force Band of the Pacific at the Discovery Theatre, Anchorage, AK.

After the Light

Composed August 2001. Taiga Press, 2001.

For alto flute, vibraphone, harp. 8:45.

Commissioned by the CrossSound Festival.

First performed November 16–18, 2001, at the CrossSound Festival, Ketchikan and Juneau, AK.

Always Very Soft

Composed April 1973. This version has been withdrawn. Unpublished (manuscript reproduction at the NYPL).

For cello (or double bass), three percussionists. 6:30.

First performed 1973 by the Cal Arts Percussion Ensemble, Valencia, CA.

Composed June 2007. Taiga Press, 2007.

For three percussionists. 9:00.

Dedicated to Percussion Group Cincinnati.

First performed July 18, 2009, by TimeTable Percussion at the Festival Salihara, Jakarta, Indonesia.

Among Red Mountains

Composed 2001. Taiga Press, 2001.

For piano. 10:30.

Dedicated to Peter Garland.

First performed December 7, 2001, by Emily Manzo at Oberlin College, Oberlin, OH.

Recorded on Red Arc/Blue Veil (Cold Blue CB0026).

Five Athabascan Dances

Composed 1992/1996. Taiga Press, 1995.

Includes Grandpa Joe's traveling song—They will all go—Deenaadai' (Long ago)—Grandpa Joe's hunting song—Potlatch song of a lonely man.

For guitar, harp, percussion. 16:00.

Composed 1992/1996. Taiga Press, 2000.

Includes Grandpa Joe's traveling song—Deenaadai' (Long ago)—They will all go—Shik'eenoohtii (My Relatives)—Grandpa Joe's hunting song.

For harp, percussion. 16:00.

Commissioned by the U.S Embassy, in Tokyo, Japan.

First performed September 21, 1995, at the Interlink Festival by Just Strings, Tokyo, Japan.

. . . and bells remembered

Composed 2005. Taiga Press, 2005.

For crotales (bowed), orchestra bells, chimes, vibraphone (bowed), vibraphone (struck). 10:15.

Commissioned by the University of Wisconsin–River Falls.

First performed April 6, 2006, at the University of Wisconsin-River Falls, River Falls, WI.

Recorded on *Four Thousand Holes* (Cold Blue CB0035).

Clouds of Forgetting, Clouds of Unknowing

Composed 1991–1995. Revised July 1996. Taiga Press, 1995 and 1996.

For two violins, viola, cello, double bass, two flutes/piccolos, clarinet, bass clarinet, two horns, trumpet, bass trombone, piano, celesta, two percussionists. 62:00.

First performed February 26, 1996, by JoAnn Falletta and the Apollo Chamber Orchestra, Norfolk, VA.

Recorded on *Clouds of Forgetting, Clouds of Unknowing* (New World 80500-2).

Confluence

Composed 1981. This work has been withdrawn. Unpublished.

For cello percussion.

Coyote Builds North America [Giving Birth to Thunder, Sleeping With His Daughter, Coyote Builds North America]

Composed 1986/1990. Complete work unpublished.

Music composed for the theatrical production. Text by Barry Lopez.

For violin, double bass, e-flat clarinet, bass clarinet, dancers (two minimum), storyteller, four percussionists. 70:00.

Commissioned by Perseverance Theater, Juneau, AK.

First performed 1987 by Perseverance Theater, Juneau, AK.

Two sets of published excerpts are available separately:

Four Pieces From Coyote Builds North America

Taiga Press, 1990 and 2000.

Includes Coyote's dance—Water music—A little joke—Death and the meadowlark—Coyote finishes his work.

For violin, double bass, clarinet, two percussionists. 21:00.

First performed separately in 1996 at the Juilliard Focus Festival, New York City, NY.

Five Percussion Quartets From Coyote Builds North America

Taiga Press, 1990 and 2003.

Includes Invocation—Consecration—Giving birth to thunder—Playing with fire—Always coming home.

For four percussionists. 18:00.

First performed separately in 1993 by Amy Knoles and the Paul Dresher Ensemble, San Francisco, CA.

Crow and Weasel

Composed 1993–1994. Unpublished.

Music composed for the theatrical production. Story by Barry Lopez, stage adaptation by Jim Leonard, script and performance recording published by Samuel French.

For string quintet, piccolo/bass clarinet, celesta, harp, four percussionists. 90:00.

Commissioned by the Sundance Institute and the Children's Theatre Company.

First performed January1994 by John Luther Adams and musicians at the Children's Theatre, Minneapolis, MN.

Dark Waves

Composed 2007. Taiga Press, 2007.

For two pianos, electronically processed sounds. 12:00.

First performed 2007 by Stephen Drury and Yukiko Takagi, Boston, MA.

Recorded on *Red Arc/Blue Veil* (Cold Blue CB0026).

Composed 2007. Taiga Press, 2007.

For strings (minimum twelve violins [I], twelve violins [II], nine violas, nine cellos, six double basses), two piccolos, two oboes, two clarinets, contrabass clarinet, two bassoons, contrabassoon, two horns, two trumpets, two trombones, bass trombone, tuba, piano, celesta, bass drum, suspended cymbal, orchestra bells, two vibraphones, electronically processed sounds. 12:00.

Commissioned by Music Nova, for the Anchorage Symphony Orchestra.

First performed February 17, 2007, by Randall Craig Fleischer and the Anchorage Symphony, Anchorage, AK.

Dark Wind

Composed September–October 2001. Taiga Press, 2001.

For bass clarinet, piano, vibraphone (or electronic mallet instrument), marimba (or electronic mallet instrument). 13:15.

Commissioned by Marty Walker.

First performed November 11, 2002, at Vanderbilt University, Nashville, TN.

Recorded on *Adams Cox Fink Fox* (Cold Blue CB0009).

Dream In White On White

Composed March 1992. Taiga Press, 1992 and 2002.

For strings (minimum two violins, two violas, two cellos, double bass), string quartet, harp (or piano). 16:45.

First performed May 25, 1992, by JoAnn Falletta and the Virginia Symphony at Old Dominion University, Norfolk, VA.

Recorded on *The Far Country* (New Albion NA061).

Earth and the Great Weather (A Sonic Geography of the Arctic)

Composed 1990–1993. Taiga Press, 1993.

Includes The place where you go to listen—Drums of winter—Pointed mountains scattered all around—The circle of suns and moons—The circle of winds—Deep

and distant thunder—River with no willows—One that stays all winter—Drums of fire, drums of stone—Where the waves splash, hitting again and again.
For violin, viola, cello, double bass, two sopranos, alto, bass, four speaking voices, four percussionists, digital delay, recorded natural sounds. 90:00.
Commissioned by the Alaska Festival of Native Arts.
First performed February 27, 1993, by John Luther Adams and musicians at the University of Alaska, Fairbanks, AK.
Recorded on *Earth and the Great Weather* (New World 80459-2).

A set of published excerpts is available separately:

Three Drum Quartets from Earth and the Great Weather
Taiga Press, 1993 and 1996.
Includes Drums of winter—Deep and distant thunder—Drums of fire, drums of stone.
For four percussionists (with optional recorded sounds). 25:30.
First performed separately in 1995 by Percussion Group Cincinnati, Cincinnati, OH.

The Far Country of Sleep (In Memoriam Morton Feldman)
Composed July 1988. Taiga Press, 1988 and 2005.
For strings (minimum six violins [I], six violins [II], four cellos, two double basses), two flutes, two oboes, two clarinets, two bassoons, two horns, two trumpets, trombone, two percussionists. 15:45.
Commissioned by the Arctic Chamber Orchestra.
First performed October 1, 1988, by John Luther Adams and the Arctic Chamber Orchestra, Haines, AK.
Recorded on *The Far Country* (New Albion NA061).

The Farthest Place
Composed 2001. Taiga Press, 2001.
For violin, double bass, piano, vibraphone (or electronic mallet instrument), marimba (or electronic mallet instrument). 11:00.
Recorded on *The Light That Fills the World* (Cold Blue CB0010).

Floating Petals
Composed April 1973. Unpublished (manuscript reproduction at the NYPL and U. of Memphis).
For violin, flute, piano, harp, vibraphone.
First performed 1973 by the Cal Arts Chamber Players, Valencia, CA.

Forest Without Leaves
Composed 1984. Complete work unpublished (manuscript reproduction at the NYPL).
Poems by John Haines.
For soprano, mezzo-soprano, alto, tenor, bass, SATB chorus, chamber orchestra. 75:00.
Commissioned by the Arctic Chamber Orchestra.

First performed November 11, 1984, by Byron McGilvray and the Arctic Chamber Orchestra and Chamber Choir, Fairbanks, AK.

Recorded on *Forest Without Leaves* (Owl 32).

Two sets of published excerpts with equivalent instrumentation are available separately:

Excerpts from Forest Without Leaves

Taiga Press, © 1984.

Includes Prologue: In the forest without leaves—Anthem: This earth written over with words—Madrigal: One rock on another—Hymn: And sometimes through the air—Cantilena: How the sun came to the forest—Prophecy: A coolness will come to their children—Benediction: In the forest without leaves.

Soundings 14-15

Soundings Press (Santa Fe, NM), 1986.

Includes One rock on another.

Four Thousand Holes

Composed 2010. Taiga Press, 2010.

For piano, percussion, electronically processed sounds.

Commissioned by Stephen Drury.

First performed June 23, 2011, by Stephen Drury (piano) and Scott Deal (percussion), at the New England Conservatory of Music, Boston.

Recorded on *Four Thousand Holes* (Cold Blue CB0035).

Green Corn Dance

Composed April 1974. Taiga Press, 1989 and 2004.

For six percussionists. 7:30.

Dedicated to James Tenney.

First performed March 26, 1977, by the New Music Ensemble at Memphis State University, Memphis, TN.

The Immeasurable Space of Tones

Composed 1998/2001. Taiga Press, 2001.

For violin, contrabass instrument (double bass, contrabass clarinet, or contrabassoon), piano, electronic keyboard (or organ), vibraphone (or electronic mallet instrument). 27:00.

First performed April 18, 1998, by Scott Deal at the University of Alaska, Fairbanks.

Recorded on *The Light That Fills the World* (Cold Blue CB0010).

In a Treeless Place, Only Snow

Composed 1999. Taiga Press, 1999.

For string quartet, harp (or piano), celesta, two vibraphones. 18:00.

Commissioned by the Third Angle New Music Ensemble.

First performed November 5, 1999, by Tim Weiss and the Oberlin Contemporary Music Ensemble at the Cleveland Museum of Art, Cleveland, OH.

In Search of the Long Line

Composed September–December 1985. This version has been withdrawn.

Unpublished (manuscript reproduction at the NYPL).

For piano. 9:30.
First performed 1985 by Thomas Dickinson, New York City, NY.

Composed 1986. This version has been withdrawn. Unpublished.
For orchestra.
First performed 1988 by Gordon Wright and the Fairbanks Symphony Orchestra,
Fairbanks, AK.

In the White Silence

Composed 1998. Taiga Press, 1998.
For string quartet, strings (minimum two violins [I], two violins [II], two violas, two
cellos, two double basses), celesta, harp, two vibraphones. 75:00.
First performed November 11, 1998, by Tim Weiss and the Oberlin Contemporary
Music Ensemble in Finney Chapel at Oberlin College, Oberlin, OH.
Recorded on *In the White Silence* (New World 80600-2).

Inuksuit

Composed 2009. Taiga Press, 2009.
For 9–99 percussionists. 75:00–90:00.
First performed June 21, 2009, by Steven Schick and percussionists at the Banff
Centre, Banff, Canada.

for Jim (rising) (In Memory of James Tenney)

Composed August 1986. *Perspectives of New Music* (Princeton, NJ) 25, nos. 1–2
(Winter 1987): 447–54.
For four horns. 5:10.

Composed 2006. Taiga Press, 2006.
For three trumpets, three trombones. 5:30.
First performed October 30, 2007, by the Orkest de Volharding, Rotterdam,
Netherlands.

The Light That Fills the World

Composed 1999–2000. Taiga Press, 2000.
For strings, piccolo, two flutes, three oboes, three clarinets, two bassoons,
contrabassoon, four horns, two trumpets, two trombones, tuba, vibraphone,
marimba, suspended cymbal, timpani. 13:00.
First performed February 2000 by Gordon Wright and the Fairbanks Symphony
Orchestra, Healy, AK.

Composed Winter 1999–2000. Taiga Press, 2001.
For violin, contrabass instrument (double bass, contrabass clarinet, or
contrabassoon), electronic keyboard (or organ), vibraphone (or electronic mallet
instrument), marimba (or electronic mallet instrument). 13:00.
Commissioned by the Paul Dresher Ensemble.
First performed November 20, 1999, by the Paul Dresher Ensemble, San Francisco, CA.
Recorded on *The Light That Fills the World* (Cold Blue CB0010) and *Musicworks* 82
(Winter 2002).

The Light Within
Composed November 2007. Taiga Press, 2007.

For violin, cello, alto flute, bass clarinet, piano, vibraphone, crotales, electronically processed sounds. 12:00.

Commissioned by the Seattle Chamber Players and the California EAR Unit.

First performed January 28, 2008, by the Seattle Chamber Players at On the Boards, Seattle, WA.

Composed 2010. Taiga Press, 2010.

For strings, piccolo, oboe, clarinet (or bass clarinet), bassoon (or contrabassoon), horn, trumpet, bass trombone, tuba, piano, harp, vibraphone (or crotales), timpani, bass drum, electronically processed sounds. 12:00.

Commissioned by the American Composers Orchestra.

First performed October 16, 2010, by George Manahan and the American Composers Orchestra, New York, NY.

Little Cosmic Dust Poem
Composed 2007. Taiga Press, 2007.

Poem by John Haines.

For medium voice, piano. 5:00.

Dedicated to Fred and Alexandra Peters.

First performed February 15, 2009, by Brenda Patterson (mezzo-soprano) and Myra Huang (piano) at Eastern University, St. Davids, Pennsylvania.

for Lou Harrison
Composed 2003. Taiga Press, 2007.

For string quartet, strings (minimum two violins, two violas, two cellos, double bass), two pianos. 65:00.

First performed September 27, 2005, by Stephen Drury and the Callithumpian Consort at the New England Conservatory of Music, Boston, MA.

Recorded on *for Lou Harrison* (New World 80669-2).

magic song for one who wishes to live
and the dead who climb up to the sky
Composed 1990. Taiga Press, 1990.

For medium voice, piano. 5:00.

Commissioned by New Songs.

First performed April 21, 1991, by New Songs at the Security Pacific Gallery, Seattle, WA.

Composed 1992. Taiga Press, 1992.

For medium voice, strings, two flutes, two oboes, two clarinets, two bassoons, two horns, trombone, harp, percussion.

Commissioned by Anchorage Opera.

First performed 1992 by James Demmler with Karen Keltner and the Anchorage Opera Orchestra, Anchorage, AK.

Make Prayers to the Raven

Composed 1996–1998. Taiga Press, 1998.

Music composed for the 1987 TV series of the same name. Written by Richard K. Nelson, narrated by Barry Lopez, directed by John Luther Adams, and produced by Mark O. Badger for KUAC-TV, Fairbanks, AK.

Includes In the forest—Deenaadai' (Long ago)—Snow falling—Shik'eenoohtii (My Relatives)—Night.

For violin, cello, flute, harp (or piano), percussion. 16:30.

First performed November 9, 2000, by the MiN Ensemble, Bergen, Norway.

The Mathematics of Resonant Bodies

Composed 2002. Taiga Press, 2003, and 2007 for CD of electronically processed sounds for use during performance.

Includes burst—rumble—shimmer—roar—thunder—wail—crash—stutter.

For solo percussionist (with electronically processed sounds). 70:00.

Commissioned by the Los Angeles County Museum of Art (LACMA), WNYC and the Subtropics Festival.

First performed April 28, 2003, by Steven Schick at the LACMA, Los Angeles, CA.

Recorded on *The Mathematics of Resonant Bodies* (Cantaloupe CA 21034).

Night Peace

Composed November 1976–January 1977. Taiga Press, 1989 and 2004.

For double SATB chorus (antiphonally placed), solo soprano, harp, percussion. 14:00.

Commissioned by the Atlanta Singers.

First performed 1977 by Kevin Culver and the Atlanta Singers, Atlanta, GA.

Recorded on *A Northern Suite/Night Peace* (Opus One 88) and *The Far Country* (New Albion NA061).

∧ Northern Suite

Composed 1979–1980. Revised 2004. Taiga Press, 2004.

For strings, two flutes (1st doubles piccolo), two oboes (2nd doubles English horn), two clarinets, two bassoons, four horns, two trumpets, two trombones, piano (or celesta), harp, three percussionists. 19:00.

Commissioned by the Arctic Chamber Orchestra.

First performed October 4, 1981, by Gordon Wright and the Arctic Chamber Orchestra, Galena, AK.

Recorded on *A Northern Suite/Night Peace* (Opus One 88).

Nunataks (Solitary Peaks)

Composed 2007. Taiga Press, 2007.

For piano. 7:00.

Commissioned by Music Northwest.

First performed March 29, 2008, by Jane Harty at Music Northwest, Seattle, WA.

The Place Where You Go To Listen

Created 2004–2006.

Sound and light environment started March 21, 2006, at the University of Alaska Museum of the North, Fairbanks, AK. Ongoing.

Poem of the Forgotten

Composed 2004. Taiga Press, 2004.

Poem by John Haines.

For medium voice, piano. 5:00.

First performed October 23, 2005, at Music Northwest by Thomasa Eckert (soprano) and Jane Harty (piano), Seattle, WA.

Prelude for Organ

Composed 1973. This work has been withdrawn. Unpublished (manuscript reproduction at the NYPL).

For organ. 15:00.

First performed September 30, 1973, by G. Thomas Hazleton at Stanford University, Palo Alto, CA.

Qilyaun

Composed 1998. Taiga Press, 1998.

For four bass drums (or bass drum with electronic delay). 15:00.

Commissioned by the Fairbanks Symphony Association.

Dedicated to Scott Deal.

First performed April 18, 1998, by Scott Deal, Fairbanks, AK.

Recorded on *Red Arc/Blue Veil* (Cold Blue CB0026).

Red Arc/Blue Veil

Composed 2002. Taiga Press, 2001, and 2007 for CD of electronically processed sounds for use during performance.

For mallet percussion, piano, electronically processed sounds. 12:00.

Commissioned by Ensemble Sirius.

First performed 2002 by Ensemble Sirius, Boston, MA.

Recorded on *Red Arc/Blue Veil* (Cold Blue CB0026) and the accompanying CD to *Winter Music* (Middletown, CT: Wesleyan University Press, 2004).

Resurrection Dance

Composed 1983. Unpublished (manuscript reproduction at the NYPL).

For violin, cello, piccolo, vibraharp, congas, percussion. 7:00.

First performed 1983 by Newband, Bronx, NY.

Sky With Four Suns *and* Sky With Four Moons

Composed 2007–2008. Taiga Press, 2008.

For four SATB choirs. 8:00.

First performed July 3, 2008, by Chamber Choir Kamer, Riga, Latvia.

songbirdsongs

Composed 1974–1979. Alry Publications (Denver, CO), 1983 [Book 1]. Taiga Press, 2003 and 2009. [Books 1 and 2].

For two piccolos and two-three percussionists. 40:00.

Grant funding by the NEA.

First performed 1974 by John Luther Adams and musicians, Atlanta, GA.

Recorded on *songbirdsongs* (Opus One 66) [Books 1 and 2] and *Exotic Chamber Music* (Centaur CRC 2273) [Book 1].

The Sound Goes Round and Round

Composed June 1974. This work has been withdrawn. Unpublished (manuscript reproduction at the NYPL).

For violin, viola, cello, piano, harp. 12:30.

Grant funding by the NEA.

Spring Rain

Composed 1975/1985. Unpublished (manuscript reproduction at the NYPL).

Poem by Chiyo Ni.

For two sopranos, two altos, piano. 3:15.

First performed 1985 by Kevin Culver and the Atlanta Singers, Atlanta, GA.

Strange and Sacred Noise

Composed 1991–1997. Taiga Press, © 1997, 2003 and 2007.

Includes . . . dust into dust, solitary and time-breaking waves, velocities crossing in phase-space, triadic iteration lattices, clusters on a quadrilateral grid, . . . and dust rising . . .

For four percussionists. 75:00.

First performed November 25, 1998, by Percussion Group Cincinnati, Cincinnati, OH.

Recorded on *Strange and Sacred Noise* (Mode 153).

Strange Birds Passing (In Memory of Tadashi Miyashita)

Composed 1983. Taiga Press, 1983 and 2003.

For two piccolos, three flutes, two alto flutes, bass flute. 6:30.

Dedicated to Dorli McWayne and the Fairbanks Flutists.

First performed 1983 by the Fairbanks Flute Choir, Fairbanks, AK.

Three High Places (In Memory of Gordon Wright)

Composed 2007. Taiga Press, 2007.

For solo violin. 10:00.

First performed April 11, 2007, by Erik Carlson, New York, NY.

Three on Hira

Composed 1978. This work has been withdrawn. Unpublished.

For solo koto.

The Time of Drumming (Sauyatugvik)

Composed 1995. Revised June 1996. Taiga Press, 1995.

For strings, piccolo, two flutes, three oboes, three clarinets, two bassoons, contrabassoon, four horns, three trumpets, two trombones, bass trombone, tuba, two pianos, timpani, four percussionists. 10:30.

Commissioned by the Anchorage Symphony Orchestra.

First performed February 17, 1996, by George Hanson and the Anchorage Symphony Orchestra, Anchorage, AK.

Composed December 1996 (revisions). Taiga Press, 1997.

For two pianos, timpani, four percussionists. 10:30.

First performed November 8, 1997, by Richard Brown and the Shepherd School of Music Percussion Ensemble at Rice University, Houston, TX.

Time Undisturbed

Composed 1999. Unpublished.

For cello, piccolo, flute, alto flute (or three shakuhachis), sustaining keyboard (or sho), three harps (or celesta, piano and harp, or three kotos).

Commissioned by the Kanagawa Cultural Council.

First performed December 5, 2000, by the Monophony Consort, Kanagawa, Japan.

up into the silence

Composed 1978. Taiga Press, 2003.

Poem by ee cummings.

For medium voice, piano (or harp). 3:30.

First performed 1978 by Cheryl Bray (voice), Atlanta, GA.

Composed 1984. Unpublished (manuscript reproduction at the NYPL).

For medium voice, strings, harp, percussion. 3:30.

First performed 1984 by Lauren Pelon (voice) with Gordon Wright and the Fairbanks Symphony Orchestra, Fairbanks, Alaska.

Veils *and* Vesper

Sound and light installation first exhibited May 6–27, 2006, at the Diapason Gallery, New York, NY.

Additional exhibitions September 23–October 8, 2006, at the Happy New Ears Festival, Kortrijk, Belgium; April 25–27, 2007, at the Arizona State University Art Museum, Tempe, Arizona; and March 8–25 at the Arts@29 Garden, Cambridge, MA.

The Wind in High Places

Composed 2011. Taiga Press, 2011.

For string quartet. 16:00.

First performed October 26, 2011, by Ethel at the Cerritos Center for the Performing Arts, Cerritos, CA.

Five Yup'ik Dances

Composed 1991–1994. Taiga Press, 1991 and 2002.

Includes Invitation to dance—Jump rope song—Shaman's moon song—Juggling song—It circles me.

For harp. 12:00.

First performed 1991 by Heidi Lehwalder, Seattle, WA.

Composed 1995. This work has been withdrawn. Unpublished.

Includes Invitation to dance—Jump rope song—Shaman's moon song—Juggling song—It circles me.

For piano. 12:00.

First performed October 27, 1995, by Juliana Osinchuk at the Kennedy Center's Terrace Theater, Washington, D.C.

Discography

Listed chronologically

songbirdsongs

Opus One 66 | 1980 | LP; 39:00

songbirdsongs (Books 1 and 2) recorded December 28–29, 1979, in the Glenn Memorial Chapel at Emory University, Atlanta, GA.

Michel Cook, Anne McFarland, piccolos/ocarina; John Luther Adams, Kevin Culver, Scott Douglas, Tim Embry, percussion/ocarina.

A Northern Suite/Night Peace

Opus One 88 | 1982 | LP; 37:12

A Northern Suite recorded October 1 and 3, 1982, at the University of Alaska, Fairbanks, AK.

Arctic Chamber Orchestra. Gordon Wright, conductor.

Night Peace recorded November 5–6, 1982, at the Northside United Methodist Church, Atlanta, GA.

Atlanta Singers. Kevin Culver, conductor.

Cheryl Bray, soprano; Joan Rubin, harp; Billy Traylor, percussion.

Forest Without Leaves

Owl 32 | 1987 | LP; 52:34

Arctic Chamber Choir and Arctic Chamber Orchestra. Byron McGilvray, conductor.

The Far Country

New Albion NA061 | 1993 | CD; 48:08

Dream In White On White recorded May 25, 1992, in Chandler Hall at Old Dominion University, Norfolk, VA.

Apollo Quartet and Apollo Strings. JoAnn Falletta, conductor.

Night Peace recorded September 27, 1992, in St. David's Episcopal Church, Roswell, GA.

Atlanta Singers. Kevin Culver, conductor.
Cheryl Bray Lower, soprano; Nella Rigel, harp; Michael Cebulski, percussion.

The Far Country of Sleep recorded July 29, 1991, in Performing Arts Concert Hall at the University of California at Santa Cruz, Santa Cruz, CA.
Cabrillo Festival Orchestra. JoAnn Falletta, conductor.

Earth and the Great Weather
New World 80459-2 | 1994 | CD; 75:50
Earth and the Great Weather recorded March 8–11, 1993, in the Charles W. Davis Concert Hall at the University of Alaska, Fairbanks, AK.
Robin Lorentz, violin; Ron Lawrence, viola; Michael Finckel, cello; Robert Black, double bass; John Luther Adams, Robert Black, Amy Knoles, Robin Lorentz, percussion; James Nageak, Doreen Simmonds [Iñupiaq and English]; Adeline Peter Raboff, Lincoln Tritt [Gwich'in and English]; Dave Hunsaker [Latin].
John Luther Adams, Michael Finckel, directors.

Exotic Chamber Music [selection]
Centaur CRC 2273 | 1996 | CD; 65:52 [13:16]
songbirdsongs (Book 1) recorded May 1995 at the Pennsylvania State University School of Music, University Park, PA.
Armstrong Flute and Percussion Duo.

Clouds of Forgetting, Clouds of Unknowing
New World 80500-2 | 1997 | CD; 61:24
Clouds of Forgetting, Clouds of Unknowing recorded February 27 and 29, 1996, in Chandler Hall at Old Dominion University, Norfolk, VA.
Apollo Chamber Orchestra. JoAnn Falletta, conductor.

Adams Cox Fink Fox [selection]
Cold Blue CB0009 | 2002 | CD; 41:01 [13:22]
Dark Wind recorded November 2001, Los Angeles, CA.
Marty Walker, clarinet; Bryan Pezzone, piano; Amy Knoles, vibraphone/marimba.

The Light That Fills the World
Cold Blue CB0010 | 2002 | CD; 50:58
The Farthest Place, *The Light That Fills the World*, and *The Immeasurable Space of Tones* recorded August 2002, Los Angeles, CA.
Robin Lorentz, violin; Barry Newton, double bass; Bryan Pezzone, piano; Amy Knoles, vibraphone [The Farthest Place].
Robin Lorentz, violin; Barry Newton, double bass; Marty Walker, contrabass clarinet; Amy Knoles, vibraphone/marimba; Nathaniel Reichman, keyboard/sound design [The Light That Fills the World].
Robin Lorentz, violin; Barry Newton, double bass; Marty Walker, contrabass clarinet; Bryan Pezzone, piano; Amy Knoles, vibraphone/marimba; Nathaniel Reichman, keyboard/sound design [The Immeasurable Space of Tones].

Musicworks *82* [selection]

2002 (Winter) | CD; 64:37 [12:56]

The Light That Fills the World included on CD accompanying Musicworks print edition.

Paul Dresher Ensemble.

In the White Silence

New World 80600-2 | 2003 | CD; 75:07

In the White Silence recorded November 11, 1998, in Finney Chapel at Oberlin College, Oberlin, OH.

Oberlin Contemporary Music Ensemble. Tim Weiss, conductor.

Winter Music: Composing the North

2004 | CD; 32:51

Music included on CD accompanying Adams's book of the same name (Middletown, CT: Wesleyan University Press, 2004).

roar early release of a section of the recording *The Mathematics of Resonant Bodies* (Cantaloupe CA 21034).

Steven Schick, percussion (tam-tam/electronically processed sounds).

velocities crossing in phase-space early release of a section of the recording *Strange and Sacred Noise* (Mode 153).

Percussion Group Cincinnati.

Red Arc/Blue Veil recorded October 26, 2002, in the Center for Audio Recording Arts at Georgia State University, Atlanta, GA.

Ensemble Sirius.

Strange and Sacred Noise

Mode 153 | 2005 | CD/DVD; 73:06

DVD version equivalent to CD, but includes the video interview "A Brief History of Noise: John Luther Adams and Allen Otte in Conversation."

Strange and Sacred Noise recorded November 12–15, 1998, in the Patricia Corbett Theater at the University of Cincinnati, Cincinnati, OH.

Percussion Group Cincinnati.

Russell Burge, James Culley, and Allen Otte.

With Stuart Gerber, Brady Harrison, and Matt McClung.

The Mathematics of Resonant Bodies

Cantaloupe CA 21034 | 2006 | CD; 69:09

The Mathematics of Resonant Bodies recorded January 19–21, 2002, and January 15–18, 2003, in the Charles W. Davis Concert Hall at the University of Alaska, Fairbanks, AK.

Steven Schick, percussion.

The Place Where You Go to Listen: Interactive Guide

CD-ROM | 2007

Guide to John Luther Adams's sound and light environment, *The Place Where You Go to Listen*, at the University of Alaska Museum of the North, Fairbanks, AK. Produced by the UA Museum, includes interviews, instruments, music excerpts, satellite updates, and composer notes.

for Lou Harrison

New World 80669-2 | 2007 | CD; 66:00

for Lou Harrison recorded September and December 2005 in Jordan Hall at the New England Conservatory, Boston, MA.

Callithumpian Consort. Stephen Drury, conductor.

Red Arc/Blue Veil

Cold Blue CB0026 | 2007 | CD; 51:48

Dark Waves, *Among Red Mountains*, and *Red Arc/Blue Veil* recorded September 2005 to July 2007 in Jordan Hall at the New England Conservatory, Boston, MA. *Qilyaun* recorded March 17–20, 2004, in the Charles W. Davis Concert Hall at the University of Alaska, Fairbanks.

Stephen Drury, Yukiko Takagi, piano [Dark Waves].

Stephen Drury, piano [Among Red Mountains].

Scott Deal, Stuart Gerber, bass drum [Qilyaun].

Stephen Drury, piano; Scott Deal, vibraphone/crotales [Red Arc/Blue Veil].

the place we began

Cold Blue CB0032 | 2009 | CD; 51:32

Four electro-acoustic soundscapes—*in a room, at the still point, in the rain, the place we began*—composed and performed by John Luther Adams.

Four Thousand Holes

Cold Blue CB0035 | 2011 | CD; 42:59

Four Thousand Holes recorded June 21–22 and November 21, 2010, in Jordan Hall at the New England Conservatory, Boston, MA.

Stephen Drury, piano; Scott Deal, percussion.

. . . and bells remembered recorded October 3, 2006, in Jordan Hall at the New England Conservatory, Boston, MA.

Callithumpian Consort. Stephen Drury, conductor.

Writings By John Luther Adams

Listed alphabetically

[CD liner notes]

Details concerning the works contained on the commercial recordings: The Far Country (New Albion NA061, 1993); *Earth and the Great Weather* (New World 80459-2, 1994); *Clouds of Forgetting, Clouds of Unknowing* (New World 80500-2, 1997); *In the White Silence* (New World 80600-2, 2003); *Strange and Sacred Noise*

(Mode 153, 2005); *for Lou Harrison* (New World 80669-2, 2007); *Red Arc/Blue Veil* (Cold Blue CB0026, 2007); *the place we began* (Cold Blue CB0032, 2009); and *Four Thousand Holes* (Cold Blue CB0035, 2011).

See Cold Blue Music (www.coldbluemusic.com) and New World Records (http://www .newworldrecords.org/liner_notes.cgi?rm=list&imprint=NWR) for liner notes.

Credo (In Memory of Gordon Wright)
Limited edition broadside of 97 signed and numbered copies. Hand-set and printed by Mary Ellen Niedenfuer of Midnight Sun Paper Sales. June 2007. http://www.johnlutheradams.com/writings/credo.html.

Forest Without Leaves
Ear Magazine 10, no. 3 (January/February/March 1986): 5 and 20.
Abbreviated version in *Winter Music: Composing the North*, 37-39. Middletown: Wesleyan University Press, 2004.

From the Ground Up
Utne Reader, no. 68 (March/April 1995): 86.

Global Warming and Art
(Originally published in slightly different form as "Alaska Is Melting; Can Art Help?" *Anchorage Daily News*, December 4, 2002, B6.)
Musicworks, no. 86 (Summer 2003): 8-9.
Reprinted in *Orion* 22, no. 5 (September/October 2003): 11;
and *Winter Music: Composing the North*, 177–83. Middletown: Wesleyan University Press, 2004.

The Immeasurable Space of Tones
Winter Music: Composing the North, 162–64. Middletown: Wesleyan University Press, 2004.
Abbreviated version in *Musicworks*, no. 91 (Spring 2005): 7–8.

In Search of an Ecology of Music
Unpublished. http://www.johnlutheradams.com/writings/ecology.html.

John Luther Adams Writes Editorial
Cantaloupe Records, October 10, 2008. http://www.cantaloupemusic.com/news.php ?story_id=55.

[*NewMusicBox* web publications]
31 articles published between April 1, 2000, and May 5, 2010, and posted on the American Music Center's online magazine, *NewMusicBox*. http://newmusicbox .org.

Nude Rolling Down An Escalator: Studies For Disklavier
Liner notes for Kyle Gann's 1994 CD recording of the same name (New World 80633), 2005. http://www.newworldrecords.org/linernotes/80633.pdf.

The Place Where You Go to Listen
Terra Nova 2, no. 3 (Summer 1997): 15–16.

Reprinted in *North American Review* 283, no. 2 (March/April 1998): 35;
and *The Book of Music & Nature: An Anthology of Sounds, Words, Thoughts*, edited by David Rothenberg and Marta Ulvaeus, 181–82. Middletown: Wesleyan University Press, 2001.

http://www.johnlutheradams.com/writings/place.html.

The Place Where You Go to Listen: In Search of an Ecology of Music
Middletown: Wesleyan University Press, 2009.

Remembering James Tenney
Musicworks, no. 98 (Summer 2007): 7–8.

Resonance of Place: Confessions of an Out-of-town Composer
Early version in the *Planet Drum Foundation*, Spring/Summer 1993, 2 and 11.

North American Review 279, no. 1 (January/February 1994): 8–18.

http://www.johnlutheradams.com/writings/resonance.html.

Sonic Geography: Alaska
(Originally published in slightly different form as "Aesthetic Belongs to Artist, Not to North." *Anchorage Daily News*, September 11, 2005, Special section, final edition.)

Musicworks, no. 93 (Fall 2005): 5.

Strange and Sacred Noise
Northern Soundscapes: Yearbook of Soundscape Studies (vol. 1), edited by R. Murray Schafer and Helmi Järviluoma, 143–46. Tampere, Finland: University of Tampere, Dept. of Folk Tradition, 1998.

Visitations
Manoa 20, no. 1 (June 2008): 73–76.

Winter Music: Composing the North
Middletown: Wesleyan University Press, 2004.

Selections, pp. 57–77, reprinted as *Winter Music: A Composer's Journal: Reflections on American Music: The Twentieth Century and the New Millennium*, edited by James R. Heintze and Michael Saffle, 31–48. College Music Society: Pendragon Press, 2000;

Also *Musicworks*, no. 82 (Winter 2002): 32–39;

and *The Best Spiritual Writing 2002*, edited by Philip Zaleski, 1–21. New York: HarperCollins, 2002.

Writings About John Luther Adams
Listed chronologically and alphabetically within each year

Salzman, Eric. "Two John Adamses." *Stereo Review* 46, no. 10 (1981): 140.

Harrison, Thomas B. "To Hear the Unheard." *Alaska Magazine*, February 1993, 96.

Gann, Kyle. "Downtown Beats for the 1990s." *Contemporary Music Review* 10, no. 1 (1994): 33–49.

Klein, Howard. *Earth and the Great Weather* (New World 80459-2), 5–6. Liner notes for 1994 CD release. http://www.newworldrecords.org/linernotes/80459.pdf.

Gann, Kyle. *American Music in the Twentieth Century*, 368–71. New York: Schirmer, 1997.

Klein, Howard. *Clouds of Forgetting, Clouds of Unknowing* (New World 80500-2), 2–4. Liner notes for 1997 CD release. http://www.newworldrecords.org/linernotes/80500 .pdf.

Gann, Kyle. "A Forest from the Seeds of Minimalism: An Essay on Postminimal and Totalist Music." Program Notes for the Minimalism Festival of the Berliner Gesellschaft für Neue Musik, Berlin, Germany, Fall 1998. http://home.earthlink .net/~kgann/postminimalism.html.

Morris, Mitchell. "Ecotopian Sounds; or, The Music of John Luther Adams and Strong Environmentalism." In *Crosscurrents and Counterpoints: Offerings in Honor of Bengt Hambraeus at 70*, edited by P. F. Broman, N.A. Engebretsen and B. Alphonce, 129–41. Göthenburg: University of Sweden Press, 1998.

Young, Gayle. "Sonic Geography of the Arctic: An Interview with John Luther Adams." *Musicworks* 70 (1998): 38–43.

Alburger, Mark. "A to Z: Interview with John Luther Adams." *21st Century Music* 7, no. 1 (2000): 1–12.

Gann, Kyle. "New Currents Coalesce: Since the Mid-1980s." In *Music in the United States*, edited by H. Wiley Hitchcock, 363–94. Upper Saddle River, NJ: Prentice-Hall, 2000. Section concerning John Luther Adams's work: 381–82.

Kosman, Joshua. "John Luther Adams." In *The New Grove Dictionary of Music and Musicians*, edited by Stanley Sadie and John Tyrell, Vol. 1, 2nd edition. New York: Macmillan, 2000.

Feisst, Sabine."Klanggeographie—Klanggeometrie: Der US-amerikanische Komponist John Luther Adams." *Musiktexte* 91 (2001): 4–14.

Slonimsky, Nicolas, editor. "John Luther Adams." In *Baker's Biographical Dictionary of Musicians*, Vol. 1, 8th edition. New York: Schirmer, 2001.

Gann, Kyle. "American Composer: John Luther Adams." *Chamber Music* 19, no. 1 (2002): 46–47.

Feisst, Sabine. *In the White Silence* (New World 80600-2), 2–8. Liner notes for 2003 CD release. http://www.newworldrecords.org/linernotes/80600.pdf.

Baechtel, Mark. "Seeing in the Dark; Winter can be an inspiring and productive season for Alaska artists." *Anchorage Daily News*, December 19, 2004, Life section, final edition.

Feisst, Sabine. "Discography," "Selected Bibliography," and "Catalog of Works" in *Winter Music*, by John Luther Adams, 185–98. Middletown, CT: Wesleyan University Press, 2004.

Gann, Kyle. "John Luther Adams: Music as a Geography of the Spiritual." Introduction to *Winter Music: Composing the North*, xi–xix. Middletown, CT: Wesleyan University Press, 2004.

Mayer, Amy. "Musician's Work Reflects Alaskan Landscape." *Voice of America News*, August 13, 2004, Arts and Culture section.

Oteri, Frank J. "Ready for Anything: Steven Schick talks with Frank J. Oteri."

NewMusicBox, April 1, 2004. http://www.newmusicbox.org/articles/ready-for-anything-steven-schick-talks-with-frank-j-oteri/.

Sheridan, Molly. "In Conversation with John Luther Adams." *NewMusicBox*, October 25, 2004. http://www.newmusicbox.org/articles/In-Conversation-with-John-Luther-Adams/.

Schick, Steven. *Strange and Sacred Noise* (Mode 153). Liner notes for 2005 CD release.

Smith, Dawnell. "Fairbanks Composer Seeks Unification of Sound and Scene." *Anchorage Daily News*, September 4, 2005, Life section, final edition.

Varela, Daniel. "From the Ends of the Earth: JLA (in Alaska) in conversation with Daniel Varela (in Argentina)." 2005. http://www.johnlutheradams.com/interview/endsoftheearth.html.

Bryson, George. "Just a Sip, Please; More Alaska new-car buyers are choosing to go easy on the gas; A gas miser sampler." *Anchorage Daily News*, July 2, 2006, Life section, final edition.

Dunham, Mike. "The Harmony of the Spheres." *Orion Magazine* (Great Barrington, MA), March/April 2006, 7.

Schick, Steven. *The Percussionist's Art: Same Bed, Different Dreams*. Rochester, NY: University of Rochester Press, 2006. Section concerning *The Mathematics of Resonant Bodies*: 79–89.

Garland, Peter. *for Lou Harrison* (New World 80669-2), 2–12. Liner notes for 2007 CD release. http://www.newworldrecords.org/uploads/file8Wiaq.pdf.

Ross, Alex. "Song of the Earth." *The New Yorker*, May 12, 2008, 76–81. http://www.newyorker.com/reporting/2008/05/12/080512fa_fact_ross.

"Alaska Photojournal." *The Rest Is Noise*, May 7, 2008. http://www.therestisnoise.com/2008/05/alaska-photojou.html.

Sheridan, Molly. "Tell Me Something, John Luther Adams." *Mind the Gap*, June 20, 2008. http://www.artsjournal.com/gap/2008/06/tell_me_something_john_luther/. Also http://www.johnlutheradams.com/interview/sheridan.html.

Herzogenrath, Bernd. "The 'Weather of Music': Sounding Nature in the Twentieth and Twenty-First Centuries." In *Deleuze/Guattari & Ecology*, edited by Bernd Herzogenrath, 216–23. Basingstoke, England; New York: Palgrave Macmillan, 2009.

Ross, Alex. Foreword to *The Place Where You Go to Listen: In Search of an Ecology of Music*, by John Luther Adams, ix–xii. Middletown, CT: Wesleyan University Press, 2009. Reprinted as "Gleanings: Seismic Symphony." *Utne Reader*, November–December 2009, 34–35. http://www.utne.com/GreatWriting/Alaskas-Seismic-Symphony.aspx.

Smith, Steven Ross. "Hearing, Listening and Composing for Outside: Interview with John Luther Adams & Steven Schick." *BOULDERPAVEMENT*, June 2009. http://www.johnlutheradams.com/interview/jlaschick.html.

Tarantino, Todd. "Wayfinding in John Luther Adams's *for Lou Harrison*." *Perspectives of New Music* 47, no. 2 (2009): 196–227.

Feisst, Sabine. "Composing the North: John Luther Adams's Sonic Geography." Paper presented at the annual conference for the Society for American Music, Ottawa, Canada, March 17–21, 2010. Also "John Luther Adams—An Avant-garde Composer in Alaska." Paper presented at the international musicological conference "Beyond the Centres:

Musical Avant-gardes Since 1950" at Aristotle University, Thessaloniki, Greece, July 1–5, 2010.

And "Music as Eco-Criticism: John Luther Adams's Creative Activities in Alaska." Paper presented at the international conference "Creative Americas: Crossed Perspectives on Discourses and Practices" at the University of Toulouse, France, October 6–7, 2010.

Hall, Lawton. "Sound Walks: James Tenney/John Luther Adams." *Footholds*, December 23, 2010. http://www.lawtonhall.com/?p=407.

Ross, Alex. "Song of the Earth: The Arctic Sound of John Luther Adams," in *Listen to This*, 176–87. New York: Farrar, Straus, and Giroux, 2010.

Wells, James. "John Luther Adams, Finding a Way to Get Lost." *BMI: Musicworld Feature*, September 1, 2010. http://www.bmi.com/news/entry/549097.

Giovetti, Olivia. "Two Adams Combine their Ribs for an Operatic Eve." *WQX-Aria: WQXR's Opera Blog*, April 11, 2011. http://www.wqxr.org/blogs/wqx-aria/2011/apr/01/two-adams-combine-their-ribs-operatic-eve/.

Reviews (and previews) of John Luther Adams's Works

Listed chronologically and alphabetically within each year
(All reviews are of sound recordings unless otherwise noted)

Dawson, Eric. "Holst Sung With Charm." Calgary Herald (Alberta, Canada), April 7, 1994, Entertainment section, final edition. Reviews *The Far Country*.

Nappi, Peter. "John Luther Adams: Earth and the Great Weather." *allmusic* [1994]. http://www.allmusic.com/cg/amg.dll?p=amg&sql=10:fifrxquhldae.

Vaughan, Peter. "A Rare Work Is Staged; 'Crow, Weasel' Is Entrancing." *Star Tribune* (Minneapolis, MN), January 25, 1994, Variety section, metro edition. Reviews performance of *Crow and Weasel* at the Children's Theatre, Minneapolis, MN.

Dunham, Mike. "In Review: Anchorage." *Opera News* 60, no. 3 (1995): 62. Reviews the Anchorage Opera's performance of *Earth and the Great Weather* at the Alaska Center for the Performing Arts, Anchorage, AK.

Hahn, Noelle. "Wieler and Velichko Great Pairing at UAA." *Anchorage Daily News*, January 31, 1995, Impulse Section, final edition. Reviews Sherri Weiler and Svetlana Velichko's performance of *magic song for one who wishes to live* and *the dead who climb up to the sky* at the University of Alaska, Anchorage, AK.

Page, Tim. "New York Music Critic Reviews John Luther Adams' 'Earth'." *Anchorage Daily News*, May 11, 1995, Lifestyle section, final edition. Reviews the Anchorage Opera's performance of *Earth and the Great Weather* at the Alaska Center for the Performing Arts, Anchorage, AK.

Weaver, Howard. "Home-grown Composition Is Living Culture." *Anchorage Daily News*, May 7, 1995, Forum section, final edition. Preview of the Anchorage Opera's performance of *Earth and the Great Weather* at the Alaska Center for the Performing Arts, Anchorage, AK.

Hahn, Noelle. "Ozinchuck [*sic*] Formidable in Wide Ranging Recital." *Anchorage Daily News*, February 29, 1996, Lifestyles section, final edition. Reviews Juliana Osinchuk's performance of *Five Yup'ik Dances* at the Anchorage Festival of Music, Anchorage, AK.

Johnston, Colleen. "Percussionist's Music Rings True: Beverley Johnston Delights Audience at NUMUS Concert." *The Record* (Kitchener-Waterloo, Ontario), October 19, 1996, Entertainment section, final edition. Reviews Beverley Johnston's performance of *Three Drum Quartets from Earth and the Great Weather* at the Seagram's Museum, Waterloo, Ontario.

Kosman, Joshua. "Dresher Ensemble's Heady Stew." *The San Francisco Chronicle*, June 3, 1996, Daily Datebook section, final edition. Reviews the Paul Dresher Ensemble's performance of percussion works from *Coyote Builds North America* at the Yerba Buena Center for the Arts, San Francisco, CA. http://articles.sfgate.com/1996-06-03/entertainment/17777654_1_vicki-ray-musical-spike-jones-ensemble.

Teply, Lee. "Apollo Premieres 'Clouds' at ODU." *The Virginian-Pilot*, February 27, 1996, Local section, final edition. Reviews the Apollo Chamber Ensemble's performance of *Clouds of Forgetting, Clouds of Unknowing* at Old Dominion University, Norfolk, VA.

Wright, Rickey. "'Clouds' Premiere Culminates Adams' 6-Year Effort." *The Virginian-Pilot*, February 26, 1996, Daily Break section, final edition. Preview of the Apollo Chamber Ensemble's performance of *Clouds of Forgetting, Clouds of Unknowing* at Old Dominion University, Norfolk, VA.

Lange, Art. "Collections: Vocal." *Fanfare* 20, no. 4 (1997): 60. Reviews the Armstrong Flute and Percussion Duo's *Exotic Chamber Music* [*songbirdsongs*].

Roca, Octavio. "Paul Dresher Ensemble Gets 'Fresh'; Unfinished work tantalizes listeners." *The San Francisco Chronicle*, March 31, 1997, Daily Datebook section, final section. Reviews the Paul Dresher Ensemble's performance of *Sauyatugvik* at the Yerba Buena Center for the Arts, San Francisco, CA. http://articles.sfgate.com/1997-03-31/entertainment/17745864_1_paul-dresher-ensemble-violin-concerto.

Gann, Kyle. "Clouds of Forgetting, Clouds of Unknowing." *The Village Voice*, February 24, 1998, 136.

Johnson, Lawrence A. "Classical Recordings." *Fanfare* 21, no. 5 (1998): 60. Reviews *Clouds of Forgetting, Clouds of Unknowing*.

Stabler, David. "Third Angle Makes All the Pieces Fit in Concert." *The Oregonian*, April 19, 1998, Arts and Books section, sunrise edition. Reviews the Third Angle Ensemble's performance of percussion works from *Coyote Builds North America* at The Old Church, Portland, OR.

Verna, Paul. "John Luther Adams: Clouds Of Forgetting, Clouds Of Unknowing, Apollo Chamber Orchestra, Joann Falletta." *Billboard*, February 21, 1998, 63.

Furtwangler, Carol. "Music in Time is Hypnotizing and Familiar." *The Post and Courier*, May 30, 1999, A18, Sunday edition. Reviews the Spoleto Festival performance of *Clouds of Forgetting, Clouds of Unknowing* at the College of Charleston's Simons Center, Charleston, SC.

Hicken, Stephen D. "The Newest Music." *American Record Guide* 62, no. 2 (1999): 324. Reviews *Clouds of Forgetting, Clouds of Unknowing*.

Jones, Robert. "In 'Mamba's Daughters,' staging overwhelms story." *The Post and Courier*, May 31, 1999, A1. Reviews the Spoleto Festival performance of *Clouds of Forgetting, Clouds of Unknowing* at the College of Charleston's Simons Center, Charleston, SC.

Kakinuma, Toshie. "John Luther Adams: Earth and the Great Weather." In *Avant Music Guide*, edited by Shiba Shun'ichi, 238–39. Tokyo: Sakuhinsha, 1999.

Ashley, Tim. "Arts: Music reviews: Opera Earth and the Great Weather, Almeida, London." *The Guardian* (London), July 10, 2000, Features section. http://www.guardian.co.uk/culture/2000/jul/10/artsfeatures2.

Bündler, David. "Recent Works by John Luther Adams." *21st Century Music* 7, no. 2 (2000): 14. Reviews *In the White Silence*, *Strange and Sacred Noise*, and *Clouds of Forgetting, Clouds of Unknowing*.

England, Phil. "A Music Drama Celebrating Alaska's Arctic Refuge." *The Wire*, September 2000, 66. Reviews performance of *Earth and the Great Weather* at the Almeida Theatre, London.

Kimberley, Nick. "British Opera Diary: 'Earth and the Great Weather': Almeida Opera at the Almeida Theatre, July 6." *Opera* 51, no. 10 (2000): 1239–40.

Milnes, Rodney. "Wild is the wind." *The Times* (London), July 10, 2000, Features section. Reviews performance of *Earth and the Great Weather* at the Almeida Theatre, London.

Potter, Keith. "Opera: Earth and the Great Weather, Almeida Theatre London." *The Independent* (London), July 12, 2000, Features section.

Alburger, Mark. "The Big Picture." *21st Century Music* 8, no. 10 (2001): 19. Reviews *The Far Country*, *Earth and the Great Weather*, and *Clouds of Forgetting, Clouds of Unknowing*.

Blanchard, Jayne M. " 'Coyote' Tricks Don't Always Work; Folklore figure dances merrily, trips over tale." *The Washington Times*, March 17, 2001, Arts and Entertainment, Theater section, final edition. Reviews performance of *Coyote Builds North America* at the Arena Stage, Washington D.C.

Gann, Kyle. "Credo In Unum Tonum." *The Village Voice*, April 24, 2001, 127. Reviews the Flux Quartet and musicians' performance of *In a Treeless Place, Only Snow* at Church of the Ascension, New York, NY.

McQuillen, James. "A Crumb from Third Angle." *The Oregonian*, February 11, 2001, Arts and Living section, sunrise edition. Reviews the Third Angle Ensemble's performance of percussion works from *Coyote Builds North America* at the First Christian Church, Portland, OR.

Pressley, Nelson. "Great Spirit Meets Okay Spirit." *The Washington Post*, March 12, 2001, Style section, final edition. Reviews performance of *Coyote Builds North America* at the Arena Stage, Washington D.C.

Alburger, Mark. "Cold Comfort." *21st Century Music* 9, no. 4 (2002): 9. Reviews *Adams Cox Fink Fox*.

Couture, François. "Adams, Cox, Fink, Fox." *allmusic* [2002]. http://www.allmusic.com/cg/amg.dll?p=amg&sql=10:wnfwxqeoldoe.
    And "The Light that Fills the World." *allmusic* [2002]. http://www.allmusic.com/cg/amg.dll?p=amg&sql=10:j9ftxq8aldje.

Moore, David W. "Contemporary Chamber Music." *American Record Guide* 65, no. 4 (2002): 186–87. Reviews *Adams Cox Fink Fox*.

Tuttle, Raymond. "John Luther Adams; Fink; Cox; Fox; 'Cold Blue'." *Fanfare* 25, no. 6 (2002): 253–54. Reviews *Adams Cox Fink Fox*.

Alburger, Mark. "The Gorgeous White North." *21st Century Music* 10, no. 10 (2003): 9–11. Reviews *In the White Silence* and *The Light That Fills the World*.

Carl, Robert. "J. L. Adams: 'The Farthest Place; The Light that Fills the World; The Immeasurable Space of Tones'." *Fanfare* 26, no. 4 (2003): 54–55. Reviews *The Light That Fills the World*.

Dunham, Mike. "Fairbanks Musicians Featured On Albums." *Anchorage Daily News*, July 18, 2003, H17, final edition. Reviews *In the White Silence*.

Gann, Kyle. "Erasing the Lines: John Luther Adams Explores a New Landscape of Pure Harmony." *The Village Voice*, June 18–24, 2003, 101. Reviews *The Light That Fills the World*, *Adams Cox Fink Fox*, and *In the White Silence*.

Gimbel, Alan. "Adams, JL: The Farthest Place; The Light That Fills the World; The Immeasurable Space of Tones (music release)." *American Record Guide* 66, no. 2 (2003): 67. Reviews *The Light That Fills the World*.
    And "In the White Silence." *American Record Guide* 66, no. 5 (2003): 66.

Kozinn, Allan. "Recent Looks at Tonality and Thorns." *The New York Times*, August 25, 2003, Arts/Cultural Desk, final late edition. Reviews the Locrian Chamber Players' performance of *Make Prayers to the Raven* at Riverside Church, New York, NY. http://www.nytimes.com/2003/08/25/arts/music-review-recent-looks-at-tonality-and-thorns.html.

Ruhe, Pierre. "Bent Frequency Proves Itself Master of the Eclectic." *The Atlanta Journal-Constitution*, May 14, 2003, Features section, home edition. Reviews the Bent Frequency Ensemble's performance of *The Light That Fills the World* at Eyedrum Art and Music Gallery, Atlanta, GA.

Story, John. "Classical Recordings: J. L. Adams — In the White Silence." *Fanfare* 27, no. 1 (2003): 78–79.

Warburton, Dan. "John Luther Adams: In the White Silence." *allmusic* [2003]. http://www.allmusic.com/cg/amg.dll?p=amg&sql=43:105200.

Loydell, Rupert. "The Great White Wonder." *Tangents*, November 2004. Reviews *Winter Music* (Wesleyan University Press, 2004). http://www.tangents.co.uk/tangents/main/2004/nov/whitewonder.html.

Varela, Daniel. "John Luther Adams: The Light That Fills the World." *Musicworks*, no. 88 (2004).

Volmers, Eric. "Ten Tales Unravel Mysteries of Coyote Figure." *Guelph Mercury* (Ontario, Canada), May 1, 2004, Arts and Leisure section, final edition. Preview of performance of *Coyote Builds North America* at the Guelph Youth Music Centre, Ontario, Canada.

Cole, Dermot. "New England Conservatory to Premiere Work of John Adams." *Fairbanks Daily News-Miner*, September 18, 2005, "Cole Column". Preview of the Callithumpian Consort's performance of *for Lou Harrison* at the New England Conservatory, Boston, MA.

Grimley, Daniel M. "Winter Music: Composing the North (review)." *Music & Letters* 86, no. 4 (2005): 669–71.

Lewis, Uncle Dave. "John Luther Adams: Strange and Sacred Noise." *allmusic* [2005]. http://www.allmusic.com/cg/amg.dll?p=amg&sql=43:129446.

Moore, Stephanie. "Mature Composer's Musings On Art and Environment." *Musicworks*, no. 92 (2005): 62. Reviews *Winter Music* (Wesleyan University Press, 2004).

Smith, Ken. "Book Review: 'Winter Music: Composing the North,' by John Luther Adams." *Gramophone* 82, no. 991 (2005): A14.

Von Glahn, Denise. "Winter Music." *Notes* 62, no. 2 (2005): 378–79.

Carl, Robert. "Classical Recordings: J. L. Adams—Strange and Sacred Noise." *Fanfare* 29, no. 6 (2006): 40–41.
> And "Classical Recordings: J. L. Adams—The Mathematics of Resonant Bodies." *Fanfare* 30, no. 2 (2006): 105–6.

Dunham, Mike. "Composer Captures Alaska's Rhythms; 'Place Where You Go to Listen': Adams' sonic installation keeps tabs on planet's progress." *Anchorage Daily News*, March 20, 2006, Life Section, final edition.

Gann, Kyle. "Long Ride in a Slow Machine." *NewMusicBox*, March 29, 2006. Reviews *The Place Where You Go to Listen*, Fairbanks, AK. http://www.newmusicbox.org/articles/Fairbanks-A-Long-Ride-in-A-Slow-Machine/.

Gimbel, Alan. "Winter Music." *American Record Guide* 69, no. 1 (2006): 295–97.

Hertzog, Christian. "Once-in-a-lifetime Concert Opportunity." *Sequenza 21*, February 25, 2006. Reviews red fish blue fish performance of *Strange and Sacred Noise* at UCSD, San Diego, CA. http://www.sequenza21.com/2006/02/once-in-lifetime-concert-opportunity.html.

Joling, Dan. "Natural Phenomena Drive Listening Gallery at University of Alaska Museum." *The Associated Press*, July 24, 2006, Entertainment News section. Reviews *The Place Where You Go to Listen*, Fairbanks, AK.

Mayer, Amy. "Northern Exposure." *The Boston Globe*, April 16, 2006, Travel section, third edition. Reviews *The Place Where You Go to Listen*, Fairbanks, AK. http://articles.boston.com/2006-04-16/travel/29245811_1_fairbanks-university-of-alaska-museum-northern-lights.
> And "Museum: Where Geophysics Sings." *Discover Magazine*, August 2006. Reviews *The Place Where You Go to Listen*, Fairbanks, AK. http://discovermagazine.com/2006/aug/reviews.

Ortiz, Edward. "Recent Releases." *Sacramento Bee*, April 23, 2006, Ticket section, metro final edition. Reviews *The Mathematics of Resonant Bodies*.

Reverter, Arturo. "Discos: Música que Viene del Frío [Discs: Music That Comes from the Cold]." *Scherzo—Revista de Música* 21, no. 209 (2006): 64, 66–67. Reviews *In the White Silence* and *Strange and Sacred Noise*.

Sheckter, Alan. "Buzz Editor's Column: Natural Phenomena Drives Perpetual Alaskan 'Concert'." *Chico Enterprise-Record*, July 26, 2006, Entertainment section. Reviews *The Place Where You Go to Listen*, Fairbanks, AK.

Sheridan, Molly. "Cold Spell." *Time Out New York*, May 4, 2006. Reviews *Veils* and *Vesper* at the Diapason Gallery, New York, NY.

Smith, Ken. "North America: Reviews - JL Adams." *Gramophone* 84, no. 1010 (2006): A7. Reviews *The Mathematics of Resonant Bodies*.

Lewis, Uncle Dave. "John Luther Adams: for Lou Harrison." *allmusic* [2007]. http://www.allmusic.com/cg/amg.dll?p=amg&sql=43:160707.
> And "John Luther Adams: Red Arc/Blue Veil." *allmusic* [2007]. http://www.allmusic.com/cg/amg.dll?p=amg&sql=43:161690.

Nolan, Maia. "Symphony Bids Farewell to Friends, Then Plays Superbly." *Anchorage*

Daily News, February 20, 2007, Life section, final edition. Reviews Anchorage Symphony Orchestra's performance of *Dark Waves* at the Atwood Concert Hall, Anchorage, AK.

Smith, Dawnell. "Musicians, Composer Imagine Sound Never Before Heard; Premiere: John Luther Adams work a challenge for Anchorage Symphony." *Anchorage Daily News*, February 11, 2007, Life section, final edition. Preview of the Anchorage Symphony Orchestra's performance of *Dark Waves* at the Atwood Concert Hall, Anchorage, AK.

Carl, Robert. "Classical Recordings: J. L. Adams—'Dark Waves'; 'Among Red Mountains'; 'Qilyuan' [*sic*]; 'Red Arc/Blue Veil'." *Fanfare* 31, no. 6 (2008): 48–49. Reviews *Red Arc/Blue Veil*.

Clark, Colin. "Classical Recordings: J. L. Adams—'for Lou Harrison'." *Fanfare* 31, no. 4 (2008): 58–59.

And "Reviews: North America - J L Adams: 'Red Arc/Blue Veil,' 'Dark Waves,' 'Among Red Mountains,' 'Qilyuan' [*sic*]; J L Adams: 'For Lou Harrison'." *Gramophone* 85, no. 1027 (2008): A5. Reviews *Red Arc/Blue Veil* and *for Lou Harrison*.

Gimbel, Alan. "Adams, JL: For Lou Harrison." *American Record Guide* 71, no. 1 (2008): 51–52. Reviews *for Lou Harrison* and *Red Arc/Blue Veil*.

Mamou, Pierre Élie. "Discos: La Liga de los Hombres Extraordinarios [Discs: The League of Extraordinary Men]." *Scherzo—Revista de Música* 23, no. 234 (2008): 68. Reviews *for Lou Harrison*.

Smith, Craig. "Pasa Tempos." *The Santa Fe New Mexican*, March 21, 2008, Pasatiempo section. Reviews *Red Arc/Blue Veil*.

Acoustic Ecology Institute. "John Luther Adams: The Place Where You Go to Listen (new book)." *Acoustic Ecology Institute*, August 24, 2009. http://aeinews.org/archives/345.

Brown, Kevin Macneil. "John Luther Adams—'in a room' (the place we began)." *Dusted*, May 8, 2009. http://www.dustedmagazine.com/reviews/4980.

Carl, Robert. "Book Reviews—'The Place Where You Go to Listen: In Search of an Ecology of Music,' by John Luther Adams." *Fanfare* 33, no. 2 (2009): 405–6.

CBC News. "Banff Premieres Alaskan Composer's Percussion Music for the Outdoors." *CBC Arts*, June 19, 2009. Preview of Steven Schick and musicians' performance of *Inuksuit* at the Banff Centre, Banff, Canada. http://www.cbc.ca/arts/music/story/2009/06/19/banff-centre.html.

Clark, Bob. "Inuksuit Concert a Musical Adventure." *The Calgary Herald* (Alberta), July 18, 2009, Entertainment section, final edition. Preview of Steven Schick and musicians' performance of *Inuksuit* at the Banff Centre, Banff, Canada.

Distler, Jed. "Reviews: Books—'The Place Where You Go to Listen: In Search of an Ecology of Music,' by John Luther Adams." *Gramophone* 87, no. 1050 (2009): 127.

Farach-Colton, Andrew. "Reviews: North America - J L Adams: 'The Place We Began' 'At a Still Point'; 'In a Room'; 'In the Rain'." *Gramophone* 87, no. 1050 (2009): A5. Reviews *the place we began*.

Gimbel, Alan. "Adams, JL: In a Room; At a Still Point; In the Rain; The Place We Began." *American Record Guide* 72, no. 5 (2009): 52. Reviews *the place we began*.

Ginnell, Richard S. "Ojai Festival: A Raging Contemporary Success." *American Record Guide* 72, no. 5 (2009): 14–16. Reviews eighth blackbird and musicians' performance of *Dark Waves* in Ojai, CA.

Kozinn, Allan. "Ensemble That Plays By Its Own Rules." *The New York Times*, May 25, 2009, Arts/Cultural Desk, final late edition. Reviews Either/Or's performance of *Red Arc/Blue Veil* at the Tenri Cultural Institute, New York, NY. http://www.nytimes .com/2009/05/25/arts/music/25eith.html.

McCallum, Peter. "Spectral sounds from the edge of the unknown." *Sydney Morning Herald*, June 2, 2009, News and Features section, first edition. Reviews the Ensemble Offspring's performance of "roar" from *The Mathematics of Resonant Bodies* at the Sydney Conservatorium of Music, Sydney, Australia.

Oteri, Frank J. "Sounds Heard: John Luther Adams—The Place We Began." *NewMusicBox*, September 28, 2009. http://www.newmusicbox.org/articles/Sounds-Heard-John-Luther-Adams-The-Place-We-Began/.

Sawyer, Jill. "Song of the Earth." *The Banff Centre*, "Report to the Community," Summer 2009. Review of Steven Schick and musicians' performance of *Inuksuit* at the Banff Centre, Banff, Canada. http://www.banffcentre.ca/about/inspired/2009/summer/ articles/song.aspx.

Tuttle, Raymond. "Classical Recordings: J. L. Adams—'in a room'; 'at the still point'; 'in the rain'; 'the place we began.'" *Fanfare* 33, no. 1 (2009): 79-80. Reviews *the place we began*.

Upchurch, Michael. "First Seattle Concert Devoted to John Luther Adams' Works Is Nov. 21." *The Seattle Times*, November 19, 2009, Arts section. Preview of Steve Schick's performance of *The Mathematics of Resonant Bodies* and Cristina Valdes's performances of *Nunataks* and *Among Red Mountains* at the Good Shepherd Center, Seattle, WA. http://seattletimes.nwsource.com/html/thearts/2010302581_adams19 .html.

Artner, Alan G. "Chamber works by CSO's Golijov unfold solemly [*sic*]." *Chicago Tribune*, March 17, 2010. Reviews the Chicago Symphony Orchestra's MusicNOW performances of Adams's *Qilyaun*, . . . *and bells remembered* . . . , and *for Jim (rising)*. http://articles.chicagotribune.com/2010-03-17/news/ct-live-0317-musicnow-review-20100317_1_dreams-and-prayers-drums-clarinet.

Halverson, Seré Prince. "The Place Where You Go To Listen." *Who Moved My Buddha*, September 12, 2010. Reviews *The Place Where You Go to Listen*, Fairbanks, AK. http://whomovedmybuddha.blogspot.com/2010/09/place-where-you-go-to-listen .html.

Ricci, Massimo. "John Luther Adams- the place we began." *Brain Dead Eternity*, April 5, 2010. http://touchingextremes.wordpress.com/2010/04/05/john-luther-adams-%E2%80%93-the-place-we-began/.

Robin, Billy. "Now and Then." *Seated Ovation*, March 16, 2010. Reviews the Chicago Symphony Orchestra's MusicNOW performances of Adams's *Qilyaun*, . . . *and bells remembered* . . . , and *for Jim (rising)*. http://seatedovation.blogspot.com/2010/03/ now-and-then.html.

Smith, Steve. "Light and Color in an Undulating Cloud." *The New York Times*, October 19, 2010, Arts/Cultural Desk, late final edition. Reviews the American Composers

Orchestra's performance of *The Light Within* at Zankel Hall, New York, NY. http://www.nytimes.com/2010/10/19/arts/music/19mystics.html?emc=eta1.

Brown, Kevin Macneil. "John Luther Adams—Four Thousand Holes." *Dusted*, May 13, 2011. http://dustedmagazine.com/reviews/6449.

Couture, François. "John Luther Adams / Four Thousand Holes." *Monsieur Délire*, April 29, 2011. http://blog.monsieurdelire.com/2011/05/2011-04-29-john-luther-adams-olivier.html.

Delacoma, Wynne. "'Silence' is Golden for Composer Adams; Alaska piece kindled by vast, strange, beautiful, scary place." *Chicago Sun-Times*, February 20, 2011, 5. Preview of the International Contemporary Ensemble's performance of *In the White Silence* and Steven Schick's performance of *The Mathematics of Resonant Bodies* at the Museum of Contemporary Art, Chicago, IL. http://www.suntimes.com/entertainment/music/3862191-421/silence-is-golden-for-composer-adams.html.

Dervan, Michael. "Isabelle O Connell (piano)." *The Irish Times*, March 30, 2011, Features section. Reviews Isabelle O'Connell's performance of *Among Red Mountains* at the NCH Kevin Barry Room, Dublin, Ireland. http://www.irishtimes.com/newspaper/features/2011/0330/1224293350663.html.

Downey, Charles. "On the Verge of Experimental Dissolution." *The Washington Post*, January 25, 2011, Style section, regional edition. Reviews the Verge Ensemble's performance of *Red Arc/Blue Veil* at the National Gallery of Art, Washington, D.C. http://www.washingtonpost.com/lifestyle/style/on-the-verge-of-experimental-dissolution/2011/01/24/ABm7BzD_story.html.

Dunham, Mike. "The New Two Spirits Gallery Debuts Tuesday [Big sound in New York]." *Anchorage Daily News*, February 27, 2011, Life section, final edition. Reviews performance of *Inuksuit* at the Park Avenue Armory, New York, NY.

Eddins, Stephen. "John Luther Adams: Four Thousand Holes." *allmusic* [2011]. http://www.allmusic.com/album/john-luther-adams-four-thousand-holes-w266563/review.

Gardner, Alexandra. "Creating a World." *NewMusicBox*, February 24, 2011. Reviews performance of *Inuksuit* at the Park Avenue Armory, New York, NY. http://www.newmusicbox.org/articles/Creating-A-World/.

Huizenga, Tom. "Music Review: Cloudscapes from the Great Noise Ensemble." *The Washington Post*, April 25, 2011, Lifestyle section. Reviews the Great Noise Ensemble's performance of *Clouds of Unknowing, Clouds of Forgetting* at the Unitarian Universalist Church in Silver Spring, MD. http://www.washingtonpost.com/lifestyle/style/music-review-cloudscapes-from-the-great-noise-ensemble/2011/04/24/AFQpAAiE_story.html.

Hurd, Devin. "Boring Like a Sunset." *Hurd Audio*, February 27, 2011. Reviews the International Contemporary Ensemble's performance of *In the White Silence* and Steven Schick's performance of *The Mathematics of Resonant Bodies* at the Museum of Contemporary Art, Chicago, IL. http://hurdaudio.blogspot.com/2011/02/boring-like-sunset.html.

Ross, Alex. "Musical Events: Reverberations." *The New Yorker*, March 14, 2011, 74. Reviews performance of *Inuksuit* at the Park Avenue Armory, New York, NY. http://www.newyorker.com/arts/critics/musical/2011/03/14/110314crmu_music_ross?currentPage=2.

Smith, Steve. "Turning It Outside-In at Armory." *The New York Times*, February 22, 2011, Arts/Cultural Desk, late final edition. Reviews performance of *Inuksuit* at the Park Avenue Armory, New York, NY. http://www.nytimes.com/2011/02/22/arts/music/22luther.html?src=twrhp.

Taub, David. "John Luther Adams: Four Thousand Holes / . . . and bells remembered. . . ." *Sequenza 21*, May 11, 2011. http://www.sequenza21.com/cdreviews/2011/05/john-luther-adams-four-thousand-holes-and-bells-remembered/.

Waard, Frans de. "John Luther Adams—Four Thousand Holes." *Tokafi*, April 27, 2011. http://www.tokafi.com/news/vital-weekly-776-777/.

John Luther Adams in Audiovisual Media

Listed chronologically and alphabetically within each year

Hansen, Liane. "Alaska Inspires New Soundscape from John Luther Adams." *Weekend Edition* (National Public Radio), February 12, 1995. Radio interview.

Casey, George, director. *Alaska: Spirit of the Wild*, 1998. Film produced by George Casey et. al for Alaska Film Partners Ltd. Selections from *Earth and the Great Weather* are featured.

Boudart, Bo, and Djerassi, Dale, directors. *Oil on Ice*, 2004. Film produced by Oil on Ice Partners. The work "Shik'eenoohtii" [*Five Athabascan Dances*] is featured.

Mayer, Amy. "Meditative Music from Alaska." *All Things Considered (National Public Radio)*, September 26, 2004. Radio interview. Audio (streaming): http://www.npr.org/templates/story/story.php?storyId=3937518.

Grossman, Roberta, director. *Homeland: Four Portraits of Native Action*, 2005. Film produced by the Katahdin Foundation. The work "Shik'eenoohtii" [*Five Athabascan Dances*] is featured.

Unrein, Scott. "NonPop Show 006—'The Place' interview." *NonPop*, April 24, 2006. Audio (downloadable MP3): http://www.nonpopmusic.com/2006/04/24/nonpop-show-006-the-place-interview.

Arizona State University, Herberger College of the Arts School of Music. "Sonic Geography: A Conversation with Composer John Luther Adams." *The Library Channel*, Episode 43, April 25, 2007. Audio (downloadable MP3): http://lib.asu.edu/librarychannel/2007/04/25/sonic-geography-a-conversation-with-composer-john-luther-adams.

Banyard, Rory, director. *Gates of the Artic: Alaska's Brooks Range*, 2008. Film produced by North Shore Productions. Selections from *Make Prayers to the Raven* are featured.

Feraca, Jean. "An Ecology of Music." *Here on Earth: Radio Without Borders*, August 25, 2008. Radio interview. Audio (streaming): "JLA Here on Earth," http://johnlutheradams.com/interview/index.html.

YouTube. "John Luther Adams." 2008-present. Assorted musical performances and interviews. Video (streaming): http://youtube.com/results?search_query=%22john+luther+adams%22&aq=f.

Ross, Alex, and Hurd, Evan. "John Luther Adams's 'Inuksuit'." *The New Yorker*, News Desk blog, September 2, 2009. Video (streaming): http://www.newyorker.com/online/blogs/newsdesk/2009/09/video-john-luther-adams-inuksuit.html.

Curran, John, director. *Stone*, 2010. Film produced by René Besson et. al. for Mimran Schur Pictures. The work "in a room" from *the place we began* is featured.

Elkins, Steve, director. *The Reach of Resonance*, 2010. Film produced by David Marks for Candela Films. The work *The Place Where You Go to Listen* is featured. Video (streaming) preview: http://vimeo.com/3019076.

Numata, Yuki. "The Best New York Alt-Classical Concerts Of 2010." *NPR Classical, Deceptive Cadence (National Public Radio)*, December 29, 2010. The works *The Farthest Place* and *In a Treeless Place, Only Snow* are featured. Audio (streaming): "American Contemporary Music Ensemble," http://www.npr.org/blogs/deceptivecadence/2011/01/05/132409680/the-best-new-york-alt-classical-concerts-of-2010.

Ross, Alex. "A Conversation with John Luther Adams and Alex Ross." *Pick Staiger Concert Hall, Bienen School of Music*, October 2010. Video (streaming): http://www.pickstaiger.org/video/conversation-john-luther-adams-and-alex-ross.

Simanis, Davis, director. *Sounds Under the Sun*, 2010. Film produced by Inese Boka-Grube for Mistrus Media Ltd. The work *Sky With Four Suns* is featured. Video (streaming) preview: http://www.youtube.com/watch?v=4_8DPP01wTU.

WFMT. "03-29-2010: John Luther Adams (composer)." *WFMT: Critical Thinking*, April 6, 2010. Radio interview. Audio (downloadable MP3): http://wttw.vo.llnwd.net/o16/wfmt/critical_thinking/100329_JohnLutherAdams.mp3.

International Contemporary Ensemble. "John Luther Adams and Steven Schick in conversation." *ICEcast*, February 12, 2011. Audio (downloadable MP3): http://itunes.apple.com/us/podcast/icecast/id368042982.

Kamerling, Leonard, director. *Strange and Sacred Noise*, 2011. Film produced with support from the Alaska State Council on the Arts, National Endowment for the Arts, and American/Alaskan Masterpieces Project. Features an outdoor performance of percussion work of the same name.

> Spielberger, Katie. "UAF filmmaker debuts new work in New York." *Capital City Weekly*, February 14, 2011. http://www.juneaublogger.com/preview/?p=318.

Moon, H. Paul. "Inuksuit by John Luther Adams." *Vimeo*, February 27, 2011. Video (streaming): http://vimeo.com/20436428.

Sheridan, Molly. "John Luther Adams: The Music of a True Place." *NewMusicBox*, March 1, 2011. Video (streaming): http://www.newmusicbox.org/articles/john-luther-adams-the-music-of-a-true-place/.

Sirota, Nadia. "Large Scale Awesomeness." *WQXR*, February 28, 2011. Audio (streaming): http://www.wqxr.org/programs/nadiasirota/2011/feb/28/.

United States Artists. "John Luther Adams—Listen." 2010. Video (streaming): http://www.facebook.com/video/video.php?v=886576850748.

Notes

1. Sabine Feisst, "Discography," "Selected Bibliography," and "Catalog of Works," in *Winter Music*, by John Luther Adams (Middletown, CT: Wesleyan University Press, 2004), 185–98. Also see Sabine Feisst, "Klanggeographie—Klanggeometrie: Der US-amerikanische Komponist John Luther Adams," *Musiktexte* 91 (2001): 4–14.

2. John Luther Adams, "Writings," "Interviews," "Works," and "Calendar," http://www.johnlutheradams.com/index.html.

3. Lexis-Nexis Academic," www.lexisnexis.com.

4. International Index to Music Periodicals, http://iimp.chadwyck.com/marketing .do.

5. Worldcat, www.worldcat.org.

6. Cantaloupe Records, "John Luther Adams," http://www.cantaloupemusic.com/art-ists.php?artist_id=91.

7. Cold Blue Music, http://www.coldbluemusic.com.

8. Mode Records, "John Luther Adams," http://www.moderecords.com/profiles/john-lutheradams.html.

9. New Albion Records, "John Luther Adams," http://www.newalbion.com/artists/adamsjl/index.htm.

10. New World Records, "Liner Notes," http://www.newworldrecords.org/liner_notes .cgi?rm=list&imprint=NWR.

CATALOGUE OF WORKS * 299

Contributors

ROBERT CARL is chair of the composition department at The Hartt School, University of Hartford, and the author of *Terry Riley's In C.*

SCOTT DEAL has appeared at performance venues, festivals and conferences in North America and Europe. He has premiered dozens of solo, chamber and mixed media works, and can be heard on the Albany, Centaur, Cold Blue and SCI labels. Continually inspired by new and emerging artistic technologies, Deal is the founder of the *Telematic Collective*, an Internet performance group comprised of artists and computer specialists. Deal currently resides in Indianapolis, Indiana where he is a professor of music and director of the Donald Tavel Arts Technology Research Center at Indiana University Purdue University Indianapolis. He is a research affiliate for the Arctic Region Supercomputing Center at the University of Alaska Fairbanks, where he was a professor of music from 1995–2007. He also serves as artist-faculty on the Summer Institute for Contemporary Performance Practice (Sick Puppy) at the New England Conservatory. Deal holds a Doctor of Musical Arts degree from the University of Miami, a Master of Music degree from the University of Cincinnati College-Conservatory of Music, and a Bachelor of Arts degree from Cameron University.

ROBERT ESLER is a percussionist and educator currently living in Arizona. He serves on the faculty at Arizona State University, Polytechnic and in the Maricopa Community College District. Esler performs regularly with the local Phoenix ensemble Crossing 32nd Street, which has been hailed as one of Phoenix's best new classical music ensembles. Esler was also a long-time member of the critically acclaimed percussion group red fish blue fish. As a soloist Esler is a lone pioneer in the field of percussion and interactive computer media. He is currently producing a series of performed sound installations called "Performing Data," which are inspired by meaningful global data sets. Esler is also actively commissioning new works for computer media and percussion. He has performed on six albums for the Cantaloupe, CIEM, Mode, and Tzadik labels. Esler will be featured in a full-length documentary to be released in the next year. The film documents one of Esler's renegade performances of *Strange and Sacred Noise* on the Alaskan tundra. Esler has written articles for the ICMA (International Computer Music Association) and contributes regularly to the website doctorrhythm.com. Dr. Esler holds degrees from the University of California San Diego, Yale University, and the Cleveland Institute of Music.

SABINE FEISST holds a Ph.D. in musicology from the Free University of Berlin and is associate professor of Music History and Literature at Arizona State University. Her research interests focus on the music of the twentieth and twenty-first centuries, including experimental music, improvisation, eco-criticism, film music and the music of Arnold Schoenberg. Her publications include the monographs *Schoenberg's New*

World: The American Years (2011) and *Der Begriff "Improvisation in der neuen Musik"* (The Idea of Improvisation in New Music, 1997) and chapters in *Schoenberg and His World* (1999), *Edgard Varèse. Composer, Sound Sculptor, Visionary (1883-1965)* (2006), and *Geschichte der Musik im 20. Jahrhundert, 1925-1945* (2006). She also contributed numerous articles to such journals as *Archiv für Musikwissenschaft, The Musical Quarterly, Journal of the Arnold Schönberg Center,* and *MusikTexte.*

KYLE GANN is a composer and teaches music theory and history at Bard College in upstate New York. From 1986 to 2005 he was the new-music critic for the *Village Voice*, and he is the author of several books on American music, including *The Music of Conlon Nancarrow, American Music in the Twentieth Century, Music Downtown: Writings from the Village Voice, No Such Thing as Silence: John Cage's 4'33",* and (upcoming) *Robert Ashley*. His music is available on the New Albion, New World, Lovely Music, Cold Blue, Mode (upcoming), Meyer Media, and Monroe Street labels.

PETER GARLAND, composer, has been a friend and colleague of John Luther Adams for over thirty-five years, since their student days at the brand new Cal Arts in the early 1970s. Like Adams, he was a student of James Tenney and a good friend of Lou Harrison. From 1971 to 1991 he edited and published *SOUNDINGS Press*, which printed scores and essays by multiple generations of composers, and which played a major role in the rediscovery and re-evaluation of the so-called American Experimental Tradition. He has done years of research and fieldwork on Native American musics, in California, the Southwest, and Mexico; and is the author of several books on American experimental and Mexican traditional musics.

DAVE HERR, born 1987 in New York, holds a B.A. in musicology and electroacoustic composition from Hampshire College under the tutelage of professors Dan Warner and Becky Miller. He has also studied piano with Judith Gordon at Smith College, composition with Eric Sawyer at Amherst College, and musical aesthetics with Simon Frith at the University of Edinburgh. His Bachelor's thesis, an essay entitled *Process in the Music of John Luther Adams: A Study of Strange and Sacred Noise*, is a musicological analysis of the use of (and deviation from) musical processes in *Strange and Sacred Noise*, Adams's 1991-1997 extended cycle for percussion quartet.

BERND HERZOGENRATH is professor of American Literature and Culture at Goethe University of Frankfurt/Main, Germany. He is the author of *An Art of Desire: Reading Paul Auster* (1999), and the editor of *From Virgin Land to Disney World: Nature and Its Discontents in the USA of Yesterday and Today* (2001), *The Cinema of Tod Browning* (2006), *Deleuze|Guattari & Ecology* (2008), *Edgar G. Ulmer: Essays on the King of the B's* (2008), *An [Un]likely Alliance: Deleuze|Guattari & Thinking Environment[s]* (2009). His fields of interest are ninteenth and twentieth century American literature and culture, critical theory, and film/media Studies. He has just published *An American Body|Politic: Deleuzian Approach* (2010)—future publications include the edited collections *Travels in Intermedia[lity]: ReBlurring the Boundaries* (2011), and *Time and History in Deleuze and Serres* (2011). At the moment, Bernd is planning the project *CINAPSES: Thinking|Film*, that brings together scholars from film studies, philosophy, and the neurosciences (members include a.o. Antonio Damasio).

GLENN KOTCHE is a Chicago-based percussionist and composer. He is most widely recognized for his work in the Grammy-award-winning rock band Wilco. Kotche is also an active composer who has been commissioned by and performed with the Kronos Quartet, Bang on a Can All-Stars, and Eighth Blackbird. As a drummer, he has played on over eighty recordings to date, including three of his own solo percussion records, most recently *Mobile* on Nonesuch Records. He has written for *Percussive Notes* and *Modern Drummer* magazine, appearing on the January 2007 cover of the latter. His music is available through Alfred publishing.

NOAH POLLACZEK is a graduate of Oberlin College with an M.S. in library and information science from the University of Illinois, and has worked in a variety of academic, government, and music libraries as a digitization specialist, collections cataloger, database manager, and archivist to John Luther Adams. His long-term aim is to preserve unique audiovisual materials and make them more broadly available to the public.

ALEX ROSS has been the music critic of *The New Yorker* since 1996. From 1992 to 1996 he wrote for the *New York Times*. His first book, *The Rest Is Noise: Listening to the Twentieth Century*, a cultural history of music since 1900, won the 2007 National Book Critics Circle Award for criticism, was a finalist for the 2008 Pulitzer Prize in general nonfiction, and received the Guardian First Book Award. His second book, the essay collection *Listen to This*, appeared in 2010 and received an ASCAP-Deems Taylor Award. He is now at work on a book called *Wagnerism*. He has received the Belmont Prize in Germany, an Arts and Letters Award from the American Academy of Arts and Letters, fellowships from the American Academy in Berlin and the Banff Centre, and a Letter of Distinction from the American Music Center for contributions to the field of contemporary music. In 2008, he was named a MacArthur Fellow.

DAVID ROTHENBERG is professor of Philosophy and Music at the New Jersey Institute of Technology, author of *Thousand Mile Song* and *Why Birds Sing*, which has appeared in six languages and was the basis of a BBC television documentary. He also edited the *Book of Music and Nature*, and has released numerous CDs of his own music, which usually involves sounds of the natural world.

STEVEN SCHICK was born in Iowa and raised in a farming family. For the past thirty years he has championed contemporary percussion music as a performer and teacher, by commissioning and premiering more than one hundred new works for percussion. Schick is Distinguished Professor of Music at the University of California, San Diego and a consulting artist in percussion at the Manhattan School of Music. In 2008 Schick received the "Distinguished Teaching Award" from UCSD. He was the percussionist of the Bang on a Can All-Stars of New York City from 1992-2002, and from 2000 to 2004 served as Artistic Director of the Centre International de Percussion de Genève in Geneva, Switzerland. Schick is founder and Artistic Director of the percussion group red fish blue fish, and in 2007 assumed the post of music director and conductor of the La Jolla Symphony and Chorus. Steven Schick recently released three important publications. His book on solo percussion music, *The Percussionist's Art: Same Bed, Different Dreams*, was published by the University of Rochester Press; his recording of *The Mathematics of Resonant Bodies* by John Luther Adams was released by Cantaloupe Music; and, a three-CD set of the complete percussion music of Iannis Xenakis, made in collaboration with red fish blue fish, was issued by Mode Records.

MOLLY SHERIDAN is the managing editor of NewMusicBox.org and the director of CounterstreamRadio.org, both programs of the American Music Center. She is also the host of Carnegie Hall's *Sound Insights* podcasts and maintains the ArtsJournal blog *Mind the Gap*. An ASCAP-Deems Taylor Award winner, her writing also appears in publications such as *The Washington Post* and *Time Out New York*. Prior to joining the AMC staff, Sheridan was associate editor of *Symphony* magazine. She attended the Honors Tutorial College at Ohio University, earning a bachelor's in journalism with a specialization in violin performance and French in 1999.

DAVID SHIMONI has performed as a solo and collaborative pianist throughout the United States, including New York's Carnegie Hall, Alice Tully Hall, and Museum of Modern Art, as well as the Barns at Wolf Trap, Dallas Museum of Art, Caramoor Center, and Chicago Cultural Center. He has been a guest artist at the Chautauqua, Brevard, Moab, Foothills, and Rockport music festivals, and his performances have been broadcast on radio stations WGBH-Boston, WFMT-Chicago, and WQXR-New York. He has served on the accompanying and teaching staff of The Juilliard School, Brooklyn College, New School for Jazz and Contemporary Music, and Ravinia Steans Institute. He has degrees from Swarthmore College and The Juilliard School and is currently completing a DMA at The Graduate Center of the City University of New York, where his dissertation is on the music of John Luther Adams. He has also researched birdsong at Rockefeller University and interned with the New Jersey Audubon Society and Congressional Research Service.

TODD TARANTINO is a New York City–based composer. He holds a doctorate in composition from Columbia University and has taught music theory, music history, and aural skills at Columbia University and the Manhattan School of Music. His music has been performed throughout America as well as in Europe, Asia, and Africa by musicians such as Ensemble Moderne Akademie, Manhattan Sinfonietta under the direction of Jeffrey Milarsky, Second Instrumental Unit, saxophonist Eliot Gattegno, pianists Barbara Lieurance and Kathleen Tagg, and the OCNM Ensemble under the direction of Zsolt Nagy at venues as varied as the ISCM World Music Days, the Ostrava Days New Music Festival in the Czech Republic, the Pacific Music Festival in Japan, the Aspen Music Festival in America, the Arab Perspectives Festival in Egypt as well as throughout New York.

Index

Symmetry, 42, 52–53, 55–57, 75, 170, 173–75, 179n17, 191, 198

Tempo layers, 163, 176, 199, 201, 204
Tenney, James, 10, 16, 23, 81, 85, 105, 117, 122, 207, 210–11, 228; *Koan*, 210
Thoreau, Henry David, 1, 6, 10, 17, 107, 114, 208, 219–28, 231, 231nn1–3, 232n7
Timbre, 9, 42, 46n19, 128, 183, 188–204, 215, 238, 241, 252, 262–63
Tolentino, Lisa, 89
Transcendentalism, 208, 220–24, 231n3
Tritt, Lincoln, 31
Turner, J.M.W., 191
Turner, Victor, 134, 135
Turrell, James, 109, 180–81,191

Ultramodernism, 10, 206–16, 217n1
Ung, Chinary, 137
Unity, 1, 44, 70, 120–21, 132, 192, 224, 226

Varèse, Edgard, 16, 81, 84, 103, 117, 125, 207, 228

Wagner, Richard, 20, 200, 251; *Siegfried*, 251
Wright, Gordon, 19, 144

Xenakis, Iannis, 16, 83, 95, 103, 140; *Psappha*, 103, 140

Young, La Monte, 23, 43, 45n11, 45n18, 216